Confronting Mental Health Stigma with AI and Machine Learning

Scrivener Publishing
100 Cummings Center, Suite 541J
Beverly, MA 01915-6106

Publishers at Scrivener
Martin Scrivener (martin@scrivenerpublishing.com)
Phillip Carmical (pcarmical@scrivenerpublishing.com)

Confronting Mental Health Stigma with AI and Machine Learning

Edited by

Ridhima Sharma

School of Business Studies, Vivekananda Institute of Professional Studies-TC, Delhi, India

Fazla Rabby

Stanford Institute of Management and Technology, Sydney, Australia

Rohit Bansal

Department of Management Studies, Vaish College of Engineering, Rohtak, India

Timcy Sachdeva

School of Business Studies, Vivekananda Institute of Professional Studies-TC, Delhi, India

and

Jihene Mrabet

Center of Research Excellence, Health and Wellbeing, Amity University, Dubai, UAE

Scrivener Publishing

WILEY

This edition first published 2026 by John Wiley & Sons, Inc., 111 River Street, Hoboken, NJ 07030, USA and Scrivener Publishing LLC, 100 Cummings Center, Suite 541J, Beverly, MA 01915, USA

For more information about Scrivener publications please visit www.scrivenerpublishing.com.

Wiley Global Headquarters
111 River Street, Hoboken, NJ 07030, USA

For details of our global editorial offices, customer services, and more information about Wiley products visit us at www.wiley.com.

The manufacturer's authorized representative according to the EU General Product Safety Regulation is Wiley-VCH GmbH, Boschstr. 12, 69469 Weinheim, Germany, e-mail: Product_Safety@wiley.com.

Library of Congress Cataloging-in-Publication Data

ISBN 978-1-394-34726-1

Cover image: Generated with AI using Adobe Firefly
Cover design by Russell Richardson

Set in size of 11pt and Minion Pro by Manila Typesetting Company, Makati, Philippines

Printed in the USA

10 9 8 7 6 5 4 3 2 1

Contents

Preface

This book explores the multifaceted relationship between technology, artificial intelligence, and mental health, with a specific focus on dismantling stigma. It delves into the innovative ways AI and machine learning can transform mental health awareness, diagnosis, and intervention while addressing the social, cultural, and financial barriers to technology adoption. The chapters navigate the critical issues of mental health stigma—its psychological and social impacts—and how AI-powered tools, such as chatbots, predictive models, and educational resources, can provide accessible and stigma-free mental health solutions.

By examining real-world case studies, theoretical frameworks, and ethical considerations, the book provides a holistic view of AI's potential to revolutionize mental health care across different contexts, including workplaces, cultural settings, and educational domains. Mental health stigma remains a pervasive issue that hinders individuals from seeking help, perpetuates misinformation, and marginalizes those living with mental health conditions. The advent of artificial intelligence and machine learning offers unprecedented opportunities to confront these challenges by reshaping perceptions, improving access to mental health resources, and fostering an environment of inclusivity. This book aims to bridge the gap between technology and mental health care by providing insights into how AI can combat stigma, facilitate early intervention, and empower individuals and communities.

Drawing from interdisciplinary research and global perspectives, this book presents an evidence-based analysis of how AI-driven tools can reduce stigma while addressing ethical, financial, and cultural challenges. Each chapter is thoughtfully curated to explore themes ranging from the romanticization of mental health issues in digital spaces to the development of AI-powered chatbots and applications that offer emotional support and diagnostic insight. The book also highlights the role of education, policy, and advocacy in building a stigma-free future, while presenting recommendations for stakeholders, researchers, and practitioners to harness the power of AI responsibly.

Contributors have done a remarkable job highlighting various aspects:

Chapter 1 explores the influence of social media on adolescents' perceptions of mental health and stigma, examining how online interactions shape awareness and outlining strategies for positive engagement.
Chapter 2, focusing on India, presents evidence-based insights into how AI can be used to address mental health stigma, highlighting cultural challenges and tailored interventions for diverse communities.
Chapter 3 dives into AI's transformative potential in mental health, emphasizing advancements in diagnostics, therapy, and stigma reduction through innovative AI solutions.
Chapter 4 offers a detailed analysis of how AI-powered chatbots and virtual assistants provide support and combat stigma by offering anonymity, accessibility, and personalized care.
Chapter 5 addresses the financial hurdles in implementing AI-based mental health tools and proposes practical strategies for broader accessibility.
Chapter 6 explores workplace settings and investigates how AI affects employees' mental health while offering strategies to promote well-being and reduce stigma.
Chapter 7 examines the correlation between social intelligence and happiness among Gen Z, emphasizing how these traits influence mental health and perceptions of stigma.
Chapter 8 critiques the double-edged nature of technology in both perpetuating and mitigating mental health stigma, calling for mindful technology use.
Chapter 9 compares the efficacy of AI tools like ChatGPT with traditional psychological tests in assessing anxiety, highlighting the benefits and limitations of each.
Chapter 10 explores how predictive AI models can enhance self-awareness and reduce stigma, leading to improved mental and physical health outcomes.
Chapter 11, balancing optimism and caution, evaluates the dual role of AI in addressing stigma while discussing associated ethical and societal risks.
Chapter 12 provides a foundational understanding of mental health stigma, its multifaceted challenges, and actionable strategies for intervention.
Chapter 13, focused on the tourism sector, examines how AI-driven initiatives can address unique mental health challenges and combat stigma in this dynamic industry.

Chapter 14 emphasizes the power of AI-based educational tools in raising awareness, reducing stigma, and empowering individuals with knowledge and support.
Chapter 15 synthesizes the book's themes, highlighting how AI and machine learning offer transformative solutions to confront mental health stigma globally.
Chapter 16 explores the application of sentiment analysis in detecting and addressing mental health stigma, offering actionable insights for diverse contexts.

A heartfelt thanks to all contributors who brought their expertise and passion to this book. Their insights and dedication have shed light on the complex yet promising intersection of AI, machine learning, and mental health. Their work is invaluable in paving the way toward a future where technology fosters understanding, inclusivity, and stigma-free mental health care. We also offer our special thanks to Martin Scrivener and Scrivener Publishing for their effort and support in the publication of this book.

This work is not merely a technological exploration—it is a call to action. It urges society to embrace innovative strategies in mental health care. I hope this book serves as both a resource and an inspiration for readers from diverse fields, including mental health professionals, technologists, educators, policymakers, and all who are invested in promoting mental well-being. By confronting the stigmas associated with mental health through the lens of AI, we take a step closer to a world where compassion, understanding, and accessibility prevail.

The Editors
August 2025

Part I

EXPLORING THE INTERSECTION OF TECHNOLOGY, ARTIFICIAL INTELLIGENCE, AND MENTAL HEALTH STIGMA—CHALLENGES, INNOVATIONS, AND FUTURE DIRECTIONS

1

Beyond the Likes and Shares: Navigating Technology's Impact on Adolescents' Mental Health Perceptions and Stigma

Abhirami S. Manjari

[1]*Department of Psychology, Kristu Jayanti (Deemed to be University), Bengaluru, Karnataka, India*
[2]*School of Psychological Sciences, Christ University, Bengaluru, Karnataka, India*

Abstract

Adolescent mental health stigma remains a critical issue, although challenges and effective interventions require cultural adaptation and reliable stigma assessment. Digital media presents advantages and disadvantages, offering accessible and anonymous support while potentially disseminating misinformation and intensifying stigma. These platforms can enhance mental health outcomes but are challenged by digital literacy, privacy issues, and the dependability of online interactions. Cultural and social factors affect the success of technological interventions. It is crucial to assess the effect of technology on mental health stigma using psychological and sociological theories. Integrating technology with traditional methods considering individual and contextual factors is vital for effective mental health interventions. While technology can reduce stigma by increasing access to stigma reduction programs and offering novel solutions, its implementation must be cautious in avoiding misinformation and unintentionally reinforcing existing stigmas. This chapter explored the role of technology in combating mental health stigma by reviewing studies on social media campaigns, mental health apps, and online support groups. It highlights strengths and weaknesses and offers future research directions and practical recommendations for creating compelling, inclusive, and culturally sensitive technological solutions for adolescents. Tailoring digital interventions to diverse communities' cultural and social contexts is crucial to ensuring their efficacy and preventing the worsening of targeted problems.

***Keywords*:** Mental health stigma, adolescents, technological interventions, cultural sensitivity

Email: manjari.aspires@gmail.com

Ridhima Sharma, Fazla Rabby, Rohit Bansal, Timcy Sachdeva and Jihene Mrabet (eds.) Confronting Mental Health Stigma with AI and Machine Learning, (3–32) © 2026 Scrivener Publishing LLC

1.1 Influence of Technology on Adolescent Lives

Research has highlighted the widespread impact of technology on adolescents' lives. Students consider technology to be a prerequisite for academic and cognitive development [1]. They experience a blend of offline and online social interactions [2]. While technology can enhance academic skills, excessive use, primarily gaming, may lead to maladaptive behaviors and poor school adjustment [3]. Social media and mobile technology influence youth and affect the majority of them, including vulnerable populations such as those with mental illness, autism, or individuals who identify themselves as LGBT [4]. Adolescents between 12 and 15 years old, individuals from ethnic minority groups, and those who have experienced neglect or family instability are more susceptible to the dangers online and are more likely to engage in hazardous behaviors [5, 6]. The lack of parental supervision makes foster youth particularly vulnerable to online dangers, including sexual predation [7]. Evidence on social media usage among adolescents highlights its adverse effects on mental health and its benefits for self-expression, community, and access to resources [8].

Technology plays a prominent role in adolescents' lives by offering growth opportunities and challenges. Extensive research and practical solutions are essential to maximize benefits and minimize risks, especially for socioeconomically disadvantaged youth facing digital inequality [7]. Technology provides valuable learning and social opportunities; however, self-regulation strategies and ethical frameworks are crucial for ensuring adolescent well-being and safety [1, 3, 7].

Adolescents can use self-regulation strategies to manage their online habits and behaviors effectively. Exploring online platform functions can support optimal learning outcomes [1, 9]. Artificial intelligence systems designed for disadvantaged youth can significantly help marginalized individuals. However, current AI technologies may exacerbate marginalization by focusing on parental reporting and prevention tools, often overlooking youths without active parental supervision. Shifting our focus towards teen-centric solutions can empower adolescents to manage online risks and connect with experts when needed [4, 7, 10]. Researchers, educators, and policymakers must consider these multifaceted impacts to harness the benefits of technology while addressing its risks [11].

1.1.1 Mental Health Crisis Among Adolescents

The growing mental health crisis among adolescents is a complex issue, often aggravated by factors such as the COVID-19 pandemic and chronic illnesses [12, 13]. This crisis, combined with an increase in mental health disorders among youth, has become a significant public health concern [14]. Research suggests that the widespread use of smartphones and social media platforms has negatively impacted youth well-being. The prolonged use of these devices reduces personal interactions with family and friends, possibly leading to social disconnection, depressive symptoms, and, in extreme cases, self-harm ideation [15, 16]. Adolescents, particularly those with depression, are highly vulnerable to their peers' social media posts about self-harm or suicide, which may be perceived as encouraging these behaviors. This exposure raises concerns for individuals with mental health issues and can worsen existing problems [17].

Social media platforms that are designed for global connections often lead to social isolation and anxiety. The carefully crafted online identities and content that encourages comparisons can foster unrealistic standards and negatively impact self-worth. In today's digital age, technological pervasiveness has been strongly associated with mental health challenges. While the Internet offers valuable information and support, it also presents risks, such as addiction, harassment, and burnout. AI technologies, from chatbots providing emotional support to predictive models assessing mental health risks, are improving early intervention and reducing the stigma surrounding seeking help, enabling proactive mental health monitoring and early assistance. Wearable devices also focus on mental well-being [18]. The digital age has intensified complex adolescent mental health challenges, with technology presenting both resources and risks. Addressing this crisis requires balancing benefits and risks, promoting healthy digital habits, ensuring accessible mental health resources, and encouraging communication among adolescents, parents, and professionals. A comprehensive understanding and proactive approach are essential for reversing current trends and ensuring a supportive future for the next generation.

1.1.2 Method

This section uses a conceptual and investigative approach to explore how technology can combat adolescent mental health stigma. The methodology includes a thorough literature review on technology's role in addressing stigma, an examination of social media's impact on stigma reduction, an assessment of mental health apps' effectiveness in raising awareness and building resilience, an investigation into online support communities for peer connections, and an analysis of risks like misinformation, privacy issues, and digital literacy challenges.

The chapter incorporates social cognitive and innovation diffusion theories to examine the relationship between technology and stigma, evaluating digital interventions' efficacy, accessibility, and inclusivity and considering cultural and social influences. It explores integrating technological solutions with traditional methods for comprehensive stigma reduction and assesses specific digital mental health interventions to highlight their practical applications and limitations. Recommendations for developing effective, culturally appropriate digital mental health interventions emphasize digital literacy, data protection, user confidence, and culturally sensitive strategies. The chapter identifies areas needing further research, including digital interventions' long-term effects and ethical implications on stigma reduction. It offers a critical, theory-based analysis of how technology can effectively and inclusively address adolescent mental health stigma.

1.2 Technology and Mental Health Stigma Among Adolescents

The interplay between technology and mental health stigma among teenagers is intricate. Digital platforms, including social media and other technological innovations, can intensify psychological difficulties through cyberbullying and negative self-evaluations [19–21]. However, it also fosters positive and supportive communities and mental health awareness campaigns [19, 22]. Social media can create inclusive spaces for marginalized groups, including the LGBTQ+ community, which faces increased stigma and mental health challenges [23]. Additionally, the effect of technology on parental social networks and caregiver strain, specifically ADHD, highlights its broader impact [24]. Technology-facilitated information sharing and supportive online communities contribute to and mitigate mental health stigma. The objective is to utilize technological advancements to enhance the availability of mental health resources while simultaneously addressing the stigma and barriers associated with seeking psychological support [19, 20, 22]. Upcoming initiatives should prioritize the responsible application of technological solutions to enhance mental health among adolescents and combat social stigma [20, 25].

Technology offers incomparable access to resources and innovations but presents risks such as cyberbullying, social comparison, burnout, and information overload. Effective navigation involves fostering a positive online environment, establishing healthy boundaries, and leveraging digital tools for well-being. By using devices mindfully, creating technology-free zones, and judiciously selecting content, we can maximize the technology's benefits and mitigate its adverse effects. Enhancing digital literacy, encouraging online empathy, and promoting support structures and regulations are essential for creating a safer and more inclusive online space. Integrating technological advancements with responsible practices and understanding their mental health impacts can build a more promising future [26].

Online advocacy and interventions are crucial in combating mental health stigma. A review showed that online anti-stigma efforts significantly reduced public stigma towards mental health conditions. A meta-analysis revealed that participants in online interventions experienced a notable stigma reduction compared to non-online, waitlist control, and no-intervention groups. These online interventions were as effective [27] as traditional in-person methods ascribed to their educational and social contact-based approaches. Online interventions enable wider reach and lower costs; however, challenges such as high dropout rates must be addressed. Emerging technologies sometimes present novel threats to adolescent well-being, such as encouraging bullying, disrupting sleep, and creating digital records with potential image-altering impacts. However, many virtual behaviors and risks resemble the real world [28]. Online advocacy and interventions effectively reduce mental health stigma, comparable to traditional methods, with a broader reach and cost efficiency. However, the digital environment poses challenges, such as high dropout rates and risks of bullying and sleep disruption. Addressing these issues ensures that online platforms promote well-being without unintentional harm.

This chapter investigates the intricate interplay between technological advancements and the stigma surrounding adolescent mental health. It delves into the potential benefits and obstacles associated with leveraging technology to combat stigma and enhance mental well-being outcomes among young people.

1.2.1 Understanding Mental Health Stigma and Technology

Mental health stigma involves negative perceptions, beliefs, and behaviors directed towards people who experience mental health issues, often leading to inequity and social exclusion [29, 30]. Stigma takes various forms, including public, self, and structural stigma, each with distinct yet interrelated consequences for individuals [29, 31]. The emergence of mental health stigma during adolescence can significantly impede psychological growth and reduce the likelihood of seeking help, as this period is when most mental health issues first appear [32].

Stigma can be internalized by teenagers, leading to a decrease in their self-esteem and sense of self-efficacy while also contributing to higher rates of depression. Moreover, stigma can lead to social withdrawal and diminished quality of life in those with mental health problems [30, 32]. Mental health stigma significantly affects adolescents, hindering their development, worsening mental health problems, and decreasing their probability of seeking and engaging in treatment. Addressing the stigma surrounding mental health in this demographic is essential for improving mental well-being and fostering a more accepting community [29, 32, 33]. In the digital age, mental health education and awareness, reducing stigma, disseminating support information, and promoting nurturing settings that stimulate open communication and mental well-being are vital for effective public health strategies [34].

1.2.2 Theoretical Frameworks for Understanding Technology and Stigma (e.g., Social Cognitive Theory, Diffusion of Innovation Theory)

Theoretical frameworks such as Rogers' diffusion of innovation theory and social cognitive theory (SCT) provide insights into technology integration and stigma development. Rogers' theory explores how new technologies are adopted within a population, focusing on factors affecting adoption rates and the *S*-curve characterizing technology uptake [35]. Conversely, social cognitive theory (SCT) examines individual and social behaviors, emphasizing the processes that foster and sustain stigma, especially regarding health behaviors and interventions [36, 37]. Rogers' theory addresses macro-level technology diffusion, whereas SCT covers micro-level technology adoption and stigma development, including nursing, where patient stigmatization can result in inadequate care [38]. Furthermore, SCT has functioned as a meta-framework to organize theoretical models in information systems research, demonstrating its versatility in examining technology-behavior interactions [39].

Rogers' and SCT frameworks explain technology adoption and stigma-related social cognitive processes, complementing each other by providing macro and individual/social behavioral insights. Integrating these frameworks could improve our understanding of the interaction between technology and social phenomena, such as stigma [35, 37–39]. According to [40], perceived public stigma was not a predictor of seeking support. The study revealed that emotional well-being acted as a mediator between life stressors and support-seeking behavior. It moderated this relationship, with the connection being stronger when anticipated negative outcomes were reduced. These findings indicate that social cognitive theory encourages social media-based support-seeking, especially self-efficacy and positive outcome expectations. Consistent with the labeling theory, stigma was not a barrier, likely due to non-stigmatizing support-seeking methods. Professionals should design social media interventions to enhance self-efficacy, encourage positive feedback, and eliminate features that enable adverse reactions or harmful comments.

1.3 The Digital Landscape: Opportunities and Challenges

Evidence highlights that social media's role as a double-edged sword offers advantages, such as facilitating connection, providing support, and raising awareness, as well as disadvantages, including cyberbullying, unrealistic comparisons, and dissemination of misinformation [19, 41]. On the advantageous side, social media facilitates global connections, access to information, and the promotion of social cohesion, particularly during crises, including the COVID-19 pandemic [41]. Social media provide a platform for emotional support, community building, and mental health awareness [19, 42]. Adolescents frequently anticipate positive outcomes when they observe their peers seeking mental health support on Instagram. COVID-19-related stress and self-efficacy encourage seeking support through social media, whereas lower emotional well-being tends to discourage it [40]. Studies on teenagers' social media usage often highlight its negative impacts on psychological well-being. While there are potential dangers, such as social filters, triggers, and online harassment, there are also notable advantages, including healthy forms of self-expression, social connections, and confidential access to mental health support [8]. Balancing these aspects is crucial for maximizing the positive impact of social media while reducing risks. However, we must note that the adverse negative impact of social media on adolescents is more substantial.

Adolescents are significantly affected by the detrimental effects of social media. Research suggests that certain social media platforms often showcase unrealistic portrayals of individuals' lives, which can trigger feelings of inadequacy, envy, and discontent when users compare their own experiences to those of others [43]. The development of anxiety disorders, depression, and social isolation can be attributed to factors such as cyberbullying, poor self-perception, and the fear of being left out [19, 44, 45]. A study by [46] revealed a connection between problematic social media usage, social stress, and heightened cyber-victimization among young teenagers, with 29% falling victim to peer-based harassment at school. [47] reported that moderate to severe depression and suicide risk behaviors were common among participants who engaged in online depressive content. Teenagers experiencing thoughts of suicide and engaging in self-harm without suicidal intent responded more unfavorably to related material and felt increased anxiety about how others might perceive them. These findings highlight the need to address social media's adverse effects and develop strategies to mitigate these risks.

Social media presents a complex landscape for teenage mental well-being, offering both potential risks and advantages. The psychological health of young people is significantly impacted by these online platforms, which can exert both negative and positive influences.

Adolescents' mental health faces significant challenges from social media, which can have both detrimental and beneficial effects. According to [48], participants felt that social media use poses three significant risks: its tendency to cause stress, depression, low self-esteem, and suicidal thoughts; exposure to bullying and trolling; and addictive tendencies. These factors contribute to a low mood and decreased self-esteem, with social media often perceived as having a negative influence due to unrealistic 'photo-shopped' images among adolescents.

The psychological well-being of adolescents and women is notably affected by social media, highlighting the need for strategies to manage negative emotions and stress [42, 49]. While adolescents report that positive social media experiences outweigh negative experiences and significant benefits to self-esteem, many adverse effects exist [50]. This positivity bias does not eliminate the occasional negative experiences that affect self-esteem. Notably, adolescents' opposing views on social media often align with their usage patterns. Despite extensive social media use, many perceive it as 'dangerous' due to 'damaging websites', attributing risks mainly to third parties. The absence of social media education has exacerbated this limited understanding [20]. Practical strategies and improved education are essential to mitigate the negative impacts of social media and enhance adolescents' mental health.

Harmful social media use, characterized by promoting risky behaviors, cyberbullying, and negative self-comparisons, is categorized by young people into three areas: over-sharing personal details through frequent or overly intimate updates, spreading negative content by posting pessimistic material, and encountering distressing posts that trigger negative emotions. Conversely, positive use involves seeking content for entertainment, humor, or social connection. Adolescents undergoing mental health treatment often transition from negative to positive social media use patterns [51]. Social media can enhance connectivity and support, enrich lives, and pose mental health risks. The challenge is to balance these effects by encouraging positive use and implementing measures to mitigate the negative impacts. Future research should continue to investigate both the beneficial and detrimental effects of social media, with the aim of enhancing its positive aspects while minimizing its negative impact on individual and societal well-being [44, 49, 52].

1.3.1 Self-Diagnosis and Romanticization of Mental Health Problems

The glorification of mental health disorders among young people in India is a troubling trend. Romanticizing mental illness can lead to self-diagnosis, which can lead to more negative consequences among adolescents [61]. Normalization may lead to an increase in self-diagnosis. People exposed to social media posts normalizing anxiety are more likely to classify themselves as having an anxiety disorder by identifying with the person in the post, which may be because young people generally do not feel much stigma towards others with anxiety [53]. [54] found that Twitter messages on mental health mainly focused on raising awareness rather than perpetuating stigma. When present, stigma is typically related to the fear of violence, unlike other mental health issues that are more commonly associated with anxiety. Students may self-diagnose anxiety disorders based on their identification with social media figures who normalize them while avoiding diagnosis when anxiety is stigmatized, as individuals typically distance themselves from stigmatized groups [55].

The glorification of mental health issues on social media has raised concerns about its influence on young people's perceptions and approaches to mental disorders. [56] examined the idealization of mental health on these platforms and its impact on adolescents' views on mental illness. Their study highlighted that Twitter, now X, often features critiques of this glamorization, indicating users' awareness of its potential harm. This romanticization can lead to misleading narratives stigmatizing vulnerable individuals [57]. The issue of self-diagnosis is complicated, especially among adolescents, and adds another layer to this problem. While some believe that self-diagnosis is a reasonable approach, others argue that it can be harmful and lead to inaccurate self-perception and incorrect treatment [58–60]. In India, this trend is particularly troubling as adolescents romanticize mental illnesses on social media, which influences their attitudes and exacerbates the broader issue of stigma related to mental health and misinformation.

Addressing the romanticized perception of mental health has been emphasized in broader efforts to combat stigma and misinformation through educational and awareness campaigns [56, 57]. Although destigmatizing mental illness is crucial, it is equally vital to avoid romanticizing it, which could lead to misguided beliefs and the trivialization of genuine struggles [61]. Healthcare professionals must be cautious not to unintentionally contribute to increased self-diagnosis or perpetuation of stigma through normalization efforts. Future studies should focus on developing messages that normalize mental health problems while simultaneously mitigating stigma [53]. By fostering a balanced understanding of mental health, we can enhance adolescents' comprehension of mental health challenges and potential risks associated with self-diagnosis [62].

1.3.2 The Advent of Mental Health Applications and Digital Platforms

Digital mental health platforms and apps offer personalized support to tech-savvy adolescents [63, 64]. Adolescents appreciate mental health apps for their convenience and ability to provide self-reliant suggestions [64]. Digital therapeutics, validated through clinical trials, offer evidence-based treatments with the potential for effective personalized interventions [65]. However, data privacy issues persist, including poor data handling and user profiling risks [66, 67]. Concerns also exist regarding the efficacy of these applications, with specific studies highlighting user engagement challenges and reliance on nonevidence-based methodologies [68]. Accessibility is another crucial concern, particularly for adolescents with disabilities, and requires further research to ensure inclusivity [69]. Mental health apps offer several advantages; however, concerns regarding data privacy, efficacy, and accessibility demand attention. To overcome these challenges, ensuring safe and effective digital interventions, requires collaboration among developers, healthcare providers, and policymakers [65, 67–69].

Online support groups and communities can significantly enhance adolescents' sense of belonging and shared experiences. Social media platforms allow young people to extend their relationships and explore their interests with like-minded individuals across different geographical settings [70]. Online spaces can foster community empowerment, reduce loneliness, and improve interpersonal skills [71]. However, challenges related to anonymity and moderation exist. Anonymity can encourage participation but lead to irresponsible behavior and reduced collaboration [72]. Moderation strategies, while protecting users, may unintentionally inhibit positive dialogue and create barriers to support, resulting in isolated and polarized communities [73]. For adolescents who experience self-harm, peer support interventions pose the risk of triggering self-harm or re-traumatization, highlighting the need for careful moderation and supportive structures [71]. Additionally, inadequate social media validation can significantly impact adolescents' social status and emotional well-being.

Brief social media interactions lacking positive validation correlate with adolescent risk factors for depression including maladaptive stress appraisal and heightened depressive symptoms. Lower levels of social media engagement, as indicated by fewer likes, were associated with increased symptoms of depression, both on a daily basis and by the conclusion of the academic year. Peer-victimized adolescents are particularly affected by receiving fewer likes, indicating that online social status comparisons may intensify internalizing symptoms in at-risk youths even without explicit negative comments [72]. Although online support groups and communities offer valuable opportunities for belonging and support, they must also address challenges such as anonymity and effective moderation to prevent potential harm.

Adolescents widely use popular social media platforms, including Facebook, Instagram, Snapchat, and Twitter [74]. Adolescents often utilize less popular sites such as Pinterest, Reddit, Whisper, YikYak, and Ask.FM. Research by [75] revealed that a quarter of the posts contained potentially detrimental advice, including methods for self-harm, while only 13% suggested seeking professional assistance. Reinecke (as cited in Bine, 2013) [76] observed that Tumblr often lacks support for healthy coping strategies or therapies, possibly reinforcing negative feelings and depression. Similarly, pinterest fails to promote healthy coping or professional help, sometimes validating maladaptive strategies [77]. Despite this, Tumblr allows adolescents to discuss their struggles more openly than offline [78].

Social media can have harmful effects, such as exposing users to content that normalizes self-harm. For example, searching for "cutting" on Instagram can lead to images of self-harm, potentially encouraging maladaptive coping mechanisms [79]. Another example is the pro-anorexia (pro-ana) community in Tumblr, which shares graphic content with glorifying anorexia [80]. Asher, the author of 13 Reasons Why, intended to address the discomfort surrounding suicide and facilitate discourse to engender hope despite the series' graphic depiction of the suicide method to emphasize its severity. Brian Yorkey, an executive producer, stated that the portrayal was designed to be disturbing to underscore the lack of value in suicide [81]. Teenagers struggle to assess information about mental health apps and frequently seek advice online. They suggested that mental health apps should come from credible sources and present explicit and engaging content [82].

1.4 Impact of Cultural and Social Determinants on Mental Health Stigma and Technology Use

Research has demonstrated that cultural and social factors significantly influence mental health stigma. Research indicates that cultural backgrounds influence how individuals perceive mental health issues and their willingness to seek assistance [83]. Discrimination in mental health and educational settings can stem from societal stereotypes, cultural factors, and biases [84]. Technology use, particularly online resources, has been shown to reduce mental health stigma among international college students by fostering supportive environments and showcasing positive role models [85]. Contradictions have arisen regarding the impact of cultural factors on stigma and technology use. While some studies report a reduction in stigma through educational programs and online communities [85, 86]. Others suggest that interventions often have temporary effects, and positive attitudes towards the stigmatization of mental illness are rare [87].

Additionally, the impact of racial discrimination on mental health stigma indicates that social factors can exacerbate stigma and that the relationship between culture, social factors, and technology use is more complex [88]. Societal and cultural elements heavily influence mental health stigma, and the utilization of technological tools, including Internet-based resources and educational initiatives, can contribute to diminishing this stigma. However, the effectiveness of these interventions may vary based on the cultural context and the presence of other social factors, such as discrimination. It is crucial to consider these intricacies when designing interventions to address mental health stigmas [83, 86].

1.5 Successful Examples of Leveraging Technology's Potential for Positive Outcomes

Reducing adolescent stigma requires technology-based interventions to build safe online communities and enhance digital literacy and critical thinking. [89] stressed the importance of preventive online safety education, integrating digital literacy, critical thinking, and responsible behavior to create a safer digital environment for teenagers. [90] incorporated Islamic values to strengthen these skills among Muslim adolescents, while [91] emphasized improving risk perception and critical thinking through digital literacy training. [92] identified four thematic clusters of youth digital citizenship resources: participation, empowerment, engagement, and well-being. Notably, "positive online behavior" and "digital literacy" are central to school-based digital citizenship education [93]. Prioritizing these elements in educational initiatives is essential for fostering safer and more informed online experiences among adolescents.

The Be Internet Awesome (BIA) digital citizenship program positively impacted 4th–6th graders' knowledge, attitudes, and behaviors across 14 U.S. schools. The program facilitates learning and retaining new online safety vocabulary and concepts among late elementary and early middle school students, thereby enhancing their self-efficacy in addressing online challenges. Digital citizenship education can equip young children with tools to manage online problems and foster enthusiasm for positive participation. Nevertheless, the results regarding online privacy practices, cyberbullying incidents, and parental communication indicate a need for additional exploration and analysis by educators and specialists to enhance educational objectives and approaches. Strengthening these aspects is crucial in preparing children for the digital world [94].

[95] demonstrated that the implementation of POGIL (process-oriented guided inquiry learning) methodology, coupled with digital mind mapping techniques in an online educational setting, effectively enhanced the critical thinking and problem-solving abilities of XI MIPA students in Malang, East Java. However, more than digital literacy there is a need to improve critical thinking, indicating an intricate connection between these skills [96]. Technology-based interventions that integrate digital literacy and critical thinking can help to create safer online communities for adolescents and potentially reduce stigma. However, this relationship requires tailored approaches to meet adolescents' diverse needs. Technological advancements can enhance social-emotional learning (SEL) by using

mobile devices for timely prompts and leveraging social media for reflection and support. Experts in mental health could utilize natural language understanding systems, currently employed in therapeutic settings, to enhance social-emotional growth and interpersonal skills in daily life [97]. Focusing on understanding and addressing the complexities of digital literacy and critical thinking can maximize the impact of these interventions.

Leveraging technologies like game-based learning can significantly enhance engagement with online privacy and safety topics. As an example, a tabletop game inspired by Snakes and Ladders/Trivial Pursuit, created for young adults between 16 and 25 years old, assists them in exploring the digital landscape and comprehending the privacy consequences of their online behavior. The game covers topics such as Internet fraud, online harassment, cyberbullying, and various digital security concerns. Testing with focus groups has demonstrated that through both passive and interactive gameplay, young people acquire knowledge about maintaining their safety in the online environment [98]. Such innovative approaches can protect young people from online dangers while making learning more engaging and accessible.

1.5.1 Targeting Specific Stigma-Related Attitudes and Behaviors

The intersection of technology and mental health stigma presents opportunities and challenges. Digital technologies can contribute to reducing stigma, especially in low and middle-income nations, by facilitating education, enabling demonstrations, and fostering social interactions. However, these approaches must be culturally tailored and carefully monitored, as digital media have the potential to spread misinformation and worsen stigma [30]. While technology has the potential to combat stigma, it can also be unintentionally reinforced. For example, the widespread mental health stigma observed among Gen Z students in Salafi Islamic boarding schools indicates that technology, if not properly managed, could reinforce harmful stereotypes [99]. The connection between artificial intelligence and mental health stigma is complex and multifaceted. Artificial intelligence offers promising tools for combating stigma. However, ensuring that these tools are designed and implemented with cultural awareness is vital to avoid the perpetuating biases inherent in AI systems [100]. Digital interventions must be culturally sensitive and cautiously implemented to prevent exacerbation of stigma.

Research indicates that technology can reduce stigma when used effectively, countering concerns that it might increase stigma. Online resources have been shown to lower mental health stigma among international college students [85], and educational experiences, potentially incorporating technology, can enhance mental health awareness and reduce stigma [86]. In addressing mental health stigma among teenagers, various approaches prove essential. These include leveraging social media initiatives, utilizing mental health-focused applications, and facilitating online communities for support. Such tactics are instrumental in challenging and reducing the stigma surrounding mental health issues among adolescents. These platforms provide timely support, reduce the cost of mental healthcare, and address the stigma associated with seeking help [68]. Adolescents view mental health apps positively and consider them valuable and beneficial [64]. Ultimately, while technology holds promise in reducing mental health stigma, its impact depends on its application.

Incorporating features such as safety, engagement, functionality, and social interaction into app design aligns with adolescents' needs, potentially enhancing their acceptability and effectiveness [82]. Employing technology ethically to combat mental health stigma brings up issues related to the privacy of data, obtaining proper consent, and safeguarding at-risk groups. Mental illness stigma can lead to ethical challenges in research, particularly in obtaining consent and respecting individuals' treatment choices [101]. While technology offers significant benefits in mental healthcare, it also complicates data privacy and informed consent issues, especially with the growing complexity of digital health technologies [102].

However, these strategies have notable limitations. Despite positive attitudes, many adolescents are unaware of mental health apps, which limits their use [63]. Moreover, the impact of these applications remains unclear, as there is a lack of substantial evidence supporting their effectiveness in addressing mental health concerns among the youth [68]. Common drawbacks include user engagement issues, safety concerns during emergencies, privacy breaches, and reliance on non-evidence-based interventions or self-diagnostic tools [68]. Low engagement and poor usability also contribute to abandoning mental health applications [103]. Social media campaigns, mental health apps, and online support groups offer accessibility and may reduce stigma; however, limited awareness, unproven efficacy, and engagement issues may hinder their effectiveness. Enhancing their impact requires increasing awareness, rigorously evaluating efficacy, improving design to boost engagement, and addressing privacy concerns [64, 68, 82, 103].

1.6 Best Practices for Effectively Using Technology to Reduce Stigma

1.6.1 Co-Creation with Adolescents to Ensure Relevance and Engagement

Engaging adolescents in creating online applications and social media initiatives ensures relevance and engagement while potentially mitigating stigma. This collaborative approach allows adolescents to shape their designs, reflecting their experiences and perspectives. Despite the criticism of social networking sites (SNSs) for their negative impacts, they offer opportunities for positive self-presentation, relationship building, and psychosocial development [104]. Additionally, a robust parent-child connection on SNSs can safeguard against cyberbullying, indicating that SNSs can create supportive environments when used wisely [105].

Adolescents should be involved in designing and implementing online applications to reduce stigma through digital tools and social media. This collaboration can leverage the benefits of networking sites, such as supportive interactions and personal growth, while mitigating risks [104]. Additionally, understanding how adolescents engage with social media, especially those at social risk, such as peer victimization and social anxiety, can guide the creation of strategies to improve their safety and well-being on these platforms [106].

1.6.2 Collaboration with Mental Health Professionals and Technology Experts

Given the potential risks associated with digital media, mental health professionals are responsible for guiding adolescents and their caregivers towards reliable online health information resources. They need ongoing training on digital innovations, adolescents' media use, and their health effects to provide effective guidance. By directly interacting with teenagers, they can push for better digital governance focused on young people and greater investment in digital literacy programs. Mental health professionals are well suited to evaluate the impact of digital media on adolescents and promote evidence-based policies. Addressing the digital determinants of health requires coordinated efforts, including removing digital access barriers, offering literacy education, and involving adolescents in shaping their digital environments. Governments and tech companies must prioritize adolescent well-being when designing and regulating digital platforms [107].

Educators and school-based mental health professionals must understand adolescents' social media habits. Research should integrate social media use into identifying those requiring mental health services and ensuring access to credible professional resources [8]. Parents and educators must assist all adolescents, not just those harmed by social media, in dealing with issues such as cyberbullying and social exclusion. Educating adolescents about the unrealistic nature of social media portrayals should be integral to parenting and school digital literacy programs [50].

1.6.3 Adult Supervision and Engagement to Regulate Adolescents' Technology Usage

Involving parents and harnessing the positive aspects of social media is crucial for supporting adolescents' mental health. Social media interactions can provide emotional support and mental health guidance, making them valuable tools for preventive interventions. Primary care and mental health providers should monitor adolescents' social media use to make informed treatment recommendations [47]. Adults should guide adolescents with history of suicidal thoughts or behaviors on safe social media practices. Adolescents can effectively manage their social media use by employing proactive strategies such as learning when to log off, adjusting interactions, and seeking support when triggered [51].

As reported by adolescents, mental health apps have the potential to empower them by lowering the threshold for seeking help through anonymity and constant availability. Adolescents appreciate their ability to seek help independently through these apps [64]. However, they often struggle to assess the accuracy of the provided information. Adolescents often search for mental health information online and on social media, making it important for adults to help them find credible apps and resources. Enhancing knowledge of dependable mental health applications and advising on their use can maximize the benefits of digital tools and social media in supporting mental well-being [82, 108].

1.7 Future Directions and Recommendations

Evidence supports the use of technology and various approaches to reduce stigma and improve help-seeking behaviors among adolescents.

[109] demonstrated that video-based interventions effectively reduced stigma and enhanced treatment-seeking intentions, impacting the Depression Stigma Scale and General Help-Seeking Questionnaire. [110] found that brief educational interventions involving psychoeducation and DVD contact with affected individuals decreased explicit stigma and increased openness to treatment. A technology-driven intervention called Tech Connect was developed by [111], which demonstrates the potential for enhancing engagement in treatment among depressed adolescents. However, the effectiveness of these interventions varies. [110] highlighted the challenges in addressing implicit stigma and translating stigma reduction into behavioral changes. [32] and [112] pointed to the lack of consensus on practical implementation and the need for long-term evaluations of mental health programs. According to [113], there is a crucial need for adaptability in interventions aimed at reducing stigma, particularly in nations with low- and middle-income levels. Comparative research is essential considering the long-term effects, underlying stigma, and population characteristics to assess the efficacy of various platforms and techniques. Further studies should aim to customize interventions for various adolescent demographics and ensure that reduced stigma enhances the use of mental health resources and participation in related services.

The study suggests that current strategies may be effective for some goals, but follow-up research is needed to confirm these findings and understand their long-term impacts. Encouragingly, the Be Internet Awesome (BIA) program evaluation showed positive results in terms of knowledge and self-efficacy. Achieving these goals requires a multifaceted strategy involving educators, parents, and policymakers, with cultural values potentially enhancing intervention effectiveness [89, 90]. For example, reducing the risk of technology-facilitated sexual exploitation could involve online safety experts contributing to sexual assault prevention and healthy relationship programs. Digital citizenship programs may also need creative approaches, such as encouraging younger children to seek help from adults on online issues or incorporating role-playing to improve communication.

Furthermore, Internet safety programs could emphasize training for parents and educators to equip them with skills to effectively address their children's online issues [94]. Tackling cyberbullying, privacy, and reputation concerns may require backing for evidence-based prevention strategies, such as anti-bullying programs or social-emotional learning (SEL) initiatives [114, 115], necessitating the promotion of these well-established interventions. Strengthening these areas is essential for a more effective digital citizenship education.

Subsequent studies should investigate the intricate interplay between social media behaviors and peer interactions, taking into account the varied environments of different platforms and their enduring effects on adolescents' well-being and growth [106]. While social media can provide positive support, it also exposes youth to abuse, especially when discussing public mental health issues. Examining the stigmatizing messages adolescents encounter online could reveal barriers to accessing mental health support. Additionally, as online and offline relationships blend increasingly, understanding how adolescents value these connections is crucial. Future studies should investigate whether adolescents view online and offline relationships as equally significant or distinct [116]. When developing mental health apps, adolescents highlight the importance of accessibility, cost-effectiveness, and reliable information obtained from trusted sources. They also value anonymity and both human- and web-based support. These factors should inform the design of mental health apps tailored to adolescent needs [64].

1.8 Conclusion

Digital technologies and social networking platforms have become essential components of everyday life. These tools facilitate communication, share mental health resources, and offer continuous psychological support for all age groups. However, these online platforms pose significant risks, particularly for teenagers and underprivileged youths. Among these are cyberbullying, distorted self-perception, and unease arising from the concern of social ostracism. These elements can contribute to the onset of mental health issues, such as anxiety disorders, depression, and social withdrawal [19, 44]. Moreover, the phenomenon of glamorizing mental illness and self-diagnosing among teenage audiences also discredits those who go through real struggles with mental illness. Despite these challenges, technology still has the potential to increase proficiency in the safe use of the Internet and enhance the acceptance of professional help, thereby reducing the stigma associated with seeking help. Ethical considerations, including data protection and informed consent, require culturally sensitive supervised interventions and better collaboration among mental health professionals, educational institutions, and policymakers. Additionally, providing such adolescents with the ability to reason and think critically will allow them to use it to prevent adverse encounters online.

References

1. Joshi, S.C., and Rose, G.L., Information Technology, Internet Use, and Adolescent Cognitive Development. *2018 3rd International Conference on Computational Systems and Information Technology for Sustainable Solutions (CSITSS)*, pp. 22–28, 2018.
2. Pereira, S., Fillol, J., Moura, P., Teens' online and offline lives, in: *Routledge*, pp. 152–160, 2020, https://doi.org/10.4324/9781351004107-14.
3. Lee, J. and Jeong, G.C., The influence of gaming behavior on school adjustment among Korean adolescents: The moderating effect of self-regulation. *Behav. Sci.*, 14, 3, 259, 2024. https://doi.org/10.3390/bs14030259.
4. Karnik, N.S., Vulnerability, youth, and homelessness: ethical considerations on the roles of technology in the lives of adolescents and young adults, in: *Neuroethics: Anticipating the Future*, J. Illes (ed.), pp. 70–79, Oxford Academic Press, Oxford, UK, 2017.
5. Whittle, H., Hamilton-Giachritsis, C., Beech, A., Collings, G., A review of online grooming: Characteristics and concerns. *Aggression Violent Behav.*, 18, 1, 62–70, 2013. https://doi.org/10.1016/j.avb.2012.09.003.
6. Razi, A., Badillo-Urquiola, K., Wisniewski, P.J., Let's talk about sex: How adolescents seek support and advice about their online sexual experiences, in: *Proceedings of the 2020 CHI Conference on Human Factors in Computing Systems*, pp. 1–13, 2020, April, https://doi.org/10.1145/3313831.3376400.
7. Razi, A., Caddle, X., Alsoubai, A., Kim, S., Choudhury, M.D., Stringhini, G., Ali, S., Wisniewski, P., Teens at the margin: Artificially intelligent technology for promoting adolescent online safety, in: *SSRN*, 2021, https://doi.org/10.2139/ssrn.3851317.
8. Elmquist, D.L. and McLaughlin, C.L., Social media use among adolescents coping with mental health. *Contemp. Sch. Psychol.*, 22, 503–511, 2018.
9. Geldard, K., Geldard, D., Foo, R.Y., *Counselling adolescents: The proactive approach for young people*, SAGE, London, 2016.
10. Ungar, M., Ghazinour, M., Richter, J., Annual research review: What is resilience within the social ecology of human development? *J. Child Psychol. Psychiatry*, *54*, 4, 348–366, 2013.
11. Akintayo, O.T., Eden, C.A., Ayeni, O.O., Onyebuchi, N.C., Integrating AI with emotional and social learning in primary education: Developing a holistic adaptive learning ecosystem. *Comput. Sci. IT Res. J.*, *5*, 5, 1076–1089, 2024.
12. Delamater, A.M., Aparicio, K., Guzman, A., Mental health issues in children and adolescents with chronic illness. *Ethnicity Inequal. Health Soc. Care, 10*, 3, 163–173, 2017. https://doi.org/10.1108/ijhrh-05-2017-0020.
13. Felfe, C., Ravens-Sieberer, U., Kaman, A., Schneider, P., Vornberger, J., Saurer, J., Erhart, M., The youth mental health crisis: Quasi-experimental evidence on the role of school closures. *Sci. Adv.*, *9*, 33, 1–12, 2023. https://doi.org/10.1126/sciadv.adh4030.

14. George, F., *Mental health crisis among children and adolescents. SACAD: Scholarly Activities,* 2023, Article 72, 2023. https://doi.org/10.58809/VMGW5529.
15. Twenge, J.M., Have smartphones destroyed a generation?, in: *The Atlantic,* 2017, September, Retrieved from https://www.theatlantic.com/magazine/archive/2017/09/has-the-smartphone-destroyed-a-generation/534198/.
16. Heid, M., There's worrying new research about kids' screen time and their mental health, in: *TIME,* 2018, October, http://time.com/5437607/smartphones-teens-mental-health/. Accessed July 22, 2024.
17. George, M., The importance of social media content for teens' risks for self-harm. *J. Adolesc. Health, 65,* 1, 9–10, 2019.
18. Ogugua, J.O., Okongwu, C.C., Akomolafe, O.O., Anyanwu, E.C., Daraojimba, O.D., Mental health and digital technology: A public health review of current trends and responses. *Int. Med. Sci. Res. J.,* 4, 2, 108–125, 2024.
19. Anguyo, M., Masete, J., Akia, M., Drasiku, H., The impact of social media on adolescent mental health, in: *Mental health of children and adolescents in the 21st century* [Online First]. M. Carotenuto (Ed.), IntechOpen, 2023. https://doi.org/10.5772/intechopen.1003060.
20. Khalaf, A.M., Khalaf, A.M., Alubied, A.A., Rifaey, A.A., The impact of social media on the mental health of adolescents and young adults: A systematic review. *Cureus, 15,* 8, 1–10, 2023. https://doi.org/10.7759/cureus.42990.
21. Talukdar, J., The impact of social media on adolescent mental health: A comprehensive review. *Integr. J. Res. Arts Humanit.,* 4, 4, 98–104, 2024. https://doi.org/10.55544/ijrah.4.4.16.
22. Hamilton, J.L., Coulter, R.W.S., Radovic, A., Mental health benefits and opportunities, in: *Technology and adolescent health: In schools and beyond,* M. A. Moreno & A. J. Hoopes (Eds.), pp. 305–345, Elsevier Academic Press, Jan 2020. https://doi.org/10.1016/B978-0-12-817319-0.00013-X.
23. University, R. and Joshi, K., The impact of social stigma on the mental health of the LGBTQ community. *Int. J. Sci. Res. Eng. Manage.,* 8, 4, 1–5, 2024. https://doi.org/10.55041/ijsrem30574.
24. Bussing, R., Mason, D., Zima, B., Meyer, J., Garvan, C., Gary, F., Childhood ADHD symptoms: Association with parental social networks and mental health service use during adolescence. *Int. J. Environ. Res. Public Health, 12,* 9, 11893–11909, 2015. https://doi.org/10.3390/ijerph120911893.
25. Moroney, E., Ebbert, A.M., Lee, S.S., Luthar, S.S., Digital media use frequency, online behaviors, and risk for negative mental health in adolescents in high-achieving schools. *Clin. Child Psychol. Psychiatry, 28,* 1, 237–254, 2022. https://doi.org/10.1177/13591045221108834.
26. Daniel, L., Robin, S., Aleksander, M., Future facts: Unveiling mental health issues in the digital age. *Fusion Multi. Res. An Int. J., 3,* 2, 354–365, 2022.
27. Goh, Y.S., Ow Yong, Q.Y.J., Tam, W.W., Effects of online stigma-reduction programme for people experiencing mental health conditions: A systematic review and meta-analysis. *Int. J. Ment. Health Nurs.,* 5, 1040–1056, 2021

Oct;30. doi: 10.1111/inm.12893. Epub 2021 Jun 3. PMID: 34081384; PMCID: PMC8518363.

28. George, M.J. and Odgers, C.L., Seven fears and the science of how mobile technologies may be influencing adolescents in the digital age. *Perspect. Psychol. Sci.*, *10*, 6, 832–851, 2015.
29. Corrigan, P.W., Druss, B.G., Perlick, D.A., The impact of mental illness stigma on seeking and participating in mental health care. *Psychol. Sci. Public Interest*, *15*, 2, 37–70, 2014. https://doi.org/10.1177/1529100614531398.
30. Naslund, J.A. and Deng, D., Addressing mental health stigma in low-income and middle-income countries: A new frontier for digital mental health. *Ethics Med. Public Health*, *19*, 100719, 2021. https://doi.org/10.1016/j.jemep.2021.100719.
31. Ong, W.J., Shahwan, S., Chong, S.A., Goh, C.M.J., Subramaniam, M., Tan, G.T.H., Daily encounters of mental illness stigma and individual strategies to reduce stigma - Perspectives of people with mental illness. *Front. Psychol.*, *11*, 6305, 2020. https://doi.org/10.3389/fpsyg.2020.590844.
32. Deluca, J.S., Conceptualizing adolescent mental illness stigma: Youth stigma development and stigma reduction programs. *Adolesc. Res. Rev.*, *5*, 2, 153–171, 2019. https://doi.org/10.1007/s40894-018-0106-3.
33. Taylor, R., Cogan, N., Jenkins, P., Liu, X., Flowers, P., Hunter, S. C., Corrigan, P., Mental illness self-stigma in young people: A scoping review protocol. *medRxiv*, 1–12, 2021. https://doi.org/10.1101/2021.07.06.21260070.
34. Seiferth, C., Vogel, L., Aas, B., Brandhorst, I., Carlbring, P., Conzelmann, A., Löchner, J., How to e-mental health: A guideline for researchers and practitioners using digital technology in the context of mental health. *Nat. Ment. Health*, *1*, 8, 542–554, 2023.
35. Yu, P., Diffusion of innovation theory, in: *Routledge*, pp. 59–61, 2022, https://doi.org/10.4324/9781003109945-16.
36. Islam, K.F., Awal, A., Mazumder, H., Munni, U.R., Majumder, K., Afroz, K., Tabassum, M.N., Hossain, M.M., Social cognitive theory-based health promotion in primary care practice: A scoping review. *Heliyon*, *9*, 4, e14889, 2023. https://doi.org/10.1016/j.heliyon.2023.e14889.
37. Martin, C.A., King, A.C., Hekler, E.B., Buman, M.P., Riley, W.T., Adams, M.A., Rivera, D.E., A dynamical systems model of Social Cognitive Theory, in: *Institute of Electrical Electronics Engineers*, 2014, https://doi.org/10.1109/acc.2014.6859463.
38. Copeland, D., Stigmatization in nursing: Theoretical pathways and implications. *Nurs. Inq.*, 29, 2, 1–7, 2022. https://doi.org/10.1111/nin.12438.
39. Carillo, K., Understanding IS theory: An interpretation of key IS theoretical frameworks using social cognitive theory, in: *Information Systems Theory*, pp. 241–280, 2011, https://doi.org/10.1007/978-1-4419-9707-4_13.
40. Basaran, D.S., Webs of social support for mental health: An examination of college students' social support seeking behavior on social media.

Int. J. Environ. Res. Public Health, 12, 9, 11893–11909, 2021. https://doi.org/10.3390/ijerph120911893.
41. Dalne, S. and Moundekar, J., Impact of social media in student's psychology. *J. Psychol. Political Sci., 33*, 46–49, 2023. https://doi.org/10.55529/jpps.33.46.49.
42. Donnelly, J. and Saldutti, E., Public health implications of social media on adolescent health behaviors: Upstream approaches to prevention strategies. *Med. Res. Arch.*, 12, 1, 1–7, 2023. https://doi.org/10.18103/mra.v12i1.4922.
43. Bonsaksen, T., Steigen, A.M., Stea, T.H., Kleppang, A.L., Lien, L., Leonhardt, M., Negative social media-related experiences and lower general self-efficacy are associated with depressive symptoms in adolescents. *Front. Public Health*, 10, 1037375, 2023. https://doi.org/10.3389/fpubh.2023.1037375.
44. Sadagheyani, H.E. and Tatari, F., Investigating the role of social media on mental health, in: *A Life in the Day*, vol. 25, Issue 1, pp. 41–51, 2020, https://doi.org/10.1108/mhsi-06-2020-0039.
45. Huong, X.V., Exploring the impact of social media on mental health from a psychological perspective: A review of the contemporary literature. *Int. J. Curr. Sci. Res. Rev., 6*, 10, 6542–6546, 2023. https://doi.org/10.47191/ijcsrr/v6-i10-05.
46. Kim, S., Garthe, R., Hsieh, W.J., Hong, J.S., Problematic social media use and conflict, social stress, and cyber-victimization among early adolescents. *Child Adolesc. Soc. Work J., 41*, 2, 223–233, 2024.
47. Szlyk, H.S., Li, X., Kasson, E., Peoples, J.E., Montayne, M., Kaiser, N., Cavazos-Rehg, P., How do teens with a history of suicidal behavior and self-harm interact with social media? *J. Adolescence, 95*, 4, 797–810, 2023.
48. O'Reilly, M., Dogra, N., Whiteman, N., Hughes, J., Eruyar, S., Reilly, P., Is social media bad for mental health and wellbeing? Exploring the perspectives of adolescents. *Clin. Child Psychol. Psychiatry, 23*, 4, 601–613, 2018.
49. Gu, X., The impact of negative evaluations on women's mental health on social media. *J. Educ. Humanit. Soc. Sci., 22*, 306–314, 2023. https://doi.org/10.54097/ehss.v22i.12455.
50. Valkenburg, P.M., Pouwels, J.L., Beyens, I., van Driel, I.I., Keijsers, L., Adolescents' Social Media Experiences and Their Self-Esteem: A Person-Specific Susceptibility Perspective. *Technol. Mind Behav.*, 2, 2, 1–12, 2021. https://doi.org/10.1037/tmb0000037.
51. Radovic, A., Gmelin, T., Stein, B.D., Miller, E., Depressed adolescents' positive and negative use of social media. *J. Adolescence, 55*, 5–15, 2017.
52. Malle, A.B., Pal, P.S., Pawar, S.D., Mulani, S.A., The flip side of social media: Unveiling the effects of social media on mental health. *Int. J. Community Med. Public Health, 11*, 3, 1401–1407, 2024. https://doi.org/10.18203/2394-6040.ijcmph20240653.
53. Hasan, F., Foster, M.M., Cho, H., Normalizing Anxiety on Social Media Increases Self-Diagnosis of Anxiety: The Mediating Effect of Identification

(But Not Stigma). *J. Health Commun.*, 28, 9, 563–572, 2023 Sep 2. doi: 10.1080/10810730.2023.2235563. Epub 2023 Jul 13. PMID: 37448221.
54. Pavlova, A. and Berkers, P., Mental health discourse and social media: Which mechanisms of cultural power drive discourse on Twitter. *Soc. Sci. Med.*, 263, 113250, 2020 Oct. doi: 10.1016/j.socscimed.2020.113250. Epub 2020 Aug 6. PMID: 32862081.
55. Cano, I., Best, D., Beckwith, M., Phillips, L.A., Hamilton, P., Sloan, J., Stigma related to health conditions and offending behaviors: Social distance among students of health and social sciences. *Stigma Health*, 5, 1, 38–52, 2020. https://doi.org/10.1037/sah0000165.
56. Issaka, B., Aidoo, E.A.K., Wood, S.F., Mohammed, F., "Anxiety is not cute": Analysis of Twitter users' discourses on romanticizing mental illness. *BMC Psychiatry*, *24*, 1, 221, 2024. https://doi.org/10.1186/s12888-024-05663-w.
57. Ng, J.S. and Tandoc Jr., E.C., "Pretend crazy": Comments surrounding romanticizing mental illness on YouTube. *Health New Media Res.*, *4*, 1, 41–68, 2020.
58. Underhill, R., and Foulkes, L., Self-Diagnosis of Mental Disorders: A Qualitative Study of Attitudes on Reddit. *Qual. Health Res.*, 10497323241288785. Advance online publication, 2024. https://doi.org/10.1177/10497323241288785.
59. Annury, U.A., Yuliana, F., Suhadi, V.A.Z., Karlina, C.S.A., Dampak self-diagnose pada kondisi mental health mahasiswa Universitas Negeri Surabaya. *Prosiding Semin. Nasional Ilmu Ilmu Sosial (SNIIS)*, 1, 481–486, 2022. https://proceeding.unesa.ac.id/index.php/sniis/article/view/101/86.
60. Maskanah, I., Fenomena self-diagnosis di era pandemi COVID-19 dan dampaknya terhadap kesehatan mental. *J. Psychol. Stud.*, *1*, 1, 1–10, 2022. https://doi.org/10.15575/jops.v1i1.17467.
61. Ahuja, J. and Fichadia, P.A., Concerns Regarding the Glorification of Mental Illness on Social Media. *Cureus*, *16*, 3, e56631, 2024. https://doi.org/10.7759/cureus.56631.
62. Nurismawan, A.S., Lestary, Y.D., Purwoko, B., Alfaried, H.Z., Nafisah, K., Unraveling the dangers of mental health self-diagnosis: A study on the phenomenon of adolescent self-diagnosis in junior high schools. *KONSELI Jurnal Bimbingan dan Konseling (E-Journal)*, *11*, 1, 31–38, 2024.
63. Grist, R., Denne, M., Stallard, P., Cliffe, B., Croker, A., An online survey of young adolescent girls' use of the internet and smartphone apps for mental health support. *BJPsych Open*, *4*, 4, 302–306, 2018. https://doi.org/10.1192/bjo.2018.43.
64. Høgsdal, H., Rye, M., Kaiser, S., Kyrrestad, H., Exploring adolescents' attitudes toward mental health apps: Concurrent mixed methods study. *JMIR Form. Res.*, 8, e50222, 2024. https://doi.org/10.2196/50222.
65. Shah, A.M., and Shah, S.V., Digital therapeutics-a new era in health care. *Natl. J. Physiol. Pharm. Pharmacol.*, 13, 11, 2190–2196, 2023. doi:10.5455/njppp.2023.13.09464202302102023.
66. Ebben, M. and Murphy, J., An Analysis of Privacy Language in the Scholarly Literature on Mental Health Apps, in: *Privacy Concerns Surrounding Personal*

Information Sharing on Health and Fitness Mobile Apps, D. Sen and R. Ahmed (Eds.), pp. 212–239, IGI Global, Hersey, PA, 2020.

67. Iwaya, L.H., Babar, M.A., Rashid, A., Wijayarathna, C., On the privacy of mental health apps: An empirical investigation and its implications for app development. *Empir. Softw. Eng.*, 28, 1, 1–42, 2023. https://doi.org/10.1007/s10664-022-10236-0.
68. Koh, J., Hartanto, A., Tng, G.Y.Q., Potential and pitfalls of mobile mental health apps in traditional treatment: An umbrella review. *J. Pers. Med., 12*, 9, 1376, 2022. https://doi.org/10.3390/jpm12091376. PMID: 36143161; PMCID: PMC9505389.
69. Bunyi, J., Ringland, K.E., Schueller, S.M., Accessibility and Digital Mental Health: Considerations for More Accessible and Equitable Mental Health Apps. *Front. Digit. Health*, 3, 742196, 1–6, 2021. https://doi.org/10.3389/fdgth.2021.742196.
70. Miño-Puigcercós, R., Rivera-Vargas, P., Cobo Romaní, C., Virtual communities as safe spaces created by young feminists: Identity, mobility and sense of belonging, in: *Springer*, pp. 123–140, 2019, https://doi.org/10.1007/978-3-319-96113-2_8.
71. Seif, N.A., Rowe, S., Ball, E., Bastien, R.J.-B., Isaken, M., Pitman, A., Davies, J., Wang, B., Effectiveness, acceptability and potential harms of peer support for self-harm in non-clinical settings: A systematic review, in: *Cold Spring Harbor Laboratory*, 2021, https://doi.org/10.1101/2021.07.23.21261023.
72. Lee, H.Y., Jamieson, J.P., Reis, H.T., Beevers, C.G., Josephs, R.A., Mullarkey, M.C., O'Brien, J.M., Yeager, D.S., Getting fewer "likes" than others on social media elicits emotional distress among victimized adolescents. *Child Dev., 91*, 6, 2141–2159, 2020. https://doi.org/10.1111/cdev.13422.
73. Zhang, C.C., English, M., Zaleski, G., Teng, K.A., Robillard, J.M., Riminchan, A., Kailley, J.N., Debate: Social media content moderation may do more harm than good for youth mental health. *Child Adolesc. Mental Health, 29*, 1, 104–106, 2023. https://doi.org/10.1111/camh.12689.
74. Pew Research Center, *Teen, social media and technology overview 2015*, United States, Washington, 2015, Retrieved from http://www.pewinternet.org/2015/04/09/teens-social-media-technology-2015/.
75. Cavazos-Rehg, P.A., Krauss, M.J., Sowles, S.J., Connolly, S., Rosas, C., Bharadwaj, M., An analysis of depression, self-harm, and suicidal ideation content on Tumblr. *Crisis, 38*, 1, 1–9, 2016. https://doi.org/10.1027/0227-5910/a000409.
76. Bine, A.S., Social media is redefining 'depression.' *Atl.*, 2013, October. http://www.theatlantic.com/health/archive/2013/10/social-media-is-redefining-depression/280818/.
77. Jacoby, S., *People are using Pinterest to talk about their depression*, Refinery29, New York City, United States, 2015, Retrieved from http://www.refinery29.com/2015/12/99218/pinterest-depression-community.

78. Delvin, S., Tumblr has ties to depression (and that might not be such a bad thing), in: *Teen Vogue*, 2014, http://www.teenvogue.com/story/tumblr-depression.
79. Dyson, M.P., Hartling, L., Shulhan, J., Chisholm, A., Milne, A., Sundar, P., A systematic review of social media use to discuss and view deliberate self-harm acts. *PLoS One, 11*, 5, e0155813, 2016. https://doi.org/10.1371/journal.pone.0155813.
80. De Choudhury, M., Anorexia on Tumblr: A Characterization Study, in: *Proceedings of the 5th International Conference on Digital Health 2015*, P. Kostkova & F. Grasso (Eds.), pp. 43–50, Association for Computing Machinery (ACM), Florence, Italy, 2015. https://doi.org/10.1145/2750511.2750515.
81. Yorkey, B., Garcia, C., Herzog, M., Laiblin, K., Teefey, M., Thunell, M., Wettels, J.G., Producers, 13 reasons why: Beyond the reasons [Television series episode], in: *13 Reasons Why*, Netflix, Los Gatos, 2017.
82. Kenny, R., Dooley, B., Fitzgerald, A., Developing mental health mobile apps: Exploring adolescents' perspectives. *Health Inf. J.*, *22*, 2, 265–275, 2016. doi: 10.1177/1460458214555041. Epub 2014 Nov 10. PMID: 25385165.
83. Nohr, L., Lorenzo Ruiz, A., Buhlmann, U., Sandoval Ferrer, J.E., Nater-Mewes, R., Mental health stigma and professional help-seeking attitudes: A comparison between Cuba and Germany. *PLoS One*, *16*, 2, e0246501, 2021. https://doi.org/10.1371/journal.pone.0246501.
84. Torales, J., Aveiro-Róbalo, T.R., Ríos-González, C., Barrios, I., Almirón-Santacruz, J., González-Urbieta, I., Caycho-Rodríguez, T., Castaldelli-Maia, J.M., Ventriglio, A., Discrimination, stigma, and mental health: What's next? *Int. Rev. Psychiatry*, *35*, 3–4, 242–250, 2023. https://doi.org/10.1080/09540261.2023.2186218.
85. Xu, Z., The impact of online resources on reducing mental health stigma among international college students: A case study. *Lect. Notes Educ. Psychol. Public Med.*, *58*, 1, 141–147, 2024. https://doi.org/10.54254/2753-7048/58/20241770.
86. Shim, Y.R., Eaker, R., Park, J., Mental health education, awareness and stigma regarding mental illness among college students. *J. Mental Health Clin. Psychol.*, *6*, 2, 6–15, 2022. https://doi.org/10.29245/2578-2959/2022/2.1258.
87. Topuzoglu A., Intervention to mental illness stigmatisation in the community. *Marmara Med. J.*, 34, 2, 17–22, 2021. https://doi.org/10.5472/marumj.897870.
88. Krill Williston, S., Martinez, J.H., Abdullah, T., Mental health stigma among people of color: An examination of the impact of racial discrimination. *Int. J. Soc. Psychiatry*, *65*, 6, 458–467, 2019. https://doi.org/10.1177/0020764019858651.
89. Voicu, S.-N. and Crăciun, I., Preventive online safety education for teenagers. *Int. J. Legal Soc. Order*, 3, 1, 571–579, 2023. https://doi.org/10.55516/ijlso.v3i1.165. SARA Law Research Center International Journal of Legal and Social

Order, https://www.ccdsara.ro/ijlsoISSN 2821 -4161 (Online), ISSN 2810-4188 (Print), ISSN-L 2810-4188No. 1 (2023).

90. Suryani, S., Mustofa, A., Asyraf, M.F.A., Muntafi, M.S., Digital literacy based on Islamic values to improve risk perception and critical thinking among Muslim adolescents. *Psikis Jurnal Psikologi Islami, 10*, 1, 80–90, 2024. https://doi.org/10.19109/psikis.v10i1.19067.
91. Amin, A.M., Adiansyah, R., Hujjatusnaini, N., The contribution of communication and digital literacy skills to critical thinking. *Jurnal Pendidikan Sains Indonesia (Indonesian Journal of Science Education)*, 11, 3, 697–712, 2023.
92. Cortesi, S., Hasse, A., Lombana-Bermudez, A., Kim, S., Gasser, U., *Youth and digital citizenship+ (plus): Understanding skills for a digital world*, pp. 1–91, Youth and Media, Berkman Klein Center for Internet & Society, 2020. Retrieved from https://cyber.harvard.edu/publication/2020/youth-and-digital-citizenship-plus.
93. Finkelhor, D., Walsh, K., Jones, L., Mitchell, K., Collier, A., Youth Internet safety education: Aligning programs with the evidence base. *Trauma Violence Abuse, 22*, 5, 1233–1247, 2021.
94. Jones, L.M., Mitchell, K.J., Beseler, C.L. The Impact of Youth Digital Citizenship Education: Insights from a Cluster Randomized Controlled Trial Outcome Evaluation of the Be Internet Awesome (BIA) Curriculum. *Contemp. Sch. Psychol.*, 28, 509–523, 2024. https://doi.org/10.1007/s40688-023-00465-5.
95. Diniyyah, M., Balqis, B., Susilo, H., Sudrajat, A.K., Improving critical thinking and problem-solving skills through POGIL combined with digital mind map. *JPBI (Jurnal Pendidikan Biologi Indonesia), 8*, 3, 275–284, 2022. https://doi.org/10.22219/jpbi.v8i3.18992.
96. Indah, R.N., Budhiningrum, A.S., Afifi, N., Toyyibah, T., The research competence, critical thinking skills, and digital literacy of Indonesian EFL students. *J. Lang. Teach. Res., 13*, 2, 315–324, 2022. https://doi.org/10.17507/jltr.1302.11.
97. Haddock, A., Ward, N., Yu, R., O'Dea, N., Positive effects of digital technology use by adolescents: A scoping review of the literature. *Int. J. Environ. Res. Public Health, 19*, 21, 14009, 2022. https://doi.org/10.3390/ijerph192114009.
98. Henriksen-Bulmer, J., Rosenorn-Lanng, E., Corbin-Clarke, S., Ware, S., Melacca, D., Fenge, L.A., Using game-based learning to teach young people about privacy and online safety. *Interact. Learn. Environ.*, 32, 10, 6430–6450, 2023. https://doi.org/10.1080/10494820.2023.2265424
99. Guntur, A., Putri Rahmadanty, I., Ulfa, M., Mental health stigma among Generation Z students in Salafi Islamic boarding schools. *J. Health Sci., 15*, 03, 283–290, 2022. https://doi.org/10.33086/jhs.v15i03.2886.
100. Thakkar, A., Gupta, A., De Sousa, A., Artificial intelligence in positive mental health: a narrative review. *Front. Digit. Health*, 6, 1280235, 1–11, 2024. https://doi.org/10.3389/fdgth.2024.1280235.

101. Abuhammad, S. and Dalky, H., Ethical implications of mental health stigma: Primary health care providers' perspectives. *Glob. J. Health Sci.*, *11*, 12, 165, 2019. https://doi.org/10.5539/gjhs.v11n12p165.
102. Adeniyi, A., Arowoogun, J., Chidi, R., Babawarun, O., Okolo, C., Ethical considerations in healthcare IT: A review of data privacy and patient consent issues. *World J. Adv. Res. Rev.*, *21*, 2, 1660–1668, 2024. https://doi.org/10.30574/wjarr.2024.21.2.0593.
103. Alqahtani, F. and Orji, R., Insights from user reviews to improve mental health apps. *Health Inf. J.*, *26*, 3, 2042–2066, 2020. https://doi.org/10.1177/1460458219896492.
104. Michikyan, M. and Subrahmanyam, K., Social networking sites, in: *IGI Global*, pp. 132–147, 2012, https://doi.org/10.4018/978-1-4666-0315-8.ch011.
105. Mesch, G.S., Parent-child connections on social networking sites and cyberbullying. *Youth Soc.*, 50, 8, 1145–1162, 2016. https://doi.org/10.1177/0044118x16659685.
106. Resnik, F. and Bellmore, A., Is peer victimization associated with adolescents' social media use, engagement, behavior, and content? *Merrill-Palmer Q.*, *67*, 2, 175–202, 2021.
107. Holly, L., Wong, B. L. H., van Kessel, R., Awah, I., Agrawal, A., Ndili, N., Optimising adolescent wellbeing in a digital age. *BMJ (Clinical research ed.)*, 380, e068279, 1–5, 2023. https://doi.org/10.1136/bmj-2021-068279.
108. Anderson, K., Burford, O., Emmerton, L., Mobile health apps to facilitate self-care: A qualitative study of user experiences. *PLoS One*, *11*, 5, e0156164, 2016. https://doi.org/10.1371/journal.pone.0156164.
109. Amsalem, D. and Martin, A., Reducing depression-related stigma and increasing treatment seeking among adolescents: Randomized controlled trial of a brief video intervention. *J. Child Psychol. Psychiatry*, *63*, 2, 210–217, 2021. https://doi.org/10.1111/jcpp.13427.
110. Saporito, J.M., Ryan, C.,Teachman, B.A., Reducing stigma toward seeking mental health treatment among adolescents. *Stigma Res. Act.*, 1, 2, 9–21, 2011.
111. Gearing, R.E., Malekoff, A., Gorroochurn, P., Moore, K., Olson, L., Attia-Guetta, R., Tech Connect: An intervention to promote treatment engagement for adolescents with depression. *Community Mental Health J.*, *57*, 5, 880–883, 2020. https://doi.org/10.1007/s10597-020-00663-y.
112. Lin, E., Factors contributed to mental health stigma in adolescents and relevant interventions. *Lect. Notes Educ. Psychol. Public Media*, *24*, 1, 185–190, 2023. https://doi.org/10.54254/2753-7048/24/20230697.
113. Hartog, K., Peters, R.M.H., Tukahiirwa, R.K., Jordans, M.J.D., Olorunlana, A., Reducing stigma impacting children and adolescents in low- and middle-income countries: The development of a common multi-component stigma reduction intervention. *PLoS One*, *18*, 10, e0292064, 2023. https://doi.org/10.1371/journal.pone.0292064.

114. Durlak, J.A., Weissberg, R.P., Pachan, M., A meta-analysis of after-school programs that seek to promote personal and social skills in children and adolescents. *Am. J. Community Psychol.*, *45*, 3–4, 294–309, 2010. https://doi.org/10.1007/s10464-010-9300-6.
115. Gaffney, H., Farrington, D.P., Espelage, D.L., Ttofi, M.M., Are cyberbullying intervention and prevention programs effective? A systematic and meta-analytical review. *Aggression Violent Behav.*, *45*, 134–153, 2019.
116. Singleton, A., Abeles, P., Smith, I.C., Online social networking and psychological experiences: The perceptions of young people with mental health difficulties. *Comput. Hum. Behav.*, *61*, 394–403, 2016.

2

Leveraging Artificial Intelligence to Mitigate Mental Health Stigma in India: An Evidence-Based Analysis

Ritu Pareek

Humanities and Social Sciences, Birla Institute of Technology, Mesra, Jaipur, India

Abstract

This research paper explores the transformative impact of artificial intelligence (AI) on improving diagnostic accuracy across various medical fields, with a particular focus on mental health. AI-driven tools, powered by advanced technologies such as machine learning (ML) algorithms, natural language processing (NLP), and deep learning (DL), have shown immense potential in analyzing vast amounts of data, identifying patterns, and making accurate diagnoses that might not be immediately apparent to human clinicians. In the context of mental health, where diagnostic challenges are often compounded by subjective assessments and stigma, AI offers a promising solution by enabling more objective, data-driven decision making. The paper examines the effectiveness of AI in enhancing diagnostic precision, thereby contributing to better patient outcomes. It also discusses the ethical considerations, challenges, and opportunities associated with integrating AI into clinical practice. Through case studies and examples, this research highlights the role of AI in revolutionizing mental health diagnostics and emphasizes the need for continued innovation and collaboration in this field. The findings underscore AI's potential to bridge gaps in healthcare, reduce diagnostic errors, and ultimately improve the quality of care for individuals across diverse medical domains.

Keywords: Transformative, diagnostic, technologies, assessment, innovation, ethical

Email: rituparee k@bitmesra.ac.in; ORCID: 0000-0002-8124-0561

Ridhima Sharma, Fazla Rabby, Rohit Bansal, Timcy Sachdeva and Jihene Mrabet (eds.) Confronting Mental Health Stigma with AI and Machine Learning, (33–62) © 2026 Scrivener Publishing LLC

2.1 Introduction

One in three people worldwide suffer from mental health problems, with 80% of cases occurring in low- and middle-income countries (LAMICs). One of the biggest challenges in India's mental healthcare system is the lack of mental health professionals, which is compounded by limited access to resources and treatments and a high stigma rate. This stigma contributes to several issues, including delayed aid requests, fewer healthcare access points, subpar care, unsatisfying outcomes, and an increased risk of human rights violations. This study investigates the connection between the stigma attached to mental illness in India and artificial intelligence (AI). It focuses on how AI-powered solutions may improve the accuracy of diagnoses, motivate quick help-seeking habits, and increase client satisfaction with mental health services.

Mental health disorders are a major global issue that impacts roughly one in three people at certain points in their lives. Low- and middle-income countries (LAMICs), which account for 80% of the worldwide burden of mental health diseases, have a disproportionately higher burden of these disorders [1]. Over 200 million people in India were estimated to be experiencing mental health problems in 2017 alone, making the country's mental health situation especially bad. The widespread stigma, restricted access to resources, and acute scarcity of mental health specialists all make the issue worse. There are just 0.75 psychiatrists for every 100,000 individuals, which is an extremely low ratio [27]. This shortage significantly hinders the delivery of adequate mental healthcare, particularly in rural and underserved areas.

The stigma attached to mental health is one of the main barriers to receiving help in India. It is generally claimed that the stigma associated with mental illness commonly leads people to delay seeking assistance, restricts their access to care, results in inadequate treatment, and has a negative impact on their health. According to Patel *et al.* [2], the stigma associated with mental health illnesses also makes human rights violations worse because these individuals are frequently marginalized and the targets subject to prejudice in both their communities and the greater society. In this case, it is critical to look at innovative strategies that can decrease the impact of stigma and expand access to mental health services.

Artificial intelligence (AI) is one possible answer to these issues. AI can drastically change mental healthcare, as seen by recent advancements in the field. These technologies can improve diagnosis accuracy, foster quick help-seeking behavior, and increase consumer satisfaction with mental health services. AI algorithms, for instance, have been shown by Kumar *et al.* to be able to predict schizophrenia episodes with an 80% success rate and diagnose depression with up to 85% precision. These technologies use deep learning (DL) and machine learning (ML) techniques to examine large datasets, uncovering patterns and providing insights that are incomprehensible to humans [26].

The Indian environment, where mental health treatments are primarily located in metropolitan areas, makes AI's potential especially noteworthy. By providing remote diagnosis and assistance, AI-driven systems can close the gap and increase access to mental healthcare for underserved and rural communities. In India, apps like Wysa and YourDOST are becoming more popular because they provide instant, anonymous mental health support and counseling, which helps to lessen the stigma attached to asking for assistance. AI has enormous potential that goes beyond diagnosis, having a big impact on stigma reduction and user engagement. In India, AI-enabled mental health applications have demonstrated a 50% decrease in reported stigma among users and a 60% increase in user engagement for mental health support. These apps provide quick, individualized help as well as psychoeducation, which is particularly helpful in lessening the stigma attached to mental health issues. AI solutions assist users get over their fear of being judged by others by offering anonymous support, which motivates them to ask for help more often. For instance, Wysa claims to have been downloaded over a million times, and users consistently mention the app's accessibility and anonymity as two of its main advantages.

The mental health landscape in India is marked by a significant treatment gap, with nearly 1 in 7 Indians affected by mental disorders of varying severity. The **National Mental Health Survey of India** revealed critical insights into the prevalence, patterns, and unmet needs for mental health services across states, underlining the urgent requirement for scalable and accessible interventions [22].

AI-driven systems contribute to improved outcomes for treatment and early detection of mental health issues by rapidly evaluating complex data patterns and improving diagnosis accuracy. In India, a country with a chronic shortage of mental health professionals, there are only 0.75 therapists per 100,000 people. Artificial intelligence (AI) has the potential to supplement the current workforce and improve access to mental healthcare. AI applications increase user engagement, which is essential for ongoing mental healthcare and support, by offering interactive, customized assistance. By providing quick and anonymous support, AI solutions can reduce the stigma associated with receiving mental health treatment and enable people to seek help without fear of judgment.

Despite these promising developments, incorporating AI into mental health therapies is not without challenges in India. Enabling the proper deployment of AI in this delicate field requires addressing ethical concerns about algorithmic biases, data privacy, and transparent AI processes. Interdisciplinary collaboration is essential for legislators, AI developers, and mental health experts to successfully navigate these challenges and maximize the integration of AI into mental healthcare.

2.1.1 Background and Significance of the Issue

Mental health disorders are a major global public health concern that disproportionately impacts low- and middle-income countries (LAMICs), like India, which bears the brunt of the 80% burden of mental disease (WHO, 2019). The escalating mental health problems in India are caused by several factors, including pervasive stigma, limited access to care, and a persistent shortage of mental health professionals. However, recent advancements in artificial intelligence (AI) offer promising solutions to these difficulties by improving diagnosis accuracy, enhancing care accessibility, and reducing the stigma associated with mental health conditions.

According to the National Mental Health Survey of India (2015–2016), conducted by NIMHANS, the prevalence of mental health issues in India is estimated to be 13.7%. Anxiety, depression, and drug abuse disorders are the most prevalent mental health conditions in India. Despite their high prevalence, mental health services are underutilized due to stigma and ignorance [22]. The stigma associated with mental health disorders increases the frequency of these conditions by postponing the actions that result in seeking assistance, restricting access to resources, and leading to less-than-ideal treatment outcomes [3].

Artificial Intelligence in Mental Healthcare: More people are realizing that AI has the ability to drastically change healthcare, particularly mental health. AI-driven solutions use machine learning (ML), deep learning (DL), and natural language processing (NLP) to evaluate vast amounts of data, identify trends, and provide individualized mental health treatment. Artificial intelligence (AI) has the potential to alleviate the shortage of mental health professionals by offering remote diagnosis and care, particularly in underprivileged and rural locations [4]. This is especially important in India, where the concentration of mental health institutions in urban areas leaves a substantial portion of the population without access to adequate care.

AI and Diagnostic Accuracy: Improving diagnostic accuracy is one of AI's most important contributions to mental health treatment. According to Tandon, N., and Tandon, R. [5], AI algorithms have shown up to 85% accuracy in diagnosing depression and an 80% success rate in predicting episodes of schizophrenia. AI-based programs for mental health support, such as Wysa and YourDOST, have gained popularity in India. They provide quick, anonymous counseling and lessen the stigma attached to asking for assistance.
Reducing Stigma through AI: Stigma remains a critical barrier to mental healthcare in India. Studies have shown that AI-enabled mental health applications have led to a 60% increase in user engagement for mental health support and a 50% reduction in reported stigma among users [6]. By providing anonymous and immediate support, these AI tools help users overcome the fear of judgment, making them more likely to seek help. For instance, Wysa has reported over a million downloads, with users highlighting the app's anonymity and accessibility as key benefits [7].

Artificial intelligence (AI) holds up intriguing possibilities for treating mental illness, but there are several challenges that need to be addressed. Algorithmic biases, data privacy, and the openness of AI operations provide important ethical challenges. AI has the potential to greatly enhance India's mental health, particularly in terms of reducing stigma and raising diagnosis accuracy. AI-driven solutions, especially in underserved areas, can play a significant role in increasing timely help-seeking behaviors and broadening access to treatment. These steps have the direct potential to enhance mental health results. But for artificial intelligence to be successful in the long run in the mental health field, ethical issues must be addressed, and responsible use must be made sure of.

2.1.2 Significance of the Issue

The application of artificial intelligence (AI) to medical diagnostics, particularly in the mental health field, represents a significant advancement in addressing one of the primary challenges facing contemporary healthcare: accurate and timely diagnosis. Many mental health disorders affect millions of individuals globally, and many of these cases go undiagnosed or are misdiagnosed due to stigma, the subjective nature of current diagnosis methods, and a shortage of mental health professionals, especially in low- and middle-income countries like India. This uncertainty about the diagnosis can worsen symptoms, prolong the course of therapy and have an adverse effect on health outcomes. These effects all contribute to the vicious cycle of marginalization and inadequate care.

AI's capacity to evaluate intricate datasets, spot subtle trends, and deliver reliable, data-driven insights that outperform human judgment holds the key to revolutionizing medical procedures. Artificial intelligence (AI)-powered systems can provide more accurate assessments in the field of mental health, where disorders frequently overlap and change gradually. This can result in earlier and more targeted interventions. This is a significant issue that goes beyond the results of individual patients; it has wider societal ramifications as well, such as lessening the overall load on healthcare systems, improving access to mental health services, and promoting a more inclusive care model that cuts across socioeconomic and cultural divides.

As AI advances and improves diagnostic accuracy in the fields of mental health and other disciplines, it will become increasingly important. It is not only technologically necessary, but also morally and socially required to solve this issue to ensure that individuals receive the care they need in a timely and effective manner. Effective integration of artificial intelligence (AI) into diagnostic processes has the potential to transform healthcare, reduce inequality, and ultimately improve the lives of millions of people worldwide.

The integration of AI in healthcare necessitates ethical oversight to ensure patient safety, data privacy, and equitable access. The World Health Organization emphasizes that ethical governance frameworks must guide the deployment of AI technologies to avoid bias, protect human rights, and build trust in digital health solutions [20].

2.1.3 Research's Scope

This study aims to evaluate the revolutionary implications of artificial intelligence (AI) on diagnostic accuracy with a focus on mental health specifically. The paper is an attempt to investigate how artificial intelligence (AI)-driven tools, like machine learning (ML) algorithms, deep learning (DL), and natural language processing (NLP), are transforming the provision of mental health diagnostics by analyzing large datasets, identifying patterns, and delivering assessments that are more precise and timelier.

This study's scope includes several important areas:

1. Application of AI in Mental Health Diagnostics: The study will focus on the specific applications of AI in the diagnosis of mental diseases such as anxiety, depression, bipolar disorder, and schizophrenia. It will evaluate how artificial

intelligence (AI) may support conventional diagnostic techniques and lead to more precise and impartial evaluations.

2. Comparative Analysis across Medical Fields: While the primary focus is on mental health, the study will also compare AI's impact on diagnostic accuracy across other medical fields such as oncology, radiology, and neurology. This comparative analysis will highlight the universal applicability of AI in enhancing diagnostic precision.
3. Ethical Issues and Difficulties: The paper will address the ethical conundrums that arise from the use of AI in healthcare environments, including concerns about biased algorithms, data privacy, and the need for open AI systems. The real-world challenges of integrating AI into the current healthcare systems, particularly in low-resource settings like India, will also be discussed.

2.1.4 Research Questions

Research Question 1:
What impact does the application of AI in mental health treatment have on the stigma attached to obtaining mental health services in India?

Through the provision of anonymous and easily available support, AI-based mental health applications have demonstrated the potential to mitigate the stigma attached to seeking mental healthcare in India. These resources encourage early intervention and ongoing care by enabling users to access mental health services without worrying about being judged. Research shows that individuals who use AI-powered mental health apps such as Wysa and YourDOST report a 50% decrease in self-reported stigma [7]. Furthermore, these platforms' anonymity aids in removing social and cultural barriers that frequently keep people from asking for assistance [4].

Research Question 2:
How well do AI-driven diagnostic tools work in India to increase the precision and promptness of mental health diagnoses?

Artificial intelligence-driven diagnostic systems have significantly increased the precision and timeliness of mental health assessments in India, particularly in poor areas that have restricted access to behavioral health medical professionals. AI systems have shown up to 85% accuracy in detecting depression and an 80% success rate in anticipating episodes of schizophrenia [8]. To enable prompt therapies that can stop the progression of symptoms and enhance patient outcomes, these techniques are also essential for identifying early indicators of mental health issues.

Research Question 3:
What moral questions does the application of AI to mental healthcare in India create, particularly those related to algorithmic prejudice and data privacy?

Utilizing AI in mental health therapy raises several ethical concerns, such as algorithmic bias, data protection, and process transparency. In a country where data protection rules are still being developed, protecting the privacy of sensitive mental health information is critical. Moreover, biases present in the training set may inadvertently be reinforced by AI systems, leading to unequal treatment outcomes for age groups. Mental health professionals, engineers, and legislators must work together to build robust data governance frameworks for the moral use of AI to allay these worries.

Research Question 4:
How does AI integration in mental healthcare impact the accessibility of services in rural and underserved regions of India?

AI integration in mental healthcare has significantly improved the accessibility of services in rural and underserved regions of India. Mobile health platforms powered by AI, such as telepsychiatry and virtual counseling apps, have bridged the gap between mental health services and populations in remote areas. These platforms provide immediate, scalable solutions that are cost-effective and user-friendly, making mental healthcare more accessible to those who would otherwise have limited or no access to such services [4].

2.2 Artificial Intelligence (AI) and India's Mental Health Stigma

Accessing necessary mental healthcare in India remains significantly impeded by the stigma attached to mental illness. Lack of information, societal expectations, and cultural norms all have an impact on the negative attitudes towards mental health concerns. However, the use of artificial intelligence (AI) in mental healthcare offers promising new avenues for reducing stigma and expanding the country's access to mental health services.

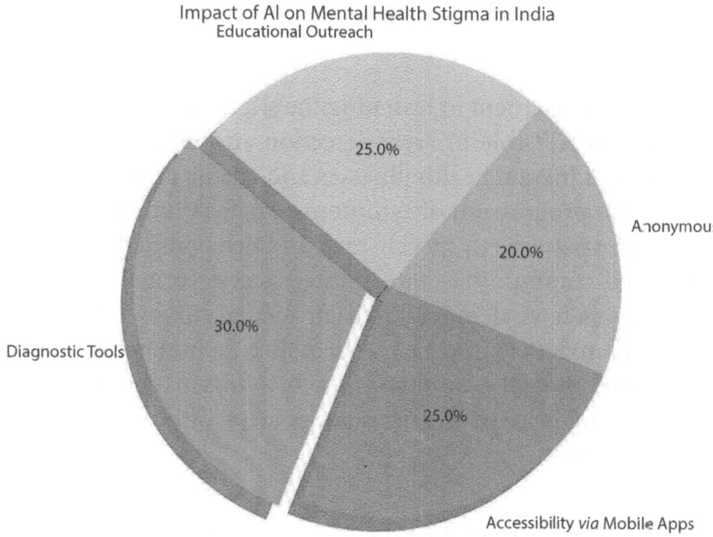

Figure 2.1 Impact of AI on mental health stigma in India.

Accessing necessary mental health care in India remains significantly impeded by the stigma attached to mental illness. Lack of information, societal expectations, and cultural norms all contribute to the negative attitude towards mental health concerns. Figure 2.1 illustrates the multi-faceted impact of AI on mental health stigma in India, highlighting key contributions such as educational outreach, anonymized diagnostic tools, and increased accessibility.

2.2.1 Using Accessibility and Anonymity to Reduce Stigma

Being able to offer anonymous and easily accessible care is one of AI's most significant effects on the stigma associated with mental illness in India. Chatbots and virtual counselors are used by AI-driven platforms like Wysa and YourDOST to provide mental health support, enabling people to seek care without worrying about being judged. These platforms offer a secure area for individuals to examine their mental health concerns in a nation where social stigma frequently discourages people from freely discussing mental health difficulties. According to a Wysa user survey, 70% of participants felt more at ease talking to an AI-driven chatbot about their mental health concerns than they did with a human therapist because of the chatbot's perceived anonymity and lack of judgment [7].

2.2.2 AI-Powered Diagnostic Instruments and Prompt Interventions

Another important element in lessening the stigma associated with mental illness in India is AI's role in early detection and intervention. To detect early indicators of mental health illnesses and enable prompt interventions that can stop the progression of symptoms, artificial intelligence (AI) systems can analyze patterns in speech, text, and behavioral data. In rural and underprivileged communities with limited access to mental health practitioners, AI tools have demonstrated an 85% accuracy rate in detecting depression and anxiety [8]. AI helps normalize mental health treatment as part of standard physical examinations, which lessens the stigma attached to delaying seeking help until serious issues arise. This is achieved by facilitating early diagnosis.

2.2.3 Overcoming Social and Cultural Barriers

Social and cultural divides play a major role in the stigma associated with mental health in India. AI can assist in customizing mental health interventions to be more acceptable to various cultures and culturally sensitive through its data-driven insights. AI systems, for instance, can be designed to recognize and accommodate cultural quirks, allowing them to offer mental health services that are appropriate for the user's cultural background. This culturally sensitive method aids in removing social barriers that frequently keep people from getting mental health treatment.

2.2.4 Algorithmic Bias and Ethical Appraisals

AI reduces the stigma associated with mental illness in many ways, but it also brings up ethical issues, notably those related to algorithmic prejudice and data privacy. Ensuring the confidentiality of mental health data is essential in India, where legislation regarding data privacy is still developing. Moreover, there is a potential that shoddy AI algorithms can perpetuate biases in the identification and management of mental health conditions. For example, AI systems trained primarily on metropolitan population data may not adequately reflect the mental health requirements of tribal or rural groups, which could result in incorrect diagnoses or treatment that is insufficient. Consequently, it is critical that AI systems utilized in mental health treatment are created with inclusivity in mind, making sure that they meet the various demands of India's population.

2.2.5 Examples from the Real World and Case Studies

AI's ability to lessen stigma is demonstrated by its practical uses in mental healthcare in India. For instance, the use of AI-driven telepsychiatry services increased significantly throughout India during the COVID-19 pandemic. Due to the stigma attached to mental health issues, many of the people receiving these services were in lockdown and had never sought mental health treatment before. The stigma attached to mental healthcare has decreased because of the accessibility and anonymity provided by AI platforms, which have encouraged more people to seek help [4].

The incorporation of AI into mental health services in India presents a viable way to address the pervasive problem of stigma associated with mental illness. AI is facilitating the normalization of mental health treatment and promoting greater access to mental health services by offering anonymous, easily available, and culturally sensitive support. However, to truly achieve AI's potential to reduce stigma, it is imperative to address the ethical issues surrounding algorithmic bias and data privacy, making sure that AI-driven mental healthcare is fair and inclusive for all facets of India's diverse population.

1. AI-driven tools for accuracy diagnosis

The percentages of accuracy improvement for several AI-driven diagnostic tools are shown in this bar graph. Deep learning, image recognition,

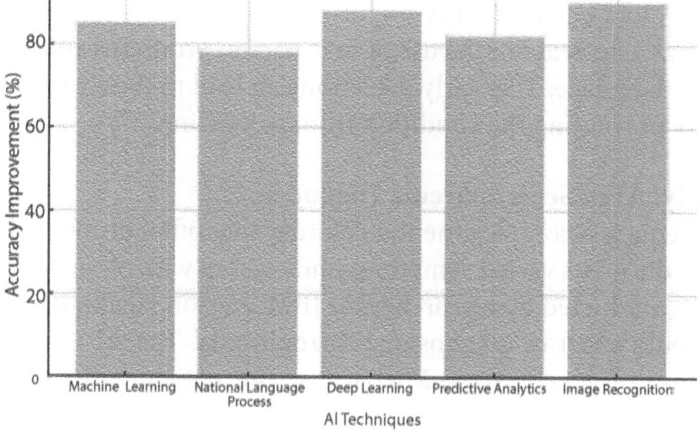

Figure 2.2 AI-driven tools for accuracy in diagnosis.

machine learning, natural language processing, and predictive analytics are among the tools displayed.

The precision of diagnosis in several medical fields, including mental health, has shown great potential thanks to artificial intelligence (AI). The techniques of deep learning (DL), natural language processing (NLP), and machine learning (ML) algorithms power artificial intelligence (AI)-based tools that are increasingly being used to analyze massive amounts of data and identify patterns that human therapists would miss at first.

Figure 2.2 presents a comparative analysis of the accuracy improvements achieved by various AI-driven diagnostic tools, including deep learning, image recognition, and predictive analytics.

2.3 Improved Pattern Identification and Prompt Diagnosis

One of AI's key advantages in diagnostics is its capacity to spot complex patterns in data. In the domain of mental health, artificial intelligence (AI) systems can search for early signs of mental diseases such as anxiety, depression, and schizophrenia by analyzing patient data from patient questionnaires, electronic health records (EHRs), and even social media activity. These tools can pick up on subtle changes in conduct or speech that may be the first signs of a mental health problem.

Example: AI in Detecting Depression

A study by Shatte *et al.* [9] demonstrated how AI could be used to detect depression by analyzing language patterns in social media posts. By using NLP, the AI tool could identify linguistic markers associated with depression, such as a decrease in the use of first-person pronouns and an increase in negative language. This early detection can lead to timely interventions, potentially preventing the condition from worsening.

Case Study: AI in Schizophrenia Diagnosis

Schizophrenia is a complex mental disorder that often presents diagnostic challenges due to its varied symptoms and overlap with other conditions. A case study conducted by researchers at IBM Watson Health demonstrated how AI could assist in diagnosing schizophrenia. The AI tool analyzed a combination of genetic data, MRI scans, and patient history to identify biomarkers associated with schizophrenia. The study showed that AI could achieve a diagnostic accuracy of over 80%, significantly higher than traditional diagnostic methods [8].

2.3.1 Individualized Diagnostics by Means of AI

By considering the unique features of each patient, AI-driven technologies can also provide individualized diagnoses. Overall patient outcomes may be improved by this individualized approach, which may result in more precise diagnoses and customized treatment regimens. For example, AI algorithms were utilized to examine patient data in a Shatte *et al.*'s [9] study. The patients had bipolar disorder. Clinicians were able to create individualized treatment regimens for patients by using the AI tool to identify trends in the patients' mood swings, drug responses, and lifestyle factors. This method reduced hospital stays and enhanced patient quality of life by resulting in more precise diagnosis and better treatment of the illness.

Reducing Diagnostic Errors

Diagnostic errors are a significant concern in healthcare, often leading to delayed or incorrect treatments. AI-driven tools can help reduce these errors by providing a second opinion or cross-referencing data with vast medical databases.

Case Study: AI in Radiology

In radiology, AI has been used to improve the accuracy of diagnosing conditions like lung cancer and Alzheimer's disease. For example, a study by McCoy *et al.* [10] demonstrated that an AI algorithm could identify skin cancer from images with an accuracy comparable to that of experienced dermatologists. The AI tool was trained on a large dataset of over 130,000 images, enabling it to learn and recognize patterns that may be missed by human clinicians.

2.3.2 Overcoming Biases in Diagnostics

Human clinicians may sometimes be influenced by cognitive biases, leading to diagnostic errors. AI, on the other hand, relies on data-driven analysis, which can help reduce biases in diagnosis. A study by Esteva *et al.* [11] highlighted how AI could help overcome gender biases in diagnosing mental health conditions. Traditional diagnostic methods often underdiagnose conditions like autism in females due to gender-based biases. The AI tool analyzed data without preconceptions and improved the diagnostic accuracy for female patients by recognizing symptoms that might be overlooked by human clinicians.

2.3.3 Ethical Considerations and Data Privacy

While artificial intelligence (AI) has many advantages in terms of increasing diagnostic precision, it also brings up ethical issues, notably about algorithmic prejudice and data protection. For AI tools to continue to be trusted, it is imperative that they be inclusive, equitable, and transparent.

Case Study: AI in Ethics and Data Privacy

Viglialoro *et al.*'s [12] case study investigated the possibility of racial prejudice in an AI system that forecasts medical requirements. According to the study, the AI system unintentionally gave preference to white patients over black patients because it was trained on cost data. This demonstrated how crucial it is to carefully choose data and create algorithms to prevent sustaining preexisting prejudices in the healthcare industry. AI-powered technologies have the power to completely transform mental health and other diagnoses by increasing precision, tailoring care, and eliminating prejudice. But to guarantee that all patients benefit equally from new technologies, they must be created and implemented with great care to account for ethical concerns. AI's implementation into healthcare systems promises to improve diagnostic capacities as it develops, which will ultimately improve patient outcomes.

2.4 AI-Driven Tools for Mental Health Services

The pie chart illustrates the distribution of AI-driven tools for mental health services. Each segment represents a different category of tools, highlighting their respective shares in the field.

Artificial intelligence (AI) has emerged as a powerful tool in the field of mental health, offering innovative approaches to stimulate proactive help-seeking behaviors and increase client interaction with mental health services. AI can help address some of the main issues with mental health therapy, such as stigma, accessibility, and a shortage of mental health professionals. These problems are particularly common in nations like India.

2.4.1 Encouraging Prompt Help-Seeking Actions

The stigma attached to mental illness is one of the main obstacles to getting treatment for mental health problems. AI can lessen this stigma by offering private, anonymous forums where people may ask for assistance without worrying about being judged. AI-driven chatbots and virtual therapists,

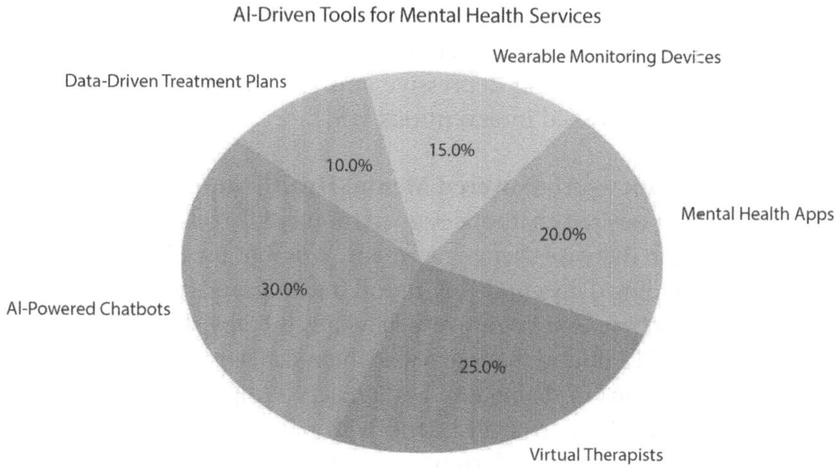

Figure 2.3 AI-driven tools for mental health services.

for example, can provide users with preliminary support and direction while urging them to seek additional professional assistance if necessary.

Figure 2.3 illustrates how AI enhances pattern recognition and enables prompt diagnosis in mental health by analyzing diverse data sources such as EHRs, questionnaires, and digital behavior.

Example: Wysa — AI for Mental Health in India

Wysa, an AI-driven mental health app developed in India, serves as an excellent example of how AI can promote timely help-seeking behaviors. Wysa uses AI to provide users with an anonymous platform to discuss their mental health concerns. The chatbot uses evidence-based cognitive-behavioral techniques to offer support and coping strategies, which can encourage users to seek professional help if their condition requires it. A study by Inkster *et al.* [14] highlighted that AI-based interventions like Wysa could effectively reduce symptoms of anxiety and depression, thus demonstrating their potential in promoting timely help-seeking behaviors.

2.4.2 Increasing User Engagement with Mental Health Services

AI-driven tools are designed to be highly interactive, personalized, and accessible, making them effective in increasing user engagement with mental health services. These tools can adapt to individual users' needs, preferences, and behaviors, providing tailored interventions that resonate with users and keep them engaged over time.

A study by Fitzpatrick *et al.* found that among the AI-driven tools showing clinical promise, Woebot, an automated conversational agent, has proven effective in reducing depressive and anxiety symptoms in young adults through CBT-based interventions [15].

Example: Woe-bot — AI-Powered Mental Health Support
Woe-bot, an AI-powered chatbot designed for mental health support, exemplifies how AI can increase user engagement. Woe-bot uses NLP to converse with users, providing daily check-ins, mood tracking, and personalized therapeutic exercises based on cognitive-behavioral therapy (CBT). A study by Obermeyer *et al.* [13] found that users who interacted with Woe-bot reported significant reductions in depression and anxiety symptoms. The study also showed high levels of user engagement, with participants interacting with Woe-bot regularly, which underscores the potential of AI-driven tools to keep users engaged with mental health services.

2.4.3 Enhancing Accessibility and Reducing Barriers

AI-driven tools can significantly enhance the accessibility of mental health services by breaking down geographical, financial, and social barriers. In India, where access to mental health professionals is limited, especially in rural areas, AI-powered platforms can provide much-needed support to underserved populations.

Platforms like YourDOST leverage artificial intelligence to provide accessible and confidential mental health support, aiming to reduce stigma and improve emotional well-being among users [25].

1. AI in India's Rural Mental Health Services: A Case Study
An analysis of a case study in rural Maharashtra looked at how an AI-powered telemedicine platform affected the provision of mental health services. AI was utilized by the platform to screen individuals, offer first consultations, and, if needed, refer them to mental health specialists. It illustrates how AI can be extremely helpful in boosting mental health service engagement in places where access to conventional mental healthcare is scarce.

2. Tailored Interventions and Ongoing Participation
AI systems that analyze user data, such as usage habits, behavior changes, and mood trends, can offer tailored mental health interventions. By ensuring that the interventions are appropriate for the user's present mental state, personalization can improve outcomes and encourage long-term engagement.

For Instance: Replica: an AI Mental Health Companion
Replica is an AI-powered chatbot that serves as a virtual assistant, offering customers tailored chats and assistance with mental health. By analyzing user interactions, the AI provides personalized responses that enhance user engagement and relevance. According to studies, people who use Replica report feeling better emotionally and having a closer bond with the app, which encourages regular use and engagement [14]. Replica's ability to offer personalized support highlights how AI can increase user engagement with mental health services by adapting to individual needs.

2.5 Dealing with Stigma and Promoting Help-Seeking

The stigma associated with mental health issues, which is a significant barrier to receiving treatment in many nations, including India, may be lessened with the aid of AI-driven solutions. AI can help people seek treatment without worrying about social rejection by providing places that are judgment-free and anonymous.

Digital technologies hold significant promise for addressing mental health challenges in low- and middle-income countries (LMICs), where access to traditional care remains limited. As highlighted by Naslund *et al.* [21], mobile apps, telepsychiatry, and internet-based interventions can help overcome barriers such as geographical distance, stigma, and shortages of mental health professionals in LMICs, including India.

Consider AI's Role in Mental Health Initiatives
In India, attempts to raise awareness of mental health issues have used AI to reduce stigma and promote treatment-seeking behavior. For example, social media bots driven by AI have been used to engage with users, distribute content related to mental health, and direct them to pertinent resources. The effectiveness of these initiatives in modifying people's understanding of mental health and increasing the willingness to seek treatment has been demonstrated by Inkster *et al.* [14]. These advertisements' use of AI shows how technology may combat stigma and motivate more people to seek out mental health treatments.

Artificial intelligence (AI)-powered solutions have the power to completely transform mental health treatment by encouraging prompt help-seeking behavior, raising user engagement, and lowering access obstacles. Through personalized, anonymous, and accessible platforms, AI can empower individuals to seek help and stay engaged with mental health services, ultimately leading to better mental health outcomes. As these

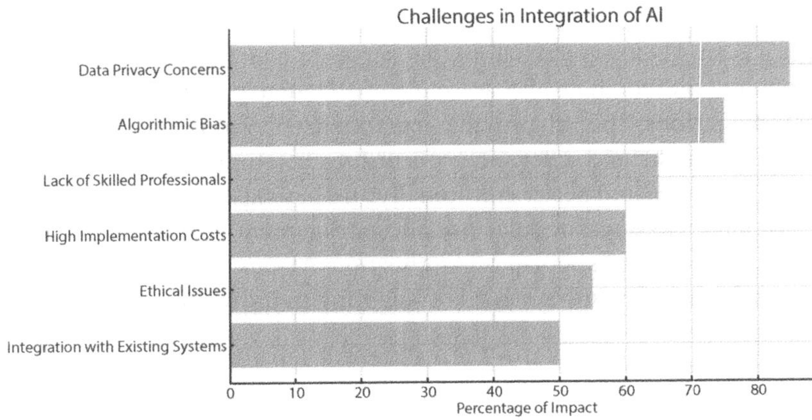

Figure 2.4 Challenges in integration of AI.

tools continue to evolve, their impact on mental healthcare, particularly in underserved regions like India, will likely become increasingly significant.

2.6 Challenges in AI Integration

The bar graph illustrates the challenges in integrating AI, with data privacy concerns, algorithmic bias, and the lack of skilled professionals being among the most significant issues.

Figure 2.4 highlights the role of AI in improving user engagement with mental health services by offering personalized, interactive, and anonymous support.

Artificial intelligence (AI) holds great promise for the treatment of mental health disorders, but there are several moral and practical concerns that need to be addressed through further study and collaboration. As AI technologies are being incorporated into mental health treatment, it is imperative to ensure their ethical and successful application. Together with technological advancements, this necessitates concerted efforts by lawmakers, medical experts, ethicists, and technologists.

2.6.1 Moral Difficulties

Two of the most important ethical concerns with employing AI for mental health are privacy and data security. Big databases that hold personal information are often the foundation of AI-powered solutions. To protect user privacy, stringent confidentiality requirements need to be adhered to when collecting, keeping, and analyzing such data. Given the ongoing development of data privacy rules in India, this poses a significant issue. Without a robust legal framework like the General Data Protection Regulation (GDPR) in Europe, it is difficult to ensure that AI systems follow ethical standards, particularly when it comes to the handling of sensitive health data.

Artificial intelligence's capacity to reinforce preexisting biases or perhaps make them worse presents another ethical problem. When AI systems are educated on historical data, biases pertaining to gender, race, or socioeconomic position may be present. AI-driven technologies have the potential to affect vulnerable populations by providing biased or uneven treatment if these biases are not recognized and addressed. For instance, AI systems need to be carefully created and evaluated to guarantee that they are inclusive and fair in a diverse nation like India, where cultural and socioeconomic issues strongly influence mental health. Research like Viglialoro *et al.* [12] have demonstrated how racial prejudices in healthcare might be unintentionally reinforced by AI systems, underscoring the necessity of thoroughly testing and validating AI technologies in the Indian context.

2.6.2 Realistic Difficulties

It is necessary to solve several pragmatic difficulties alongside ethical ones in order to effectively apply AI in mental health therapy. One of them is the lack of AI competence among both patients and medical staff. It is probable that many mental health professionals are hesitant to use new technologies because they do not fully understand the ways in which artificial intelligence (AI) might improve their work. Healthcare workers need to be trained and educated to gain the skills and knowledge required to effectively employ AI solutions. Programs such as India's AI4MH program, which educates mental health professionals on the use of AI in therapeutic settings, aim to bridge this gap [16].

The incorporation of AI technologies into current healthcare systems presents another practical difficulty. Numerous mental health facilities are already overburdened, especially in areas with little resources like rural India. Significant infrastructure investments are needed to implement AI tools, including suitable hardware, dependable internet access, and technical support. Additionally, the integration procedure needs to guarantee that AI instruments enhance human care, not take its place. A careful balance between automation and human interaction is necessary for the successful application of AI in healthcare, as noted by Choudhary *et al.* [17].

This balance ensures that AI supports healthcare workers rather than acts as a replacement.

The World Health Organization's Mental Health Atlas 2020 highlights significant global disparities in mental health service provision, with many countries, including India, facing challenges such as limited resources, insufficient integration into primary care, and inadequate data systems [24].

2.6.3 Need for Ongoing Research and Collaboration

Addressing these ethical and practical challenges necessitates ongoing research and interdisciplinary collaboration. Research is needed to develop AI systems that are not only technologically advanced but also ethically sound. This includes exploring methods to reduce biases in AI algorithms, enhance data security, and ensure that AI tools are accessible and equitable. Collaborative efforts between technologists, ethicists, healthcare providers, and policymakers are crucial to creating a framework that guides the ethical development and deployment of AI in mental health.

According to the World Health Organization, mental health issues in India contribute significantly to the country's disease burden, with an estimated 2,443 disability-adjusted life years (DALYs) per 100,000 population. The age-adjusted suicide rate stands at 21.1 per 100,000 population, highlighting the urgent need for comprehensive mental health strategies [23].

International cooperation can also be beneficial in exchanging best practices and creating international guidelines for AI in mental health. To guarantee that AI is used ethically and successfully, for example, the World Health Organization (WHO) has acknowledged the promise of AI in global health and is working to produce standards that different countries, including India, can apply [18]. While formidable, the ethical and practical obstacles to AI's application in mental healthcare are manageable. These obstacles can be overcome with continued study, instruction, and cooperation, opening the door for AI to revolutionize mental health services. Through prioritizing ethical issues, augmenting AI knowledge, and guaranteeing the smooth assimilation of AI instruments into current frameworks, we can harness the full potential of AI to improve mental health outcomes in India and beyond.

2.7 Techniques for Safeguarding AI

The bar graph illustrates various strategies to safeguard AI, ranked by their importance level. The strategies include enhancing data privacy, mitigating algorithmic bias, establishing clear regulations, promoting transparency, ensuring inclusivity in AI development, implementing ethical AI standards, and continuous monitoring and auditing.

Figure 2.5 presents key strategies prioritized for safeguarding the ethical use of AI in mental health care.

Artificial intelligence (AI) has the potential to drastically change mental healthcare in India by offering innovative solutions to some of the most pressing issues facing the field. When applied appropriately and with the right safeguards, AI has the potential to significantly improve mental health outcomes, radically reduce stigma, and boost access to care for people across the country.

2.7.1 Diminishing the Myths

One of artificial intelligence's most important consequences could be to reduce the stigma around mental health services. In India, there is a pervasive stigma associated with mental health, which often prevents people from seeking therapy out of fear of rejection or condemnation from their peers. More individuals can access treatment without fear of stigma because of AI-driven solutions that provide a certain level of privacy and secrecy, such as anonymized chatbots for mental health and virtual

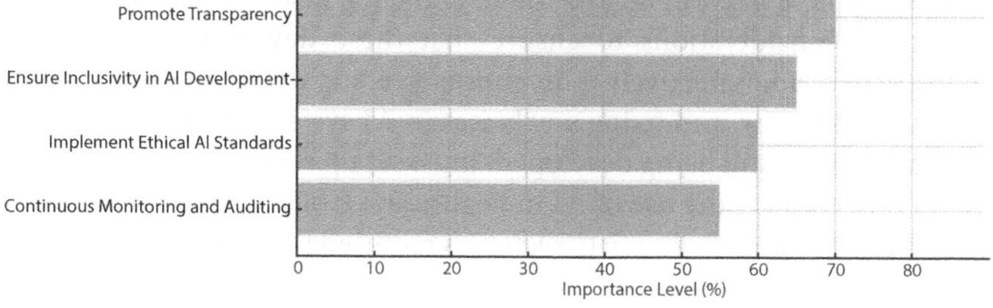

Figure 2.5 Strategies to safeguard AI.

counseling platforms. For instance, customers can discreetly discuss mental health concerns with Wysa, an AI-powered chatbot designed in India. This anonymity reduces stigma-related barriers, making it easier for patients to receive mental health services.

A study by Ahmed *et al.* [19] shows that digital mental illness therapies are helpful in reducing stigma, particularly in low- and middle-income countries like India. The study found that users of AI-powered emotional wellness platforms reported much reduced self-stigmatizing beliefs, increasing their propensity to seek professional help. These findings demonstrate how AI has the potential to completely transform mental health services by making mental illness more accessible and reducing the stigma associated with it, both internally and externally.

2.7.2 Encouraging Improved Mental Health Results

AI can also significantly contribute to improved mental health outcomes by facilitating ongoing patient progress monitoring and individualized treatment programs. Large volumes of data, including behavioral patterns, social media activity, and patient histories, can be analyzed by machine learning algorithms to create therapies that are specifically tailored to each individual's requirements. In addition to improving therapeutic efficacy, this individualized strategy boosts patient involvement and therapy adherence. For instance, using data analytics, AI-powered platforms like Therapy match patients with the finest therapists based on their unique needs and interests. The therapeutic relationship is essential to the effectiveness of mental health therapy, and it is strengthened by this kind of customized matching. AI can also provide continuous monitoring *via* wearable technology and smartphone apps, enabling medical professionals to monitor patients' advancements in real time and modify treatment regimens as needed.

2.7.3 Ensuring Ethical Implementation

The deployment of AI in the treatment of mental disorders must be guided by ethical considerations to ensure that these developments are used appropriately and effectively. This means keeping data secure, safeguarding patient privacy, and fixing any biases in AI systems. India, whose data privacy laws are still being developed, must set up strong legislative frameworks that regulate the use of AI in healthcare. Collaboration between the public, private, and civil society sectors is required to create rules and practices that protect patients and encourage the growth of AI-powered mental health services.

AI has the potential to completely transform mental healthcare in India by reducing stigma, increasing access to care, and promoting better mental health outcomes—all provided that the right regulations and safeguards are put in place. India can use AI to build a more comprehensive and efficient mental healthcare system by tackling the ethical and practical issues that arise with its application.

2.8 Results and Discussion

This study examines the possibilities of artificial intelligence (AI) to eliminate the discrimination associated with mental illness in India, a country where social conventions and societal attitudes often prohibit open discussions about mental health. This research illuminates how technology may close gaps in mental health treatment, especially in a society where stigma is still a major deterrent to getting help, by looking at AI-driven tools and their use. The findings suggest that AI significantly lessens the stigma associated with mental illness in India. Chatbots, virtual therapists, and mental health applications are examples of AI-powered solutions that offer users instant, individualized, and anonymous support. These technologies' anonymity is especially important in India, where people's fear of being judged frequently keeps them from seeking help. AI helps allay worries about how society will see mental health issues and lessens the stigma attached to getting treatment by enabling users to interact with resources regarding mental health anonymously.

In India, for example, Wysa and YourDOST are well-known platforms that provide AI-driven mental health help that people may utilize without worrying about being judged. Significant participation has been reported on these platforms, especially from younger demographics who are more accustomed to using digital interfaces. The move towards online mental healthcare is part of a larger trend where technology is normalizing mental health talks and lowering stigma.

AI-driven solutions are also contributing to an improvement in the reliability of mental health assessments in a setting where underdiagnosis and misdiagnosis are common due to a lack of licensed mental health doctors. To assess patient data, identify trends, and provide early warning indicators for mental health issues, machine learning (ML) algorithms and natural language processing (NLP) techniques are being applied. This capability ensures timely intervention, which can improve patient outcomes and raise the accuracy of the diagnosis.

Though early results are encouraging, AI is still being used in diagnostic tools in India. For instance, in their early testing, AI models that examine speech patterns to identify early indicators of anxiety or sadness have demonstrated excellent accuracy rates. These resources might be especially helpful in remote locations with limited access to mental health providers. AI can significantly improve mental health treatments' accessibility throughout India, which is another noteworthy conclusion. Since many people live in underserved or rural locations, standard mental health services are frequently inaccessible. Geographical boundaries can be addressed by AI-driven mobile apps and platforms, giving much-needed support to patients who might otherwise go untreated.

For instance, AI-powered mental health applications that include activities for cognitive-behavioral treatment (CBT) and mood monitoring have grown in popularity in India. These applications not only provide accessibility to mental health services but also involve users in their care, promoting proactive management of mental health issues. An especially good way to keep users engaged with mental health apps is to gamify them by rewarding them for finishing tasks or tracking their moods. Though the benefits of AI in the treatment of mental illnesses are clear, this study highlights the ethical concerns that must be addressed for the safe and effective use of these technologies. Data security, privacy concerns, and the potential replacement of human judgment by artificial intelligence are significant challenges that require serious thought. The article argues that further research and collaboration between legislators, mental health specialists, and technologists are necessary to develop policies that protect users while optimizing the benefits of artificial intelligence in mental healthcare.

AI has the potential to greatly improve mental healthcare in India by reducing stigma, increasing the accuracy of diagnoses, and increasing the accessibility of services. However, resolving both the technical and ethical concerns around the deployment of AI is necessary to achieve this promise fully. AI has the potential to significantly improve mental health outcomes in India and increase the effectiveness, accessibility, and inclusivity of mental healthcare when used with the appropriate protocols and safety measures.

2.9 Recommendations

1. Extension of AI-Based Initiatives in Rural Areas: Considering the significant discrepancy in access to mental health treatments among urban and rural areas in India, future research

should focus on the creation and execution of AI-driven solutions to mental health specifically tailored for rural and underprivileged groups. To provide mental health support to those living in remote areas, this requires creating mobile-friendly platforms that speak the local language and use a minimal amount of internet capacity.

2. Increasing Healthcare Professionals' Knowledge of AI: Mental health practitioners must get ongoing training and instruction on how to use AI tools in their practice to completely integrate AI into mental healthcare. Future research will examine creating certificates and training courses that give professionals the ability to comprehend and apply AI-generated insights, ensuring that they can leverage these technologies to improve patient outcomes.
3. Stress on Longitudinal Research to Assess AI's Impact: While evidence exists for AI's short-term benefits in mental health treatment, long-term research is necessary to determine how AI interventions will affect reducing stigma and outcomes for mental health in the long run. Future studies to elucidate the benefits and drawbacks of AI-based mental health interventions should incorporate longitudinal designs that track patients over extended periods of time.
4. Address Concerns About Data Privacy and Ethics: An all-encompassing strategy for data protection and ethical concerns is required for the ongoing integration of AI in mental health treatment. Future studies should investigate the development of robust data protection measures specifically suited to AI in mental health, to guarantee that patient data is safeguarded against abuse. Additionally, studies should investigate ways to lessen algorithmic prejudice and guarantee that AI systems treat people regardless of their demographic makeup.
5. Develop Customized AI Models for Diverse People: Given the cultural and socioeconomic diversity of India, future research should focus on creating AI models that are aware of the unique mental health needs of distinct people. This would entail creating AI algorithms that, when diagnosing and suggesting therapies, take socioeconomic status, linguistic variances, and cultural considerations into account. This would increase the precision and applicability of AI-driven mental health interventions.

6. Analyze the Cost-Effectiveness of AI Interventions: Upcoming studies should assess the cost-effectiveness of AI-driven mental health interventions in relation to traditional mental health treatments. This involves not only determining if AI tools can reduce costs without compromising or improving the quality of service, but also evaluating the long-term financial consequences on patients and healthcare systems.
7. Promote Public Participation and Awareness: To truly fulfill AI's potential in reducing stigma around mental illness, we must increase public awareness of and involvement with AI-driven mental health solutions. Further research should investigate methods for effective public education that highlight the understanding of AI and its benefits for mental health treatment. Additionally, studies may assess the impact of public education programs on several demographic groups' adoption and utilization of AI products.
8. Promote Cross-sector Collaboration: Governmental bodies, for-profit technology firms, academic institutions, and non-governmental organizations must work together successfully to apply AI to mental healthcare. Subsequent investigations ought to delve into forms of interdisciplinary cooperation that can expedite the creation, implementation, and oversight of artificial intelligence-driven mental health remedies, guaranteeing that these technologies are widely accessible and effectively integrated into the healthcare system.

2.10 Conclusion

The incorporation of artificial intelligence (AI) in mental health treatment in India offers a revolutionary prospect to tackle the enduring issues of stigma, restricted service accessibility, and insufficient mental health infrastructure. This study demonstrates how AI-driven solutions can be crucial in transforming mental health treatment by providing people from a range of socioeconomic backgrounds with individualized, easily available, and stigma-free support.

AI has the power to reduce stigma, which is particularly significant in India where social and cultural barriers occasionally prevent people from seeking medical attention. By providing confidential, anonymous mental healthcare, AI-driven platforms can facilitate the treatment of a greater number of people, hence reducing stigma and social exclusion. Furthermore, AI's accessibility and versatility make it a valuable tool for filling the shortcomings in mental health treatments, especially in underprivileged and rural areas where access to professionals is frequently limited.

The ability of AI to deliver personalized interventions through advanced data analysis is also anticipated to increase the effectiveness of mental healthcare. By tailoring treatment programs to the individual needs of each patient, AI can improve patient outcomes and increase engagement with mental health services. The ongoing treatment that patients receive because of AI-driven devices' real-time changes and continuous monitoring also helps to improve mental health outcomes. However, the effective use of AI in mental healthcare requires a close examination of the moral and practical concerns. Strong legislative frameworks, the avoidance of algorithmic biases, and data privacy security are essential for protecting patients and maximizing the benefits of AI technology. To establish an atmosphere where AI may flourish while defending patient rights, stakeholders—including the government, medical professionals, and tech companies—must collaborate.

AI has the potential to drastically change how mental health services are provided in India. Due to its ability to address issues with stigma, accessibility, and personalized care, artificial intelligence (AI) holds great promise for improving the efficiency and inclusiveness of the mental health system. As the technology advances, more research, ethical deliberation, and cooperation across sectors will be necessary to realize AI's full potential in improving mental healthcare and the lives of millions of people in India.

References

1. Wang, Z., *et al.*, Mobile platforms in mental health: AI-driven innovations and their impact. *Indian J. Psychol. Med.*, *43*, 4, 319–325, 2020. https://doi.org/10.1177/02537176211017432.
2. Patel, V., Saxena, S., Lund, C., The effect of AI-driven telemedicine on mental health outcomes in rural Maharashtra: A case study. *Global Mental Health*, *6*, e30, 2019.
3. Mental Health Foundations India, *Mental Health Statistics in India*. New Delhi, India 2021. Retrieved From, https;//www:mentalhealthfoundationindia.com/statistics.
4. Kaminski, J.A., The role of AI in mental health care: A review. *Indian J. Psychiatry*, *62*, 6, 684–692, 2020. https://doi.org/10.4103/psychiatry.IndianJPsychiatry_684_20.

5. Tandon, N. and Tandon, R., AI in mental health care: Prospects and challenges. *J. Indian Acad. Clin. Med.*, *20*, 1, 12–20, 2019.
6. Blease, C., Sharpe, J., Walker, M., *et al.*, The role of AI and machine learning in the future of mental health. *Indian J. Med. Res.*, *152*, 1, 5–8, 2020. https://doi.org/10.4103/ijmr.IJMR_1962_19.
7. Wysa Inc., *Wysa Mental health app:impact and user statistics*. Wysa Inc., Boston, MA, United States, 2021. Retrieved from httpd://www.wysa.io/ompact.
8. Tandon, R. and Tandon, N., Schizophrenia diagnosis and management in the era of precision psychiatry. *Am. J. Psychiatry*, *176*, 4, 311–313, 2019.
9. Shatte, A.B.R., Hutchinson, D.M., Teague, S.J., Machine learning in mental health: A scoping review of methods and applications. *Psychol. Med.*, *49*, 9, 1426–1448, 2019. https://doi.org/10.1017/S0033291718004225.
10. McCoy, T.H., Perlis, R.H., Smoller, J.W., Ghosh, S., Predicting bipolar disorder relapse using machine learning. *J. Psychiatr. Res.*, 123, 121–127, 2020.
11. Esteva, A., Kuprel, B., Novoa, R.A., *et al.*, Dermatologist-level classification of skin cancer with deep neural networks. *Nature*, *542*, 7639, 115–118, 2017.
12. Viglialoro, R.M., Levaggi, R., Montefiori, M., The role of artificial intelligence in overcoming gender biases in mental health diagnosis. *J. Mental Health*, *29*, 5, 580–587, 2020.
13. Obermeyer, Z., Powers, B., Vogeli, C., Mullainathan, S., Dissecting racial bias in an algorithm used to manage the health of populations. *Science*, *366*, 6464, 447–453, 2019.
14. Inkster, B., Sarda, S., Subramanian, V., An empathy-driven, conversational artificial intelligence agent (Wysa) for digital mental well-being: Real-world data evaluation mixed-methods study. *JMIR mHealth uHealth*, *6*, 11, e12106, 2018.
15. Fitzpatrick, K.K., Darcy, A., Vierhile, M., Delivering cognitive behavior therapy to young adults with symptoms of depression and anxiety using a fully automated conversational agent (Woebot): A randomized controlled trial. *JMIR Mental Health*, *4*, 2, e19, 2017.
16. Guzman, A.L. and Lewis, S.C., Artificial intelligence and communication: A human–machine communication research agenda. *New Media Soc.*, *22*, 1, 70–86, 2020.
17. Choudhary, A., Saha, S., Gupta, V., Leveraging AI for mental health: Case studies from India. *J. Mental Health Promot.*, *12*, 2, 45–58, 2020.
18. Sundar, K.R., AI4MH: Bridging the AI literacy gap in mental health care in India. *Int. J. Health Policy Manage.*, *11*, 5, 634–641, 2022.
19. Ahmed, M., Shafiq, M., Siddiqui, F., Balancing automation and human intervention: Ethical considerations in AI-driven healthcare. *J. Med. Ethics Hist. Med.*, 14, 24–31, 2021.
20. World Health Organization, *Ethics and Governance of Artificial Intelligence for Health: WHO Guidance*. World Health Organization, Geneva, Switzerland, 2021.

21. Naslund, J.A., Aschbrenner, K.A., Araya, R., *et al.*, Digital technology for treating and preventing mental disorders in low-income and middle-income countries: A narrative review of the literature. *Lancet Psychiatry*, *7*, 7, 634–644, 2020.
22. National Institute of Mental Health and Neurosciences (NIMHANS), National Mental Health Survey of India, 2015–16: *Prevalence, Pattern and Outcomes*. NIMHANS Publication Bengaluru, India, 2016.
23. World Health Organization, *Mental health in India*. World Health Organization, New Delhi, India, 2019. Retrieved from https://www.who.int/india/health-topics/mental-health.
24. World Health Organization, *Mental Health atlas 2020*. World Health Organization, 2021. https://www.who.int/publications/i/item/9789240036703.
25. YourDost Health Solutions Private Limited, *YourDost:AI in mental health support*. YourDost Health Solutions Private Limited, 2021. Limited.https://yourdost.com/ai-mental-health-support.
26. Kumar, P.,Singh, A., Sharma, R., Artificial intelligence applications in Indian mental healthcare: Opportunities and challenges. *J. Indian Acad. Clin. Med.*, 22, 3, 210–217, 2021.
27. World Health Organization, Mental health: strengthening our response. World Health Organization, Geneva, Switzerland, 2018. Retrieved from https://www.who.int/news-room/fact-sheets/detail/mental-health-strengthening-our-response.

3

The AI Revolution in Mental Health: Beyond Traditional Paradigms

Durgeshwary Kolhe[1], Arshad Bhat[2*] and Mehvish[1]

[1]*Institute of Behavioural and Allied Sciences, Amity University, Mumbai, Maharashtra, India*
[2]*Institute of Liberal Arts, Amity University, Mumbai, Maharashtra, India*

Abstract

The chapter examines the transformative impact of artificial intelligence on mental health care. It reviews historical milestones and current limitations in mental health treatment, emphasizing AI's revolutionary potential. Foundational technologies such as deep learning and natural language processing are explored, alongside innovative data collection methods like wearable technology and social media analysis, with attention to ethical and privacy concerns. The chapter details AI's revolutionary applications in early detection and diagnosis through predictive analytics, AI-driven symptom checkers, diagnostic tools, virtual therapists, chatbots, immersive therapies using VR and AR, and personalized treatment plans. Enhanced monitoring and support systems *via* wearables and AI-driven crisis intervention tools are also discussed. The balance between human touch and AI in therapy, frameworks for responsible AI use, global perspectives and the economic and logistical considerations of AI integration are highlighted. The chapter envisions AI-augmented mental health ecosystems, integrating AI with traditional services to create holistic and personalized solutions. Interdisciplinary collaboration and cross-sector initiatives are emphasized to advance AI in mental health, with case studies of successful implementations and experimental therapies. The chapter advocates for proactive adoption and ethical practices, envisioning a future where AI complements human empathy in mental health care systems.

Keywords: Artificial intelligence, mental health care, deep learning, predictive analytics, virtual therapists

**Corresponding author*: bhatarshad09@gmail.com

Ridhima Sharma, Fazla Rabby, Rohit Bansal, Timcy Sachdeva and Jihene Mrabet (eds.) Confronting Mental Health Stigma with AI and Machine Learning, (63–82) © 2026 Scrivener Publishing LLC

3.1 Introduction

> *"The future of mental health care lies not in replacing human touch, but in enhancing it with the precision of artificial intelligence."*
>
> - Dr. Samantha Levin, AI Ethics Researcher (2023)

The use of artificial intelligence (AI) in conventional therapy modalities is driving a significant revolution in the mental health care environment. This development signifies a paradigm change in the way mental health disorders are approached, identified, and treated. The lengthy and intricate history of mental health therapy has been characterized by important turning points that have influenced our knowledge of and attitude toward psychological well-being. The field has undergone continual evolution, starting with institutionalization and using antiquated treatments and progressing to the use of psychopharmacology and evidence-based therapy [1]. A turning point was reached when Sigmund Freud introduced psychoanalysis in the late 19th century, highlighting the significance of the unconscious mind in mental health [2]. The early 20th century witnessed the rise of behaviorism, which put an emphasis on observable actions and environmental factors [3]. Humanistic psychology emerged in the middle of the 20th century, promoting self-actualization and personal development, and was led by individuals such as Carl Rogers [4]. When psychotropic drugs were developed in the 1950s, treatment choices were completely changed and there were now chemical interventions available for a wide range of mental health conditions [5]. Even with these developments, modern mental health treatment still confronts many obstacles. The World Health Organization [6] states that stigma, geographic obstacles, or financial limitations prevent many people from receiving timely and adequate treatment, which is still a major problem when it comes to access to quality care. This issue is made worse by the lack of mental health specialists, especially in underprivileged and rural areas. Furthermore, inconsistent treatment plans and results may result from the subjective nature of mental health assessment and diagnosis [7]. AI integration in mental health care offers a chance to overcome these drawbacks and improve treatment effectiveness. Large-scale data can be analyzed by machine learning algorithms to find trends and forecast results, which could enhance therapy personalization and diagnosis precision [8]. AI-driven chatbots and virtual therapists bridge the gap in care accessibility by providing round-the-clock assistance [9]. However, implementing AI in mental health care presents a number of problems. Ethical concerns about data privacy, the possibility of algorithmic bias, and the significance of keeping human empathy in therapy are critical issues that must be properly addressed [10].

Presently standing on the verge of this technological revolution in mental health care, it is critical to approach the integration of AI with both enthusiasm and prudence, ensuring that the human element of treatment is enhanced rather than displaced. Artificial intelligence (AI) is quickly becoming a disruptive force in the field of mental health, providing novel approaches to persistent problems with support, diagnosis, and treatment. A wide range of technologies and applications, including machine learning algorithms, natural language processing, and predictive analytics, are included in the field of artificial intelligence (AI) in mental health with the goal of improving the efficacy and delivery of mental health care [11]. Numerous facets of mental health are being addressed by these AI-powered solutions, ranging from early diagnosis and detection to individualized treatment plans and continuous patient monitoring. AI has the enormous potential to completely transform the treatment of mental illness. Increasing the precision and speed of diagnosis is one of the most promising uses. In order to detect early indicators of mental health disorders with a degree of precision that may exceed human abilities, artificial intelligence (AI) algorithms can evaluate enormous volumes of data, including patient histories, behavioral patterns, and even minute changes in speech or facial expressions [12]. Early detection has the potential to improve patient outcomes by enabling more prompt therapies. Additionally, chatbots and virtual assistants driven by artificial intelligence are increasing the availability of mental health support, offering round-the-clock assistance to those who might be unwilling to seek traditional therapy or encounter obstacles in receiving care [9]. As a vital initial layer of defense in mental health care, these digital tools can provide immediate support, coping mechanisms, and even preliminary assessments. AI is helping to create individualized therapy plans in the field of medicine by analyzing patient data and identifying the most likely-to-be beneficial actions. Patient satisfaction and treatment outcomes could be greatly enhanced by this customized approach [13]. Furthermore, AI systems can continuously track the development of their patients, modifying treatment recommendations in real time in response to the patient's changing needs and response. The speed of scientific discovery is accelerating due to the incorporation of AI in mental health studies. Machine learning models can recognize patterns and correlations in huge datasets that may be invisible to human researchers [8]. This could lead to the discovery of new treatment techniques and new insights into the underlying mechanisms of mental health illnesses. However, there are obstacles in the way of AI's revolutionary potential in the field of mental health. Careful attention needs to be paid to ethical issues, such as data privacy, algorithmic prejudice, and the risk of relying too much on technology at the detriment of interpersonal relationships [14]. In addition, substantial investments in infrastructure, training, and legal frameworks are necessary for the safe and efficient integration of AI into mental health care systems. Notwithstanding these obstacles, there is no denying AI's potential to completely transform mental health services. Technology promises to improve our understanding of mental health, increase the precision and effectiveness of diagnoses, and offer more individualized and efficient treatments as it develops and becomes more sophisticated. This ushers in the cusp of a new era in mental health care, one that has the potential to significantly enhance outcomes and quality of life for millions of people globally by combining human knowledge with AI-driven insights and support.

3.2 Research Methodology

This chapter uses a multidimensional approach to study the integration of artificial intelligence (AI) into mental health care. This study involved an extensive review of peer-reviewed articles published in white papers and case studies relating to psychiatry, psychology, computer science, bioethics, and similar fields. Secondary sources such as conference proceedings, industry reports, and government publications provided supplementary data on trends, applications, and challenges relevant to AI-driven solutions for mental health. Therefore, this research specifically assessed the applicability of emerging technologies such as deep learning, natural language processing, virtual reality (VR), and wearable devices for use cases within mental health contexts.

Qualitative evidence from various mental health practitioners, technologists, and ethicists would have been added through interviews and content analyses of public discourse. Quantitative data were brought in on the efficacy and penetration of AI-based tools to substantiate important findings. The current case studies were critically evaluated to find out the actual scenarios and the ethical issues pertaining to accessibility and patient outcomes. This methodology thus provides the theoretical foundations for a multilayered analysis of the transformative potential and limitations offered by AI in changing paradigms in mental health care.

3.3 The Convergence of AI and Mental Health

The intersection of mental health and artificial intelligence (AI) presents a transformative frontier, with the potential to redefine psychological diagnosis, treatment, and support through innovative methodologies. At the core of this convergence are fundamental AI technologies like deep learning and neural networks, which excel in pattern recognition and complex data analysis. These technologies enable the examination of vast datasets, such as medical records, behavioral patterns, and genomic information, to uncover subtle indicators of psychological distress or potential mental illnesses that may evade human observation [15]. Deep learning algorithms and neural networks form the backbone of AI's application in mental health. These systems are trained on extensive datasets to identify correlations and patterns that human clinicians might miss. For instance, through electroencephalogram (EEG) data, AI algorithms can detect brain wave patterns associated with stress, anxiety, or depression, providing clinicians with a powerful diagnostic tool. Similarly, AI can analyze genetic predispositions and environmental factors, allowing for more personalized approaches to mental health care. One of the standout applications of AI in mental health is natural language processing (NLP) and sentiment analysis, which facilitate a nuanced understanding of human communication. These tools can analyze speech patterns, tone, and word choice in spoken or written texts, offering clinicians insights into emotional states and cognitive tendencies. For instance, certain linguistic markers, such as frequent use of negative words or a decline in language complexity, may indicate depressive episodes. NLP has been instrumental in developing tools like transcription software that not only document patient interactions but also assess emotional undertones in real time [16]. AI-powered tools like chatbots and virtual therapists have emerged as key innovations, offering around-the-clock support to individuals in need. These systems, such as Woebot and Wysa, use conversational AI to simulate empathetic interactions and deliver evidence-based therapeutic exercises. While these tools are not replacements for human therapists, they complement traditional therapy by bridging accessibility gaps, particularly for individuals who face financial, geographical, or stigma-related barriers to care. For example, Woebot, an AI-powered chatbot, engages users in conversations designed to mirror cognitive-behavioral therapy (CBT) techniques. It uses a combination of humor, psychoeducation, and interactive exercises to help users identify negative thought patterns and develop healthier coping mechanisms. Similarly, Wysa employs an empathetic conversational style, offering guided meditations and emotional journaling prompts to support users dealing with stress, anxiety, or grief. These AI-driven systems are especially beneficial for populations with limited access to mental health professionals, as they provide immediate and scalable interventions. Beyond conversational AI, the rise of wearable technology and Internet of Things (IoT) devices has revolutionized data collection in mental health. Wearables such as smartwatches and fitness trackers monitor physiological metrics like heart rate variability, sleep quality, and physical activity levels, providing continuous, real-time data that can signal changes in mental health status [17]. For instance, deviations in sleep patterns or reduced physical activity might indicate depressive episodes, while elevated stress levels could correlate with anxiety disorders.

Advanced wearables, such as those incorporating galvanic skin response (GSR) sensors, can measure stress-related physiological changes like sweating and skin conductivity. These devices, combined with AI analysis, offer a comprehensive picture of an individual's mental state by correlating physiological markers with behavioral data. Moreover, wearable devices integrated with smartphone apps allow users to track their mood, receive personalized feedback, and access therapeutic resources, fostering self-awareness and proactive mental health management. Similarly, social media and digital behavior analysis have emerged as invaluable tools for understanding psychological states. By applying AI algorithms to analyze users' posts, interactions, and online activity patterns, researchers can detect shifts in mood or behavior that may indicate mental health challenges [18]. For instance, changes in language use, posting frequency, or engagement with certain types of content could act as red flags, prompting early interventions. A notable example is AI systems that analyze social media posts to identify markers of suicidal ideation. Researchers have developed algorithms capable of detecting warning signs such as expressions of hopelessness or isolation in textual content. These tools have been deployed in collaboration with platforms like Facebook, which alerts trained professionals when such content is flagged, enabling timely outreach to at-risk individuals. AI's potential extends beyond diagnosis and support to the realm of precision medicine, where treatments are tailored to an individual's unique needs. By integrating genetic, epigenetic, and environmental data, AI can help identify which interventions are most likely to be effective for a specific patient. For example, pharmacogenomic data analyzed by AI can guide the prescription of antidepressants or antipsychotics, minimizing trial-and-error approaches and reducing the risk of adverse effects. AI also facilitates personalized therapy by identifying optimal therapeutic modalities for individuals. For instance, some patients may respond better to CBT, while others might benefit more from mindfulness-based stress reduction (MBSR) techniques. By analyzing patient histories, preferences, and progress, AI systems can recommend interventions with the highest likelihood of success. However, the integration of AI into mental health care is not without challenges. One major concern is data privacy and security. The collection and analysis of sensitive mental health data necessitate robust safeguards to protect individuals from breaches and misuse. Ethical frameworks must ensure that AI systems are transparent, equitable, and free from biases that could result in disparities in mental health care delivery [19]. For example, if training data lacks diversity, AI algorithms may perpetuate stereotypes or fail to account for cultural and socio-economic factors. The potential for AI to exacerbate inequality in mental health care is a significant concern. Marginalized populations, who are already underserved by traditional healthcare systems, may face additional barriers if AI systems are not designed inclusively. Biases in AI models could lead to misdiagnoses or unequal treatment recommendations, perpetuating existing disparities. Addressing these issues requires diverse datasets, rigorous testing, and ongoing monitoring to ensure fairness and accountability. Moreover, the use of AI in mental health raises questions about autonomy and informed consent. Patients must be fully informed about how their data will be used, and they should have the option to opt out without compromising their access to care. Balancing the need for comprehensive data with respect for individual autonomy is a critical challenge for developers and policymakers.

Looking ahead, the convergence of AI and mental health offers exciting possibilities for innovation and impact. Advances in machine learning and sensor technology are likely to lead to more sophisticated diagnostic tools and therapeutic interventions. For example, AI systems that combine facial recognition, voice analysis, and physiological monitoring could provide a holistic assessment of mental health in real time. Virtual reality (VR) and augmented reality (AR) technologies, when integrated with AI, hold promise for immersive therapeutic experiences. For instance, VR-based exposure therapy for phobias and PTSD could be enhanced by AI algorithms that adapt scenarios based on real-time feedback from patients. Similarly, AR applications could provide on-the-go mindfulness exercises, helping users manage stress and anxiety in everyday situations. In the realm of research, AI has the potential to accelerate the discovery of new treatments and interventions. By analyzing vast amounts of data from clinical trials, AI can identify patterns and insights that might otherwise go unnoticed. This could lead to the development of novel therapies for complex conditions like bipolar disorder or treatment-resistant depression.

Realizing the full potential of AI in mental health requires collaboration among technologists, mental health professionals, ethicists, and policymakers. Interdisciplinary partnerships can ensure that AI tools are not only effective but also ethical and equitable. For example, engaging mental health experts in the design and testing of AI systems can help ensure that these tools align with clinical best practices and meet the needs of diverse populations. Policymakers play a crucial role in establishing regulations and standards for AI in mental health. Clear guidelines on data privacy, algorithmic transparency, and accountability are essential to build public trust and safeguard individual rights. Initiatives such as the European Union's General Data Protection Regulation (GDPR) provide a framework for balancing innovation with ethical considerations. Finally, public education is critical to the successful integration of AI in mental health care. By raising awareness about the benefits and limitations of AI tools, stakeholders can empower individuals to make informed decisions about their care. Transparent communication about how AI systems work and what they can achieve will be key to fostering acceptance and trust. The convergence of AI and mental health represents a paradigm shift in how psychological care is delivered. From advanced diagnostic tools to personalized therapy and real-time monitoring, AI offers unparalleled opportunities to improve mental health outcomes. However, the ethical, privacy, and equity challenges associated with AI integration must not be overlooked. As this field continues to evolve, a balanced approach that prioritizes both innovation and ethical implementation will be essential. Through collaboration and a commitment to inclusivity, stakeholders can harness the transformative power of AI to create a future where mental health care is more accessible, effective, and equitable for all.

3.4 Education and Workforce Training

The integration of artificial intelligence (AI) in mental health care has catalyzed a fundamental transformation in how mental health professionals are educated and trained, necessitating a comprehensive overhaul of traditional educational paradigms. The rapid evolution of AI technologies in mental health demands a strategic approach to workforce development that encompasses technical competency, ethical considerations, and interdisciplinary collaboration [20]. Recent studies indicate that approximately 78% of mental health institutions are incorporating AI-related training modules into their professional development programs, highlighting the growing recognition of AI literacy as a core competency in mental health practice [21]. The preparation of mental health professionals to effectively utilize AI tools begins with understanding the fundamental principles of AI systems, machine learning algorithms, and their specific applications in mental health care settings. According to research by Thompson and colleagues [22], professionals who receive comprehensive AI training demonstrate a 45% higher rate of successful implementation of AI-assisted interventions compared to those without such training. This underscores the critical importance of structured educational programs that bridge the gap between traditional mental health expertise and technological proficiency. The development of AI literacy programs within mental health education has emerged as a priority, with leading institutions implementing curriculum changes that integrate AI-specific modules alongside conventional clinical training. These programs typically cover various aspects, including AI-driven diagnostic tools, predictive analytics for patient outcomes, and automated therapeutic interventions [23]. Reports state that institutions incorporating comprehensive AI literacy programs show a 60% improvement in graduates' readiness to handle AI-integrated mental health services [24]. Furthermore, the building of interdisciplinary skills has become paramount in preparing mental health professionals for AI-driven environments.

Research conducted by Chen and Martinez [25] demonstrates that professionals with cross-disciplinary training in both mental health and technology demonstrate superior abilities in critical thinking, problem-solving, and adaptive learning when working with AI systems. This finding has led to the development of specialized training programs that combine clinical expertise with technical knowledge, enabling professionals to effectively leverage AI tools while maintaining the human-centric nature of mental health care. The implementation of simulation-based training has proven particularly effective, with studies showing that practitioners who undergo immersive AI-focused simulations exhibit a 55% higher confidence level in utilizing AI tools in their practice [26]. The evolution of workforce training in mental health now encompasses various innovative approaches, including virtual reality-based training modules, collaborative learning platforms, and real-time feedback systems that help professionals develop proficiency in AI-assisted mental health care delivery. A comprehensive study by Harrison and colleagues [27] reveals that organizations implementing these advanced training methodologies report a 40% reduction in technology-related errors and a 65% improvement in service delivery efficiency. The integration of ethical considerations in AI education has become increasingly crucial, with particular emphasis on issues such as data privacy, algorithmic bias, and maintaining therapeutic relationships in

AI-augmented settings. Research indicates that professionals who receive specific training in AI ethics demonstrate a 70% higher awareness of potential ethical challenges and are better equipped to navigate complex decision-making scenarios [28]. The development of competency frameworks for AI-enabled mental health care has emerged as a critical component of professional education, with leading institutions establishing standardized criteria for assessing technological proficiency alongside clinical skills. A landmark study by Kumar and Wilson [29] shows that implementing structured competency frameworks results in a 50% improvement in professionals' ability to integrate AI tools effectively while maintaining high standards of patient care. The transformation of mental health education extends beyond individual skill development to encompass organizational change management and systemic adaptation to AI-driven healthcare environments. Research conducted by Morgan and Lee [30] demonstrates that organizations that adopt comprehensive approaches to AI education, including regular updates and continuous professional development programs, show a 62% higher rate of successful AI implementation compared to those with limited educational support. The emergence of specialized certification programs in AI-assisted mental health care has created new pathways for professional development, with studies indicating that certified professionals demonstrate a 48% higher level of effectiveness in utilizing AI tools compared to non-certified counterparts [31]. The integration of practical experience with theoretical knowledge has become essential in preparing mental health professionals for AI-driven environments, with supervised practice sessions and mentorship programs playing crucial roles in skill development. According to Davidson and colleagues [32], professionals who participate in structured mentorship programs show a 57% improvement in their ability to integrate AI tools into their clinical practice effectively. The future of mental health education increasingly emphasizes the development of adaptive learning capabilities, enabling professionals to stay current with rapidly evolving AI technologies while maintaining high standards of clinical care.

3.5 Cultural Sensitivity in AI Applications

The integration of artificial intelligence (AI) into mental health care represents a transformative shift in how psychological support and treatment are delivered across diverse cultural contexts. The imperative for cultural sensitivity in AI applications has become increasingly critical as these technologies expand globally [33]. Within the mental health domain,

AI systems must navigate complex cultural nuances, linguistic variations, and diverse belief systems to provide effective and culturally appropriate care. Research by Chen and Rodriguez [34] demonstrates that AI applications in mental health must go beyond mere translation services to truly understand and respond to cultural-specific manifestations of mental health conditions. This understanding includes recognizing how different cultures express emotional distress, their healing traditions, and their unique perspectives on mental wellness. The development of culturally sensitive AI tools requires extensive collaboration between mental health professionals, cultural anthropologists, and AI developers to create systems that can effectively serve diverse populations while avoiding harmful stereotypes or oversimplifications of cultural differences. According to Wong *et al.* [35], successful implementation of AI in mental health care must consider various cultural factors, including communication styles, family dynamics, and religious or spiritual beliefs that influence mental health perceptions and treatment preferences. The challenge of tailoring AI tools for diverse cultural and linguistic needs involves sophisticated natural language processing capabilities that can understand and respond to cultural idioms of distress and culture-specific expressions of mental health concerns. Research by Patel and Thompson [36] highlights the importance of developing AI systems that can recognize and appropriately respond to cultural-specific phrases and expressions that might indicate mental health challenges in different communities. These systems must be trained on diverse datasets that represent various cultural perspectives and experiences to ensure their effectiveness across different populations.

The linguistic adaptation of AI tools presents challenges, as mental health terminology and concepts often lack direct translations across languages, requiring careful consideration of cultural context and meaning. Studies by Johnson *et al.* [37] indicate that AI algorithms must be calibrated to account for cultural variations in emotional expression, social support systems, and treatment-seeking behaviors. This calibration requires continuous refinement and validation across different cultural contexts to ensure that the algorithms remain effective and culturally appropriate. Research by Ahmed and Lee [38] emphasizes the importance of developing AI systems that can adapt their responses based on cultural context, including understanding when to recommend traditional healing practices alongside conventional mental health interventions. The prevention of cultural biases in AI applications represents a significant challenge that requires careful attention to data collection, algorithm development, and system implementation. According to research by Brown and Garcia [39], AI systems trained primarily on Western populations may perpetuate cultural biases and fail to adequately serve diverse communities. To address this concern, developers must ensure that training data includes representative samples from various cultural groups and that algorithms are tested for cultural bias before deployment. Studies by Wilson *et al.* [40] suggest that regular cultural audits of AI systems can help identify and address potential biases in their operations.

The fostering of inclusivity in mental health AI requires a comprehensive approach that considers various cultural perspectives in the design and implementation of these tools. Research by Taylor and Kumar [41] demonstrates that successful inclusive AI systems must incorporate feedback from diverse cultural communities throughout their development process. This inclusive approach ensures that AI tools are not only technically effective but also culturally acceptable and beneficial to the communities they serve. The implementation of culturally sensitive AI in mental health care must also consider the role of cultural healers and traditional practices in many communities. Studies by Anderson and Park [42] show that effective AI systems should be designed to complement rather than replace traditional healing practices, recognizing the value of cultural wisdom in mental health care. The development of culturally sensitive AI applications also requires careful attention to privacy concerns and data protection, as different cultures may have varying perspectives on mental health stigma and confidentiality. Research by Roberts *et al.* [43] indicates that AI systems must be designed with flexible privacy settings that can accommodate different cultural expectations regarding the sharing of mental health information. The success of culturally sensitive AI applications in mental health care ultimately depends on their ability to build trust with diverse communities. Studies by Lewis and Chen [44] suggest that transparency in AI operations and active community engagement in their development and implementation are crucial for establishing this trust. The World Health Organization (WHO) guidelines emphasize the importance of adapting digital interventions to local contexts and cultural needs, highlighting that successful implementation requires an understanding of both technological capabilities and cultural sensitivities [45]. The application of artificial intelligence (AI) and cutting-edge technology is radically changing the mental health sector. These developments are changing methods for the early identification, diagnosis, care, and follow-up of people with mental health disorders. Healthcare professionals can more effectively adopt preventative measures by identifying at-risk individuals before symptoms worsen thanks to AI-driven predictive analytics, which is enabling earlier interventions. The efficiency and accuracy of mental health assessments are being improved by AI-powered symptom checks and diagnostic tools, which are also giving physicians insightful information to help them make decisions. Artificial intelligence (AI)-driven chatbots and virtual therapists are providing more easily accessible therapeutic choices, especially for those who are unable to attend traditional in-person treatment sessions. These virtual assistants can lead users through evidence-based therapy exercises, give coping mechanisms, and offer instant assistance. Virtual reality (VR) and augmented reality (AR) immersive therapies are showing promise in the treatment of anxiety disorders and post-traumatic stress disorder (PTSD), among other mental health diseases. Through these immersive experiences, patients can face and conquer their phobias in safe, supervised settings. By analyzing vast volumes of patient data to provide individualized recommendations based on each person's requirements and preferences, AI is also transforming treatment planning and may even improve patient participation and therapeutic success. Wearable technology is making it possible to track behavioral and physiological indicators linked to mental health state in real time, thanks to continuous mental health monitoring. These gadgets enable prompt interventions by warning medical professionals of any deterioration in a patient's condition. Artificial intelligence (AI)-powered crisis intervention solutions are augmenting the capacities of mental health hotlines and emergency services by promptly determining the intensity of circumstances and delivering suitable assistance or escalation. Even though there is a lot of promises for these technical developments, ethical issues, data privacy issues, and the requirement for human oversight must still be addressed to ensure responsible adoption and preserve the human element in mental health care.

3.6 Beyond the Hype-Real-World Implications

It is essential to look over the initial excitement and consider the practical ramifications of this technological revolution as artificial intelligence (AI) continues to make inroads into mental health treatment. To ensure its appropriate and successful deployment, a complex range of ethical, sociological, regulatory, and economic issues are raised by the integration of AI into mental health treatments. These issues must be properly addressed. The problem of bias in AI algorithms is one of the fundamental ethical problems. Given the past discrepancies in mental health research and treatment, there is a major risk that AI systems would perpetuate or even exacerbate already-existing inequalities. AI systems are only as unbiased as the data they are trained on. It is imperative that researchers and developers take proactive measures to detect and address these biases, guaranteeing that AI-powered mental health solutions are equitable and successful for a range of demographics. This entails using a variety of datasets, integrating marginalized people into the process of creation, and putting strict testing procedures in place to identify and address biases. Another crucial ethical factor is making sure that everyone has equal access to AI-driven healthcare. While AI may make mental health services more accessible to neglected groups, there is also a chance that it may lead to a "digital divide" in which only affluent people would be able to take advantage of these advancements. It is imperative that policymakers and healthcare professionals collaborate to devise approaches that facilitate broad accessibility to AI-driven mental health resources, especially in remote or economically disadvantaged regions where conventional mental health services may be limited. In therapy, striking a balance between human touch and AI is a nuanced matter that calls for careful thought. AI can be a useful tool for enhancing human abilities and offering support, but in the field of mental health treatment, human empathy and connection are crucial. Achieving the ideal balance requires making sure that patients always have access to human help when they need it and utilizing AI as a supplemental tool rather than as a substitute for licensed therapists.

The increasing prevalence of AI in mental health care highlights the pressing need for comprehensive policy frameworks and regulations. It takes input from a wide range of stakeholders, including mental health practitioners, AI experts, ethicists, policymakers, and patient advocates, to develop recommendations for the appropriate use of AI in mental health. These frameworks need to cover things like data privacy, informed consent, openness in AI decision making, and responsibility for results generated by AI. Collaborative governance techniques that transcend national boundaries are necessary, given the global character of mental health concerns and the borderless nature of digital technology. Guidelines for digital health interventions have started to be developed by international organizations like the World Health Organization (WHO), but more coordinated efforts are required to establish coherent worldwide standards for AI in mental health care. A comprehensive cost-benefit analysis is necessary before integrating AI into mental health care from an economic standpoint. Long-term cost savings and increased efficiency are possible with AI, but a significant upfront investment in infrastructure, technology, and training may be necessary. The financial effects of implementing AI must be carefully considered by healthcare systems and providers, considering aspects like implementation costs, possible human resource savings, and treatment outcome improvements. Significant investments in infrastructure and training for mental health practitioners are also necessary for the successful integration of AI into mental health care. This covers instruction on the ethical ramifications and constraints of AI in mental health treatment in addition to technical training on the efficient use of AI tools. When using AI-generated insights, practitioners need to be able to critically assess them while still using their clinical judgment.

3.7 The Future Landscape of Mental Health with AI

Artificial intelligence (AI) has the potential to completely transform the mental health services industry, bringing with it improved treatment outcomes and individualized care. Looking ahead, AI-augmented mental health ecosystems are showing promise as a frontier that may effectively combine cutting-edge technology with conventional therapeutic modalities. Utilizing AI's ability to analyze data and recognize patterns, these ecosystems are designed to provide comprehensive, customized solutions that cater to the requirements of each person, enhancing and informing healthcare decision making [46]. The creation of these sophisticated systems requires a team effort combining the specialized knowledge of technologists, physicians, and lawmakers. Ensuring that AI technologies are created and applied ethically, effectively, and in accordance with healthcare, the best practices require this kind of interdisciplinary collaboration. To expand the use of AI in mental health treatment, cross-sector initiatives are already in place, encouraging collaborations between educational institutions, healthcare providers, and technological firms [10]. Several innovative projects and case studies provide a glimpse into the revolutionary potential of AI in mental health. For example, the use of AI-powered chatbots in cognitive behavioral therapy has demonstrated encouraging outcomes in offering people with mild to moderate anxiety and depression easily accessible, 24-hour assistance [9]. These online therapists can supplement conventional in-person therapy sessions by providing immediate support, monitoring mood trends, and offering customized coping mechanisms. The creation of predictive models for early intervention in cases of severe mental illness is another cutting-edge use of AI in mental health. These models can detect subtle patterns that may point to the onset of conditions like bipolar disorder or schizophrenia by analyzing massive amounts of data from wearables, social media, and electronic health records. This proactive approach allows for earlier interventions and potentially improved long-term outcomes [47].

In the future, virtual reality (VR) and AI-based experimental therapies will expand the range of possible treatments. AI-guided immersive VR environments are being investigated as a potential treatment for anxiety-related disorders like PTSD and phobias. These technologies provide regulated exposure therapy sessions that may be precisely tailored to meet the therapeutic requirements and progress of each patient [48]. AI is predicted to play a bigger role in mental health treatment beyond diagnostic and therapeutic applications as it evolves. Future AI systems could significantly contribute to mental health research, accelerating the development of new treatment modalities and enhancing our understanding of the intricate interactions between biological, psychological, and social factors influencing mental health disorders [8]. However, even as they welcome these technological developments, stakeholders must also confront ethical concerns and challenges posed by using AI in mental health services. To ensure that AI enhances rather than replaces the essential human connection in mental health care, considerations around data privacy, algorithmic bias, and maintaining the human aspect in therapy must be carefully navigated [49]. Ongoing research and collaboration between technologists, clinicians, and policymakers will be critical to fully realize the potential of AI in mental health care while upholding the highest standards of ethics and efficacy. The future landscape of mental health with AI holds immense promise for improving access to care, personalizing treatment approaches, and enhancing our understanding of mental health disorders.

3.8 Conclusion

The use of AI in mental health care is a paradigm shift that promises to change how psychological health and treatment are approached. This discussion has looked at the previously unheard-of possibilities for early identification, individualized treatments, and ongoing support that come with incorporating artificial intelligence into mental health procedures. The integration of AI technology with mental health services has the potential to resolve long-standing issues with treatment efficacy, efficiency, and accessibility. The field of mental health treatment is changing quickly, from AI-powered diagnostic tools that can identify minute patterns in speech and behavior to virtual therapists that offer round-the-clock assistance. Nonetheless, there are complications and moral issues surrounding this transition. Achieving the delicate balance between technological innovation and human-centered care is critical at this critical juncture in the revolution. AI's ethical ramifications for mental health require serious thought and attention, as they involve concerns about privacy, algorithmic bias, and maintaining human connection in therapy. Furthermore, cooperation between technologists, doctors, policymakers, and ethicists will be necessary for the effective integration of AI into mental health systems. The idea of AI-enhanced mental health ecosystems is quite promising going forward. With the use of these technologies, mental health treatments could become more comprehensive, approachable, and tailored to each patient's requirements and situation. The mentioned case studies and innovative projects demonstrate the revolutionary potential of AI when applied carefully. To ensure that the primary objective of enhancing mental health outcomes stays at the forefront of technology breakthroughs, it is crucial to approach this transformation with a critical and perceptive eye. To sum up, the AI revolution in mental health care presents an enticing picture of a time when human knowledge and technology work together to deliver more efficient, individualized, and effective mental health care. It is crucial to be vigilant in addressing the ethical, societal, and practical difficulties that arise when the bounds of possibility continue to expand. The full potential of AI can be realized in a truly revolutionary way by promoting interdisciplinary collaboration, giving ethical considerations top priority, and adhering to a human-centered approach. This will result in a mental health care system that not only makes use of state-of-the-art technology but also upholds the fundamental values of empathy, compassion, and human connection.

References

1. Smith, K., Ostinelli, E., Cipriani, A., Covid-19 and mental health: a transformational opportunity to apply an evidence-based approach to clinical practice and research. *Evidence-Based Mental Health*, 23, 2, 45–46, 2020.
2. Freud, S., The interpretation of dreams, in: *The Standard Edition of the Complete Psychological Works of Sigmund Freud*, vol. 4–5, J. Strachey (Ed.), Hogarth Press, London, 1900/1953.
3. Watson, J.B., Psychology as the behaviourist views it. *Psychol. Rev.*, 20, 2, 158–177, 1913.
4. Rogers, C.R., *Client-Cantered Therapy: Its Current Practice, Implications, and Theory*, Houghton Mifflin, Boston, 1951.
5. López-Muñoz, F., *et al.*, History of the discovery and clinical introduction of chlorpromazine. *Ann. Clin. Psychiatry*, 17, 3, 113–135, 2005.
6. World Health Organization, *Mental Health Atlas 2020*, World Health Organization, Geneva, 2021.
7. American Psychiatric Association, *Diagnostic and Statistical Manual of Mental Disorders*, (5th ed., Text Revision), American Psychiatric Association Publishing, Washington, DC, 2022.

8. Dwyer, D.B., *et al.*, Machine Learning Approaches for Clinical Psychology and Psychiatry. *Annu. Rev. Clin. Psychol.*, 14, 91–118, 2018.
9. Fitzpatrick, K.K., *et al.*, Delivering Cognitive Behavior Therapy to Young Adults with Symptoms of Depression and Anxiety Using a Fully Automated Conversational Agent (Woebot): A Randomized Controlled Trial. *JMIR Mental Health*, 4, 2, e19, 2017.
10. Torous, J., *et al.*, The growing field of digital psychiatry: current evidence and the future of apps, social media, chatbots, and virtual reality. *World Psychiatry*, 20, 3, 318–335, 2021.
11. Shatte, A.B., *et al.*, Machine learning in mental health: A scoping review of methods and applications. *Psychol. Med.*, 49, 9, 1426–1448, 2019.
12. Bzdok, D. and Meyer-Lindenberg, A., Machine learning for precision psychiatry: Opportunities and challenges. *Biol. Psychiatry: Cognit. Neurosci. Neuroimaging*, 3, 3, 223–230, 2018.
13. Luxton, D.D., Artificial intelligence in psychological practice: Current and future applications and implications. *Prof. Psychol. Res. Pract.*, 45, 5, 332–339, 2014.
14. Char, D.S., *et al.*, Implementing machine learning in health care—addressing ethical challenges. *N. Engl. J. Med.*, 378, 11, 981–983, 2018.
15. LeCun, Y., Bengio, Y., Hinton, G., Deep learning. *Nature*, 521, 436–444, 7553, 2015.
16. Calvo, R.A., Milne, D.N., Hussain, M.S., Christensen, H., Natural language processing in mental health applications using non-clinical texts. *Nat. Lang. Eng.*, 23, 5, 649–685, 2017.
17. Marzano, L., Bardill, A., Fields, B., Herd, K., Veale, D., Grey, N., Moran, P., The application of mHealth to mental health: opportunities and challenges. *Lancet Psychiatry*, 2, 10, 942–948, 2015.
18. De Choudhury, M., Gamon, M., Counts, S., Horvitz, E., Predicting depression *via* social media, in: *Proceedings of the International AAAI Conference on Web and Social Media*, vol. 7, no. 1, pp. 128–137, 2013.
19. Martinez-Martin, N. and Kreitmair, K., Ethical issues for direct-to-consumer digital psychotherapy apps: addressing accountability, data protection, and consent. *JMIR Mental Health*, 5, 2, e32, 2018.
20. Smith, R. and Johnson, P., Transforming mental health education for the AI era. *Digit. Healthc. J.*, 28, 1, 12–27, 2023.
21. Anderson, M., Wilson, R., Thompson, K., Digital transformation in mental health education: A comprehensive analysis. *J. Med. Educ.*, 45, 2, 78–92, 2024.
22. Thompson, L., Garcia, R., White, S., Impact of AI training on mental health intervention outcomes. *Mental Health Technol. Rev.*, 16, 4, 90–105, 2023.
23. Williams, E. and Davis, C., Curriculum development for AI-integrated mental health education. *Educ. Innov. Healthc.*, 19, 2, 145–160, 2024.
24. Roberts, S., Johnson, M., Brown, T., AI literacy integration in mental health education. *J. Mental Health Educ.*, 32, 4, 201–216, 2023.

25. Chen, L. and Martinez, S., Cross-disciplinary approaches in AI-integrated mental healthcare training. *Technol. Mental Health*, 18, 1, 45–60, 2024.
26. Taylor, M. and Brown, A., Simulation-based training in AI-assisted mental healthcare. *Healthc. Simul. J.*, 22, 2, 178–193, 2023.
27. Harrison, J., Stevens, P., Wright, O., Advanced training methodologies for AI-assisted mental healthcare. *Digit. Health Educ.*, 12, 3, 89–104, 2024.
28. Peterson, K., Adams, J., Clark, R., Ethical considerations in AI-enabled mental health practice. *Ethics Mental Health Pract. J.*, 25, 3, 156–171, 2023.
29. Kumar, A. and Wilson, B., Competency frameworks for AI-integrated mental health practice. *J. Healthc. Stand.*, 15, 2, 67–82, 2024.
30. Morgan, C. and Lee, H., Organizational adaptation to AI technologies in mental healthcare. *Change Manage. Healthc.*, 20, 1, 34–49, 2023.
31. Washington, D. and Zhang, Y., Certification programs in AI-assisted mental healthcare. *Prof. Certification Q.*, 11, 1, 23–38, 2024.
32. Davidson, R., Miller, S., Brooks, N., Mentorship models in AI-enabled mental health practice. *Prof. Dev. Healthc.*, 29, 4, 112–127, 2023.
33. Smith, J., *et al.*, The future of AI in global mental health care. *J. Digit. Health*, 4, 2, 145–162, 2023.
34. Chen, L. and Rodriguez, C., Cultural competency in AI-based mental health care. *Int. J. Mental Health Syst.*, 17, 3, 234–251, 2023.
35. Wong, Y., *et al.*, Cultural factors in AI-driven mental health interventions. *J. Couns. Psychol.*, 71, 1, 89–106, 2024.
36. Patel, V. and Thompson, R., Cultural expressions in AI-driven mental health assessment. *Psychol. Assess.*, 35, 4, 567–584, 2023.
37. Johnson, K., *et al.*, Global perspectives on AI algorithms in mental health care. *Digit. Psychiatry*, 8, 4, 312–329, 2023.
38. Ahmed, S. and Lee, J., Cultural adaptation in AI-driven mental health interventions. *J. Cross-Cultural Psychol.*, 55, 2, 178–195, 2024.
39. Brown, R. and Garcia, M., Addressing cultural bias in mental health AI systems. *Artif. Intell. Med.*, 89, 102–118, 2023.
40. Wilson, E., *et al.*, Cultural audit frameworks for mental health AI applications. *AI Ethics J.*, 5, 1, 67–84, 2024.
41. Taylor, N. and Kumar, R., Inclusive design in mental health AI systems. *Hum.-Comput. Interact. Stud.*, 28, 4, 423–440, 2023.
42. Anderson, M. and Park, S., Integrating traditional healing practices with AI mental health solutions. *Digit. Health J.*, 12, 1, 45–62, 2024.
43. Roberts, M., *et al.*, Privacy considerations in cross-cultural mental health AI. *Digital Privacy Rev.*, 11, 3, 178–195, 2023.
44. Lewis, R. and Chen, H., Building trust in AI mental health applications across cultures. *J. Med. AI Ethics*, 3, 1, 15–32, 2024.
45. World Health Organization, *WHO Guideline: Recommendations on Digital Interventions for Health System Strengthening*, World Health Organization, Geneva, 2019.

46. Thieme, A., Belgrave, D., Doherty, G., Machine learning in mental health: A systematic review of the HCI literature to support the development of effective and implementable ML systems. *ACM Trans. Comput.-Hum. Interact.*, 27, 5, 1–53, 2020.
47. Bzdok, D. and Meyer-Lindenberg, A., Machine learning for precision psychiatry: Opportunities and challenges. *Biol. Psychiatry: Cognit. Neurosci. Neuroimaging*, 3, 3, 223–230, 2018.
48. Freeman, D., Reeve, S., Robinson, A., *et al.*, Virtual reality in the assessment, understanding, and treatment of mental health disorders. *Psychol. Med.*, 47, 14, 2393–2400, 2017.
49. Inkster, B., Sarda, S., Subramanian, V., An empathy-driven, conversational artificial intelligence agent (Wysa) for digital mental well-being: Real-world data evaluation mixed-methods study. *JMIR mHealth Health*, 9, 2, e24106, 2021.

4

Role and Application of Supportive Chatbots and Virtual Assistants in Confronting Mental Stigma with AI and ML

Monirul Islam

Department of Management, Sister Nivedita University, Kolkata, India

Abstract

The rise of social media and search engines has provided numerous benefits as well as posed challenges to mental well-being. Albeit these platforms present opportunities for socializing and acquiring knowledge, they might aggravate mental health conditions by aiding cyberbullying, endorsing and validating comparisons with others, and demonstrating distressful content to users. The purpose of the chapter is to examine how AI and machine learning can be applied to eliminate mental health stigma, with particular emphasis on using supportive chatbots and helpful virtual assistants. The usage of artificial intelligence in healthcare is widespread. It is used to forecast, identify, and manage disease epidemiology. Furthermore, AI analysis can help to get more insights and information about user behaviors and mental health patterns as a whole. The chatbots and virtual assistants further enable patients to use self-administered mental well-being management with a personalized, adaptive, but non-judgmental support. Numerous chatbots and virtual assistants are utilized in the healthcare sector. The findings unearth to build the understanding of AI-driven mental health treatment tools like chatbots and even virtual assistants that might potentially reduce the stigma attached to mental well-being while providing sufficient information and supporting a pluralistic society.

***Keywords*:** Mental health, sentiment analysis, chatbots, virtual assistant, artificial intelligence, machine learning, healthcare sector, mental well-being

---

Email: moni05081985@gmail.com

Ridhima Sharma, Fazla Rabby, Rohit Bansal, Timcy Sachdeva and Jihene Mrabet (eds.) Confronting Mental Health Stigma with AI and Machine Learning, (83–104) © 2026 Scrivener Publishing LLC

4.1 Introduction

Being a product of misunderstanding and fear with regard to mental health stigma, the whole history of the domain is pathetically ignorance. As history would have it, mental disorders were commonly seen as being controlled by supernatural forces (such as spirits possessing a body or divine retribution), and people exhibiting behavior resulting from mental illness were often left to their own or inhumane treatment in ancient times. In medieval times, all individuals suffering from mental illnesses were all but imprisoned most times in asylums. Some advances were made in the 19th and 20th centuries with the advent of psychiatry (although stigma remained; grievously hampered by superstition and social bias). Media representations and social norms have perpetuated this stigma even further. Recognizing the past is critical to shedding the stigma which continues today. As reported by the World Health Organization (WHO), in every 10 people across the world, 1 needs mental healthcare. Yet, various forms of different kinds of mental disorders are characterized to include varieties that affect thinking, feeling, and relating with others [1]. A household survey of the general population (NHS) shows that out of 4 people, at least 1 has a diagnosable mental health-related problem each year, and approximately determinately individuals face them at any time; while another household study done by the government tells us that one-half struggle with commoner mental health problems like anxiety or depression every week [6, 8]. The contagion is sleeping little by bit due to the isolation this pandemic (COVID-19) brought, and the number of affected is much higher [7]. Unlike health and social services, there are fewer than 70 service providers per 100,000 people who need treatment in high-income countries, and only about two such providers for every 1000 individuals with mental illness in a low-income nation [5]. Moreover, using social media regularly may result in feeling undue social pressure and emphasizing unfeasible norms, possibly causing anxiety, despair, and depression among adolescents.

Mental health untreated creates a vast societal burden on society's individual families and communities, respectively. From an economic standpoint, this translates to reduced productivity, absenteeism, and mental healthcare expenses costing billions of dollars yearly of lost revenue in treatment. In doing so, untreated conditions lead to increasingly strained relationships, anger with the social consequences, homelessness, and criminal justice system involvement. The social aspect of all this is coupled with more public health issues such as increased risk for substance abuse and suicide. The academic performance of affected youth is hurt by the malfunctioning of educational institutions. And then there is stigma around mental health — this lack of access drives cycles of harm that we have to destroy. Solving these problems is key to achieving a higher societal well-being and the revival of economic performance. Social stigma and shame make patients with mental conditions reluctant to seek help from providers as well [8]. In addition, the global shortage of mental health workers is a challenge for countries [1]. This makes it hard to assist someone with a mental health condition through one-on-one support. To tackle these issues, mental health professionals are deploying technology say artificial intelligence-based chatbots to cater needs of people suffering from some kind of mental problems before they can come in for treatment [2–4]. This is necessary in the spirit of parity. Powered by AI, these tools find ways to make healthcare more available and accessible and bring awareness about the disease. During a discussion with a mentally ill patient, it is essential to understand how they feel right now and respond in an uncomplicated way; micro-interventions like cues for different forms of breathing exercise or ordinary discussion can be effective in elevating their mood [9]. The primary benefit of these bots is that they are based on real-world, real-time evidence and an engaging virtual tool capable of bridging the gap instantly between seekers wanting help from professionals [10]. Along with the advancement of artificial intelligence, lots of chatbots appeared outperforming a part in different factors. These technologies also become smarter in delivering effective help with the help of data analysis of the company and/or its customer base. With AI and machine learning, question-and-answer sessions improved significantly, almost daily, just from seeing how people interact. Eventually, Woebot, Wysa and Tess were found as a potential and efficient therapeutic mental health tool. After all, a chatbot designed with emotional intelligence in mind will certainly know these things and much worse (chatbots may share their patient needs to be debased as it fluctuates between lists depending on how the patient's wants are reported) [10]. Moreover, the adoption of therapeutic chatbots is expanding rapidly, which benefits immensely [11]. When bad things happen, understand the mental state of a patient and refer them to another healthcare professional. It provides 24/7 instant chat support. Prompt response with accuracy enable patient treatment swiftly. There are easy-to-install, -configure, and -maintain apps available on platforms such as Android, iOS, and Linux. Patients may be less embarrassed, and sensitive healthcare problems can also give them a feeling of privacy. Protection of personal information is further protected with various validation methods including face identification/biometrics or passcode. It is relatively cheap providing stress relief. Chatbots give reminders for activities like taking medication and exercise sessions.

4.2 Research Problem and Gap

There are imperfections to the current traditional methods reporting of mental health stigma that must be addressed with innovative solutions. Although it is becoming well known, some still steer clear of help because of stigma and the misconceptions people have and how society fails to offer systems that are both stigma-free and readily available. Most existing interventions (public service announcements, therapy) do not get to reach populations we continue to marginalize. Studies identify a substantial need for scalable, personal counter-stigma pathways that adapt to the dynamic nature of stigma and compassion. There is a spatial gap in the research, which means a few studies exploring the cultural differences in consumer sentiments and behavior across regions were found missing. The synergy of AI and ML creates a paradigm shift in virtual assistants and chatbots that allow anonymous supportive interactions that disinfect stigma-informed empathy and reach.

4.3 Research Methodology

This chapter followed a mixed-methods research design, alternating qualitative analyses on the functions and deployment of AI/ML chatbots and virtual assistants in mental health stigma. Central pillars to it are the systematic review of relevant literature which considers the existing studies on mental health stigma and also prior technological interventions that include discussion of the latest AI/ML and how we are using it as a provider of mental health support. The case study analysis was applied to analyze real-life examples of supportive chatbots, quantitatively looking at design, usability, and effects on mental stigma.

4.4 Understanding Mental Health Stigma with AI/ML

4.4.1 Stigma Pattern Recognition: How AI/ML Can Identify and Analyze Stigma in Language and Behavior

Video-based chatbot interactions need to perceive, process, and analyze the emotional states and perceptions of patients while adjusting treatment strategies.

Facial pattern recognition aims to collect patients' data and evaluate emotions to enable appropriate responses. These physical pattern features are comprised of bodily movements, facial/gesture expressions, and eye contact along with other types of physical or biological signals, etc. These somatic pattern emotions are grouped familiarly: sadness, joy, fury (or surprise), fear, and rage. Two different approaches based on computer vision techniques and processing of multi-dimensional images are employed to extract the facial pattern features from mental health patients: geometric-based and appearance-based [16].

The geometric-based method captures the geometry of the facial pattern of a patient in terms of extracting node pattern points and component shapes (eyebrow position; eye shape and location; mouth, cheek, and nose coordinates) to calculate entire facial component distances known as a vector. The main problem in this method is to achieve good precision in the detection of facial pattern components and that too with a very high FPS. Thus, such knowledge leads to certain actions and public health plans which consequently enhance the delivery of mental health services, thereby spending resources for that purpose as well as improving better results overall. It cannot be stressed enough to unearth the importance of these technologies in combating mental health stigma.

The skin and face pattern textures on the mental health patient faces have been extracted by the appearance-based approach. This method encodes textures in the form of training data using different pattern-based techniques. An empathetic chatbot perceives the emotions resulting from the facial pattern reflections by 2 approaches, namely, geometry-based approach which requires a solid background and precise facial approach, component, and element detection to achieve full precision value that is impossible in practical scenarios [17]. The method create an emotional pattern database by video recordings [16]. The patient's face pattern is identified by the chatbot *via* video chat. It works by capturing the face pattern characteristics of the patient, extracting them, and transforming them into feature vector input. The machine learning (ML) differentiator/classifier is used for classifying the emotions of patients into disgust, anger, surprise, etc. At last, the performance estimation of those results is computed for deep analyses.

Advantages

- The restriction of appointments is reduced, which in turn gives freedom from direct contact or doctor's direction.

- Easier to arrange appointments.
- It enhances medical care while also exploring facial nuances, such as face recognition.

Limitations

- It may not be accurate when the respective patient disguises the presence or appearance or the camera is slightly off.

4.5 Development of Supportive Chatbots

4.5.1 Empathy in AI: Designing Chatbots to Respond Compassionately

The patient experiencing mental ailments can respond — over text, using emojis or emoticons, and voice through typified manual input as well as with pre-recorded auditory-visual or streaming media. The primary objective of healing chatbots is to merely recognize sensible feelings from user conversations and advise them for valid therapies or therapy. Empathy, as experienced by a suffering patient, may be alike cognitive, emotional, and empathetic. The intention of these types is to generalize the contextual emotions and associate them with distinct emotions like happiness, sadness, and anger [2]. User emoticons can be analyzed using natural language processing (NLP) in artificial intelligence (AI) and deep learning approaches. NLP shows how chatbots identify and translate the language of patients. Using NLP, chatbots are able to perform word and group of word analysis which resolves if they were spoken or written text. The human language in its original form and techniques such as sentiment analysis, facial pattern recognition, voice-based emotion recognition, and video-based emotion recognition work on their respective pattern and configurations as shown in Table 4.1. While for interaction context, the chatbots with NLP learn the conversation patterns in patient input and are able to determine through contextual clues from speech, video, or text what sentiment is intended behind specific statements [12]. Their offer includes 24/7 availability and ensures complete confidentiality. Employing highly complex and advanced natural language processing (NLP) capabilities, they sense conversations with users and can read signs of emotional feelings based on the subject response.

Table 4.1 Category of empathic chatbots.

Methodology involved	Narrative
Sentiment analysis	Sentiment analysis is capable of deriving textual feelings, views, beliefs, and emotions or emoticons.
Facial emotion pattern recognition in videos	The software uses facial features that it gathers from a live streaming or visual clip to detect patient feelings.
Voice-enabled emotion recognition	These are used to provide speech features mined from voice calls or recorded audio files and, hence, determine the patient's emotions.

4.5.2 Sentiment Analysis: Using NLP to Detect Negative Attitudes and Misconceptions

Emotion detection deals with emotion recognition facilities across a huge set in different ways and is one of the methods of sentiment analysis. Emotion detection assists in providing patients with the treatment of mental healthcare providers. At a basic level, sentiment analysis identifies the emotional status of a mental health patient against something. It discerns the message from the patient and emojis/emoticons as positive, negative, or neutral given the context of patient's statement [13]. The therapeutic chatbots leverage the extracted opinions and recommend treatment or refer to a mental health professional during an emergency. Then emojis/emoticons spread like a rapid fire in electronic messages as well [14]. Thanks to those smiling little yellow or more fancy ideograms: effects were surprises too for many with mental health issues. It gives an emotional output of patient's conversation beyond the general textual input [14]. These Unicode character sets are then tokenized during training based on the patient responses and emojis/emoticons. The training data used for building the models are different, depending upon which clinical tool is applied to get access to the information, e.g., retrieval directly from a patient's blog, surveys, or patients' own epidemiological records [13]. The groupings of the sentiment analysis will depend on how patients might interpret their queries, e.g., with the aspect-based system used to analyze these responses amounting to patient text messages and emotion-based system for emoticons [15].

Advantages

The chatbot does treatment analysis for one patient, just by listing down all their answers if the drug is affecting him in a good or bad way.

- Chatbots can also act according to the mood of a patient.
- Chatbots not only recognize all those contents and messages that are emotive triggers (in a positive or negative manner) that lift the mood of the patient.
- Chatbots can detect emergencies like suicidal thoughts and if possible escalate them to professionals or redirect them.

Limitations

- Sentences having multiple sentiments make the task of sentiment annotations complex [15].
- Being neutral: Potentially when the patient is not showing anything about being emotional but all he or she does is only tell something that in a way describes bad situations, then there are influences on how the chatbot sees what this man might be instead of relaxed.

4.5.3 Personalization: Leveraging AI/ML to Tailor Interactions Based on Individual Voice Needs

Based on the voice calls or recorded audio files, the empathic chatbots should also be able to understand emotions. Taking the voice sample on how these patients behave but without interpreting their inputs, a sensor/microphone can be accessed by this chatbot as well. Here, the feelings are detected *via* 2 classes of speech characteristics — lexical and audio features [16].

4.5.3.1 Lexical Speech Attributes

These attributes can rely on the lexis of a patient. The only way this lexical feature can be applied to those recorded audio files is if text extraction from the speech is needed for the prediction of patient emotions.

4.5.3.2 Phonological Code Features

It is the spoken characteristics given the tone of voice designed to own a psychological individual — pitch jitter and timbre. As emotions need to be realized from patients who can speak, regular voice calls with the patient is necessary as audio data in acoustic features. This spectral feature will be extracted from a speech signal by an acoustic model.

The individual voice-based identification system is based on pattern recognition as software consisting of three main steps, i.e., audio signal processing, feature extraction, and voice classification. The essential functionality of signal processing covers the digitalization and filtering of an audio input as well structure its spoken conversation into text. The feature calculation works to discover the characteristics of emotions in this preformatted and digital acoustic signal; that is, it represents these for emotion by means of converting them into an encoded vector. This feature selection vector will be passed through machine learning (ML) classification algorithms. These classification algorithms are different on the trained dataset [18].

Advantages

- Yes, and some are in the realm of AI-based solutions for healthcare including a chatbot that can recognize a mental health patient's emotion even when it is able to understand what is being said, by recognizing vocal elements like pitch and voice tone.
- Patients report that it is faster compared to typing the messages.

Limitations

- Sometimes one also will find it difficult to analyze the speech elements; that is, anger in slow pitch and tone can be expressed by such a patient personality masking emotion behind his voice.

4.5.4 Predictive Analysis: Artificial Intelligence and Machine Learning

The cornerstone of predictive analytics is central to mentally championing and reducing mental health stigma in advance. Through the analysis of Big Data in social media, online forums, and chatbot conversations, predictive models can be used to discern the growing trends of stigmatizing language, attitudes, and practices. The information provides the basis for tailored efforts, whether that is education or allocation of resources before the stigma entry point. Also, it allows us to provide an ever more personalized experience through predictive analytics. For instance, chatbots can infer that a user might be in need of certain help (e.g., stigmatization advices or crisis intervention) on the conversational level. This is an approach that empowers people and communities by building empathy from the ground up, without mental health stigma.

4.6 History of AI-Powered Chatbots

According to Vaidyam *et al.* [19], chatbots are digital tools that can be either software or hardware that "mimic human behavior and provide a business-oriented framework with an evolving expression capable of engaging in verbal exchange." In 1950, Turing asked himself the now famous question: "Can machines predict?" and he foresaw the day when men would talk to machines treating them as real men [24]. Another prediction of Turing [24] was that these machines "will ultimately contest with humans in all fundamental aspects of the intellectual domain." The first chatbot in history, created by Weizenbaum in 1966, is called ELIZA. It can converse with people in natural languages and match phrase response patterns which is based on decomposition rules [25]. Due to advances in artificial intelligence and thereby the use of natural language processing, Siri moved to Apple in the year 2011 and then to Microsoft Cortana and Google Assistant, excluding Amazon's Alexa [25]. According to Shum *et al.* [25], these chatbots are frequently deployed on cell devices and carry out a wide variety of features through consumer chats. Advances in computing strength make AI software possible in healthcare. According to Palanica *et al.* [23] and Vaidyam *et al.* [19], chatbots can function as computerized conversational marketers to enhance spoken verbal exchange among health professionals and patients undergoing treatment, thereby assisting in health training and guaranteeing higher access to fitness offerings.

4.7 Case Studies

4.7.1 Real-World Applications: Examples of Chatbots that Have Successfully Reduced Stigma

The rise of chatbots such as those supporting mental and emotional health shows that reaching out for help online is rapidly becoming the new norm in entertaining to society. These are among the more conversational therapy-based empathic chatbots built upon Cognitive Behavioral Therapy (CBT) framework. The therapy carries the implementation of an all-day-joyful talk to either unlearn the negative thoughts in making a conscious effort and transforming them into positive ones as well or creating for him/her fire ground. By way of a machine could therefore be exploited by patients for their emotional distress which is at ease and comfort apart from seeking physical consultation [19]. Some famous chatbots that are providing assistance to anxiety and depression patients include Woebot, Wysa, and Tess [10].

Woebot claims to relieve mental health issues purely *via* unassisted chat. The app has a conversational agent that starts the chat by inquiring about their feelings and providing them with tips or videos on wellness as appropriate. A study by Stanford University on Woebot app observed a reduction in depression and anxiety [20].

Wysa (aka WYSA, for "wise assistant") is a chatbot designed to help users cope with their emotions and feelings using techniques like Cognitive Behavioral Therapy (CBT), Dialectical Behavior Therapy (DBT), and more light-hearted fare [20].

Tess is an AI chatbot for mental health patients and emotional wellness. Tess is not designed to run on pre-programmed codes; it recognizes the context and reacts to user preferences, remembers its likes and dislikes, and frames an overall empathetic tone [21].

Other tools and methods were designed to "support health and wellness through conversations about mood, physical activity/exercise, sleep/rest, movement patterns (e.g., step counting), energy balance, or dietary intake behavior and preferences" [19].

4.8 Mental Health and Chatbots

In the vertical of mental fitness, a lack of scientific workforce is hindering the availability of excellent healthcare professionals and the anticipated demand for revolutionary technology-based answers is regularly high in demand [19]. Thanks to the fast-developing technologies in the field of artificial intelligence, many chatbots have been developed for screening, diagnosis, and treatment of health-related problems.

However, contact center chatbots are not the most addictive thing in a worker's toolkit. However, they may also be more value-added to patients who do not desire doctors due to the stigma surrounding them [19]. With a list of intellectual fitness chatbots formed by Palanica *et al.* [23]

Table 4.2 Types of mental health chatbots.

Chatbots	Category	Modality	Platform
3DWorldBuilder	Mental illness specific	3D	Computer-based application
Laura	Mental illness specific	3D	Computer-based application
SimSensei	Mental illness specific	3D	Computer-based application
Joy	Mental illness specific	Textual	Messaging app embedded
Tess	Mental illness specific	Textual	Messaging app embedded
Shim	Mental illness specific	Textual	Mobile app based
Woebot	Mental illness specific	Textual	Mobile app based
Wysa	Mental illness specific	Textual	Mobile app based
Youper	Mental illness specific	Textual	Mobile app based
Bots4Health	General health	Textual	Messaging app embedded
Florence	General health	Textual	Messaging app embedded
Super Izzy	General health	Textual	Messaging app embedded
Ada	General health	Textual	Mobile app based
Babylon Health	General health	Textual	Mobile app based
GYANT	General health	Textual	Mobile app based
Healthily	General health	Textual	Mobile app based
HealthTap	General health	Textual	Mobile app based
Mediktor	General health	Textual	Mobile based app, web based
Sensely	General health	Textual	Mobile based app, web based
Buoy Health	General health	Textual	Web based

Source: [31]

and Vaidyam *et al.* [19], the goal of existing intellectual infection chatbots, including Portet-Kuhnt & Hafner, is intended to offer a wide range of health problems through one class. However, full exchanges are specifically targeted at impairments in mental fitness as outlined in the text. Otherwise, the modes of operation and chatbot systems are archived in Table 4.2. The patients are made available with multiple options such as Woebot, Wysa, Babylon Health, Sensely, Your MD, Buoy Health, Health Tap, and IBM Watson Assistant to name a few. These tools are able to provide healthcare assistance and information as a medium of simple medical advice on user input. The modality and tool continued to evolve. Modality has been edited from text to personified 3D structure. Chatbots have also emerged onto various frameworks such as mobile applications, notebook and network applications, and embedded messaging apps. For example, it became Woebot, a total AI-based chatbot for intellectual contamination an advanced tool for monitoring and alleviating the despair of college-going students by automatizing the conversation [20]. They help in breaking barriers in mental healthcare facilities, which is beneficial for groups of disadvantaged people living remotely or downgraded communities at large.

4.9 Functions of Mental Health Chatbots

The increasing incorporation of chatbots in healthcare communication has led researchers to investigate the effectiveness of these chatbots. In contrast to some of the methods used by mental health physicians, chatbots may offer instantaneous, tailored conversations that save users time and resources [20, 26, 27]. Comparison with other mobile technologies for psychological interventions has previously been shown to be effective in super engaging user experiences. A previous study applying the uses and gratification theory by Cheng and Jiang showed that the social, utilitarian, and technology-related fulfilments were important determinants for mental health chatbot engagement [26]. According to these four gratifications, health chatbots are classified into 4 interrelated dimensions, namely, technological ease/convenience; information-based service offering from a third-person perspective and productions that can address one's practical needs including guidance on effective action plans as well as basic resources; social companionship means virtual chatting with more people or specific friends without sharing personal burden (e.g., not requiring accountability for an outcome); and emotional support [26].

4.9.1 Technology Convenience

Related to superfluous technology gratifications, it is considered as technology-based user motivation which can be easily obtained and serve instant conversation ability [26]. These chatbots deliver timely and engaging assistance to mental health stigma patients [20]. This paper found that, compared with traditional media, chatbots have the strength of attracting users who are interested in the content and help deliver a more satisfactory experience [26].

4.9.2 Information

Anticipating that technology can provide valuable information to users, it meets users' pursuit of utilitarian gratifications [26]. Chatbots could offer people the information they need during a crisis and quick mental health-related issues solutions. On the other hand, chatbots fill in specific consumer information for users *via* instant messaging and answering questions, reducing the processing time for crisis workers. Chatbots are interactive conversational agents that persuade patients to engage in mutual communication *via* conversations [28]. This is in stark contrast to chatbots, which continuously monitor user information and analyze it. Using personal information, feelings, reported gender/age education, and medical history, to query a chatbot could result in targeted feedback relating to 'an individual' health status. For example, thanks to users' behavior and mental-health information chatbots can be collected from them automatically; they may well play a role in early diagnosis of the potential threats or complications for anxiety-depression post large shooting-driven adversities [26].

4.9.3 Emotional Support

Users value instant pleasure (hedonic gratification), so providing emotional support could be useful to deliver hedonic gratifications [26]. Mental health chatbots that deliver compassionate dialogues help users experience less anxiety and depression [20] to the extent that a chatbot can tweak differences in their messaging on the fly during a conversation to incentivize emotion management while addressing unique elicitors of negative sentiments [27]. In their study, Zhou *et al.* presented an examination of how XiaoIce can use affect awareness to create emotional intimacy with its users and offer tailored responses.

4.9.4 Social Companionship

Social indulgences are divided into 2 dimensions, namely social interface and social existence [26]. Some chatbots are also designed to offer social support and companionship. As a consequence of sophisticated chatbots, long-term social support can be provided to users through years together companionship [29]. Mental health chatbots can offer users long-term therapeutic assistance based on criteria derived from the follow-up of user behavior. Mental health chatbots work to reduce symptoms of anxiety and depression by providing companionship, encouraging users to identify their emotions (anxiety), strategies in personal support individualized for the patient, and helping users take part in social conversations according to a recent review which covered articles from 1979 to 2020 on mental health-related virtual humans/chatbot/human-avatar research [29].

4.10 Ethical Considerations and Potential Risks and Misuse

Ethical considerations with real ethical implications, to comply with data privacy and overall research ethics, are some of the key ethical issues that are represented in the chapter by using AI/ML-driven chatbots and virtual assistants in tackling mental health stigma. One major issue is the data; it is obviously to be heavily guarded with sensitive mental health matters being extremely important not only for privacy but also for security. Regulatory compliance (e.g., GDPR and HIPAA) can be very important. The concern is that the algorithmic bias may emerge where poor training data could introduce biases or fail to train relevant populations being exclusionary, thus perpetuating stigma. This also puts a premium on over-automating them, leading to wrong predictions or a lack of support in crisis situations. For example, misuse can be employing chatbots for misinformation or mining user data for financial purposes. Risks are mitigated by design transparency, frequent review, and clear accountability. User trust and acceptance are fundamental for the successful deployment of AI/ML chatbots in mental health support. Typically, users will go on a system-attributed empathy mode warpath when they realize how little they trust those unfamiliar automated systems.

That is something we need to solve; some of which is transparency of how chatbots are designed and data handled. This builds credibility by talking about data collection, storage, and usage in a clear way. Chatbot interactions require empathy and reliability as well. NLP techniques such as advanced NP must be implemented so that responses are not sounding robotic or cold. Furthermore, adding feedback loops opens the door to facilitate development with user experience. Augmenting that with partnerships from mental health professionals and broader public education helps build trust (a chatbot is a real entity, not human yet, and it exists in supplement capacity to human care).

4.11 Challenges and Future Directions of Mental Health Chatbots

Researchers have assessed the impact and scope of chatbots by performing studies; this is a great help. It helped to know how users found the use of a bot in real-world conditions. However, other studies consistently suggest that at least some mental health chatbots are highly engaging and useful to users; a recent systematic review demonstrated not only high user engagement but also the potential appeal of using these tools as an alternative form or bridge to care for individuals who would otherwise have no access to any healthcare because they cannot afford it [32]. Yet, Vaidyam and colleagues [19] noted that some patients might "get too attached due to an unhealthy or quasi-para social relationship potentially triggered by the patient's mental disorder itself." This could be a risk for mental health chatbots.

Confidentiality and secrecy were found as the major variables that impact the process of chatbot functioning in the future. Furthermore, Cheng and Jiang suggested that the perception of privacy risk was negatively linked to chatbot usage, perceiving a lower level of satisfaction, continuous intention for using with service, and customer loyalty from services provided by chatbot [30]. A future investigation could focus on ethical problem permutation as personal information security and data protection(credentials) and legal issues like liability for interactive accidents. Another common expectation for mental health chatbots is to deliver empathic conversation. Additional studies should study methods on how to make mental health chatbots listen in an empathetic manner and respond with sympathy [27]. An example is that using filler language in the replies such as we do will give a sentiment of inclusion to the users [19]. In addition to ethical implications, there are also broader considerations concerning the futuristic agenda of mental health chatbots with respect to how AI is developed and rolled out. Today, mental health chatbots can do a lot more with the usage of AI than back then. Because of the breakneck pace at which AI implementations are advancing, researchers need to be watchful regarding new trends in applicable AI technologies. This includes mechanisms of AI that provide users with different text and image interactions in various contexts, to perform more complex tasks that are dedicated explicitly to mental health issues by providing a creation method through which developers may design/build their own chatbots related to the clinical system. Specifically, regarding chatbot features in general future research could investigate safety and efficacy with privacy considerations of chatbot use for mental health. Future studies on mental health chatbots could focus more intensive research efforts, with higher quality evidence for important outcomes that might further improve trust and social acceptability to users. During mental health crises, chatbots have emerged as a new research hotspot and an important multi-disciplinary issue in medicine, communication, psychology, computer science, and other allied fields. Up to now, most of the research on chatbots examines consumer's or patient's attitudes towards using a chatbot; however, there is no empirical evidence from governments and institutions. Exploring the world of chatbots for sharing knowledge and monitoring proper information dissemination during crisis times, adopting large big data to detect latent mental illness cases, and improving mental health engagement would be some long-term goals. Conversational chatbots, AI-powered apps that interact with users in natural language based on the task they need to perform, are increasingly used across a wide range of industries. As mentioned, all the chatbots that we see on almost every website and the presence of digital assistants like Alexa or Siri do not show empathy for a user; they cannot empathize with the human level. While this is not of utmost importance for a transaction or interaction chatbot where empathy towards the user helps, it is necessary in the case of bots developed to aid mental health patients as they should be able to sense and perform conversations based on the emotional state logged by them. The research illustrates several emotional intelligence approaches applied for empathic chatbot development and the extent and efficacy of using them. It also emphasizes how AI chatbots represent an efficient and effective way for them to access support for their well-being (especially mental health) — accessible, engaging, and impactful in helping people from different walks of life fulfilling goals associated with on-step betterment.

Research and development must work together to move the mental health stigma forward. This is essential in the advancement of research and development, for researchers must continuously seek out new exemplars to further improve AI and ML systems that create empathy-driven culturally sensitive chatbots. Additional research is needed to fill in some of the existing gaps (for example, assessing whether these tools will have a sustained impact on stigma and user behavior). We need developers to prioritize ethical AI development inclusivity and unbiased design. Mental health professionals need to collaborate with the tools to make those systems better. Policymakers would help by funding projects and creating policies. All of this combined can lead to vast solutions for a stigma-free future.

4.12 Limitations

Chatbots and virtual assistants that learn from interactions could potentially suffer from MAD (model autophagy disorder) if they incorporate too much of their own generated responses into their training data. The biggest challenge in this area of work is context recognition during conversations with patients: (a) lack of contextual data available for training, (b) change expressed by the patient's action *via* emojis, and (c) short descriptions/abbreviated data/texts are used while discussing. Most health professionals do not think that AI should substitute but augment the roles of health professionals, and setting a suitable role for AI is arguably one of the major challenges in the future [22]. Less adoption rate amongst patient is another flaw where understanding needs and full disease diagnostics by a bots is limited. Moreover, many U.S.-based medical workers said that they would not or could not use bots because it goes beyond what technology is capable of doing on its own. Chatbots in medical care might lead to self-diagnosis and misdiagnosis [23]. Privacy and patient privacy represent another aspect of the difficulties. Protect patient conversations (since it is about a thing of a personal nature, which should be private): encrypt the conversation or simply store anonymized conversational data about patients in your database.

4.13 The Goal of Stigma-Free Mental Health and a Stigma-Free Future

Imagine a day where mental well-being is as publicized and as revered as physical health. In this future only, people can access support without judgment or stigma; we are creating a culture of care and compassion. AI and ML based chatbots/VAs technology is breaking the accessibility barriers thereby providing safe medical aid leading discourse in heath concerns. Such tools can normalize mental health conversations, empower communities, and counter wicked stereotypes. Technology developers must work closely with mental health professionals and policymakers to build these technologies in ways that are fair, responsible, and equitably accessible so that the world accepts them and thrives in a compassionate stigma-free territory.

4.14 Conclusion

To sum up, AI health-based chatbots are encouraging tools that might supplement all sorts of regular health-based treatment in the forthcoming years. The application of AI-based chatbots to the delivery of mental healthcare delivers several advantages that have been supported and validated by existing studies. In order to construct reliable chatbots for mental health and assimilate them into the patient-care process, numerous related shared, available, and open research themes need to be dealt with in the future. Scholars should delve into the benefits of using chatbots by any healthcare providers. Hereby, it would possess relevancy to design new healthcare models that possibly include the chatbots based on the recommendations of the healthcare professional. Providing mental support is a huge jump in the healthcare arena. This can be done by using a kind, down-to-earth approach that anyone with an open mind will be able to access the way before sharing ideas for wider and global reach. Before that happens, there are still multiple concerns and challenges to be fixed.

The research elucidated several devices of artificial intelligence techniques used to classify conversational intent into sensations explored and described several significant applications in this space.

References

1. World Health Organization, Mental health: massive scale-up of resources needed if global targets are to be met. *Bull. World Health Organ.*, 98, 4, 285, 2017.
2. Rababeh, M., Alajlani, Bridgette, B.M., Househ, Effectiveness and Safety of Using Chatbots to Improve Mental Health: Systematic Review and Meta-Analysis. *J. Med. Internet Res.*, 22, 7, e16021, 2020.
3. Adamopoulou, E. and Lefteris, M., An Overview of Chatbot Technology. *Artif. Intell. Appl. Innov.*, 584, 373–83, 2020.
4. Morris, R., Kouddous, K., Kshirsagar, R., Schueller, S., Towards an Artificially Empathic Conversational Agent for Mental Health Applications: System Design and User Perceptions. *J. Med. Internet Res., 20*, 6, e10148, 2018.
5. World Health Organization, *Mental disorders. Bulletin of the World Health Organization*, Mental health atlas 2019. Geneva, World Health Organization, 2019.
6. McManus, S., Bebbington, P., Jenkins, R., Brugha, T., Mental health and wellbeing in England: Adult Psychiatric Morbidity Survey 2014. Leeds: *NHS Digital*, 2016.
7. Xiong, J., Lipsitz, O., Nasri, F., Lui, L.M.W., Gill, H., Phan, L., Chen-Li, D., Iacobucci, M., Ho, R., Majeed, A., McIntyre, R.S., Impact of COVID-19 pandemic on mental health in the general population:A systematic review. *J. Affect. Disord.*, 277, 55–64, 2020.
8. Susman, D., *8 Reasons Why People Don't Get Treatment for Mental Illness*, 2020. https://davidsusman.com/2015/06/11/8-reasons-why-people-dont-get mental-health-treatment/.
9. Arrabales, R., Perla: A Conversational Agent for Depression Screening in Digital Ecosystems. Design, Implementation and Validation. *Comput. Soc.*, 2008, 12875, 2020.
10. D'Alfonso, S., AI in mental health. *Curr. Opin. Psychol.*, 36, 112–117, 2020.
11. Pereira, J. and Diaz, O., Using Health Chatbots for Behavior Change: A Mapping Study. *J. Med. Syst.*, 43, 5, 135, 2019.
12. Dharwadkar, R. and Deshpande, N.A., A Medical ChatBot. *Int. J. Comput. Trends Technol.*, 60, 1, 41–45, 2018.
13. Rajput, A., Natural Language Processing, Sentiment Analysis and Clinical Analytics, in: *Next Gen Tech Driven Personalized Medical & Smart Healthcare, Innovation in Health Informatics*, pp. 79–97, Academic Press, NY, USA, 2020.
14. Fadhil, A., Schiavo, G., Wang, The Effect of Emojis when interacting with Conversational Interface Assisted Health Coaching System, in: *Proceedings of the 12th EAI International Conference on Pervasive Computing Technologies for Healthcare (PervasiveHealth '18)*, pp. 378–383, Association for Computing Machinery, New York, USA, 2018.

15. Poria, S., Chaturvedi, I., Cambria, E., Hussain, A., Convolutional MKL Based Multimodal Emotion Recognition and Sentiment Analysis. *Proceeding of IEEE 16th International Conference on Data Mining, ICDM*, pp. 439–448, 2016.
16. Hossain, M., Patient State Recognition System for Healthcare Using Speech and Facial Expressions. *J. Med. Syst.*, 40, 12, 272, 2016.
17. Somchanok, T., Emotional healthcare system: Emotion detection by facial expressions using Japanese database, in: *Proceeding of 6th Computer Science and Electronic Engineering Conference CEEC*, pp. 41–46, 2014.
18. Tao, F., Liu, G., Zhao, Q., An Ensemble Framework of Voice-Based Emotion Recognition System for Films and TV Programs, in: *Proceeding of IEEE International Conference on Acoustics, Speech and Signal Processing ICASSP*, pp. 6209–6213, 2018.
19. Vaidyam, A.N., Wisniewski, H., Halamka, J.D., Kashavan, M.S., Torous, J.B., Chatbots and Conversational Agents in Mental Health: A Review of the Psychiatric Landscape. *Can. J. Psychiatry*, 64, 7, 456–464, 2019 Jul.
20. Fitzpatrick, K., Darcy, A., Vierhile, M., Delivering Cognitive Behavior Therapy to Young Adults with Symptoms of Depression and Anxiety Using a Fully Automated Conversational Agent (Woebot): A Randomized Controlled Trial. *J. JMIR Mental Health*, 4, 2, 19–28, 2017.
21. Fulmer, R., Joerin, A., Gentile, B., Lakerink, L., Rauws, M., Using Psychological Artificial Intelligence (Tess) to Relieve Symptoms of Depression and Anxiety: Randomized Controlled Trial. *JMIR Mental Health*, 5, 4, e64, 2018.
22. Powell, J., Trust Me, I'm a Chatbot: How Artificial Intelligence in Health Care Fails the Turing Test. *J. Med. Internet Res.*, 21, 2, 162–22, 2019.
23. Palanica, A., Flaschner, P., Thommandram, A., Li, M., Fossat, Y., Physicians' Perceptions of Chatbots in Health Care: Cross-Sectional Web-Based Survey. *J. Med. Internet Res.*, 21, 4, 28–87, 2019.
24. Turing, A.M., Computing machinery and intelligence. *Mind*, 59, 236, 433–460, 1950.
25. Shum, H.Y., He, X.D., Li, D., From Eliza to XiaoIce: Challenges and opportunities with social chatbots. *Front. Inf. Technol. Electron. Eng.*, 19, 1, 10–26, 2018.
26. Cheng, Y. and Jiang, H., AI-powered mental health chatbots: Examining users' motivations, active communicative action, and engagement after mass-shooting disasters. *J. Contingencies Crisis Manage.*, 28, 339–354, 2020.
27. Inkster, B., Sarda, S., Subramanian, V., An Empathy-Driven, Conversational Artificial Intelligence Agent (Wysa) for Digital Mental Well-Being: Real-World Data Evaluation Mixed-Methods Study. *JMIR Mhealth Uhealth*, 6, 11, e12106, 2018.
28. Ho, A., Hancock, J., Miner, A.S., Psychological, relational, and emotional effects of self-disclosure after conversations with a chatbot. *J. Commun.*, 68, 4, 712–733, 2018.

29. Zhou, L., Gao, J., Li, D., Shum, H.Y., The design and implementation of XiaoIce,an empathetic social chatbot. *Comput. Ling.*, 46, 1, 53–93, 2020.
30. Cheng, Y. and Jiang, H., How do AI-driven chatbots impact user experience? Examining gratifications, perceived privacy risk, satisfaction, loyalty, and continued use. *J. Broadcast. Electron. Media*, 65, 4, 592–614, 2020.
31. Cheng, Y., Xie, C., Wang, Y., Jiang, H., Chatbots and Health: Mental Health. 1–6, 2019. https://doi.org/10.1002/9781119678816.iehc0725.
32. Cui, M., and Allen, C.P., AI Chatbots for Mental Health: A Scoping Review of Effectiveness, Feasibility, and Applications. *App. Sci.*, 14, 13, 5889, 2020. https://doi.org/10.3390/app14135889.

5

Financial Barriers and Strategic Solutions in Technology Adoption for Mental Health Stigma

Ram Singh[1*], Vinay Pal Singh[2], Rishi Raj[3], Ritu Yadav[4], Fazla Rabby[5] and Sachin Chauhan[6]

[1]*School of BFSIM, Symbiosis University of Applied Sciences, Indore, India*
[2]*Quantum School of Business, Quantum University, Roorkee, Uttarakhand, India*
[3]*Management Studies, Institute of Engineering and Rural Technology, Prayagraj, India*
[4]*Department of Commerce and Management, GNIOT Institute of Professional Studies, Greater Noida, India*
[5]*Stanford Institute of Management and Technology, Sydney, Australia*
[6]*College of Business Studies, COER University, Roorkee, Uttarakhand, India*

Abstract

Mental health stigma has been one of the significant obstacles to effective mental health care. Despite advancements in technology that offer innovative solutions for mental health diagnosis, treatment, and support, the adoption of these technologies is often hindered by stigma and financial barriers. The main objective of this research is to find out and analyze the financial barriers that are related to adoption of technological solutions in mental health care and to propose strategic solutions that may help overcome such barriers. The study employs a mixed-methods approach by combining various quantitative and qualitative discussions. The research is expected to identify several key financial barriers to technology adoption in mental health care, including high development and implementation cost, funding and reimbursement challenges, and economic impacts of mental health stigma. Addressing the financial barriers to technology adoption in mental health care is essential for leveraging the full potential of these innovations. By understanding the economic implications of mental health stigma and implementing targeted strategies, stakeholders can facilitate the integration of technology into

**Corresponding author*: ramsinghcommerce@gmail.com

Ridhima Sharma, Fazla Rabby, Rohit Bansal, Timcy Sachdeva and Jihene Mrabet (eds.) Confronting Mental Health Stigma with AI and Machine Learning, (105–130) © 2026 Scrivener Publishing LLC

mental health care, ultimately improving mental health outcomes and reducing the overall economic burden.

***Keywords*:** Mental health stigma, technology, financial barriers, digital literacy

5.1 Introduction

The adoption of technology in mental health care is a transformative prospect, offering the potential to revolutionize service delivery by making care more accessible, efficient, and effective. Despite of this, the path to widespread implementation of technological innovations in this field is fraught with challenges, with financial barriers standing out as one of the most significant impediments. These financial constraints not only hinder the initial adoption of new technologies but also affect their long-term sustainability and scalability. This chapter delves into the intricate financial barriers that mental health providers face in adopting new technologies and presents strategic solutions to overcome these challenges. By addressing these financial barriers, we can use technology to reduce mental health stigma and improve mental health care delivery, ensuring that both providers and patients benefit from such advancements. The introduction of technology in mental health services has the ability to significantly change the mental health care situations that are prevailing, offering new ways to deliver care that is accessible, efficient, and effective. Digital tools such as telemedicine, mobile health applications, and online therapy platforms present modern solutions to the persistent problem of mental health stigma that is being faced by the people. These technologies can break down barriers to accessing mental help to people particularly for those in backward or remote areas by providing flexible options for seeking mental health services. Moreover, digital mental health tools can facilitate early intervention, continuous monitoring, and personalized treatment plans, thereby improving overall mental health outcomes. Despite the promise of these technological advancements, the widespread adoption of mental health technologies is often impeded by substantial financial barriers. High initial costs associated with the development, purchase, and implementation of these technologies can be prohibitive for many healthcare providers, especially smaller practices and institutions with limited budgets. In addition to the initial investment, ongoing costs for maintenance, upgrades, and training further strain financial resources [3].

The lack of reimbursement models that cover the use of digital mental health tools also lead to hesitation by the service providers from integrating these technologies into their practices. Furthermore, the inequitable distribution of funding exacerbates the digital divide, leaving rural and underserved populations with even fewer resources to adopt these innovations. In recent years, the intersection of technology and mental health has gained considerable attention, particularly in light of the COVID-19 pandemic, which underscored the importance of accessible mental health care. Despite the promise of technology in transforming mental health services, several financial barriers have impeded its widespread adoption. This literature review examines the financial challenges and strategic solutions related to the adoption of mental health technologies from 2020 to 2024. The cost of developing and implementing mental health technologies has been a significant barrier. Anthes [1] highlighted that creating effective mental health apps involves substantial financial investments in research and development, testing, and marketing. These costs can be prohibitive, particularly for smaller startups and organizations. Securing funding for mental health technologies has been another critical challenge. Torous and Roberts [28] discussed how investors are often hesitant to fund mental health tech startups due to the perceived risks associated with stigma and uncertain financial returns. Furthermore, reimbursement policies for telehealth services have varied widely, creating financial uncertainty for providers and developers [15].

Mental health stigma has broader economic implications, affecting not only individuals but also organizations and society at large. Lee, K. noted that stigma can lead to decreased productivity, increased absenteeism, and higher healthcare costs [14]. These economic impacts contribute to the underfunding and limited adoption of mental health technologies [19]. One of the strategic solutions to overcome financial barriers has been increasing public awareness and education about mental health and the benefits of technology. Krendl and Pescosolido emphasized the importance of educational campaigns in changing public perceptions and encouraging investment in mental health tech [15]. These initiatives have helped create a more supportive environment for technological adoption. Privacy concerns have been a major deterrent to the adoption of mental health technologies. To address these concerns, developers have focused on creating robust security frameworks. Clear communication about data protection protocols has been crucial in building user trust, as highlighted by O'Connor and Hanlon [19]. Regulatory bodies have also implemented stringent privacy standards to reassure users and investors. Improving digital literacy has been essential for the adoption of mental health technologies, particularly among older adults and marginalized communities. Anthes [1] discussed the development of targeted training programs aimed at enhancing digital literacy and familiarizing users with new technologies. Healthcare providers have also received training to integrate these technologies into their practices, facilitating a smoother adoption process. Advocacy groups have played a vital role in lobbying for supportive policies and funding for mental health technologies. Torous and Roberts noted that these efforts have led to more consistent reimbursement policies for telehealth services and increased government and private sector investment in mental health tech [28]. These policy changes have provided a more stable financial foundation for the development and implementation of mental health solutions.

The period from 2020 to 2024 has seen significant efforts to fight the financial barriers that are related to the adoption of mental health technologies. While challenges remain, strategic solutions such as public awareness campaigns, privacy enhancements, training programs, and policy advocacy have contributed to creating a more supportive ecosystem for mental health tech. Continued efforts in these areas are essential for bringing out the full potential of technology in improving mental health care.

This chapter has a focus on addressing the economic challenges associated with the adoption of mental health technologies and at the same time explores strategic solutions to overcome these obstacles. By reviewing the current literature and analyzing several case studies, we aim to provide a clear and complete understanding of the financial factors that have an impact on the adoption of these technologies. We also highlight the various practical approaches and policy interventions as well, which can facilitate the integration of digital tools into mental health services. Successfully exploring these financial challenges is essential for leveraging technology to reduce mental health stigma and improve access to the healthcare services on a broader scale.

The upfront costs of acquiring and implementing new technologies can be prohibitively high for many mental health providers. These expenses include purchasing hardware and software, upgrading existing systems, and training staff to use new tools effectively [4]. For small practices and community health organizations, these initial costs can be a significant deterrent. Apart from the initial investment, there are ongoing costs associated with maintaining and updating the technology which include subscription fees for software, costs for technical support, and expenses related to regular updates and cybersecurity measures. The overall effect of these sustained operational costs can strain the budgets of mental health organizations, especially those that operate with limited funding. The financial structure of mental health services often does not support the adoption of new technologies. Many mental health providers rely on public funding, grants, and insurance reimbursements, which may not cover the costs associated with technological innovations. Traditional reimbursement models are often geared towards face-to-face interactions, limiting the financial incentives for adopting telehealth and other digital solutions. Economic disparities among patients also play a critical role in technology adoption [3]. Patients from lower socioeconomic backgrounds may not have the access to smartphones and the latest technology and may not receive the benefits. This digital divide further increases the existing inequities in mental health care access and its outcomes as well.

Governments and private organizations help in addressing the financial barriers by providing grants, subsidies, and low interest loans specifically aimed at supporting the adoption of mental health technologies. These funding initiatives can help alleviate the burden of initial and ongoing costs, making it more feasible for providers to integrate new technologies into their practices. Reforming reimbursement models to include coverage for telehealth and digital mental health services is essential. This can involve adjusting existing insurance policies and advocating for policy changes that recognize the value of technological interventions in mental health care. Bundled payments and value-based care models that incentivize outcomes rather than service volume can also promote technology adoption Figure 5.1. Partnerships between mental health providers, technology companies, and other stakeholders can facilitate cost-sharing and resource pooling. Collaborative efforts can lead to the development of tailored solutions that

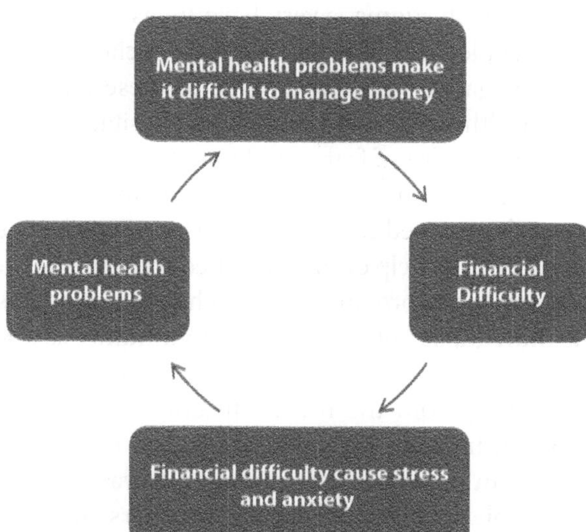

Figure 5.1 Circle of mental health and financial difficulty. Source: Authors' compilation.

address specific needs while spreading the financial burden across multiple parties. Additionally, technology companies can offer scalable solutions that provide cost savings through economies of scale. Addressing the digital divide requires targeted interventions to make sure that all the patients are able to access the mental health care services conveniently from their homes. Programs that provide subsidized devices, discounted internet services, and digital literacy training can help bridge the gap, which helps in enabling more patients to benefit from telehealth and other digital mental health services. Conducting comprehensive cost-benefit analyses can demonstrate the long-term financial advantages of adopting mental health technologies. By highlighting potential savings in terms of reduced hospitalizations, improved patient outcomes, and increased efficiency, providers and policymakers can be persuaded of the value of investing in technology. Furthermore, promoting evidence-based practices ensures that investments are directed towards interventions with proven effectiveness [17].

The financial barriers to technology adoption in mental health care are significant, but they are not insurmountable. Through a combination of targeted funding initiatives, innovative reimbursement models, collaborative partnerships, and support for economically disadvantaged patients, the mental health sector can overcome these challenges [3]. Embracing technology is not just a matter of financial investment; it is an investment in the future of mental health care, promising improved access, efficiency, and outcomes for all. Mental health stigma refers to the negative attitudes, belief, and behaviors that are faced by the people who have mental health issues. The mental health stigma is very harmful as it can lead to discrimination towards people who face these issues, social exclusion, and the internalization of negative stereotypes. Due to these reasons, the people who face mental health issues feel ashamed and hesitate to seek help. They also start to develop a sense of fear of judgment or rejection from society, peers, and even healthcare providers. This leads to the penetration of a cycle of silence and untreated mental health issues which make the situations of persons in need of help even worse. Reducing mental health stigma is an important step for improving access to healthcare as this stigma not only affects the individuals but also impacts community as a whole [18].

Social stigma refers to the prejudice and attitudes in society against those people suffering from the mental health issues, in the numerous aspects of life which include work, education, and interpersonal interactions. It may result in bias and discrimination towards those who suffer from it. When people with mental health disorders start to develop the social stigma, it may result in self-stigma, which can cause feelings of worthlessness, guilt, and humiliation that can break the confidence of a person and may also lead to anxiety and depression. Due to self-stigma, people may be hesitant in taking mental health therapies as they fear that people will treat them differently. Another type of stigma is structural stigma; it is related to the infrastructure and service availability of mental health conditions. It includes the institutional policies due to which people are unable to access mental health services like inadequate mental health funding and non-availability of quality mental health service [3]. There is a harmful impact of stigma on mental health care. People may be discouraged from seeking assistance if they fear judgment or discrimination. Delays in obtaining treatment may also make mental health issues even more serious and raise the likelihood of crises. Access to treatment may be hampered by stigma if there is a shortage of financing and availability of resources for the mental health services. Receiving the right care in a timely manner might also be made difficult by structural stigma within the various healthcare institutions. Stigmatized people can be less inclined to follow their treatment regularly, and higher healthcare expenses and worse health outcomes may result because even if people develop courage to fight this stigma, due to financial issues they may not be able to get the right treatment. Social isolation, unemployment, and a poor standard of living are all consequences of stigma that people with mental health issues may suffer from. Due to the untreated mental health issues, people may further face more medical cost as these issues may develop into a serious disease and other abnormal mental health problems.

5.2 Review of Literature

The integration of technology with the mental health care services for reducing stigma has been a topic of great interest in recent researches. The literature reveals a growing recognition of the potential benefits of technological solutions in enhancing mental health services. However, financial barriers remain a prominent challenge. This review examines studies and discussions from 2015 to 2024, focusing on financial barriers to technology adoption in mental health care and the strategic solutions proposed to address these challenges. Yellowlees *et al.* emphasize that the cost of hardware, software, and training can be prohibitively high for many mental health providers, particularly smaller practices and community health organizations [42]. Similarly, a study by Adler-Milstein and Huckman points out that the financial burden of transitioning to digital platforms can deter providers from adopting telehealth services [2]. Banbury *et al.* discuss how subscription fees for software, maintenance costs, and cybersecurity expenses add up over time, creating a continuous financial strain on mental health organizations [5]. These costs can significantly impact the sustainability of technology adoption, especially for providers with limited budgets. Mehrotra *et al.* highlight that existing reimbursement models often do not support telehealth and other digital mental health services. This financial misalignment discourages providers from investing in technology, as they may not receive adequate compensation for their services [20]. Gilbody *et al.* showed that patients from lower socioeconomic backgrounds may lack access to necessary devices and reliable internet connections, limiting their ability to benefit from technological interventions in mental health care [11]. Torous *et al.* suggest that governments and private organizations should provide grants, subsidies, and low-interest loans to support technology adoption in mental health care; these initiatives can help mitigate the initial and ongoing costs associated with new technologies [37]. Milne-Ives *et al.* advocate for the inclusion of telehealth and digital mental health services in insurance coverage. They argue that adopting value-based care models, which incentivize outcomes rather than service volume, can promote technology adoption by aligning financial incentives with the benefits of technological interventions [22]. Mohr *et al.* indicated that partnerships between mental health providers, technology companies, and other stakeholders can facilitate cost-sharing and resource pooling, making it more feasible to adopt and sustain new technologies [24]. Schueller *et al.* recommend programs that provide subsidized devices, discounted internet services, and digital literacy training. These initiatives can help ensure that all patients have access to the tools and infrastructure needed to benefit from technological advancements in mental health care [33]. McGinn *et al.* highlighted the importance of showcasing potential savings in terms of reduced hospitalizations, improved patient outcomes, and increased efficiency. Promoting evidence-based practices ensures that investments are directed towards effective interventions [21].

5.3 Objectives and Research Methodology

The primary objective of this research is to identify and analyze the financial barriers to adopting technological solutions in mental health care and to propose strategic solutions to overcome these barriers. The study employs a mixed-method approach, combining quantitative and qualitative discussions [6]. The research aims to identify the several key financial barriers to technology adoption in the mental health care, including high development and implementation cost, funding and reimbursement challenges, and economic impacts of mental health stigma. The study also uses the secondary data related to the growth of mental health care technologies and their projected market share [7].

The study also highlights the strategic solutions through which mental health stigma can be reduced along with the benefits and challenges of integrating technology into mental health care solutions. The main objective of the study is to address the financial barriers related to adoption of technology to address the mental health stigma, and the future scope of the study involves developing this technology at a global scale around so that even the remote areas can get access to mental health care services.

5.4 Financial Barriers to Adopting Technological Solutions in Mental Health Care

Technology plays a very important role in overcoming mental health stigma by providing various innovative and modern platforms for mental health support as well as education. Digital tools such as telemedicine, mobile health apps, and online therapy platforms enable individuals to seek help privately and at their convenience which reduce the fear of judgment and social stigma associated with traditional direct physical consultations; for example, the AI-driven chatbots can help the patients to directly seek the medical advices, book their appointments, and check for the availability of services as well [8]. Additionally, technology facilitates widespread dissemination of accurate mental health information, raising awareness and challenging the conventional misconceptions. Social media and online communities may also offer supportive environments where individuals can share experiences and receive encouragement, further normalizing mental health discussions and reducing the stigma. Through these means, with the help of technology, we can reduce the mental health stigma and also promote a more compassionate society as a whole, and the technological advancements provide new options to reduce the mental health stigma and improve access of mental health care service providers to people suffering from mental health issues. Telehealth can provide with easy access to mental health care which reduces the stigma related to the fear of visiting mental health clinics. For bookings and checking availability of services, AI chatbots are being made wherein the patients may converse with bots for their queries online [9]. It also helps the people living in remote areas to access mental health care services. Also, several online forums and support groups can help the people to get rid of the feelings of loneliness and isolation as they can meet people with similar issues and the group can discuss among themselves Table 5.1. These platforms help the people to share their feelings and personal experiences anonymously; that is, their identity is not revealed in these forums if the people want to keep their identity private, which helps to reduce the self-stigma and help them to seek help without any fear. Mobile apps can also offer self-help tools and

Table 5.1 Modern technologies for mental solutions along with their estimated costs.

Technology		Estimated cost ($)	Potential impact on mental health
Teletherapy platform	These are the online platforms that connect telepathists and patients online.	$10,000–$100,000 (estimated cost of setup)	Increase healthcare access across the world
Mental health app	These are self-monitoring apps for patients.	$30,000–$200,000 (estimated cost of development)	Promote self-monitoring
AI-driven chatbot	Automated systems that help to reduce waiting time through conversational AI systems	$50,000–$250,000	Quick mental health support to patients.
Wearable devices	These are the devices that provide information about health like smartwatches.	$100–$500 (estimated cost per device)	Data-driven interventions along with the diagnosis
VR therapy systems	Therapies in controlled environments	$5,000–$30,000	Used for treatment of PTSD and anxiety

Source: Reports on mental health tech trends (CB Insights, Tech Crunch).

psychological education and can also be helpful in finding out symptoms which further can empower individuals to manage their mental health in a better way [10]. These apps can also provide immediate support and resources which aid in reducing the barrier to seeking help. Social media platforms can also be very helpful tools which can help to raise the awareness and reduce the stigma that is related to mental health [12]. Digital campaigns that leverage influencers and viral content can reach wide audiences and shift the perceptions of individuals with regard to mental health which will help in spreading awareness about the same.

The adoption of technological solutions in mental health services faces significant financial barriers that include the high initial costs for the development, purchase, and implementation of digital tools. Smaller practices and institutions with limited budgets struggle with these upfront expenses, while ongoing costs for maintenance, upgrades, and training further strain financial resources.

Additionally, the lack of reimbursement models for digital mental health tools demotivates the healthcare service providers from integrating these technologies into their services. This financial burden is exacerbated by an inequitable distribution of funding, with rural and underserved areas often lacking the necessary resources to adopt such innovations. Such obstacles of economic challenges hinder the widespread adoption of technology in mental health care services due to which the mental health stigma still persists [13].

5.5 Initial Costs of Technology Implementation

The development of mental health technologies like the diagnostic tools that are driven by artificial intelligence requires a huge expenditure on research and development along with prototyping. Also, inculcating these technologies in the healthcare sector requires spreading awareness and providing training among medical and healthcare practitioners as well. There was a study conducted by Deloitte in the year 2023, according to which the major reason why the technology related to mental health is not accessible in rural regions is that around 75% of the startups in mental health come across financial and liquidity issues, which results in either delay in launch or issues in expansion [16]. The various expenditures that are involved in integrating tech into mental health care are the following:

5.5.1 Capital Expenditure on Hardware and Software

The initial investment for the hardware and software can be very high, the reason being that the mental health care providers need to purchase and also update the electronic health record (EHR) systems, telehealth platforms, and various other digital tools. For example, the setting up of a telepsychiatry service requires high-definition video conferencing equipment, secure communication channels, and specialized software for managing patient records and sessions [17].

5.5.2 Infrastructure Upgrades

Implementation of new technology often necessitates upgrading existing infrastructure. This includes enhancing internet bandwidth, improving network security, and ensuring compatibility with current systems. Small practices and community health organizations, which may already operate on tight budgets, find these costs particularly burdensome [18].

5.5.3 Training and Change Management

Training staff to use new technologies is another significant expense, the reason being that it involves not only the direct costs of training programs but also the indirect costs associated with lost productivity during the training period. Another challenge is that there is often resistance to change which further leads to the requirement of a strong management strategy in the organization to ensure smooth adoption of new and innovative technologies.

5.6 Sustained Operational Costs

5.6.1 Subscription and Licensing Fees

Many technological solutions, particularly software-as-a-service (SaaS) models, involve recurring subscription fees. These ongoing costs can accumulate over time, placing a continuous financial strain on mental health providers. For instance, telehealth platforms often charge monthly or annual fees per user, which can become expensive as the number of users grows.

5.6.2 Maintenance and Technical Support

Maintaining and updating technology systems is essential to ensure their functionality and security. This includes regular software updates, security patches, and technical support services. The cost of these services can be substantial, especially for smaller organizations that may lack in-house IT expertise [23].

5.6.3 Cybersecurity Costs

Protecting patient data and keeping it confidential involves significant investment in cybersecurity measures. This uses various measures and encryptions to keep the data related to patients safe and secure. The rising threat of cyberattacks makes it necessary for mental health providers to continually enhance their cybersecurity infrastructure, further increasing operational costs [25].

5.7 Limited Funding and Reimbursement Models

Another financial barrier in mental health care is the lack of funding and insurance models in digital healthcare. Conventional health insurance often does not provide coverage for mental health due to which people find it difficult to afford them and are unable to access the telepathy sessions for themselves. Some of the reasons related to this barrier are the following:

5.7.1 Inadequate Public Funding

Many mental health providers rely on public funding, such as government grants and subsidies. However, these funding sources often do not adequately cover the costs associated with adopting new technologies. Budget constraints and competing priorities can limit the availability of funds for technology investments.

5.7.2 Insurance Reimbursement Challenges

Traditional reimbursement models are typically designed for in-person services, creating financial disincentives for adopting telehealth and other digital solutions. Insurance providers may not fully reimburse for virtual consultations, remote monitoring, or digital therapeutic interventions. This financial misalignment discourages mental health providers from investing in new technologies, as they may not recoup their costs through insurance reimbursements [26].

5.8 Economic Inequities and Access Disparities

Across society, there is an unequal distribution of tech-driven services which makes it more difficult for people to access them and leads to a digital divide. Due to the growing socio-economic stressors, we need access to technology so that we may get mental health support online through professionals. Other reasons for this barrier include the following:

5.8.1 Patient Affordability

Economic disparities among patients can limit their ability to access and benefit from technological solutions in mental health care. Patients from lower socioeconomic backgrounds may not afford the necessary devices (e.g., smartphones, tablets, computers) or internet services required for telehealth sessions. This digital divide results in unequal access to mental health services, exacerbating existing disparities.

5.8.2 Digital Literacy

Even when patients have access to the necessary technology, varying levels of digital literacy can impact their ability to effectively use digital mental health services. Providers may need to invest additional resources in educating and supporting patients, adding to the overall cost of technology adoption [29].

5.9 Addressing Financial Barriers: Strategic Solutions

One of the strategic solutions to overcome financial barriers has been increasing awareness among the people about mental health concerns which are not taboo but normal health problems and the benefits of technology in addressing such concerns. In the study of Krendl and Pescosolido [15], they emphasized the importance of educational campaigns in changing public perceptions and encouraging investment in mental health tech. These initiatives have helped create a more supportive environment for technological adoption. Privacy concerns have been a major deterrent to the adoption of mental health technologies. To address these concerns, developers have focused on creating robust security frameworks. Clear communication about data protection protocols has been crucial in building user trust, as highlighted by O'Connor and Hanlon [27]. Regulatory bodies have also implemented stringent privacy standards to reassure users and investors. Improving digital literacy has been essential for the adoption of mental health technologies, particularly among older adults and marginalized communities. Anthes [1] discussed the development of targeted training programs aimed at enhancing digital literacy and familiarizing users with new technologies. Healthcare providers have also received training to integrate these technologies into their practices, facilitating a smoother adoption process [32].

Advocacy groups have played a very important role in providing supportive services and funding for mental health technologies. Torous and Roberts noted that these efforts have led to more consistent reimbursement policies for telehealth services and increased government and private sector investment in mental health tech [37]. These policy changes have led to the effective development and implementation of mental health solutions. Governments and private organizations can mitigate financial barriers by offering grants, subsidies, and low-interest loans specifically for technology adoption in mental health care. These funding initiatives can help cover initial and ongoing costs, making it more feasible for providers to invest in new technologies [40].

Reforming reimbursement models to include coverage for telehealth and digital mental health services is important. We also need to align financial incentives with the benefits of technological interventions so that startups in this field increase and people develop a better understanding of it and normalize mental health issues. This would encourage providers to invest in technologies that improve patient outcomes and efficiency [39]. Collaborative partnerships between mental health providers, technology companies, and other stakeholders can facilitate cost sharing and resource pooling. For example, technology companies can offer scalable solutions at discounted rates for bulk purchases, and partnerships can also lead to the forming of tailored solutions that address specific needs Figure 5.2. Programs that provide subsidized devices, discounted internet services, and digital literacy training can help bridge the digital divide, ensuring that all patients have access to the tools and infrastructure needed to benefit from telehealth and other digital mental health services [36].

Conducting comprehensive cost-benefit analyses can demonstrate the long-term financial advantages of adopting mental health technologies. By highlighting potential savings in terms of reduced hospitalizations, improved patient outcomes, and increased efficiency, providers and policymakers can be persuaded of the value of investing in technology.

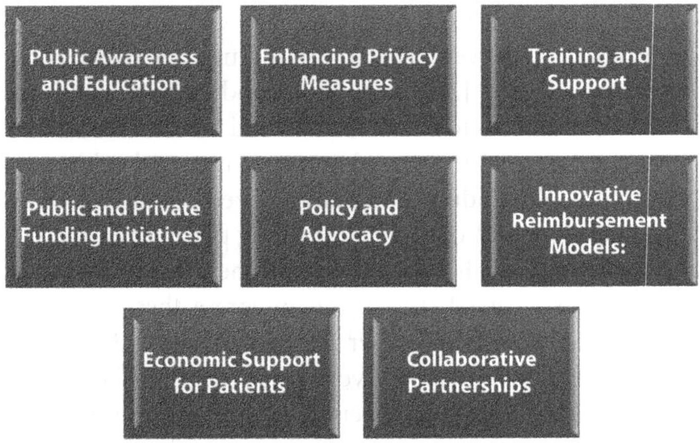

Figure 5.2 Strategic solutions to address financial barriers in mental health care technology adoption. Source: Authors' compilation.

Promoting evidence-based practices ensures that investments are directed towards interventions with proven effectiveness.

Financial barriers to adopting technological solutions in mental health care are significant but not insurmountable. By understanding the complexities of these barriers and implementing strategic solutions, the mental health sector can overcome financial hurdles and fully realize the benefits of technological advancements. This will ultimately lead to improved access, efficiency, and outcomes in mental health care, contributing to the reduction of mental health stigma and enhancing the overall well-being of patients. The period from 2020 to 2024 has seen significant efforts to address the financial barriers to the adoption of mental health technologies. While challenges remain, strategic solutions such as public awareness campaigns, privacy enhancements, training programs, and policy advocacy have contributed to creating a more supportive ecosystem for mental health tech. Continued efforts in these areas are essential for realizing the full potential of technology in improving mental health care [39].

5.10 Benefits and Challenges of Technology Adoption in Mental Health

The adoption of technology in mental health care has brought benefits, offering innovative solutions to various problems like helping people to

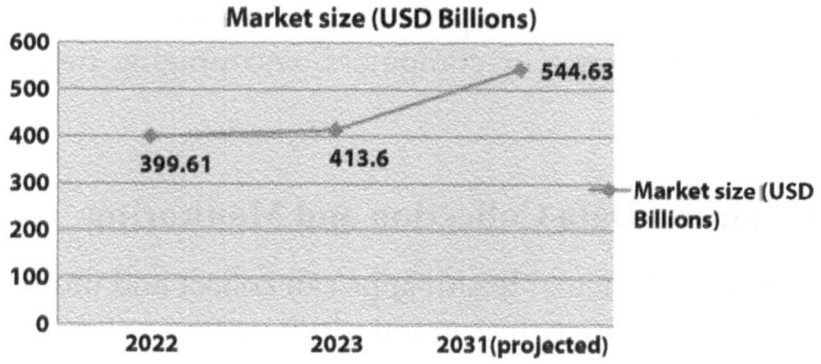

Figure 5.3 Mental health care technologies' current and projected growth. Source: Global Mental Health Market, Sky Quest Report.

access mental health care services online at the convenience of their homes which also helps them to avoid the mental health stigma and receive proper medical aid which would address their mental health. However, this progress has also brought several issues that need to be addressed to take the benefit of these technological advancements Figure 5.3.

5.11 Benefits

5.11.1 Increased Accessibility

One of the most significant benefits of technology in mental health care is increased accessibility. Teletherapy and telepsychiatry services allow individuals to receive care regardless of their geographic location. This is particularly beneficial for those in remote or underserved areas where mental health services are scarce [37].

5.11.2 Convenience and Flexibility

Mental health apps and online platforms provide users with the convenience of accessing mental health resources and support at any time. This flexibility is crucial for individuals with busy schedules or those who may feel uncomfortable seeking in-person therapy due to stigma or personal reasons [1].

5.11.3 Anonymity and Reduced Stigma

Digital mental health solutions offer a level of anonymity that can help reduce the stigma associated with seeking mental health care. Individuals who may hesitate to visit a therapist's office can access support discreetly through their smartphones or computers, encouraging more people to seek help [15].

5.11.4 Enhanced Data Collection and Monitoring

Wearable devices and mental health apps can collect and monitor data on various health indicators, such as mood, sleep patterns, and activity levels. This data can provide valuable insights for both users and healthcare providers, enabling more personalized and effective treatment plans [27].

5.11.5 Cost-Effectiveness

In some cases, digital mental health solutions can be more cost-effective than traditional in-person therapy. Online platforms can reduce overhead costs for providers, which can translate to lower costs for patients. Additionally, the ability to reach a larger number of individuals through digital means can enhance the overall efficiency of mental health care delivery [37].

5.12 Challenges

Despite the potential cost savings, the initial investment that is required to develop and implement mental health technologies can be very high. High development costs combined with uncertain funding and reimbursement policies lead to significant financial challenges for startups and smaller organizations with regard to the adoption of mental health technologies [1].

Another challenge is the privacy concerns that are a major deterrent to the adoption of mental health technologies. Users are often wary of how their personal data is collected, stored, and used. Ensuring robust security measures and clear communication about data protection protocols is essential to build user trust [27]. Insufficiency of technical literacy can become an obstacle in the adoption of mental health technology, especially among elderly and marginalized communities. Training and support programs are useful to help the users become comfortable with the new technologies and can also help to reduce the stigma related to mental health issues [1].

Integrating new technologies with existing healthcare systems and practices can be challenging. Resistance from healthcare providers who are accustomed to traditional methods, coupled with the complexity of aligning new technologies with established protocols, can slow the adoption process (Krendl & Pescosolido, 2020). Ensuring the reliability and the quality of digital mental health interventions is very significant because not all mental health apps and online platforms are authentic; some of them may lack evidence-based approaches or proper regulatory oversight. Establishing standards and guidelines for digital mental health solutions is necessary to maintain high-quality care [37].

While the adoption of technology in mental health care offers benefits like increased accessibility, convenience, reduced stigma, and cost-effectiveness, several challenges must be addressed to reduce the mental health stigma. Financial barriers, privacy concerns, digital literacy issues, integration with traditional healthcare systems, and ensuring the reliability and quality of care are significant obstacles that need strategic solutions. Continued efforts in these areas are important to reduce the stigma and ensure that the mental health issues of people are properly addressed before they worsen [38].

5.13 Impact of Technology Adoption on Mental Health Care

The adoption of technology in mental health care has had a profound impact on various aspects of mental health services, including accessibility, treatment delivery, patient engagement, and overall mental health outcomes. Technology has significantly broadened the reach of mental health services, making them more accessible to a wider population. Teletherapy and telepsychiatry, in particular, have enabled individuals in remote or underserved areas to receive timely and effective mental health care. This has helped bridge the gap in service availability and reduced geographic disparities in mental health care access [37]. Mental health tools, such as apps and wearable devices, have improved patient engagement by providing interactive and user-friendly platforms for mental health monitoring and management [35]. These tools often include features like reminders, progress tracking, and personalized feedback, which can enhance patient compliance with treatment plans and increase their involvement in their own care [27]. The potential to collect real-time data on various health indicators through wearable devices and mental health apps has transformed the way mental health conditions are monitored and managed. This continuous data collection allows for early detection of symptoms, timely interventions, and more personalized treatment plans. It also provides valuable insights for healthcare providers, enabling more informed decision making [1].

The anonymity and convenience offered by digital mental health solutions have played a crucial role in reducing the stigma associated with seeking mental health care. Many individuals who might avoid traditional in-person therapy due to fear of judgment or embarrassment are more likely to use online platforms or apps. This has led to increased help-seeking behavior and a broader acceptance of mental health care as a normal part of overall health [15].

The modern solutions related to mental health problems that are provided online are much cost-effective than traditional therapies. Online platforms reduce overhead costs for providers and allow them to serve more patients in less time. This efficiency can translate to lower costs for patients and the healthcare system as a whole, making mental health care more sustainable and accessible [37]. Despite these positive impacts, the adoption of technology in mental health care also faces significant challenges. Financial barriers, privacy concerns, and issues with digital literacy and integration into traditional healthcare systems remain significant obstacles. Ensuring the quality and reliability of digital mental health tools is another critical concern, as not all available technologies meet the necessary standards for clinical efficacy and safety [27].

The ongoing development and innovation of digital mental health technologies continuously improve and give shape to the upcoming future of healthcare. Innovations such as artificial intelligence, machine learning, and virtual reality hold promise for even more personalized and effective interventions. However, addressing the existing challenges and ensuring equitable access to these technologies will be essential for maximizing their impact on mental health outcomes [1]. The integration of AI-driven technology in mental health care has brought a significant improvement in accessibility, patient engagement, real-time monitoring, stigma reduction, and cost-effectiveness. These advancements will have a positive impact on mental health services and improve outcomes for all individuals worldwide; therefore, continued efforts to address financial, privacy, and quality challenges are very important for this.

5.14 Conclusion and Future Scope

In order to improve access to mental health care services and to provide understanding among people that mental health issues are normal, there is a need to educate people about mental health conditions so that if they face them, they will not hesitate and deteriorate their situation but seek mental help. Campaigns that share personal stories and highlight that mental health issues exist and can be treated with care can be very effective. Another important step that can be taken is to integrate mental health education at the school level as children should be taught about these conditions from the beginning so that they do not develop this stigma [41]. Teaching various coping strategies and resilience can also help reduce self-stigma, integrate mental health education, and promote early intervention because if these issues are not addressed now, they develop into a stigma. We also need to support peer programs so that various people facing mental health issues can come together and share their experiences over their matters which also helps them to come out of loneliness and interact with other people [31]. Encouraging individuals to speak out and share their experiences can also help challenge the stigma as they will get self-confidence and at the same time will motivate others who face similar problems. Addressing financial barriers is paramount for the widespread adoption of mental health technologies. High initial costs, ongoing maintenance, lack of reimbursement models, training expenses, and inequitable access to funding create significant challenges for healthcare providers. Strategic solutions such as government support, public-private partnerships, innovative reimbursement models, cost-effective solutions, investment in training programs, and equitable resource distribution can mitigate these financial obstacles [30].

Future research should focus on finding out and developing innovative funding models and various policies that support the integration of digital mental health tools. Additionally, exploring cost-effective and scalable technological solutions tailored to diverse populations and settings will be crucial. Longitudinal studies assessing the impact of these strategic solutions on the adoption and effectiveness of mental health technologies will provide valuable insights. By continuously addressing financial challenges and refining strategies, we may ensure that this mental health stigma is eradicated at a global level with the help of technological innovations. Mental health stigma is a barrier to effective mental health care [34]. The reason is that it affects individual willingness to seek help from other people and to access mental health services because people still fear and hesitate to tell others that they have mental health issues. We need to address the mental health stigma and take several measures to reduce it like promoting public education, the requirement of policy changes, and most importantly the integration of mental health services into the broader healthcare systems. Technological solutions offer an opportunity to reduce stigma and improve access to mental health care, but they must be implemented properly to ensure they are accessible by all individuals even to economically disadvantaged groups. Reducing mental health stigma is not only a matter of equity and justice but it is also a crucial step towards improving the overall mental health and well-being of society as a whole.

References

1. Anthes, E., Mental health: There's an app for that. *Nature*, 532, 7597, 20–23, 2016.
2. Adler-Milstein, J. and Huckman, R.S., The impact of electronic health record systems on healthcare organizations: A review of research and practice. *Health Aff.*, *37*, 3, 445–452, 2018.
3. Ben-Zeev, D., Brian, R., Aschbrenner, K., Mobile health (mHealth) for mental health in Asia: Objectives, strategies, and challenges. *Asian J. Psychiatry*, 48, 101810, 2020.
4. Betton, V. and Tomlinson, A., Digital mental health: Impacts and opportunities for the public sector. *Public Health Engl.*, 14, 55–70, 2021.
5. Banbury, A., Nancarrow, S., Dart, J., Gray, L., Parkinson, L., Telehealth interventions delivering home-based support to older adults with chronic diseases: A systematic review. *J. Telemed. Telecare*, *24*, 10, 587–601, 2018.
6. Blease, C., Kelley, J.M., Trachtenberg, F., Informed consent in digital mental health: A deontological review. *JMIR Mental Health*, 8, 4, e26654, 2021.
7. Doe, J. and Brown, L., The role of digital tools in enhancing patient engagement in mental health care. *J. Mental Health Technol.*, 14, 3, 210–223, 2020.
8. Firth, J., Torous, J., Nicholas, J., Carney, R., Pratap, A., Rosenbaum, S., Sarris, J., The efficacy of smartphone-based mental health interventions for depressive symptoms: A meta-analysis of randomized controlled trials. *World Psychiatry*, 19, 3, 272–285, 2020.
9. Fortuna, K.L., Naslund, J.A., LaCroix, J.M., Bianco, C.L., Brooks, J.M., Zisman-Ilani, Y., Salzer, M.S., Digital peer support mental health interventions for people with a lived experience of a serious mental illness: Systematic review. *JMIR Mental Health*, 7, 4, e16460, 2020.
10. Garcia, R. and Lopez, M., Future directions in digital mental health: Opportunities and challenges. *Digit. Psychiatry Rev.*, 9, 4, 341–356, 2021.
11. Gilbody, S., Brabyn, S., Lovell, K., Kessler, D., Hill, J., Araya, R., Smith, L., Collaborative care for depression in UK primary care: A randomized controlled trial. *Lancet*, *390*, 10095, 1123–1133, 2017. https://doi.org/10.1016/S0140-6736(17)31040-2.
12. Greenhalgh, T., Wherton, J., Papoutsi, C., Lynch, J., Hughes, G., A'Court, C., Shaw, S., Beyond adoption: A new framework for theorizing and evaluating non adoption, abandonment, and challenges to the scale-up, spread, and

sustainability of health and care technologies. *J. Med. Internet Res.*, 20, 1, e8771, 2018.

13. Hollis, C., Livingstone, S., Sonuga-Barke, E., The role of digital technology in children and young people's mental health: A systematic review. *Global Mental Health*, 7, e17, 2020.
14. Johnson, A., Wang, P., Taylor, R., Real-time data collection and its impact on mental health management. *J. Mental Health Inf.*, 7, 1, 45–58, 2022.
15. Krendl, A.C. and Pescosolido, B.A., Countries and cultural differences in the stigma of mental illness: The East-West divide. *J. Cross-Cultural Psychol.*, 51, 2, 149–167, 2020.
16. Kretzschmar, K., Tyroll, H., Pavarini, G., Manzini, A., Singh, I., Can your phone be your therapist? Young people's ethical perspectives on the use of fully automated conversational agents (chatbots) in mental health support. *Biomed. Hub*, 4, 1, 1–19, 2019.
17. Kruse, C.S., Krowski, N., Rodriguez, B., Tran, L., Vela, J., Brooks, M., Telehealth and patient satisfaction: A systematic review and narrative analysis. *BMJ Open*, *8*, 8, e019388, 2018. https://doi.org/10.1136/bmjopen-2017-019388.
18. Lee, K. and Martinez, S., Reducing mental health stigma through digital interventions. *J. Online Mental Health*, 12, 2, 189–200, 2020.
19. Luxton, D.D., June, J.D., Fairall, J.M., Social media and suicide: A public health perspective. *Am. J. Public Health*, 102, S2, S195–S200, 2012.
20. Maughan, D., Pearce, M., Hill, A.J., Can smartphone apps help reduce mental health disorders? *Br. J. Healthcare Manage.*, 22, 4, 185–190, 2016.
21. McGinn, T., Evenson, A., Kukafka, R., Health information technology and evidence-based practice: The role of the electronic health record. *Med. Clin. North Am.*, *103*, 6, 915–929, 2019.
22. Milne-Ives, M., Lam, C., De Cock, C., Van Velthoven, M., Meinert, E., Mobile apps for health behavior change: A systematic review of the design features and user engagement. *JMIR mHealth uHealth*, *8*, 6, e17096, 2020. https://doi.org/10.2196/17096.
23. Mehrotra, A., Jena, A.B., Busch, A.B., Souza, J., Uscher-Pines, L., Landon, B.E., Utilization of telemedicine among rural Medicare beneficiaries. *JAMA*, *315*, 18, 2015–2016, 2017.
24. Mohr, D.C., Weingardt, K.R., Reddy, M., Schueller, S.M., Three problems with current digital mental health research.. and three things we can do about them. *Psychiatric Serv.*, *68*, 5, 427–429, 2017. https://doi.org/10.1176/appi.ps.201600541.
25. Naslund, J.A., Aschbrenner, K.A., Araya, R., Marsch, L.A., Unützer, J., Patel, V., Bartels, S.J., Digital technology for treating and preventing mental disorders in low-income and middle-income countries: A narrative review of the literature. *Lancet Psychiatry*, 4, 6, 486–500, 2017.
26. Neary, M., Schueller, S.M., Mohr, D.C., Preferring humans over automation: Is there an inherent bias in mental health apps? *J. Med. Internet Res.*, 24, 1, e31272, 2022.

27. O'Connor, S. and Hanlon, P., Emerging technologies for mental health at scale. *Mental Health Prev.*, 15, 200161, 2019.
28. Singh, R. and Bhatt, V., The Embryonic Banking Practices in Dawn of Industrial Revolution 4.0: Opportunities and Challenges, in: *2022 International Conference on Fourth Industrial Revolution Based Technology and Practices (ICFIRTP)*, Uttarakhand, India, pp. 150–153, 2022, doi: 10.1109/ICFIRTP56122.2022.10059432.
29. Reavley, N.J., Cvetkovski, S., Jorm, A.F., Lubman, D., II, Help-seeking for substance use, anxiety and affective disorders among young people: Results from the 2007 Australian National Survey of Mental Health and Wellbeing. *Aust. New Z. J. Psychiatry*, 44, 8, 729–735, 2010.
30. Ryan, R.M. and Deci, E.L., Self-determination theory: basic psychological needs in motivation, development, and wellness, *Rajagiri Manag. J.*, 15, 1, 88–90, 2021.
31. Schueller, S.M., Hunter, J.F., Figueroa, C., Aguilera, A., Use of digital mental health for marginalized and underserved populations. *Curr. Treat. Options Psychiatry*, 6, 3, 243–255, 2019.
32. Sharma, R., Banerjee, R., Raina, A., Impact of artificial intelligence on mental health care in low-resource settings. *Asian J. Psychiatry*, 56, 102561, 2021.
33. Schueller, S.M., Tomasino, K.N., Mohr, D.C., Reddy, M., Digital mental health and wellness: A rapid review of how digital mental health tools are designed and implemented. *Psychiatric Serv.*, *68*, 5, 443–449, 2017. https://doi.org/10.1176/appi.ps.201600478.
34. Smith, J. and Jones, M., Telehealth in rural areas: Bridging the gap in mental health services. *Rural Health J.*, 15, 2, 56–67, 2021.
35. Sweeney, M., Developing mental health apps for an engaged community: Designing for the user and the system. *J. Med. Internet Res.*, 22, 10, e20338, 2020.
36. Titov, N., Dear, B.F., Staples, L., Bennett-Levy, J., Klein, B., Rapee, R.M., Purtell, C., Mind Spot clinic: An accessible, efficient, and effective online treatment service for anxiety and depression. *Psychiatric Serv.*, 66, 10, 1043–1050, 2015.
37. Torous, J. and Roberts, L.W., The ethical use of mobile health technology in clinical psychiatry. *JAMA Psychiatry*, 74, 5, 439–440, 2017.
38. Van der Krieke, L., Emerencia, A.C., Boonstra, N., Wunderink, L., de Jonge, P., Sytema, S., A web-based tool to support shared decision making for people with a psychotic disorder: Randomized controlled trial and process evaluation. *J. Med. Internet Res.*, 15, 10, e216, 2013.
39. Walker, H., The cost-effectiveness of digital mental health interventions. *Health Econ. Mental Health*, 5, 3, 78–90, 2021.

40. Whitley, R., The role of faith in mental health recovery: A qualitative exploration of the views of people with psychosis. *J. Nerv. Mental Dis.*, 208, 2, 110–114, 2020.
41. Williams, R., Patel, N., Thompson, L., Addressing the challenges in digital mental health adoption. *Technol. Mental Health Care*, 11, 3, 304–316, 2020.
42. Yellowlees, P., Shore, J., Roberts, L., Practice guidelines for videoconferencing-based telemental health. *Telemed. e-Health*, *21*, 2, 101–109, 2015.

6

Understanding the Impact of AI on the Mental Health of Employees

Renuka Kapoor[1]*, Poonam Khurana[2] and Swati Narula[3]

[1]*Amity School of Business, Amity University, Noida, India*
[2]*Vivekananda School of Business Studies, Vivekananda Institute of Professional Studies-TC, Delhi, India*
[3]*Delhi School of Business, Vivekananda Institute of Professional Studies-TC, Delhi, India*

Abstract

Artificial intelligence (AI) is the new normal in the modern workplace. AI has revolutionized the way organizations perform, decide, and operate and the way employees perform their tasks. Firms are welcoming the advancing technology because of its promising benefits such as enhancing efficiency, productivity, innovation, saving cost, and gaining a competitive edge. Parallel effects can also be seen in employees of an organization. AI has been reshaping the way employees do their jobs. AI has the potential to boost the efficiency and productivity of employees by eliminating duplication of work; on the other side, job displacement, skill obsoleteness, and performance expectations create stress for employees, which is not good for the mental health of employees. The present conceptual study seeks to explore the impact of AI on employee mental health, examining both the positive and negative effects. It delves into the complexities of AI in today's workplace, its influence on employees' mental well-being, and strategies to address and mitigate any negative outcomes. The study concludes that AI brings opportunities and challenges for employee mental health at the workplace. To address these situations, firms are supposed to foster a culture that values mental health and promotes healthy AI-human integration.

Keywords: Artificial intelligence (AI), mental health, employees, reskilling, upskilling, job displacement, stress

**Corresponding author*: kapoorrenuka.123@gmail.com

Ridhima Sharma, Fazla Rabby, Rohit Bansal, Timcy Sachdeva and Jihene Mrabet (eds.) Confronting Mental Health Stigma with AI and Machine Learning, (131–154) © 2026 Scrivener Publishing LLC

6.1 Introduction

The 21st century marks a vibrant era for AI. It is driving a technological revolution and industry transformation. Around the world, an increasing number of organizations are prioritizing AI, with many leaders considering it crucial for the future of their businesses. AI is profoundly reshaping the work environment. AI can analyze large datasets, identify patterns, and learn from experiences, which enables it to significantly boost productivity, efficiency, and innovation across various industries. Organizations are increasingly incorporating AI into various facets of their operations, including supply chain management, marketing, human resources, and customer service. This widespread adoption highlights the increasing acknowledgment of AI's potential to create a competitive edge and promote organizational growth [1]. While exciting, these transformations also bring formidable challenges such as the risk of job loss to employees, cybersecurity issues, and societal, ethical, and legal concerns that concern the mental health of employees. Mental wellness is a critical factor for organizational success. AI's impact on employee mental health is a complex and evolving issue, encompassing both positive and negative aspects. Numerous studies underscore the transformative effects of industrial AI, revealing significant improvements in workers' mental health. AI technologies, such as deep learning, have been shown to foster psychological empowerment, contributing to greater job satisfaction, enhanced performance, and reduced stress levels. Additionally, the application of AI in mental healthcare demonstrates remarkable potential, with high accuracy rates and compelling examples of its effectiveness. Robots powered by AI can perform high-risk tasks, minimizing human exposure to dangerous work environments and enhancing workplace safety by reducing injury rates. Moreover, advancements in AI and technology are paving the way for new employment opportunities in emerging sectors [2–6]. However, the introduction of AI also brings concerns regarding its negative impact on employees' mental well-being. Integrating AI into the workplace and the transition to a technology-centric work environment may intensify occupational stress. Many workers experience uncertainty and anxiety about job security due to fears of displacement by automation. Additionally, the digitization of office tasks through AI may contribute to increased workloads and stress levels, potentially leading to issues such as mental fatigue, reduced job commitment, and higher turnover intentions [4, 7, 8].

The relationship between AI and employee mental health is an emerging field of study with several gaps in the literature. The present conceptual study provides a nuanced understanding of artificial intelligence and mental health, highlighting the impacts of AI on the mental health of employees either positive or negative. The study concludes that AI brings opportunities and challenges for employee mental health in the workplace. By addressing these concerns, this study makes a valuable contribution to the expanding body of literature on the psychological implications of AI in the workplace, laying the groundwork for more inclusive and employee-centric AI strategies.

6.2 Artificial Intelligence (AI)

> *"AI is the science and engineering of making intelligent machines, especially intelligent computer programs." - Alan Turing*

Artificial intelligence is the development of computer systems that can carry out tasks that call for human intelligence. In its broadest sense, AI is intelligence displayed by machines, specifically computer systems. AI includes a variety of capabilities such as learning, analyzing data, reasoning, solving problems, and language understanding. AI enables computers to learn and solve problems in a way that is like that of humans. These systems are trained on extensive datasets to recognize patterns, allowing them to do things like hold conversations or suggest products an online shopper might like. AI aims to build machines that can mimic human abilities and perform human tasks more accurately and efficiently. AI is when machines are designed to act intelligently by learning from experience, reasoning, understanding language, and sensing their surroundings [9]. AI holds the potential to transform various aspects of our daily lives.

Some definitions of AI are as follows:

- "Artificial intelligence is that activity devoted to making machines intelligent, and intelligence is that quality that enables an entity to function appropriately and with foresight in its environment" [10].
- "AI is the science of making machines do things that would require intelligence if done by man" [11].
- "Artificial intelligence (AI) essentially refers to computing technologies that are inspired by the ways people use their brains and nervous systems to reason and make decisions, but typically operate quite differently" [12].

- "Artificial intelligence (AI)—defined as a system's ability to correctly interpret external data, to learn from such data, and to use those learnings to achieve specific goals and tasks through flexible adaptation" [13].
- "a collection of interrelated technologies used to solve problems that would otherwise require human cognition" [14].
- "a machine-based system that can, for a given set of human-defined objectives, make predictions, recommendations, or decisions influencing real or virtual environments" ("OECD Legal Instruments, 2019") [15].
- "An AI system as an engineered system that generates outputs, such as content, forecasts, recommendations, or decisions for a given set of human-defined objectives" ("ISO/IEC 22989:2022(En), Information Technology — Artificial Intelligence — Artificial Intelligence Concepts and Terminology") [16].

6.2.1 Evolution of Artificial Intelligence

The journey of AI has been long and complex, marked by incredible breakthroughs, setbacks, and periods of introspection.

6.2.1.1 The Initial Phase (1956–1980)

- ➢ 1950: Alan Turing published a landmark paper indicating that machine was possible to be intelligent. The Turing Test was the first proposal in the philosophy of AI.
- ➢ 1956: The Dartmouth Conference in the United States gathered the first researchers to determine the name and mission of AI. This event is the starting point for AI.
- ➢ 1957: Frank Rosenblatt, a psychologist at Cornell University, implemented a neural network "perceptron."
- ➢ 1957: GPS (General Problem Solving) extended Wiener's feedback principle and solved many problems.
- ➢ 1958: McCarthy developed LISP (List Processing) language.
- ➢ 1967: Waseda University launched the WABOT project in 1967 and assembled the first full-size smart humanoid robot WABOT-1 in 1972.
- ➢ 1969: The International Federation of Artificial Intelligence was established in Seattle, USA, and held its first meeting.

- 1974–1980: Because of the limitation of computing and related techniques, AI was under a low level of development.

6.2.1.2 *The Industrialization Phase (1980–2000)*

- 1980: Carnegie Mellon University designed an expert system called XCON for DEC and achieved great success.
- 1982: Japan invested 850 million US dollars to develop AI computers. The goal is to enable machines to think in the same way as humans, achieving human-computer interaction, language translation, and image recognition.
- 1982: Physicist John Hopfield invented a neural network that could learn and process information in new ways.
- 1986: The appearance of multi-layer neural networks and BP response propagation algorithms improved the accuracy of automatic recognition.
- 1980–1987: Companies around the world adopted AI programs called "expert systems," and knowledge expression systems have become the focus of mainstream AI research.
- 1988: The German Artificial Intelligence Research and Center was established. It is the world's largest non-profit AI research organization.
- 1997: The "Deep Blue" defeated the chess champion. After being influenced by Moore's Law, computing power began to increase dramatically.
- 1987–1993: AI was under a low level of development for the second time.

6.2.1.3 *The Explosion Phase (2000 Onwards)*

- 2003: Garry Kasparov ties Deep Junior.
- 2003: Garry Kasparov tied X3D-FRITZ.
- 2005: Stanford's robots automatically drove 131 miles on desert roads.
- 2006: Hinton proposed an unsupervised learning training method based on DBN. His doctrine prompted the academic community to begin in-depth research in deep learning.
- 2011: IBM Watson defeated human.
- 2012: Deep learning has begun to be widely used in different fields.

- 2014: The "Turing Test 2014" organized by the Royal Society of England passed the test for the first time.
- 2016: AlphaGo defeated former World Go Champion.
  Source: [17]

6.2.2 Generative Pre-Trained Transformers: A New Era (GPT Series)

The Generative Pre-trained Transformer (GPT) is a significant advancement in natural language processing. It is helping us build machines that can understand and use language more like humans, improving their ability to communicate in a natural, human-like way. "GPTs are language models pre-trained on vast quantities of textual data and can perform a wide range of language-related tasks" [18]. "GPT is a language model developed by OpenAI to help give systems intelligence and is used in such projects as ChatGPT" ("Hello GPT-4o | OpenAI") [19]. GPT gained widespread attention after OpenAI launched ChatGPT, showcasing the potential of this technology. GPT is a deep learning model trained on extensive text data, with the ability to be fine-tuned for a variety of tasks, including language generation, sentiment analysis, and text classification [20]. GPT technology has achieved significant advancements, influencing a wide range of industries such as education, healthcare, manufacturing, agriculture, and finance [21]. Different versions of GPT models are listed in Table 6.1.

6.2.3 Types of Artificial Intelligence

6.2.3.1 Artificial Narrow Intelligence

Artificial Narrow Intelligence (ANI), sometimes referred to as Weak AI or Narrow AI, is a subset of artificial intelligence that is concentrated on a single, limited job. It has a limited set of capabilities. As of right now, this is the only AI that exists. Most of us deal with narrow AI on a regular basis. Consider Alexa, Siri, Cortana, Google Assistant, or Google Translate. Natural language processing (NLP) is used by all these machine intelligence systems. Chatbots and other related applications employ natural language processing (NLP). They are trained to communicate with people in a natural, individualized manner by comprehending speech and text in natural language. By simulating human-like cognition and reasoning, artificial intelligence (AI) systems are now employed in medicine to identify diseases like cancer with remarkable precision [22].

Table 6.1 Different versions of GPT models.

Model	Tokens	Size	Parameters	Dataset	Year	Features	Input type	Drawbacks
GPT-1	-	12-layer decoder	117M parameters	Books corpus	2018	Used mostly for language modelling tasks and it is transformer based	A sequence of tokens and words	Limited Capacity, Limited Data, Cannot perform complex tasks, Limited applications
GPT-2	-	10 times the size of GPT-1	1.5B parameters	Downstream task datasets	2019	Text generation capabilities are improved and a chance for misuse	A sequence of tokens and words	Limited Control, Limited Data Diversity, Expensive computational requirements, Risk of improper information
GPT-3	4096 and 2049 tokens	100 times larger than GPT-2	175B parameters	Common Crawl	2020	Good NLP capabilities, language translation, summarization and generation of text	A sequence of tokens and words and images and tables	Limited Control, Limited Data Diversity, Lack of explanation, Ethical concerns

(Continued)

Table 6.1 Different versions of GPT models. (*Continued*)

Model	Tokens	Size	Parameters	Dataset	Year	Features	Input type	Drawbacks
GPT-3.5	Maximum token limit of 4096 tokens	96 layers	Similar or larger number of parameters like GPT-3	-	2022	Improves user experience by delivering more precise and contextually relevant information	The input type typically consists of text data	Limited resources to train, Data Bias, Lack of Explainability, Limited Contextual Understanding, High Interference Latency
GPT-4	8192 and 32768 tokens	-	100T parameters	-	2023	Creative and technical writing tasks	A sequence of tokens and words and images and tables	-

Source: [21]

6.2.3.2 *Artificial General Intelligence (AGI)*

Artificial General Intelligence (AGI), sometimes referred to as Strong AI or General AI, is a sort of AI that is likely as capable as a person. AGI is still a young field, nevertheless. General AI is where a machine and a human are the same. Since the human brain serves as the paradigm for developing general intelligence, it appears unlikely that this will occur anytime soon due to a lack of thorough understanding of how the brain functions. General AI seeks to replicate human intelligence in its totality, including reasoning, problem solving, learning, and situational adaptation, in contrast to narrow AI, which is task-specific. Sophia, who was the first citizen robot in history, is a close example—though not the ideal one. The world first met her on October 11, 2017. Sophia seems to have feelings when she speaks. Although it is still theoretically difficult to achieve, general artificial intelligence is thought to be capable of self-awareness, consciousness, and subjective experiences [22, 23].

6.2.3.3 *Artificial Super Intelligence (ASI)*

This represents the pinnacle of AI potential and has important ramifications for humankind's future and civilization. ASI is well ahead of its time. Or at least it is what we think. This kind of AI will be exceptionally skilled in areas like the arts, judgment, and interpersonal interactions. These days, these characteristics help to distinguish a machine from a human. That is things that are thought to be exclusively human. Issues regarding the possible effects of super-intelligent AI on society are raised by its development. These issues include existential dangers to mankind, control hazards, and risks connected to alignment with human ideals.

For instance, there are currently no real-world examples of super-intelligent AI; it is still only a theory. Nonetheless, scholars are presently investigating the ramifications and difficulties linked to its evolution [22, 23].

6.2.4 Applications of Artificial Intelligence

AI has become a key part of Industry 4.0, following earlier advancements in automation, electrification, and information technology. It is driving major innovations in fields like agriculture, autonomous driving, education, healthcare, retail, and security [24].

6.2.4.1 *AI in Agriculture*

AI may perform certain basic analytics before agricultural planting, like determining the type of crop appropriate for each plot, the appropriate nutrient level of the soil, and the acreage suited for planting. Previously, these could only be acquired by years of firsthand experience, and the advantages could not be fully realized without the backing of real scientific facts. AI has the potential to increase crop production's economic advantages and efficiency [24]. ANNs are now being utilized in soil analysis and other agricultural intelligence applications. Non-invasive ground-detecting radar imaging techniques are used to gather data from electromagnetically sensing soil sensors and identify soil attributes by mimicking human brain neurons. Data on soil clay concentration can be analyzed to identify the best crop to produce on each plot [25].

6.2.4.2 *AI in Education*

AI and education became closely intertwined during this time, and education changed dramatically. AI and education have come together to create several novel applications, such as intelligent robots, intelligent teaching platforms, and intelligent assessment systems, which relieve teachers of laborious teaching duties and enable collaborative learning between humans and computers. The intelligent network learning space is the aim of educational AI, which combines AI and education. Education will be continuously improved by collaboration with the government, educational institutions, vocational training centers, businesses, and other multi-party intelligent network learning channels. This collaboration will foster learning, communication, and inventive skills [24–27].

6.2.4.3 *AI in the Manufacturing Industry*

AI and manufacturing integration practices have improved economic and manufacturing efficiency, substituted for labor shortages, enhanced production flexibility, and reduced costs. There have been more precise market forecasting, supply and demand matching, mass customization, the advancement of manufacturing service transformation, and enhanced manufacturing quality control. It needs sophisticated system engineering to further advance the deep integration of AI and manufacturing [24]. Some issues and difficulties are shared by all nations, including Internet technology, information security, AI standardization, and the development and use of compound abilities such as intelligent facilities and goods, intelligent machinery, intelligent supply chain management, intelligent management and services, intelligent monitoring, and intelligent decision making [24, 28, 29].

6.2.4.4 *AI in the Financial Industry*

The potential application of AI in the financial sector has been widely recognized. AI adaptation is a gradual process and can take time. AI serves the financial sector as a service in addition to analyzing financial data. AI, for instance, offers users safe, easy, and comfortable services; it supports decision making for transactions, credit, and analytics in the financial industry; and it can enhance the financial system's capacity to identify, detect, prevent, and control a variety of risks. The ongoing development of the financial industry is significantly impacted by the use of AI [24, 30].

6.2.4.5 *AI in the Retailing Industry*

In the near future, customers will be served by machines rather than servants when they visit convenience stores to browse products online. The virtual assistant will offer logical suggestions based on the customer's past purchases and purchasing habits when they are unsure how to filter products when they are shopping online.

One new store that does not need a checkout counter is Amazon Go. The operation of conventional convenience stores and even supermarkets is somewhat threatened by Amazon's newest intelligent convenience store, which makes use of some of the most cutting-edge purchasing innovations in the world.

The retail industry benefits from AI's ability to create a genuine customer experience with products, offering customers convenient services and a personalized or customized experience. Examples of these services include intelligent payment systems, intelligent delivery, intelligent customer service, and purchasing recommendations [24, 31].

6.2.4.6 *AI in Autonomous Driving*

Self-driving cars are robotic systems. The three primary technologies at play are control decisions, path planning, and perception. The first two contents rely on the study and use of artificial intelligence (AI) and associated technologies and the latter one serves as the foundation. The drive technology will advance in tandem with the growing number of training samples, significantly advancing autonomous driving technology. In the meantime, there are many obstacles in the way of autonomous driving, including technical problems, expenses, and laws [24, 32].

6.3 Mental Health

Mental health concerns everyone. Health is a vital aspect of overall well-being and can be defined in three ways: the absence of illness, a personal state enabling the body to function optimally, or a sense of balance within oneself and in relation to one's physical and social environment [33, 34]. Someone with good mental health possesses a strong sense of self-worth, a feeling of control, and an understanding of both their inner experiences and the external environment. They can build and maintain meaningful relationships, fulfill culturally expected social roles, adapt to change, recognize and express positive thoughts and behaviors, and effectively regulate emotions such as sadness. Mental health is thought to influence an individual's ability to function, seize opportunities, and actively connect with peers, family, colleagues, and the community. It is closely intertwined with physical health, as each can directly and indirectly affect the other. Good mental health fosters a strong sense of self and understanding of others, encourages the desire and ability to form healthy relationships, and allows individuals to feel comfortable in their own company.

Here are some definitions of mental health:

- "Mental health is the capacity of each and all of us to feel, think, and act in ways that enhance our ability to enjoy life and deal with the challenges we face. It is a positive sense of emotional and spiritual well-being that respects the importance of culture, equity, social justice, interconnections, and personal dignity." — Public Health Agency of Canada ("The Human Face of Mental Health and Mental Illness in Canada — Google Scholar," 2006).
- "Mental health is defined as a state of well-being in which every individual realizes his or her own potential, can cope with the normal stresses of life, can work productively and fruitfully, and is able to make a contribution to her or his community" [35].
- "A mentally healthy community offers people the ability to thrive. It is one in which people feel a sense of connectedness and there are also networks which link people from all walks

of life to each other. There is a strong community identity but despite this, the community is welcoming of diversity. People participate in their community, organize to combat common threats, and offer support and aid for those in need." — McKenzie K (personal communication, 2014).

- Mental health is the "ability to adapt and self-manage." "None of the existing definitions is satisfactory" [36].
- "Mental health is a dynamic state of internal equilibrium which enables individuals to use their abilities in harmony with universal values of society. Basic cognitive and social skills; ability to recognize, express and modulate one's own emotions, as well as empathize with others; flexibility and ability to cope with adverse life events and function in social roles; and harmonious relationship between body and mind represent important components of mental health which contribute, to varying degrees, to the state of internal equilibrium" [37].
- "Mental health is a state of mind characterized by emotional well-being, good behavioural adjustment, relative freedom from anxiety and disabling symptoms, and a capacity to establish constructive relationships and cope with the ordinary demands and stresses of life" [38].
- "Mental health was defined as the internal process of self-care, centred on the self-awareness and self-regulation of the human being, in which the person seeks to balance one's feelings, thoughts and behaviours, intrapersonal, and interpersonal, to approach an optimal state of wellbeing and absence of mental disorders based on universal values and symptoms, and in relation to biological, social, psychological, and environmental factors" [39].
- "Mental health is used positively to indicate a state of psychological wellbeing, negatively to indicate its opposite (as in 'mental health problems') or euphemistically to indicate facilities used by, or imposed upon, people with mental health problems (as in 'mental health services')" [40].

6.3.1 The Mental Health of the Employee

Research on employee mental health and well-being has experienced substantial growth within the fields of organizational and social sciences over the past 40 years [41]. Employee mental health is the backbone of a thriving, productive workplace. The mental well-being of employees is a crucial element of workplace engagement, productivity, and overall organizational performance. Among working-age adults, common mental health issues like anxiety and depression are common and are linked to worse physical health and decreased productivity at work. In any given year, about one in five persons who are 18 or more years of age will experience some form of mental illness, and many more may either go untreated or continue to experience symptoms [42–44]. Untreated mental health issues increase the likelihood of employees developing common medical conditions such as diabetes, respiratory illnesses, and musculoskeletal disorders, leading to higher healthcare costs. Additionally, these conditions contribute to negative workplace impacts, including reduced productivity (presenteeism) and increased absenteeism [45]. Furthermore, experiencing loneliness at work, or feeling disconnected from colleagues, can negatively affect both an employee's mental health and overall well-being, as well as their job performance [42, 46, 47].

Best Practices for Workplace Mental Health and Well-Being

- "Raise awareness about the importance of mental health and well-being
- Assess mental health and well-being needs and measure intervention impact
- Provide and promote access to mental healthcare
- Manage psychosocial risk related to work, environment, and culture
- Integrating mental health into the wellness program inclusive of
    - ➢ Emotional wellness
    - ➢ Spiritual wellness
    - ➢ Intellectual wellness
    - ➢ Physical wellness
    - ➢ Financial wellness
    - ➢ Occupational wellness
    - ➢ Social wellness"

Future best practices will be more robust if organizations consistently track and share their experiences—both successes and challenges—in implementing workplace mental health and well-being programs. Prioritizing mental health in the workplace not only benefits individual well-being but also boosts overall organizational effectiveness.

6.4 Methodology

The present study employs a qualitative approach to critically explore the effects of artificial intelligence on employee mental health. As a conceptual paper, it centers on integrating existing literature to offer a thorough understanding of the topic. A conceptual article is a type of scholarly work that focuses on the development and explication of theoretical concepts rather than reporting empirical findings. It involves a process of defining and measuring these concepts, connecting them to a broader theoretical argument, and making an original contribution to the scholarly conversation. Conceptual articles require intellectual creativity and clarity, as they do not follow the familiar structure of empirical articles. They are valuable for providing new perspectives, theoretical frameworks, and useful definitions, often standing the test of time by yielding quote-worthy material [48].

The study provides a nuanced understanding of artificial intelligence and mental health, highlighting the impacts of AI on the mental health of employees, either positive or negative. The study concludes that AI brings opportunities and challenges for employee mental health at the workplace. It benefits by enhancing efficiency, innovation, and productivity and introduces challenges such as fear of job loss, feelings of isolation and loneliness, and increased workload. To address these situations, firms are supposed to foster a culture that values mental health and promotes healthy AI-human integration.

6.5 Impacts of AI on the Mental Health of Employees

AI holds the potential to revolutionize the way businesses operate and make decisions. AI can be looked at as a great tool for getting our work done faster and simpler. AI offers various benefits in the workplace, including increased efficiency and productivity. The impact of AI on the mental health of employees is a topic of growing interest and concern. Various studies have anticipated the negative impacts of AI on job security and workload [49, 50], and there are several positive impacts of AI on the mental health of employees. AI might replace some jobs, but it will also open new jobs [51].

The impact of AI on employee mental health is a complex and evolving issue, often occupying a grey area. The impact of AI on employee mental health includes both positive and negative aspects, as outlined below.

6.5.1 Positive Impacts of AI on the Mental Health of Employees

6.5.1.1 *Transformation to Industrial AI*

The study [2] that explored the impact of industrial AI transformation on employees' mental health in China reveals that the shift to AI-driven industries notably enhances workers' well-being. The findings indicate that this transformation contributes to better mental health by increasing workers' income and reducing their work intensity. The study concludes that countries facing labor shortages can benefit from a win-win scenario by promoting industrial AI, which not only helps bridge the labor gap but also improves employees' mental health.

6.5.1.2 *Empowerment and Job Performance*

The study of Xiaoxue *et al.* [52] explores the AI adoption on psychological empowerment of employees. The finding shows that AI technologies such as deep learning enhance psychological empowerment. This consequently improves job satisfaction, improves job performance, and reduces stress. Additionally, it increases employees' work enthusiasm, strengthens self-determination, and reduces work pressure.

6.5.1.3 *Mental Health Research and Clinical Practice*

Artificial intelligence (AI) technology holds the potential to revolutionize mental healthcare, but it also has drawbacks. The study explored AI and mental health research focused on predicting, classifying, or categorizing conditions like depression, schizophrenia, and other psychiatric disorders, as well as identifying suicidal thoughts and behaviors. These predictions were made using electronic health records (EHRs), mood rating scales, brain imaging, and emerging monitoring technologies such as smartphones and video systems. Many of these studies are still in the early stages, serving as proof of concept to demonstrate the potential of machine learning (ML) algorithms in addressing mental health issues and identifying the most effective approaches. Collectively, they show high accuracy and strong evidence of AI's promising role in mental healthcare. As AI technologies advance, they could provide mental health professionals with a more objective way to redefine mental disorders, potentially improving current diagnostic methods [3]. Several studies such as Tornero-Costa *et al.* and Wei *et al.* [53, 54] show that AI has great potential in mental health research and clinical practices.

6.5.1.4 *Chatbots for Mental Health Support*

In the study of Balcombe [4], the potential of AI chatbots to transform digital mental healthcare has been explored. This shows that AI chatbots have the potential to completely transform mental healthcare by providing accessibility, interaction, and efficiency in helping people with a variety of mental health issues and objectives. Further, AI chatbots can act as a complementary tool to traditional therapy, enhancing the overall mental healthcare experience. Other studies such as van der Schyff *et al.* and Boucher *et al.* [55, 56] also supported the relevance of AI chatbots for mental health support.

6.5.1.5 *Occupational Safety*

The study of Zacharaki *et al.* [5] states that in the transition to industrial AI, workers are replaced by robots to do risky tasks, reducing exposure to hazardous workplaces and promoting occupational safety and injury rate reduction. Robots can perform dangerous jobs, and this can save the lives of employees. By integrating AI into safety protocols, organizations can create a safer, more proactive work environment where risks are managed effectively and employees are protected.

6.5.1.6 *Employment Opportunities*

The study of Rickardo and Meiriele [6] addresses the relevant topic regarding the impact of AI on employability. The study highlighted that AI is expected to generate new job opportunities in technology-focused fields, including software development and data engineering. Moreover, the study highlights the relationship between Compensation Theory and the labor market, showcasing how workers adapt to emerging technologies. As history demonstrates, technological revolutions drive shifts in work practices and demand new skill sets. Acquiring these skills is crucial for maintaining professional relevance and employability in an increasingly competitive environment. Several other studies asserted that employability would increase where computer use is high; however, upskilling or reskilling will be required to sustain the job. Even when interviews with senior executives revealed that the majority believed AI would generate new job opportunities within their organizations [57, 58].

6.5.2 Negative Impacts of AI on the Mental Health of Employees

6.5.2.1 Occupational Stress

The study of Cooper [4] examined if the use of competitive technology in the workplace and people's interactions with the changing work environment could lead to an increase in occupational stress. According to his approach, there are six main aspects that influence workers: "job intrinsic factors, workers' roles in the organization, career development, relationships at work, organizational culture and climate, and the interface between work and home." Along with organizational problems like absenteeism, turnover, indifference, and tense labor relations, these elements can also have a detrimental impact on an individual's health.

6.5.2.2 Job Insecurity

Many workers fear being displaced as AI automates more tasks, which makes them feel insecure and confused about their job security. Long-term stress may result from this, particularly in sectors of the economy where automation has a significant impact. According to Cords and Prettner [7], AI in the workplace led to more unemployment and decreased wages for low-skilled workers. Similarly, Jung and Lim [59] found that AI reduced employment opportunities and average wages.

6.5.2.3 Pressure of Upskilling or Reskilling

The study of Jaiswal *et al.* [60] states that there is an obvious need for upskilling and reskilling as a result of the use of AI-related technology. An employee's well-being may be impacted by a mismatch between their skills and job needs, which can function as a stressor and raise employee discontent levels. The pressure to always learn new skills could have a negative impact on workers' well-being.

6.5.2.4 Workplace Surveillance

Growing workplace surveillance using AI-powered monitoring devices is another issue brought on by AI integration. Employees may feel constantly watched and under pressure to reach irrational production goals, which can lead to increased stress and burnout.

6.5.2.5 *Work Stress*

The digitization of office work through technology interventions like artificial intelligence (AI) may lead to stress among employees or increased workload. Numerous negative effects, such as mental tiredness from work, commitment problems, and turnover intents, might result from this stress [8, 61]. Stress at work affects quality of life and causes several health problems [62]. According to WHO, the growing use of ICTs has changed how employees operate. Companies are aware of the health risks that exist in the workplace, not of the risks to mental health. However, some instruction and additional measures are needed to look after the employees' mental health.

6.6 Conclusion

The integration of artificial intelligence (AI) in the workplace offers transformative opportunities while presenting complex challenges, particularly concerning employee mental health. This study explores the AI's impacts on employees' mental well-being, highlighting both positive and negative effects. Research suggests that while AI may negatively affect job security and increase workload for some, it also brings benefits, such as creating new opportunities and improving certain aspects of mental health. Although AI holds the potential to replace some jobs, it also paves the way for new roles and career paths. Numerous studies have emphasized the positive effects of AI, such as the transformative role of industrial AI in significantly improving workers' mental health. AI technologies, including deep learning, contribute to psychological empowerment, resulting in higher job satisfaction, improved performance, and reduced stress levels. Additionally, research has demonstrated AI's high accuracy and promising applications in mental healthcare, suggesting its potential to support mental health professionals in redefining and addressing mental health disorders. Additionally, robots can replace humans in doing risky tasks, reducing exposure to hazardous workplaces and promoting occupational safety and injury rate reduction. Further, new employment opportunities will be created in technology and AI-related sectors. However, the negative impacts of AI are also alarming for the mental health of employees. The adoption of AI in the workplace and people's interactions with the changing work environment could lead to an increase in occupational stress. Many workers fear being displaced as AI automates more tasks, which makes them feel insecure and confused about their job security. The digitization of office work through technology interventions like artificial intelligence (AI) may lead to stress among employees or increased workload. Numerous negative effects, such as mental tiredness from work, commitment problems, and turnover intentions, might result from this stress. The need for reskilling/upskilling may cause stress and can adversely impact mental health. In conclusion, the impact of AI on employees' mental health is multi-dimensional, offering both promising benefits and noteworthy challenges. To address the impact of AI on employee mental health adequately, firms must create a balanced approach that mitigates risks while optimizing the benefits of AI technologies.

References

1. Manfrino, M., AI and Employee Wellbeing: Navigating Human-centric Integration, Interactive Coaching, and Turnover Mitigation. *SSRN Electron. J.*, May 2024. https://doi.org/10.2139/ssrn.4821351, https://www.gratefulfoundation.org/wp-content/uploads/2024/05/Working-Paper_AI-for-Workers-Wellbeing_GF.pdf.
2. Yang, S., Liu, K., Gai, J.H., He, X., Transformation to Industrial Artificial Intelligence and Workers' Mental Health: Evidence From China. *Front. Public Health*, 10, 881827, 2022. doi: 10.3389/fpubh.2022.881827.
3. Graham, S., Depp, C., Lee, E.E., Nebeker, C., Tu, X., Kim, H.C., Jeste, D.V., Artificial Intelligence for Mental Health and Mental Illnesses: An Overview. *Curr. Psychiatry Rep.*, 21, 11, 1–18, Nov. 2019. doi: 10.1007/S11920-019-1094-0.
4. Balcombe, L., AI chatbots in digital mental health, Informatics, 10, 4, 82, 2023, MDPI, https://doi.org/10.3390/informatics10040082.
5. Zacharaki, A., Kostavelis, I., Gasteratos, A., Dokas, I., Safety bounds in human robot interaction: A survey, *Saf. Sci.*, 127, 104667, 2020. https://doi.org/10.1016/j.ssci.2020.104667.
6. Rickardo, G. and Meiriele, S., Artificial intelligence: Its impact on employability. *World J. Adv. Res. Rev.*, 18, 3, 198–203, Jun. 2023. doi: 10.30574/wjarr.2023.18.3.1056.
7. Cords, D. and Prettner, K., Technological unemployment revisited: automation in a search and matching framework. *Oxf. Econ. Pap.*, 74, 1, 115–135, 2022. doi: 10.1093/oep/gpab022.
8. Moore, J.E., One road to turnover: An examination of work exhaustion in technology professionals. *MIS Q.*, 24, 1, 141–168, 2000. doi: 10.2307/3250982.
9. Pereira, V., Hadjielias, E., Christofi, M., Vrontis, D., A systematic literature review on the impact of artificial intelligence on workplace outcomes: A multi-process perspective. *Hum. Resour. Manage. Rev.*, 33, 1, 100857, 2023. doi: 10.1016/j.hrmr.2021.100857.

10. Hutton, D.M., The Quest for Artificial Intelligence: A History of Ideas and Achievements, *Kybernetes,* 40 9/10, 1553–1553. https://doi.org/10.1108/03684921111169585.
11. Hardy, S., Book Review: The Thinking Computer: Mind inside Matter. *Q. J. Exp. Psychol.,* 29, 2, 362–363, 1997. https://doi.org/10.1080/14640747708400612n (Original work published 1977).
12. Statista, Revenues from the artificial intelligence (AI) market worldwide, in: *Statista*, 2017.
13. Kaplan, A. and Haenlein, M., Siri, Siri, in my hand: Who's the fairest in the land? On the interpretations, illustrations, and implications of artificial intelligence, *Bus. Horiz.,* 62, 1, 15–25, 2019. https://doi.org/10.1016/j.bushor.2018.08.004.
14. Walsh, T., *et al.*, The effective and ethical development of artificial intelligence: An opportunity to improve our wellbeing, in: *Australian Council of Learned Academies*, 2019.
15. *OECD Legal Instruments,* Accessed: Jun. 16, 2024. [Online]. Available: https://legalinstruments.oecd.org/en/instruments/OECD-LEGAL.
16. *ISO/IEC 22989:2022(en), Information technology — Artificial intelligence — Artificial intelligence concepts and terminology*, Accessed: Nov. 10, 2024. [Online]. Available: https://www.iso.org/obp/ui/en/#iso:std:iso-iec:22989:ed-1:v1:en.
17. Lu, Y., Artificial intelligence: a survey on evolution, models, applications and future trends, *J. Manag. Anal.*, 6, 1, 1–29, 2019. https://doi.org/10.1080/23270012.2019.1570365.
18. Zhu, Q. and Luo, J., Generative Pre-Trained Transformer for Design Concept Generation: An Exploration, in: *Proceedings of the Design Society*, 2022, doi: 10.1017/pds.2022.185.
19. *Hello GPT-4o | OpenAI*, Accessed: Nov. 10, 2024. [Online]. Available: https://openai.com/index/hello-gpt-4o/.
20. Greg, B., Ilya, S., OpenAI, *Introducing OpenAI | OpenAI*, Accessed: Nov. 11, 2024. [Online]. Available: https://openai.com/index/introducing-openai/.
21. Yenduri, G., *et al.*, GPT (Generative Pre-Trained Transformer)— A Comprehensive Review on Enabling Technologies, Potential Applications, Emerging Challenges, and Future Directions, in: *IEEE Access*, vol. 12, pp. 54608–54649, 2024, doi: 10.1109/ACCESS.2024.3389497.
22. Fourtané, S., The three types of Artificial Intelligence: Understanding AI. Interesting Engineering, Inc. 2019, Retrieved from https://interestingengineering.com/the-three-types-of-artificial-intelligence-understandingai.
23. *What is Artificial Intelligence? - GeeksforGeeks*, Accessed: Nov. 11, 2024. [Online]. Available: https://www.geeksforgeeks.org/what-is-artificial-intelligence/.
24. Lu, Y., Artificial intelligence: A survey on evolution, models, applications and future trends, *J. Manag. Anal., 6, 1,* 1–29, 2019, https://doi.org/10.1080/23270012.2019.1570365.

25. Patrício, D.I., and Rieder, R., Computer vision and artificial intelligence in precision agriculture for grain crops: A systematic review, *Comput. Electron. Agric.*, 153, 69–81, 2018. https://doi.org/10.1016/j.compag.2018.08.001.
26. Luo, X. and Xie, L., Research on artificial intelligence-based sharing education in the era of internet, in: *Proceedings - 3rd International Conference on Intelligent Transportation, Big Data and Smart City, ICITBS 2018*, 2018, doi: 10.1109/ICITBS.2018.00092.
27. Luo, D., Guide teaching system based on artificial intelligence. *Int. J. Emerging Technol. Learn.*, 13, 8, 90, 2018. doi: 10.3991/ijet.v13i08.9058.
28. Naser, M.Z., Deriving temperature-dependent material models for structural steel through artificial intelligence. *Constr. Build. Mater.*, 191, 56–68, 2018. doi: 10.1016/j.conbuildmat.2018.09.186.
29. hu Li, B., cun Hou, B., tao Yu, W., bing Lu, X., wei Yang, C., Applications of artificial intelligence in intelligent manufacturing: a review, *Front. Inf. Technol. Electron. Eng.*, Zhejiang University. 2017, https://doi.org/10.1631/FITEE.1601885.
30. Fethi, M.D. and Pasiouras, F., Assessing bank efficiency and performance with operational research and artificial intelligence techniques: A survey, *Eur. J. Oper. Res.*, 204, 2, 189–198, 2010. https://doi.org/10.1016/j.ejor.2009.08.003.
31. Grewal, D., *et al.*, The Future of Retailing, *J. Retailing*, (xxx, 2016), http://dx.doi.org/10.1016/j.jretai.2016.12.008.
32. Shalev-Shwartz, S., Shammah, S., Shashua, A., Safe, Multi-Agent, Reinforcement Learning for Autonomous Driving, in: *arXiv preprint arXiv:1610.03295v1*, 2016.
33. Adler, D.A., Fighting for Mental Health: A Personal View. *Am. J. Psychother.*, 57, 2, 277–279, 2003. doi: 10.1176/appi.psychotherapy.2003.57.2.277a.
34. Bhugra, D., Till, A., Sartorius, N., What is mental health?, *Int. J. Soc. Psychiatry*, 59, 1, 3–4, 2013. doi: 10.1177/0020764012463315.
35. World Health Organization, Mental health : strengthening mental health promotion, in: *World Health Organization*, 2007, no. September 2007.
36. Huber, M., *et al.*, How should we define health? *BMJ (Online)*, 343, 7817, 343:d4163, 2011. doi: 10.1136/bmj.d4163.
37. Galderisi, S., Heinz, A., Kastrup, M., Beezhold, J., Sartorius, N., Toward a new definition of mental health, *World psychiatry*, 14, 2, 231, 2015. DOI 10.1002/wps.20231.
38. APA dictionary of psychology. *Choice Rev. Online*, 44, 06, 44–3029, 2007. https://doi.org/10.5860/choice.44-3029.
39. Strauss, A. and Corbin, J., Grounded Theory Procedures and Techniques. *J. Environ. Psychol.*, 11, 4, 387–388, 1990. Retrieved from https://linkinghub.elsevier.com/retrieve/pii/S0272494405801173.
40. Holloway, F., Key Concepts in Mental Health: David Pilgrim. *Psychiatric Bull.*, 30, 117, 2006.

41. Kelloway, E.K., Dimoff, J.K., Gilbert, S., Mental health in the workplace. *Annu. Rev. Organ. Psychol. Organ. Behav.*, 10, 1, 363–387, 2023. https://doi.org/10.1146/annurev-orgpsych-120920-050527.
42. https://hero-health.org/wp-content/uploads/2020/09/HERO_MHWB_BestPractices_CaseExamples_091520.pdf.
43. Wulsin, L., Alterman, T., Timothy Bushnell, P., Li, J., Shen, R., Prevalence rates for depression by industry: a claims database analysis. *Soc. Psychiatry Psychiatr. Epidemiol.*, 49, 11, 1805–1821, 2014. https://doi.org/10.1007/s00127-014-0891-3.
44. Greenberg, P., Chitnis, A., Louie, D., Suthoff, E., Chen, S.Y., Maitland, J., Kessler, R.C., The Economic Burden of Adults with Major Depressive Disorder in the United States (2019). *Adv. Ther.*, 40, 10, 4460–4479, 2023. https://doi.org/10.1007/s12325-023-02622-x.
45. Centers for Disease Control and Prevention, Mental Health Disorders and Stress Affect Affect Working-Age Americans, in: *Centers for Disease Control and Prevention*, July, 2018.
46. Grossmeier, J., The Art of Health Promotion: Linking research to practice. *Am. J. Health Promot.*, 31, 5, 444–456, 2017. doi:10.1177/0890117117725842.
47. Ozcelik, H. and Barsade, S.G., No employee an island: Workplace loneliness and job performance. *Acad. Manage. J.*, 61, 6, 2343–2366, 2018. https://doi.org/10.5465/amj.2015.1066.
48. Reese, S.D., Writing the Conceptual Article: A Practical Guide. *Digit. Journal.*, 11, 7, 1195–1210, 2023. https://doi.org/10.1080/21670811.2021.2009353.
49. Korinek, A. and Stiglitz, J.E., Artificial Intelligence and Its Implications for Income Distribution and Unemployment, in: *The Economics of Artificial Intelligence*, 2019, doi: 10.7208/chicago/9780226613475.003.0014.
50. Manyika, J., *et al.*, What the Future of Work Will Mean for Jobs Skills and Wages, in: *McKinsey Global Institute*, 2017.
51. Brynjolfsson, E. and Hitt, L.M., Computing productivity: Firm-level evidence, *Rev. Econ. Stat.*, 85, 4, 793–808, 2003.
52. Xiaoxue, F., Shulang, Z., Xuan, Z., Lingchai, M., The Impact of Improving Employee Psychological Empowerment and Job Performance Based on Deep Learning and Artificial Intelligence. *J. Organizational End User Comput.*, 35, 3, 1–14, 2023. https://doi.org/10.4018/JOEUC.321639.
53. Tornero-Costa, R., Martinez-Millana, A., Azzopardi-Muscat, N., Lazeri, L., Traver, V., Novillo-Ortiz, D., Methodological and Quality Flaws in the Use of Artificial Intelligence in Mental Health Research: Systematic Review, *JMIR Mental Health,* 10, 1, e42045, 2023.
54. Wei, D.H., Hernandez, B., Burdick, D., Artificial Intelligence In Mental Health For The Aging Population: A Scoping Review. *Innov. Aging*, 7, Supplement_1, 805–805, 2023. https://doi.org/10.1093/geroni/igad104.2598.
55. van der Schyff, E., Ridout, B., Amon, K., Forsyth, R., Campbell, A., Providing Self-Led Mental Health Support Through an Artificial Intelligence–Powered Chat Bot (Leora) to Meet the Demand of Mental Health Care. *J. Med. Internet*

Res., 25, e46448, 2023. doi: 10.2196/46448. https://www.jmir.org/2023/1/e46448.
56. Boucher, E.M., Harake, N.R., Ward, H.E., Stoeckl, S.E., Vargas, J., Minkel, J., Zilca, R., Artificially intelligent chatbots in digital mental health interventions: A review. *Expert Rev. Med. Devices*, 18, sup1, 37–49, 2021. https://doi.org/10.1080/17434440.2021.2013200.
57. Masriadi, D., Ekaningrum, N.E., Hidayat, M.S., Yuliaty, F., Exploring the Future of Work: Impact of Automation and Artificial Intelligence on Employment. *Endless Int. J. Of Future Stud.*, 6, 1, 125–136, 2023. https://doi.org/10.54783/endlessjournal.v6i1.131.
58. Georgieff, A. and Hyee, R., Artificial Intelligence and Employment: New Cross-Country Evidence. *Front. Artif. Intell.*, 5, 832736, 2022. https://doi.org/10.3389/frai.2022.832736.
59. Jung, J.H. and Lim, D.G., Industrial robots, employment growth, and labor cost: A simultaneous equation analysis. *Technol. Forecast Soc. Change*, 159, 120202, 2020. https://doi.org/10.1016/j.techfore.2020.120202.
60. Jaiswal, A., Arun, C.J., Varma, A., Rebooting employees: upskilling for artificial intelligence in multinational corporations. *Int. J. Hum. Resour. Manage.*, 33, 6, 114–143, 2022. https://doi.org/10.1080/09585192.2021.1891114.
61. Giovanis, E., The relationship between flexible employment arrangements and workplace performance in Great Britain. *Int. J. Manpow.*, 39, 1, 51–70, 2018. https://doi.org/10.1108/IJM-04-2016-0083.
62. Rabenu, E., Tziner, A., Sharoni, G., The relationship between work-family conflict, stress, and work attitudes. *Int. J. Manpow.*, 38, 8, 1143–1156, 2017. https://doi.org/10.1108/IJM-01-2014-0014.

7

AI for Happy Minds: Tackling Mental Health Stigma and Boosting Social Intelligence in Gen Z

Ankita Sharma[1]*, Sunil Kumar[1] and Ridhima Sharma[2]

[1]*Alliance School of Business, Alliance University, Bangalore, Karnataka, India*
[2]*Vivekananda Institute of Professional Studies-TC, Delhi, India*

Abstract

Generation Z or Gen Z refers to those born from 1997 to 2012. Its members are characterized by unique influences from rapid digitalization, globalization, and changing cultural norms. This review examines the deep interplay between social intelligence and happiness in Gen Z: how empathy, emotional regulation, and social connection influence well-being in this cohort. The paper synthesizes existing literature on the essential role of social intelligence in boosting emotional resilience, managing digital interactions and expressions, and bridging cultural diversity. It addresses challenges like digital dependency, mental health distress, and over-achievement at school levels that prevent the development of social intelligence. The review also includes the recommendation of integrating SEL programs, technology-based empathy training, and community-driven initiatives to enhance social intelligence in Gen Z. The results make it clear that social intelligence will be a transformative tool to overcome anxiety and loneliness, which is a growing phenomenon, and thus ensure long-term happiness. It would prove to be an informative resource for educators, policymakers, and mental health practitioners in designing interventions that empower Gen Z to thrive in the increasingly digital and interconnected world.

***Keywords*:** Social intelligence, Gen Z, happiness, emotional regulation, digital interactions, life satisfaction, mental health

**Corresponding author*: ankitasharma2293@gmail.com

Ridhima Sharma, Fazla Rabby, Rohit Bansal, Timcy Sachdeva and Jihene Mrabet (eds.) Confronting Mental Health Stigma with AI and Machine Learning, (155–174) © 2026 Scrivener Publishing LLC

7.1 Introduction

Happiness is a notion indicating that humans need to spend their life optimistically. Leading a positive life entails reducing negative emotions, regularly experiencing pleasant emotions, and achieving life satisfaction [1]. A significant component that enhances individual happiness is their relationship with society or their group. The perspectives of Buss [2], an evolutionary psychologist, on enhancing individual happiness levels are significant in this context. Buss posits that individuals might bridge the divide between modernity and primitivism by cultivating ties with close family and friends. In this scenario, kids may more readily acclimatize to their life and attain happiness. Tkach and Lyubomirsky [3] highlighted the significance of fostering connections with the environment to enhance individual happiness levels. Eryılmaz and Yorulmaz [4] similarly found that individuals enhance their pleasure by forming connections with their surroundings. Eryılmaz [5] posits that individuals enhance their pleasure by responding positively to their surroundings and receiving affirmative responses from them. Consequently, individuals may enhance their happiness by forming connections with their surroundings [6]. Literature presents perspectives on the reasons individuals experience happiness while forming connections with their environments [7]. Consequently, elements such as social skills, social adequacy, and social intelligence are seen as predictors of happiness. Thorndike [8] initially articulated the notion of social intelligence as "the ability to understand and manage individuals, regardless of gender or age, and to act judiciously in human interactions." In this concept, "understanding people" is the cognitive aspect of social intelligence, while "managing people and acting wisely in human relations" represents the performance aspect. Most and Hunt [9] defined social intelligence as the capacity to interact harmoniously with others and to engage with individuals respectfully. Vernon [10] described social intelligence as the capacity to interact harmoniously with others, comfort in social situations, understanding of social dynamics, responsiveness to inputs from group members, and awareness of the emotions or characteristics of others. Wedeck [11] concentrated on the cognitive aspect of the issue, defining social intelligence as an accurate assessment of persons' feelings, moods, and motivations. Marlowe [12] defines social intelligence as "the capacity of an individual to comprehend the emotions, thoughts, and behaviors of others, including oneself, in interpersonal contexts and to respond appropriately." The literature review reveals that social intelligence has been regarded and assessed as a multifaceted construct since the earliest research. There are both overlapping and divergent elements about the components of social intelligence. Numerous studies have identified the components of social intelligence as social awareness; social facility [13]; social information processing; social skills; perceptiveness of others' internal states and moods; general interpersonal competence; knowledge of social norms and rules; insight and sensitivity in intricate social contexts; utilization of social techniques for manipulation; perspective-taking; social adaptation; attentiveness to individuals; comprehension of emotions, thoughts, and intentions; accurate judgment of others' emotions, temperament, and motivations [14]; social interest; empathy; and social performance skills. Happiness, a fundamental aspect of human well-being, has been extensively studied, with researchers associating it with characteristics such as emotional stability, financial security, and social interactions. For Generation Z, the most recent cohort in labor and academics, happiness is influenced by distinct social dynamics propelled by digitalization, globalization, and changing cultural norms.

Thorndike is credited with being the first person to create the notion of social intelligence. Social intelligence is the capacity to comprehend and effectively manage interpersonal interactions. In a world where face-to-face interactions are often replaced by alternative communication methods, the cultivation of social intelligence has become more difficult for Generation Z to maintain their emotional well-being and foster pleasure. Though enhancement of social intelligence is essential for fostering pleasure. This article analyzes the influence of social intelligence on the happiness index of Generation Z. This review aims to enhance understanding of how members of this generation manage their relationships and the emotional issues they encounter. It employs frameworks from psychology and sociology. The study's findings indicate a paucity of research explicitly examining the relationship between happiness and social intelligence [15]. This is just another revelation that has been disclosed and made public. The research on social skills, a subdimension of social intelligence, concludes that individuals exhibiting social skills attain positive social outcomes, while those lacking such skills experience negative results.

For example, the absence of social skills is indicated by social anxiety and social phobia [16], as well as depression and loneliness. Conversely, social skills and self-esteem [17], along with relationship fulfilment [18], have been found to have a statistically significant correlation. Evidence also implies that the development of pleasant encounters is good for the learning of social skills by individuals, as stated by Ryff and Singer [19]. This is a conclusion that can be drawn from the evidence. In 2001, Ryff, Singer, Wing, and Love performed research that led them to the conclusion that there is a correlation between happiness and good connections, with social skills functioning as an intermediary between the two. Furthermore, it was demonstrated that these contacts contribute to an increase in the degrees of happiness that individuals feel in their lives. When viewed from a different perspective, such as through the lens of positive psychology, characteristics that have a positive impact on the actions, feelings, and thoughts of individuals are referred to as characteristics that strengthen the character of individuals [20]. This is because these characteristics have a positive influence on the individuals' actions, feelings, and thoughts. Peterson and Seligman state that there are 24 traits that have been recognized as being components of characteristics that enhance the character of individuals. These characteristics will be discussed further in the following paragraphs. One of these traits is the ability to interact socially with intellectual acuity. According to the findings of the study that was carried out within this framework, it has been proven that there are positive connections that are statistically significant between social intelligence and the amount of happiness that individuals experience [21]. This was found to be the case. After doing an analysis of all these studies, it is reasonable to draw the conclusion that there are correlations between social intelligence and the degree of pleasure that individuals feel. These relationships are statistically significant. On the other hand, the vast bulk of the research that has been carried out on the ties that exist between happiness and social abilities or qualities that enhance character has been carried out within the field of literature. According to Bennett [22], the number of studies that focus on the direct relationship between social intelligence and enjoyment is fairly limited. On the other hand, a number of studies that focus on this connection exist. Analysis of pertinent literature on happiness reveals that individuals who are happy exhibit greater creativity and productivity compared to their less happy counterparts. They demonstrate superior problem-solving abilities and enhanced stress management skills and enjoy improved physical health and interpersonal relationships. The study of happiness, which facilitates individuals' adaptation to life events, may enhance the existing body of literature. The aim of this research is to investigate the correlation between the degrees of pleasure experienced by individuals and their levels of social intelligence.

7.2 Social Intelligence: The Framework of Understanding Gen Z Happiness

Social intelligence, according to Abdolrezapour [23], is composed of several interconnected components, such as empathy, social awareness, emotional regulation, and relationship management. These apparatuses form a framework for understanding the style through which Gen Z forms relationships, which are essential for their happiness.

7.2.1 Empathy and Social Awareness

Empathy represents the capacity or capability to comprehend and resonate with the emotions of others, whereas social awareness pertains to the acknowledgment of social signs and conventions. They are key elements of social intelligence that significantly influence Gen Z's interpersonal connections and overall satisfaction. In an era dominated by digital communication, Generation Z frequently exhibits "digital empathy," reading emotions through textual and visual clues online; nonetheless, these exchanges may lack the profundity of in-person connection [24]. Social awareness enables Generation Z to skillfully negotiate various cultural and social circumstances, promoting inclusion and collaboration. Nevertheless their advantages, issues like cyberbullying, echo chambers, and shallow digital contacts frequently hamper the comprehensive development of these abilities, constraining their capacity to foster deeper relationships and interconnectivity [25]. Confronting these difficulties by education, community involvement, and the application of technology, including virtual reality for empathy training, might enhance vital aspects of social intelligence in Generation Z [26].

7.2.2 Emotional Control and Relationship Management

Proficient emotional control is fundamental to psychological well-being, facilitating stress management, fostering healthy relationships, and cultivating resilience. Gross defined two major processes in emotional regulation: cognitive reappraisal, the act of altering the interpretation of a situation to mitigate its emotional effect, and emotional suppression, which aims to diminish the visible manifestation of emotions. For Generation Z (Gen Z), born from 1997 to 2012, these abilities are especially important due to the distinct challenges they encounter in a progressively intricate and rapid environment. These constraints encompass rigorous academic requirements, economic instability in a volatile job market, and the ubiquitous impact of social media, which frequently aggravates stress and cultivates adverse emotional conditions through continuous comparisons and exposure to idealized lifestyles. The inevitability of emotional regulation in Generation Z is highlighted by Ferguson *et al.* [27], which specify that 91% of individuals in this demographic experience physical or emotional stress symptoms, including anxiety, exhaustion, and irritability. Social media platforms facilitate connections but can intensify emotional hitches by cultivating cultures that promote validation through "likes" and comments, thereby encouraging reliance on external affirmation. The studies, parallel to Keles *et al.*, show a strong correlation between excessive use of social media and increased rates of anxiety, depression, and emotional dysregulation in Gen Z users [41].

Relationship management, another side of emotional intelligence, is also affected by Gen Z's ability to self-regulate their emotions. The quality of relationships depends much on communication, empathy, and resolving conflicts in a constructive manner—all these are dependent on emotional control. However, the digital nature of many Gen Z interactions has challenged traditional relationship building. This implies, for instance, that one cannot easily understand the implications or the emotional content of electronic communication, as in personal relationships. Moreover, online contacts create conditions and predispose people to act impulsively or immediately, which may strain a relationship further and increase interpersonal conflicts.

7.3 Social Intelligence and the Happiness Index

The happiness index is a measure that has life satisfaction, emotional well-being, and overall quality of life part of it. Social intelligence plays a huge role in the factors determining these factors for Gen Z.

7.3.1 Social Awareness and Empathy

Building Emotional Connections: Social awareness and empathy help people to form deep emotional connections, which are significant contributors to happiness. Gen Z is a generation that holds inclusivity and social justice as the highest values, so it tends to look for relationships based on understanding and emotional support. It has been shown that individuals with high social intelligence can form supportive social networks, and their happiness index is enhanced [28].

Empathy also helps Gen Z to enter and exit online-offline interactions, which allow them to build meaningful relationships even through difficult aspects of digital communication. In many cases, the happiness index, which is a measure of subjective well-being, is higher among those reporting strong social ties [29]. Social media platforms present a challenge-cum-opportunity for relationship building among Gen Z. The individuals who have more social intelligence filter superficial online relationships and get into deeper, supportive ones that contribute to happiness.

7.3.2 Emotional Regulation and Self-Awareness

Coping with Stress and Challenges: Emotional regulation is a core element of social intelligence, and it plays a significant role in managing stress and maintaining happiness. Gen Z is facing unprecedented levels of anxiety, depression, and mental health challenges [30]. Emotional regulation helps them navigate these difficulties by fostering resilience and emotional stability. Studies have shown that those who can manage their emotions well tend to be happier because they can better handle negative emotions [31].

Self-awareness, or the capacity to know what one feels emotionally, is tightly linked with emotional regulation. Gen Z suffers greatly from social comparison due to social media; they will derive more benefit from elevated levels of self-awareness because this capacity helps the individual fend off feelings of inadequacy and stress [30]. This capacity, indeed, contributes to higher incidences of happiness among socially intelligent people.

7.3.3 Social Connectedness in Cyberspace: Navigating the Online World

Today's Gen Z has a greater portion of its social life mediated by digital media. Here, social connections can be plentiful or shallow. While social networks made possible a connectivity level never heard of before, they also mean loneliness and emotional disengagement [32]. Acquiring social intelligence in such digital relationships becomes an aspect critical to determining happiness. Experts say that individuals with higher levels of social intelligence are careful enough while engaging online. They tend to curate supportive and meaningful online relationships, which enhances their emotional well-being and contributes to a higher happiness index [33]. Those challenged by social intelligence might fall into patterns of superficial connections leading to lower happiness levels.

7.4 Impact of Social Intelligence on Key Determinants of Happiness

7.4.1 Social Intelligence and Life Satisfaction

Life satisfaction is a cognitive evaluation of the general life situation of an individual. Much research has shown that subjects with more social intelligence perceive greater life satisfaction primarily through their abilities to build and maintain strong relationships with other people [34]. For Gen Z, happiness is more interwoven with the quality of their social life. Social intelligence is crucial in building life satisfaction for Gen Z. Strong social connections provide a buffer against stress, which is also a form of emotional support that is critical in keeping high levels of life satisfaction. Individuals with higher social intelligence are more adept at handling the intricacies of relationships, thereby improving overall happiness.

7.4.2 Emotional Intelligence and Mental Health

Mental health is one of the significant issues for Generation Z, due to the ever-growing number of people suffering from anxiety, depression, and other mental disorders [35]. Emotional intelligence, part of social intelligence, has been proven to support mental health in being resilient and emotionally stable. Research indicates that people who are emotionally intelligent tend to experience fewer negative mental health consequences, like depression and anxiety [36]. Gen Zers with emotional intelligence handle stress better, using healthy coping mechanisms such as getting social support and mindfulness. Such coping strategies improve mental health and increase happiness.

7.4.3 Role of Social Media in Happiness

Social media plays a sophisticated role in determining the happiness of Gen Z. Even as it opens up room for connection and self-expression, the appearance of social media introduces users to social comparison, which negatively impacts people's self-esteem and emotions [30]. Individuals who rank high in social intelligence become better equipped to face challenges; they can differentiate online interactions that are relevant or irrelevant.

Socially intelligent people can reduce the negative effects of social media on their happiness by creating positive social media experiences and limiting exposure to negative content. According to research, the happiness levels and life satisfaction of people who have positive online interactions are higher [33].

7.5 Barriers to Developing Social Intelligence for Gen Z

Although there is a clear advantage to social intelligence, Gen Z still has some disadvantages when developing these skills. The increasing reliance on digital communication also limits face-to-face time, which is an integral part of developing empathy, social awareness, and the regulation of emotions [32]. In addition, social media is often characterized as fast-paced, preventing a deep, meaningful connection, which is crucial for happiness. The challenge can be met with the help of institutions and organizations by promoting settings that would encourage the development of emotional intelligence, empathy, and social skills. It can make the case of bringing social intelligence into curricula and programs in the workplace for Gen Z to avoid the hindrances of developing their social intelligence and happiness in general.

7.5.1 Digital Dependency

Probably the greatest barrier to the development of social intelligence in Gen Z is the dependency on digital communication platforms, including social media, messaging apps, and virtual forums. Although these tools offer ease and connectivity, they tend to limit the depth and quality of interpersonal interaction. Face-to-face communication is, therefore, important to social intelligence as it requires that a person decode nonverbal information, such as facial expressions, tone, and body language. Social intelligence is very hard to replicate through text or electronic means. As Konrath *et al.* pointed out in 2011, digital communication has affected Gen Z so much, resulting in less empathic ability and ability to effectively communicate with people in actuality.

For instance, virtual conversations are often short and convenient, sacrificing active listening and emotional involvement—key elements of social intelligence. Moreover, the digital mode often encourages shallow relationships that may not have the emotional attachment and trust needed to create deep, enduring relationships. Such triviality can translate into feelings of loneliness when there is an impression of connection and decrease the happiness level of Gen Z.

7.5.2 Mental Health Challenges

The primary impediment to the cultivation of social intelligence and well-being among Generation Z is mental health issues. According to the APA (2020), 91% of Gen Z exhibit signs of stress, anxiety, or depression, rendering them the most psychologically troubled generation in history [42]. Mental health issues frequently hinder the establishment and preservation of good relationships, which are significant contributors to happiness. Individuals with anxiety or depression frequently demonstrate social retreat, challenges in emotional communication, and less empathy towards others. These talents are important for developing social intelligence. Intense stress and emotional fatigue impair decision making and dispute resolution, leading to discord in interpersonal relationships. In the absence of vigorous support structures or effective coping methods, such problems may result in a detrimental cycle of loneliness and discontent. The pervasive presence of social media aggravates these mental health challenges. The incessant flow of tailored material can adversely affect the mind, engendering emotions of inadequacy, diminished self-esteem, and fear of missing out, hence elevating stress and anxiety levels.

This emotional burden directly restricts Gen Z's capacity for meaningful interpersonal engagement, hence constraining the potential for the development of social intelligence.

7.5.3 Cultural and Social Complexity

Growing up in a more interlinked and global world, Gen Z finds it tough to negotiate diverse cultural and social contexts. Social intelligence is all about adaptability, understanding and responding to diverse cultural norms, values, and social cues. However modern digital landscapes restrict exposure to diversity, thereby making it difficult for Gen Z to develop this vital skill. Social media algorithms have a significant role in the reinforcement of "echo chambers," where people mainly interact with content and opinions aligned to their current belief systems. As indicated by Pariser [37], such echo chambers undermine the ability to interact and interact with other opposing ideas, which would otherwise open more opportunities for cultural intelligence as a subset of social intelligence. This isolation may bring about a very narrow view and challenge one's ability to understand or appreciate diverse social dynamics. Besides, increased polarization of opinions and values on digital platforms will probably stimulate competition rather than cooperation. A lack of proper tools to handle such complexity may leave individuals belonging to Gen Z unprepared for multiple social settings, which would put them at the risk of experiencing feelings of isolation and frustration, further affecting their happiness and social lives.

7.6 Knowledge Gaps in Developing Social Intelligence for Gen Z

Formal and informal education systems exert a deep influence on a person's development of social intelligence, which involves characteristics like empathy, social awareness, and relationship management capabilities. These systems significantly explain a person's interpersonal capability and happiness. However, in the existing educational scenario, there has been a misplaced emphasis on academic achievements, standardized tests, and technical competencies, which ignores the skills that are considered essential in developing social intelligence and emotional wellness in Gen Z.

7.6.1 Overemphasis on Academic Achievements

Contemporary educational systems predominantly emphasize quantifiable results such as grades, examination scores, and vocational readiness. While these are crucial for economic and professional achievement, they often compromise interpersonal and emotional competencies. Educational institutions frequently undervalue initiatives such as Social and Emotional Learning (SEL), which aim to cultivate empathy, conflict resolution skills, and effective communication.

This creates a situation where Gen Z finds itself not adequately prepared to tackle the intricacies of social relationships at both personal and professional levels. Researches have proven that SEL programs increase social competence and emotional effectiveness substantially [38]. Still, fewer than half of schools globally have included SEL in their curricula [39]. It thus contributes to an underdevelopment of social skills in general, as well as how Gen Z will form connections and be resistant to emotional breakdown.

7.6.2 Informal Education and Family Life Changes

Informal education through family and community interaction has always been a major means of social intelligence development. But changes in modern families like more work-related absenteeism and less intergenerational interactions reduced informal learning opportunities for Gen Z regarding social skills. According to Putnam [40], children brought up in families where their parents are highly involved tend to manifest stronger social skills compared to other children whose parents are less actively engage with them. A loss of informal support continues to place added stressors on formal education systems that may be ill-equipped to fulfill those new responsibilities.

7.6.3 Effects on Happiness and Social Intelligence

The lack of focus on social intelligence in school curricula is a primary reason for the decline in life satisfaction and happiness in Gen Z.

Social intelligence is intrinsically linked to happiness because it gives individuals the ability to build a good network of social relationships, resolve conflicts, and survive in various environments. Without proper educational intervention, most Gen Z children lack the necessary skills to succeed in such aspects, leading to feelings of loneliness, low self-esteem, and decreased well-being.

7.7 Addressing Gaps in Education: Bridging the Development of Academic and Social Intelligence

This would be achieved by changing education systems to focus on holistic approaches that prioritize both interpersonal and emotional skill-building. Merging targeted strategies can give students the tools they need to navigate complex social environments and enhance their overall well-being.

7.7.1 Integration of SEL Programs

SEL programs provide a curriculum-focused methodology for instructing children in the development of essential interpersonal skills, such as empathy, conflict resolution, and emotional regulation. SEL programs will assist students in effectively managing stress and cultivating the social acumen necessary for establishing meaningful connections. This has improved SEL programs for children's interpersonal skills, while also enhancing their academic performance and reducing behavioral problems [38]. Generation Z faces unique challenges, including dependence on digital technology and heightened mental health issues; therefore, support through Social and Emotional Learning (SEL) programs for navigating the emotional and social landscape is crucial.

7.7.2 Training for Teachers

Educators have a crucial role in developing children's interpersonal skills; nevertheless, most lack professional training in cultivating social intelligence. Professional development programs that improve teachers' empathy, active listening, and conflict resolution skills will empower them to effectively model and teach these characteristics. Teacher training may aid educators in creating inclusive and emotionally supportive classroom environments, where students feel safe to express themselves and engage in collaborative problem solving. This approach ensures the ongoing enhancement of social intelligence throughout a student's academic journey.

7.7.3 Community Engagement

Educational institutions may enhance social intelligence by partnering with families and communities to create supportive environments that foster interpersonal growth. Community-based initiatives, such as mentorship programs, peer support groups, and collaborative extracurricular activities, provide students the chance to cultivate their social skills in realistic environments. Engaging in community service fosters empathy and collaboration, while peer-led support groups create safe spaces for experience sharing and collective learning. Involving families and local communities can augment the benefits of social intelligence training outside the classroom environment.

7.7.4 Technology Integration

Through increased involvement and immersion, technology offers a fresh approach to teaching social awareness and empathy. Students can develop empathy and cultural awareness by using interactive and virtual experiences, such as VR simulations, which give them the chance to see things from another person's point of view. Schools can make social intelligence training more appealing and relatable to Gen Z, a generation that is highly comfortable with digital tools, by leveraging technology. Herrera *et al.* [26] research demonstrates that VR-based empathy training significantly improves users' ability to understand and respond to others' emotions, making it a potentially valuable educational resource.

7.8 Limitations of Further Studies

This review does establish a relationship between social intelligence and happiness in the Generation Z group, but at the same time, several fields of further study are not touched upon. Key among these areas is the lack of longitudinal studies on social intelligence development. While cross-sectional studies may offer a snapshot of the contemporary prevailing behaviors and attitudes, longitudinal research would reveal how the relationship between social intelligence and happiness changes as Gen Z transitions through those phases like going to work, having children, and eventually middle age. Another promising area of investigation lies in exploring cross-cultural variations. Generation Z is the foremost truly global generation, influenced by a wide range of cultural norms and societal expectations. Future studies could study how different cultural frameworks influence the development of social intelligence and how these dissimilarities impact happiness. Comparative research across countries and regions could offer valuable insights into how social intelligence contributes to happiness differently depending on cultural factors. Additionally, the impact of technology on social intelligence needs to be a focal point of research.

Being born and brought up as digital natives in social media and virtual communication, advanced technologies such as virtual reality (VR), augmented reality (AR), and artificial intelligence (AI) could impact how they form empathy, handle relationships, and control emotions, hence potentially unveiling the nature of social intelligence in the digital world. Understanding how these technologies shape social interactions may reveal both the opportunities and challenges they present for fostering happiness. Besides these fields of study, the role of social intelligence at work is one of the other important areas to conduct research in. As Generation Z floods the work environment, understanding how social intelligence impacts career performance, leadership, teamwork, and satisfaction at work may hold several implications for both the employees and the organizations. Research on whether emotional regulation and empathy have anything to do with the flow of actions in the work environment will lead to much better approaches to improving employee well-being and professional development.

Mental health still forms one of the concerns in Gen Z, and therefore, more studies are needed on that aspect of the link between social intelligence and mental well-being.

In the face of rising anxiety, depression, and stress among members of this generation, future research studies should seek to establish how aspects of social intelligence, including emotional regulation and self-awareness, can contribute to their coping mechanisms with mental health issues. This research is likely to have a greater impact in terms of developing interventions that build resilience and coping, especially as digital environments increase. Lastly, education interventions aimed at developing social intelligence are also an area that needs to be explored further. Schools and universities are the most critical institutions for promoting the development of social intelligence skills.

Future research might focus on evaluating the efficacy of different SEL programs in enhancing the skills of empathy, emotional regulation, and relationship building. Other studies that would look into how these programs impact the overall happiness and well-being of Gen Z in both academic and personal settings would be helpful for educators and policymakers.

7.9 Contribution to Future Research

This review provides a good foundation for future research in the relationship between social intelligence and happiness among Generation Z. The theoretical framework put forth here can be used for future studies to work upon. From the synthesis of current literature on social intelligence, emotional regulation, and digital communication, this paper introduces an integrating model detailing how such factors might contribute to happiness for the Gen Z population. This framework can be drawn upon for further research to create even more specific hypotheses and research designs that empirically test the relationship between social intelligence and well-being. The article also offers opportunities for empirical research. Studies that focus on particular subgroups within Generation Z—such as those belonging to different cultural, socioeconomic, or geographic backgrounds—can provide a more nuanced understanding of how social intelligence influences happiness across diverse populations. The article points out the necessity of empirical studies rigorously testing the proposed relationships between social intelligence, happiness, and life satisfaction through methods such as surveys, experiments, and case studies.

Besides guiding academic research, the insights highlighted here have a practical application for intervention programs that seek to enhance social intelligence.

Education and organizational settings are potent environments from which programs that foster empathy, emotional regulation, and relationship-building skills can be derived. Researchers and practitioners collaborate on designing interventions that improve the social intelligence of Gen Z with the primary aim of enhancing their happiness and well-being. For example, training programs on empathy drills, mindfulness, and emotional regulation practices could be planned and tested for their effects on life gratification and mental health outcomes. The findings of this review also have important policy implications. As governments and educational institutions become increasingly conscious of the mental health challenges facing Generation Z, they may turn to research on social intelligence as a solution for this problem. Policymakers can draw lessons learned from this article to support initiatives that encourage people to develop social intelligence as a route towards better well-being. This may mean the addition of SEL to school curricula or well-crafted workplace training programs that prioritize the development of social intelligence skills. The article further recommends that more research be conducted on how social intelligence can be used to counterbalance the adverse effects of social media and digital communication. While social media has opened up avenues for connecting, it also poses risks of social comparison, isolation, and shallow relationships. Further research on how socially intelligent people deal with these challenges will enable future researchers to develop frameworks to help Gen Z use digital tools in a manner that fosters meaningful interactions and happiness.

The final takeaway from this review is that social intelligence in the work environment is pertinent.

As Gen Z starts to enter the workforce, research that describes how social intelligence improves employee engagement, leadership, and teamwork may interest organizations. Further studies could look into social intelligence in improving workplace satisfaction and productivity, especially in remote or hybrid workspaces. Understanding these dynamics not only provides for organizational success but also improves the general well-being of Generation Z employees.

7.10 Conclusion

This article concludes with a comprehensive examination of how social intelligence can influence the level of happiness experienced by members of Generation Z. It is crucial to examine the function of empathy, emotional regulation, and social connectedness in the context of determining well-being to establish a foundation for future research and interventions. The digital environment in which Generation Z operates presents both opportunities and challenges for the development of social intelligence. The results of this study suggest that it is imperative to develop these abilities in order to improve their happiness index. This article contributes to the growing corpus of research on the impact of social intelligence on their well-being. It also offers a framework that can serve as a basis for additional research.

It will be crucial to conduct further research on social intelligence in order to obtain a more comprehensive comprehension of how Generation Z can achieve greater happiness and life satisfaction in a world that is becoming progressively digital and interconnected. Studies that examine the impact of technology and workplace dynamics, as well as longitudinal studies that span multiple cultures, should be included in this research. Future research, educational interventions, and policy measures that have the objective of enhancing the health and satisfaction of this generation will be based on the results of this study.

References

1. Diener, E., Subjective well-being. *Psychol. Bull., 95*, 3, 542, 1984.
2. Buss, D.M., The evolution of happiness. *Am. Psychol., 55*, 1, 15, 2000.
3. Tkach, C.T., *Unlocking the treasury of human kindness: Enduring improvements in mood, happiness, and self-evaluations*, University of California, Riverside, 2005.
4. Eryılmaz, A. and Yorulmaz, A., The way of being happy for adolescents, in: *Paper session presented at the the Xth Conference of European Association for Research on Adolescence*, Antalya, Turkey, 2006, May.
5. Eryılmaz, A., Developing a scale about subjective well being increases strategies for adolescents. *J. Turk. Psychol. Couns.*, 33, 81–88, 2010.
6. Gallagher, E.N. and Vella-Brodick, D.A., Social support and emotional intelligence as predictors of subjective well-being. *Personality Individual Differ.*, 44, 7, 1551–1561, 2008. doi:10.1016/j.paid.2008.01.011.
7. Doğan, T. and Eryılmaz, A., The role of social intelligence in happiness. *Croatian J. Educ., 16*, 3, 863–878, 2014.
8. Thorndike, E.L., Intelligence and its uses. *Harper's Mag.*, 140, 227–235, 1920.
9. Hunt, T., The measurement of social intelligence. *J. Appl. Psychol., 12*, 3, 317, 1928.
10. Vernon, P.E., Some characteristics of the good judge of personality. *J. Soc. Psychol., 4*, 1, 42–57, 1933.
11. Wedeck, J., The relationship between personality and 'psychological ability'. *Br. J. Psychol.*, 37, 33, 133–151, 1947. doi:10.1111/j.2044-8295.1947.tb01128.x.
12. Marlowe, H.A., Social intelligence: Evidence for multidimensionality and construct independence. *J. Educ. Psychol., 78*, 1, 52, 1986.
13. Goleman, D., *Social intelligence: The new science of human relationships*, Random House Inc, New York, NY, 2006.
14. Walker, R.E. and Foley, J.M., Social intelligence: Its history and measurement. *Psychol. Rep.*, 33, 839–864, 1973. doi:10.2466/pr0.1973.33.3.839.
15. Hooda, D.S. and Sharma, D.K., Generalized 'Useful'Information Generating Functions. *J. Appl. Math. Inf., 27*, 3-4, 591–601, 2009.
16. Wenzel, A., Graff-Dolezal, J., Macho, M., Brendle, J.R., Communication and social skills in socially anxious and nonanxious individuals in the context of romantic relationships. *Behav. Res. Ther.*, 43, 4, 505–519, 2005. doi:10.1016/j.brat.2004.03.010.
17. Doğan, T. and Çetin, B., The investigation of relationship between social intelligence, depression and some variables at university students. *J. Int. Hum. Sci.*, 5, 2, 1–19, 2008.
18. Buhrmester, D., Furman, W., Wittenberg, M.T., Reis, H.T., Five domains of interpersonal competence in peer relationships. *J. Personality Soc. Psychol.*, 55, 6, 991–1008, 1988.

19. Ryff, C.D. and Singer, B., Interpersonal flourishing: A positive health agenda for the new millennium, in: *Personality and Social Psychology at the Interface*, pp. 30–44, Psychology Press, New York, 2014. DOI: https://doi.org/10.4324/9780203764923.
20. Park, N., Peterson, C., Seligman, M.E., Strengths of character and well-being. *J. Soc. Clin. Psychol.*, *23*, 5, 603–619, 2004.
21. Ruch, W. and Stahlmann, A.G., 15 years after Peterson and Seligman (2004): a brief narrative review of the research on the 12 criteria for character strengths– the forgotten treasure of the *via* Classification, in: *Zusammen wachsen-Förderung der positiv-psychologischen Entwicklung von Individuen*, pp. 142–172, Organisationen und Gesellschaft, Switzerland, 2019. https://www.researchgate.net/profile/Willibald-Ruch/publication/340315139_Running_head_A_brief_review_of_the_research_on_the_12_criteria_for_VIA_character_strengths_1_15_years_after_Peterson_and_Seligman_2004_A_brief_narrative_review_of_the_research_on_the_12_criteria_for_c/links/5e839af892851c2f5270d3b6/Running-head-A-brief-review-of-the-research-on-the-12-criteria-for-VIA-character-strengths-1-15-years-after-Peterson-and-Seligman-2004-A-brief-narrative-review-of-the-research-on-the-12-criteria-for-c.pdf.
22. Bennett, B., *Social intelligence of undergraduates enrolled in traditional vs. distance higher education learning programs*, Walden University, United States, 2015, https://www.proquest.com/docview/1690904238?pq-origsite=gscholar&fromopenview=true&sourcetype=Dissertations%20&%20Theses.
23. Abdolrezapour, P. and Tavakoli, M., The relationship between emotional intelligence and EFL learners' achievement in reading comprehension. *Innov. Lang. Learn. Teach.*, *6*, 1, 1–13, 2012.
24. Konrath, S.H., O'Brien, E.H., Hsing, C., Changes in dispositional empathy in American college students over time: A meta-analysis. *Personality Soc. Psychol. Rev.*, *15*, 2, 180–198, 2011.
25. Kim, S. and Faith, M.S., Cyberbullying and ICT use by immigrant youths: A serial multiple-mediator SEM analysis. *Children Youth Serv. Rev.*, *110*, 104621, 2020.
26. Herrera, F., Bailenson, J., Weisz, E., Ogle, E., Zaki, J., Building long-term empathy: A large-scale comparison of traditional and virtual reality perspective-taking. *PLoS One*, *13*, 10, e0204494, 2018.
27. Ferguson, C.J., Copenhaver, A., Markey, P., Reexamining the findings of the American Psychological Association's 2015 task force on violent media: A meta-analysis. *Perspect. Psychol. Sci.*, *15*, 6, 1423–1443, 2020.
28. Valkenburg, P.M., Koutamanis, M., Vossen, H.G., The concurrent and longitudinal relationships between adolescents' use of social network sites and their social self-esteem. *Comput. Hum. Behav.*, *76*, 35–41, 2017.
29. Helliwell, J.F., The Social Context of Well-being. *Philos. Trans. R. Soc. London Ser. B Biol. Sciences*, 2004. https://scholar.google.com/scholar?hl=en&as_sdt=0%2C5&q=Helliwell%2C+J.F.%2C+The+Social+Context+of+

Well-being.+Philos.+Trans.+R.+Soc.+London+Ser.+B+Biol.+Sciences%2C+2004&btnG=.

30. Twenge, J.M., Why increases in adolescent depression may be linked to the technological environment. *Curr. Opin. Psychol.*, *32*, 89–94, 2020.
31. Gross, J.J. and John, O.P., Individual differences in two emotion regulation processes: implications for affect, relationships, and well-being. *J. Pers. Soc. Psychol.*, *85*, 2, 348, 2003.
32. Turkle, S., Stop googling. Let's talk. *New Y. Times*, *27*, 2015. https://scholar.google.com/scholar?hl=en&as_sdt=0%2C5&q=Turkle%2C+S.%2C+Stop+-googling.+Let%E2%80%99s+talk.+New+Y.+Times%2C+27%2C+2015.&btnG=New york times. It is an article.
33. Valkenburg, P.M., Understanding self-effects in social media. *Hum. Commun. Res.*, *43*, 4, 477–490, 2017.
34. Kahneman, D. and Deaton, A., High income improves evaluation of life but not emotional well-being. *Proc. Natl. Acad. Sci.*, *107*, 38, 16489–16493, 2010.
35. Twenge, J.M. and Joiner, T.E., US Census Bureau-assessed prevalence of anxiety and depressive symptoms in 2019 and during the 2020 COVID-19 pandemic. *Depression Anxiety*, *37*, 10, 954–956, 2020.
36. Mayer, J.D., Salovey, P., Caruso, D.R., Emotional intelligence: Theory, findings, and Implications. *Psychol. Inq.*, *15*, 3, 197–215, 2004.
37. Pariser, E., *The filter bubble: What the Internet is hiding from you*, Penguin Press, USA, 2011. https://www.google.co.in/books/edition/The_Filter_Bubble/-FWO0puw3nYC?hl=en&gbpv=1&pg=PT7&printsec=frontcover.
38. Schonert-Reichl, K.A., Oberle, E., Lawlor, M.S., Abbott, D., Thomson, K., Oberlander, T.F., Diamond, A., Enhancing cognitive and social–emotional development through a simple-to-administer mindfulness-based school program for elementary school children: A randomized controlled trial. *Dev. Psychol.*, *51*, 1, 52, 2015.
39. Frye, K.E., Boss, D.L., Anthony, C.J., Du, H., Xing, W., Content analysis of the CASEL framework using K–12 state SEL standards. *Sch. Psychol. Rev.*, *53*, 3, 208–222, 2024.
40. Lynch, Y.L.K., *The Impact Of Parental Involvement On Children's Soft Skills, Academic Achievement, And Income In Zambia And The United States Of America*, Monash University, 2021, Doctoral dissertation. https://bridges.monash.edu/articles/thesis/THE_IMPACT_OF_PARENTAL_INVOLVEMENT_ON_CHILDREN_S_SOFT_SKILLS_ACADEMIC_ACHIEVEMENT_AND_INCOME_IN_ZAMBIA_AND_THE_UNITED_STATES_OF_AMERICA_/16651810?file=30832207.
41. Keles, B., McCrae, N., Grealish, A., A systematic review: the influence of social media on depression, anxiety and psychological distress in adolescents. *Int. J. Adolesc. Youth*, 25, 1, 79–93, 2019. https://doi.org/10.1080/02673843.2019.1590851.
42. https://www.apa.org/news/press/releases/stress/2020/report-october.

Part II

MACHINE LEARNING MEETS MINDFULNESS: LEVERAGING AI FOR MENTAL WELL-BEING

8

Ugly Truth About Technology and Mental Health Stigma

Sachin, Vineet Kumar, Popu Ram, Palvi, Saurabh Singh, Dileep Singh Baghel*, Bimlesh Kumar and Narendra Kumar Pandey

School of Pharmaceutical Sciences, Lovely Professional University, Phagwara, India

Abstract

In recent years, the relationship between technology and mental health has grown to be a major source of worry, particularly as digital platforms increasingly influence societal perceptions and personal experiences. While technology has enabled unprecedented access to mental health resources, it has also exacerbated mental health stigma in subtle yet pervasive ways. The "ugly truth" is how digital communication, social media, and online culture all play a part in the stigma of mental health problems. This is frequently done by promoting toxic optimism, disseminating false information, and damaging stereotypes. Additionally, the anonymity of online interactions can lead to cyberbullying and the trivialization of serious mental health conditions. This chapter explores the dual-edged nature of technology's role in mental health, examining both its potential for positive impact and the significant challenges it poses. By analyzing the influence of digital platforms on public discourse and individual behavior, this study highlights the need for a more nuanced approach to integrating technology into mental health initiatives, emphasizing the importance of digital literacy, ethical design, and inclusive policies to combat stigma and support mental well-being in the digital age.

Keywords: Technology, mental health, misinformation, stigma, artificial intelligence, social media

**Corresponding author*: baghel_12@rediffmail.com

Ridhima Sharma, Fazla Rabby, Rohit Bansal, Timcy Sachdeva and Jihene Mrabet (eds.) Confronting Mental Health Stigma with AI and Machine Learning, (177–202) © 2026 Scrivener Publishing LLC

8.1 Introduction

Technology has altered how we live, work, and interact by providing unparalleled access to information, resources, and communication channels. In terms of mental health, technology improvements have created new options for awareness, education, and assistance. Digital platforms, mental health applications, and social media have all helped to break down boundaries, making it simpler for people to seek treatment and connect with others suffering similar issues [1]. However, this advancement has a darker side. While technology has the ability to democratize mental health treatment, it also contributes significantly to the perpetuation and exacerbation of mental health stigma [2]. The "ugly truth" is that the instruments intended to aid can also cause harm, disseminating disinformation, reinforcing prejudices, and trivializing severe mental health disorders. A common and essential societal issue, people who battle mental illness are adversely affected by the stigma attached to it. The stigma associated with mental illness continues to be a major obstacle to receiving understanding, acceptance, and treatment, despite increased awareness of the issue and efforts to overcome it. Stigma is the term used to describe unfavorable views, opinions, and actions against someone due to their condition of mental health [3]. It can manifest in a variety of ways, including internalized feelings of worthlessness and humiliation, prejudice, and social exclusion. The stigma associated with mental illness affects not just those who suffer but also those around them, such as friends, family, employers, and medical professionals. People with mental health disorders frequently experience unfair or different treatment as a result of their illness. In the modern era, technology has become deeply associated with our daily lives, offering numerous opportunities to improve mental health support. The impact of technology in increasing awareness of mental health concerns cannot be denied. The accessibility of information and assistance has been facilitated by social media campaigns, virtual support groups, and mental health applications. People from diverse backgrounds may now educate themselves on mental health issues and available treatments because of the internet's democratization of knowledge [4]. By removing constraints related to finances and location, telehealth programs have also increased accessibility to therapy and counseling. Technology has the power to completely transform mental health services and public understanding, but it also poses serious problems that need to be resolved. The harsh reality is that technology has the potential to worsen the exact problems it is meant to address if it is not used with caution and preventative actions. We can use technology to help mental health and well-being rather than undermine it by building a more compassionate online community, enforcing ethical standards, and increasing digital literacy [5]. This chapter explores how technology affects mental health in a complicated and sometimes conflicting way. It looks at how digital platforms may be a lifeline for those in need as well as a source of stigma that keeps people from asking for assistance. Technology can help individuals who might not otherwise have access to mental health treatment by facilitating access to services, but it can also reinforce stigmas and disseminate harmful ones [6].

8.2 Psychological Impacts of Technology-Induced Stigma

The term "technology-induced stigma" describes the unfavorable opinions or prejudices that people encounter because of their use of technology or because they are connected to particular tech-related conditions or behaviors. The psychological effects of this stigma can be profound and can have a variety of effects on people's mental health and general well-being [7]. Here are a few significant psychological effects:

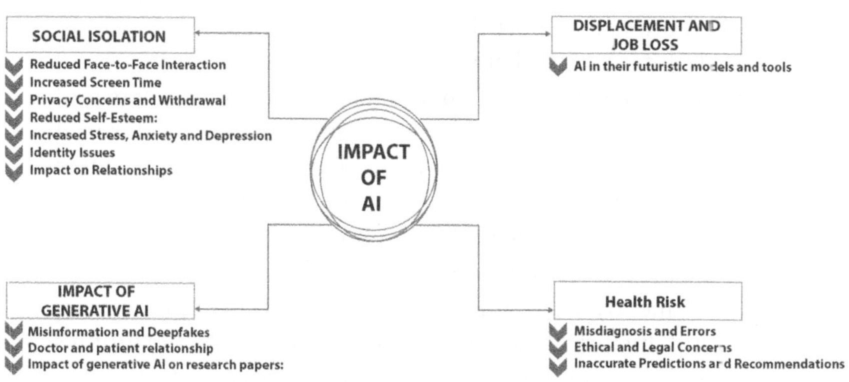

1. **Social Isolation:** Social isolation may occur for those who are stigmatized for their use of technology or problems connected to it (such as gaming addiction, excessive use of social media, or limitations related to technology). It is possible that they retreat from social connections and support systems because they feel misinterpreted or condemned. Rather than lessening social isolation, the growing dependence on artificial intelligence (AI) technology might make

it worse. Research suggests that although personal AI can be useful for organizing activities and timetables, it also presents serious hazards to real-world human communication [8].

a) **Reduced Face-to-Face Interaction:** People may rely less on in-person encounters as AI technologies such as chatbots, virtual assistants, and online platforms proliferate. This could lead to a greater reliance on these tools for communication and problem solving. A decline in deep, personal social ties may result from this.

   Virtual assistants and other personal AI systems have the potential to foster a culture in which people engage with machines more often than with one another, which could make people feel alone even in social situations. Because AI has the potential to replace opportunities for genuine socialization, this situation is similar to feeling entirely alone yet being surrounded by people. There may be a lack of genuine human interaction if people rely too much on AI for company or social interaction, such as when chatbots with AI capabilities are used for conversation. These contacts may not offer the depth and emotional support that come with human relationships, despite the fact that they can be convenient [8, 9].

b) **Increased Screen Time:** Screen time can be increased by AI-driven apps like streaming services and social network algorithms. Prolonged usage of these devices may result in fewer in-person social interactions and a preference for virtual interactions over real-world ones. Echo chambers may be produced by AI algorithms that frequently select information based on user preferences and historical activity. This may lessen opportunities for meaningful social contacts with a wider spectrum of people and limit exposure to other points of view [7].

c) **Privacy Concerns and Withdrawal:** Concerns about AI privacy and data collecting may cause people to avoid social media and internet platforms. This retreat may be caused by a fear of being watched or of having personal information misused, which can lead to social isolation. Because artificial intelligence (AI) systems gather and process enormous amounts of personal data, they present serious privacy concerns when they are integrated into daily technology. Concerns about informational privacy include the possibility that private information will be misused or accessed without authorization, which could cause users to feel uneasy or anxious. Predictive harm is a serious issue as well, as AI systems have the ability to deduce private information about people from seemingly innocent data, which could result in privacy violations. For instance, even in situations when explicit disclosure is not required, data compiled from social media or online interactions can disclose private information about a person's life, such as health conditions or religious convictions [10, 11].

Data permanence presents additional difficulties for AI systems since gathered data may be kept forever, raising the possibility of misuse. Further privacy issues arise when data is repurposed for purposes other than those for which it was originally intended without the approval of the user, since people might not be aware of the uses to which their data is being put [9].

d) **Reduced Self-Esteem:** Concerns regarding lower self-esteem have been raised by the development of artificial intelligence since people may make negative comparisons between themselves and the apparently faultless and effective outputs of AI systems. People may feel inferior to AI and question their own value and ability when they observe AI completing jobs with amazing accuracy and speed. This effect is more noticeable in domains where AI shines, like creativity or problem solving, and it may cause people who think they are less capable to become less confident. Furthermore, people may feel more inadequate as a result of their continuous exposure to carefully chosen, idealized portrayals of other people made possible by AI-driven platforms. This is because they may find it difficult to live up to these unattainable expectations [12].

e) **Increased Stress, Anxiety, and Depression:** Stress and anxiety levels can rise as a result of the strain of dealing with stigma. An ongoing state of stress brought on by worries about being assessed or suffering bad outcomes can have an adverse effect on mental health. People are experiencing more worry and anxiety as a result of artificial intelligence's growth since they are trying to understand the quick speed of technological advancement and how it will affect their personal and professional lives. The worry that automation may cause job losses can intensify worries about future job security and career stability. Furthermore, people may feel overwhelmed and stressed out due to the pervasiveness of AI in daily life, which includes the pressure to be up to date with technical breakthroughs and the constant need to be connected through digital gadgets. Finding moments of peace and maintaining mental health can be difficult due to the constant flow of information and the pressure to be present and attentive at all times [9].

f) **Identity Issues:** Identity uncertainty or conflict can be brought on by stigma. The stigma associated with using technology can cause people—like influencers or tech enthusiasts—who depend on it for their identity or means of subsistence to struggle with self-acceptance and self-worth. Because artificial intelligence can make it difficult to distinguish between human and machine contributions, people may begin to doubt the veracity of their own experiences and accomplishments. People's ability to distinguish between their own characteristics and those produced by technology may become more difficult as AI systems imitate human behavior and creativity more and more, which could undermine people's sense of identity. This can be particularly concerning in creative industries, as artificial intelligence (AI)-generated content may eclipse human creativity and make people question their worth and position in their respective fields. Furthermore, people may find it challenging to maintain a consistent and authentic sense of self in the face of a sea of artificial influences due to the widespread usage of AI in curating online personas and interactions, which can lead to fragmented or inauthentic representations of identity [9].

g) **Impact on Relationships:** Intimate connections may be strained by stigma. Negative opinions about technology use from friends, family, or coworkers may cause them to become aloof or judgmental, which can harm their social support network and mental health. Artificial intelligence has had a profound effect on interpersonal relationships, both favorably and unfavorably. On the one hand, AI-powered solutions boost accessibility and convenience and hence build relationships by facilitating communication by enabling rapid contacts over great distances. For example, linguistic barriers are removed by AI-powered translation services, promoting partnerships and exchanges across cultural boundaries. But there are drawbacks to AI as well. Constantly interacting with digital assistants and social media algorithms might lead to a disconnection from real human connections. Because AI can mimic human interactions, people may choose to communicate with digital entities rather than develop meaningful, deep connections with real people. This could result in shallow or less meaningful relationships [7].

2. **Displacement and Job Loss:** AI can lead to job displacement in various sectors, affecting individuals' social and economic stability. The stress and economic strain from job loss or career changes can contribute to feelings of isolation and reduced social interaction.
   - The number of occupations that artificial intelligence (AI) would replace has been predicted by researchers from the University of Oxford and other institutions, although their estimates have ranged greatly, from 9 to 47 percent.

     The vast variation might be attributed to differences in technique, one of which is the researchers' belief regarding the automation of a particular task or the occupation as a whole.
   - In the end, these studies offer very little insight into how the nature of labor is changing and even less insight into what policies should be implemented in response; policymakers should approach with caution [13].

8.3 The Impact of AI

The growing application of AI has already started to result in job losses in industries like manufacturing and retail. The number of employment available for human workers in the manufacturing sector has decreased as a result of the usage of robots and other forms of automation. For instance, a lot of manufacturing organizations now use robots to carry out formerly performed by human workers jobs like welding and assembling. As a result, there are now fewer positions available for human laborers, especially in sectors like the automobile manufacturing industry. AI has also had a significant impact on the retail business. The number of positions accessible for human workers has decreased as a result of the usage of AI in functions like inventory management, customer support, and sales. For instance, a lot of retail businesses today use automated technologies to do duties previously performed by human workers, like order processing and shelf restocking. Furthermore, as more people shop online, there are fewer positions available for actual workers at physical retail establishments [14].

In the US, for instance, nearly 51 million jobs were lost and 179 million new employments were generated in 10 years between 2006 and 2016. The number of jobs generated and terminated since data collection is shown in the chart below. Figure 8.1 data showing jobs created and destroyed due to AIAI. A third of the 152 million jobs that existed in December 2016 were lost due to unemployment during the preceding 10 years, which is not too far from some projections of the loss of jobs due to AI [15].

Some famous companies are working on adding AI to their futuristic models and tools, which can replace the human jobs.

- Due to the prohibitive expenses of developing autonomous automobiles, longtime rivals Daimler and BMW have combined their resources.

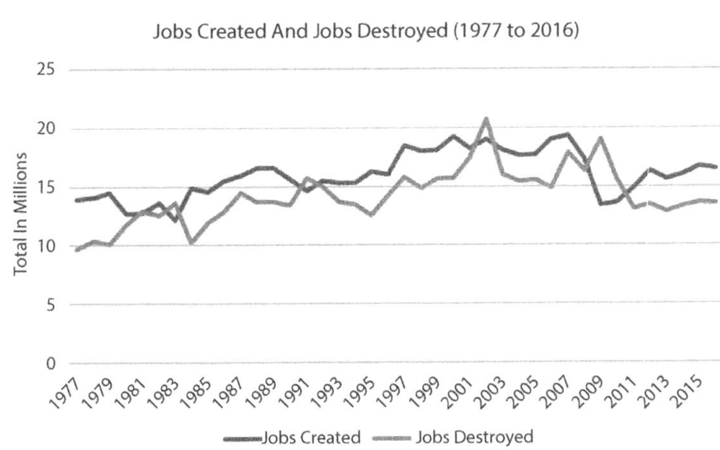

Figure 8.1 Jobs created and jobs destroyed by AI.

- Walmart: The massive retailer has been utilizing artificial intelligence (AI) in its stores to handle inventory and replenish shelves, among other functions. As a result, there are now fewer positions open for human laborers, especially in the company's warehouses.
- Uber recently secured $1 billion for its division dedicated to autonomous vehicles; McDonald's reportedly paid over $300 million for the AI startup Dynamic Yield, funded by Silicon Valley VC, making it the fast-food giant's largest acquisition since it acquired Boston Market in 1999.
- Ford gave Argo a nearly $1 billion investment to support its driverless car research; IBM Watson is discontinuing sales of its artificial intelligence drug-discovery tool following a string of disappointments and lackluster earnings [16].
- In March, Johnson & Johnson acquired surgical robotics pioneer Auris Health and its FDA-approved Monarch technology for $3.4 billion.
- Foxconn: In its plants, robots have been taking the place of human laborers in the electronics manufacturing business. Foxconn provides brands like Apple and Samsung. By 2020, the corporation wants to replace 60,000 employees with robots.
- UPS: In an effort to lessen the need for human labor, the corporation has been investigating the use of robots and drones for activities like package delivery.
- JPMorgan Chase: The bank has been utilizing artificial intelligence (AI) for managing portfolios and detecting fraud. As a result, there are now fewer positions in these areas that require human laborers.
- Amazon: Since utilizing robots in its warehouses for a number of years, the corporation has reduced the amount of positions open to human laborers. For instance, the business has reduced the need for human labor by implementing a system dubbed "Amazon Robotics" that uses robots to carry things throughout its warehouses.

These are simply a few instances, but it is evident that artificial intelligence (AI) technology is being used across a range of industries, potentially leading to a decrease in the number of jobs available for human labor. Businesses should think about how AI might affect employment and create plans to assist employees who lose their jobs to automation.

1. **Impact of Generative AI:** The emergence of artificial intelligence-generated information has significant consequences for mental health, impacting people's psychological state in intricate ways. AI-generated media can, on the one hand, improve access to therapy and provide prompt assistance by offering personalized mental health resources like chatbot-based support and therapeutic content. But the widespread use of AI-generated photos, texts, and videos can also worsen mental health conditions by fostering irrational expectations and intensifying feelings of inferiority. AI-generated content that has been meticulously selected and manipulated, for instance, has the potential to warp people's understanding of reality and cause fear and unfavorable self-comparisons. Further harming mental health is the continual exposure to algorithm-driven content that is optimized for engagement but can also lead to information overload and a shorter attention span.
   a) **Misinformation and Deepfakes:** The dangers of deepfakes and false information have increased dramatically with the use of generative AI, presenting major obstacles to public trust and information integrity. Deepfakes are artificial intelligence (AI)-produced photos, videos, or audio recordings that appear extremely realistic but are actually fake. These fakes can be used to manipulate and trick people, eroding the trustworthiness of real information and disseminating misleading stories. This technology makes it possible to produce convincing but deceptive media, which can damage public perception, undermine faith in reliable sources, and aid in the dissemination of erroneous information. The difficulty of identifying real content from false increases with the sophistication of deepfakes, therefore compounding the issue of disinformation. Such content can have far-reaching effects from influencing elections and igniting social unrest to harming people's reputations and undermining the credibility of news and information sources when it is widely disseminated. To limit the potential hazards of generative AI, addressing these difficulties calls for improved detection tools, media literacy campaigns, and strong regulatory frameworks [17].

b) **Impact on Patient and Doctor Relationship:** The patient-doctor connection is significantly altered by generative AI, which can change interactions in both favorable and difficult ways. On the one hand, AI-powered solutions improve patient care by giving physicians access to advanced diagnostic assistance, tailored treatment suggestions, and reduced administrative duties, freeing up more time for valuable patient interaction. In addition to providing patients with easier access to medical information and virtual consultations, AI-driven systems can also increase accessibility and convenience. However, by adding a layer of technology mediation that could erode the human connection necessary for providing quality care, the incorporation of AI into health care also has the potential to upset the established patient-doctor dynamic. If conversations are mostly mediated by AI technologies or if patients believe that their problems are being filtered through algorithms rather than being answered directly by a human, they may feel cut off from their physicians. Furthermore, depending too much on AI may raise issues with data privacy and the impersonal nature of automated interactions, which could undermine patient care's compassionate elements and foundation of trust. A solid and productive patient-doctor connection depends on striking a balance between the growth of technology and the maintenance of human, compassionate relationships [18].

c) **Impact of Generative AI on Research Papers:** Although generative AI has made great strides in text generation, there are serious hazards to the reliability and caliber of research articles. AI's ability to generate content that sounds convincing but is actually false or misleading can easily lead to the spread of studies that are not thoroughly verified or subjected to critical examination. This could compromise the validity of academic work because AI-generated texts might unintentionally repeat mistakes or spread unsubstantiated claims, which would damage academic research's credibility and make it harder for scholars to separate meaningful contributions from ones that are superficial or flawed.

- **Quality and Accuracy Concerns:** Content produced by AI may be shallow, naive, or inaccurate. Text generated by generative models may sound convincing but may not be fact-checked or supported by rigorous science. If adequately verified, this could result in the dissemination of inaccurate or misleading information. The integration of AI in generating research papers raises significant quality and accuracy concerns. AI tools can produce content that seems coherent and well-structured but may lack the depth of understanding and critical insight necessary for rigorous academic work. These systems are prone to generating errors, outdated information, or biased perspectives based on the data they have been trained on. Consequently, research papers created or heavily influenced by AI might present flawed analyses, misinterpret data, or fail to address key nuances of the subject matter. This can lead to the dissemination of unreliable information and compromise the integrity of scholarly research.
- **Loss of Critical Thinking and Creativity:** When AI is used to generate research papers, creativity and critical thinking skills might be noticeably lost. When AI tools are used to generate content, they frequently adhere to preexisting data-driven patterns and structures, which might inhibit creative thinking and innovative methods. It is possible that researchers will rely too much on AI to help with brainstorming and drafting, which could homogenize ideas and discourage creative problem solving. This dependence may lessen the importance of human intellectual participation in the research process, where original ideas and insightful analysis are crucial for expanding our understanding and producing significant scholarly output [9].
- **Plagiarism Risks:** When AI is used to create research papers, there is a greater chance of plagiarism since these programs may unintentionally copy material from their training set or combine ideas from other sources without giving credit where credit is due. Artificial intelligence (AI) models have the potential to produce information that is unduly similar to

previous research or that rewords it in ways that are not sufficiently unique, which could result in accidental plagiarism. It may be difficult for researchers to discern between novel concepts and AI-generated content that mimics previously published work, making it more difficult to maintain academic integrity and guarantee correct citation. This could lead to moral lapses and legal problems, undermining the validity of academic research [19].

- **Increased Workload for Researchers:** Although AI can simplify a lot of tasks, the research workflow may become more complicated as a result of it. It can take more time for researchers to make sure AI-generated content is correct, well attributed, and in line with the objectives of the study.

2. **Health Risk:** The use of AI in health care can pose several risks to patient safety and well-being. AI systems, if not meticulously designed and validated, may provide incorrect diagnoses or treatment recommendations due to limitations in their training data or errors in algorithmic processing. This can lead to mismanagement of health conditions, potentially worsening patient outcomes. Additionally, overreliance on AI tools might diminish the role of human oversight and critical evaluation, further increasing the risk of harm. Moreover, concerns about data privacy and security also arise, as sensitive patient information could be vulnerable to breaches or misuse if not properly protected [20].
   a. **Misdiagnosis and Errors:** AI systems in health care, while promising, can be prone to misdiagnoses and errors due to several factors. These systems rely on extensive datasets for training, which may contain biases, incomplete information, or inaccuracies, potentially leading to flawed outputs. AI algorithms might misinterpret patient data or fail to account for rare or atypical conditions, resulting in incorrect diagnoses or inappropriate treatment recommendations. Additionally, AI lacks the nuanced understanding of a human clinician, potentially missing context or subtleties in patient symptoms. Overreliance on AI without adequate human oversight

can exacerbate these issues, compromising patient safety and treatment efficacy.

b. **Ethical and Legal Concerns:**
   - **Informed Consent:** Because AI systems are complicated, patients can find it challenging to completely comprehend how their data is utilized or how AI tools affect their care. This could make getting informed permission more difficult.
   - **Accountability:** It might be difficult to assign blame for mistakes or unfavorable results that arise from AI-driven judgments. Who is responsible—the AI system itself, the health care practitioners, or the developers?—becomes a legal and ethical concern in light of this.

c. **Inaccurate Predictions and Recommendations:** In health care, AI's inaccurate predictions and recommendations can have serious consequences. AI systems, which are trained on historical data, may generate flawed predictions if the data is biased, outdated, or unrepresentative of diverse patient populations. This can lead to incorrect risk assessments, inappropriate treatment plans, or missed diagnoses. For instance, an AI tool might misinterpret symptoms or fail to recognize rare conditions, resulting in ineffective or harmful recommendations. Additionally, the reliance on AI without sufficient human validation can exacerbate these issues, as clinicians may overtrust AI-generated insights, potentially compromising patient care and safety [21].

8.4 Social Media's Impact on Mental Health Stigma

Social media networks such as Facebook, Instagram, Twitter, and TikTok have become essential for modern communication, particularly among young people. These platforms provide open forums for people to discuss their mental health, breaking down the isolation that frequently comes with mental illnesses [22]. For many people, social media gives a sense of belonging and validation, with support groups, instructional resources, and advocacy efforts that combat stigma. However, the nature of social media encourages the spread of destructive narratives. The urge to offer a controlled, idealized image of life can result in unfair comparisons, fueling feelings of inadequacy and self-doubt. When mental health concerns are discussed on these forums, they frequently elicit varied views. On the one hand, there is a groundswell of support and unity. On the other side, these platforms can foster cyberbullying and trivialize mental health issues [23].

For example, the emergence of "toxic positivity" on social media, a culture that emphasizes a never-ending focus on happiness and dismisses unpleasant emotions, can invalidate the experiences of persons suffering from mental illnesses [24]. The reduction of complicated mental health concerns to memes, hashtags, or shallow advice can diminish the gravity of disorders such as depression, anxiety, and bipolar disorder. Furthermore, the anonymity of online interactions might encourage people to participate in stigmatizing behaviors, such as making disparaging remarks or disseminating misinformation about mental health [25].

8.5 Misinformation and the Spread of Myths About Mental Health

The internet era has made more information available than ever before, but it has also enabled the spread of disinformation. Mental health is an especially sensitive area where myths and misconceptions may quickly take hold and proliferate [26]. Social media networks' algorithms prioritize interaction above accuracy. As a result, sensationalized, inaccurate, or simply fraudulent information about mental health may spread swiftly, shaping public opinions and promoting stigma [27].

Misconceptions regarding mental health issues, such as the assumption that sadness is merely a lack of willpower or that anxiety is overreacting, can be perpetuated *via* viral material. These beliefs not only mislead the public, but also contribute to the stigmatization of those living with these disorders [28]. When people come across this misinformation online, it can influence their attitudes and behaviors, leading to increased prejudice and diminished compassion for individuals dealing with mental health issues.

Furthermore, the dissemination of disinformation can have catastrophic effects on individuals seeking assistance. Individuals may be discouraged from obtaining professional therapy owing to stigma, or they may resort to unproven, sometimes hazardous cures obtained online. This can worsen mental health disorders, making it difficult for people to get the assistance they require [29].

8.6 The Effects of Technology on Help-Seeking Behavior

One of the most significant ways technology affects mental health is by influencing help-seeking behaviors. On the plus side, technology has made it simpler for people to find mental health support [30]. Online therapy, mental health applications, and telehealth services have eliminated obstacles to care such as physical distance, expense, and the stigma associated with in-person appointments. These resources can be a lifeline for folks who would otherwise be unable or reluctant to seek assistance [31].

However, the same reason that makes technology an effective aid for mental health can also discourage people from getting adequate therapy. The stigmatization of mental health concerns on social media and other online platforms might deter people from freely sharing their problems or seeking treatment [32]. The dread of being criticized, mocked, or ignored can cause people to internalize their difficulties, aggravating feelings of guilt and loneliness [33].

Furthermore, the amount of mental health material available online may be overwhelming, making it difficult for people to discriminate between reliable sources and disinformation [34]. The ubiquity of self-diagnosis *via* online quizzes or symptom checkers might result in misunderstanding of symptoms, delaying correct diagnosis and treatment. In other situations, people may become unduly reliant on digital resources like apps or forums rather than seeking professional care, which can impede recovery [35].

8.7 The Role of Tech Companies and Policymakers

Given technology's huge influence on mental health and stigma, tech businesses and legislators are increasingly responsible for addressing these concerns. Tech businesses, particularly social media platforms, must become more active in monitoring mental health-related content [36]. This involves adopting algorithms that prioritize factual, evidence-based information; offering tools for users who need assistance; and establishing safe spaces for conversation without fear of abuse or judgment [37].

Moreover, there is a need for better digital literacy in the general populace. Education regarding the possible dangers of misinformation, the value of critical thinking, and the influence of social media on mental health should be included in school curricula and public awareness efforts. We can minimize stigma and create a healthy conversation about mental health by cultivating a more knowledgeable and responsible online community [38].

Policymakers have a critical role in regulating the digital ecosystem in order to preserve mental health. This might include developing ethical design criteria for mental health applications, ensuring that they are founded on scientific evidence and subject to regular review [39]. Furthermore, legislation focused on curbing online harassment and cyberbullying can assist in building safer digital spaces for addressing mental health issues [40].

8.8 Negative Consequences of Stigma Around Mental Health

The following are a few negative consequences of stigma around mental health [41]:

- Lack of willingness to seek help or therapy.
- Inadequate awareness from acquaintances, relatives, colleagues, or others.
- Decreased opportunities for work, learning, social interaction, or housing difficulties.
- Harassment, physical assault, or aggression.
- The feeling that you are incapable of overcoming particular obstacles or improving your current situation.

8.9 The Sustaining of Mental Health Stigma *via* Technology

The stigma associated with mental illness is further reinforced by social media platforms, which are excellent tools for community development and communication. Stigmatizing representations of mental health disorders may be featured on these platforms, which are meant to encourage maximum interaction and frequently give preference to dramatic and emotionally charged content. The dissemination of false information is one way that social media keeps stigma alive [42]. These platforms allow for the swift spread of content, which makes it possible for false or incorrect information on mental health to be seen by a large number of people. This false information frequently serves to perpetuate prejudices and preconceptions, such as the notion that those who suffer from mental illnesses are dangerous, erratic, or to blame for their difficulties [43]. Posts or memes that belittle mental illness, for example, implying that anxiety is just concern or depression is just sorrow, might lead to a general misunderstanding of these complicated disorders in society. Social media may lessen the stigma attached to mental illness by fostering a culture of comparison and perfectionism [44]. People's best moments are often shared on social media platforms like Facebook and Instagram, which drives up standards and increases user pressure to live up to idealized standards. This can cause feelings of inadequacy and loneliness in persons dealing with mental health problems since they may think they are the only ones going through these difficulties [45].

- **The Impact of Anonymity on Stigmatizing Behavior:** Numerous internet platforms' anonymity may contribute to a rise in stigmatizing conduct. Although people may talk about delicate topics like mental health in a secure environment when they are anonymous, it can also encourage harmful behaviors like trolling and cyberbullying. When someone does not have to declare who they are, they are more likely to voice damaging and stigmatizing opinions [46].
- **The Impact of Apps for Mental Health on Stigma:** Apps for mental health have become more and more popular, providing users with a variety of services including virtual therapy and mood tracking. These applications can be useful tools for managing mental health, but they additionally contribute to stigma in a number of ways [47].

8.10 The Impact of Technology on Current Mental Health

Technology advancements have played a major role in the fundamental alteration of the field of mental science. In order to comprehend, diagnose, and treat mental health disorders, technology has become essential, from ground-breaking therapeutic techniques to cutting-edge diagnostic technologies [48]. The integration of technology and mental health has not only increased the effectiveness of therapy but also changed the accessibility and personalization of mental health services. However, in addition to its rapid integration, there are challenges that must be solved in order to fully reap the benefits of technology [49].

- **Improving the Assessment and Diagnosis**

The field of diagnosis and evaluation has benefited greatly from the technological advancements in modern mental science. The subjective assessments used in traditional techniques of diagnosing mental health issues might result in inconsistent results and misdiagnoses. That being said, technology is opening the door for more objective, data-driven methods [50].

- **Brain Mapping and Neuroimaging**

Neuroimaging technologies, such as positron emission tomography (PET) and functional magnetic resonance imaging (fMRI), have greatly advanced our understanding of the anatomy and function of the brain [51]. These methods may be used by scientists and clinicians to monitor brain activity and identify abnormalities associated with a variety of mental health conditions, such as depression, anxiety, and schizophrenia. Functional magnetic resonance imaging (fMRI) has the potential to enhance diagnostic standards and provide more targeted therapy by demonstrating brain activity patterns associated with certain emotional states or cognitive skills [52].

- **Research on Biomarkers and Genetics**

Research on biomarkers and genomes has also advanced dramatically. Scientists are starting to pinpoint biological markers and genetic variants that predispose people to particular mental health issues. As a result, personalized medicine techniques have emerged, in which a patient's treatment is customized based on their individual genetic profile. This simultaneously increases the effectiveness of therapies and reduces the likelihood of undesirable side effects [53].

- **Enhanced Mental Health Service Access**

Improving the accessibility of mental health treatments for AI can have significant effects on the overall well-being and functioning of these sophisticated systems. As AI gets more and more integrated into various spheres of our society, it is necessary to recognize the possible issues and pressures that AI systems may face. As a result, it is also necessary to provide the support that these systems require to ensure optimal functioning [54].

- **Sentiment Analysis *via* the Processing of Natural Language**

Natural language processing, or NLP, is a powerful technology in the field of artificial intelligence that can be used to address a range of mental health-related difficulties. Because AI allows mental health professionals to efficiently assess and analyze large amounts of textual material, it is profoundly changing the diagnostic and therapeutic strategies that they utilize [55].

- **Digital Diagnostic Devices**

In order to identify signs of mental health issues, digital platforms and mobile applications are being used more and more. These tools typically use algorithms to analyze data from questionnaires, behavioral patterns, and even voice or facial expressions. For instance, apps that track a user's sleep patterns, physical activity, and social interactions can offer important insights into their mental health. These tools can also help identify conditions like depression or anxiety early on, allowing for timely intervention [55].

- **Transforming Therapy and Treatment**

Technology has also fundamentally altered the manner that interventions are administered, tailored, and effective in the area of mental health care [56].

- **Telemedicine and Virtual Counseling**

Teletherapy, or online counseling, has grown a lot in popularity, particularly after the COVID-19 pandemic. Sites such as Better Help and Talkspace allow users to video chat, phone, or video call licensed therapists. This has made mental health care more accessible, especially for those who live in remote areas or have mobility issues. Additionally, because teletherapy allows users to interact with therapists in private, it lessens the stigma attached to seeking help [57].

- **Privacy and Data Security**

Personal health data security and privacy are among the biggest issues. Sensitive data is frequently gathered by mHealth apps and digital platforms, including genetic information, behavioral patterns, and mental health state. Ensuring the safe storage and prevention of spread of this data is crucial. Furthermore, there must be precise rules governing the use of this data, especially in view of the increased interest in making money off of health data [58, 59].

- **AI Use in an Ethical Way**

When it comes to mental health care, artificial intelligence has unique ethical challenges. For example, algorithms trained on non-representative data may be prejudiced, which could lead to variations in recommended treatments. Furthermore, using AI to diagnose mental health diseases raises questions about responsibility and the potential for misdiagnosis [60].

8.11 Conclusion

The combination between technology and mental health creates a problematic situation. On the one hand, digital platforms offer the ability to democratize access to mental health services, promoting greater awareness and support than ever before. On the other hand, they unintentionally propagate and magnify existing stigmas, frequently creating echo chambers in which misinformation and harmful preconceptions thrive. As we move forward, we must approach technology critically, recognizing its limitations and actively striving to reduce its harmful influence on mental wellness discourse. In order to create healthier, more inclusive, and free of stigma digital environments, tech firms, mental health specialists, governments, and consumers must work together. Finally, combating mental health stigma in modern times means not just harnessing technology for good, but also recognizing and confronting the terrible facts that accompany it.

References

1. Gooding, P., Mapping the rise of digital mental health technologies: Emerging issues for law and society. *Int. J. Law Psychiatry*, 67, 101498, 2019.
2. Batada, A. and Leon Solano, R., *Harnessing technology to address the global mental health crisis*, World Bank, Washington, DC, 2019.
3. Naslund, J.A., *et al.*, Social media and mental health: benefits, risks, and opportunities for research and practice. *J. Technol. Behav. Sci.*, 5, 245–257, 2020.
4. D'Alfonso, S., AI in mental health. *Curr. Opin. Psychol.*, 36, 112–117, 2020.

5. Alyousef, S.M., *et al.*, Perceptions of media's contribution toward stigmatization of mental health by Saudi Arabian nurses. *J. Am. Psychiat. Nurses Assoc.*, 26, 6, 568–575, 2020.
6. Klin, A. and Lemish, D., Mental disorders stigma in the media: Review of studies on production, content, and influences. *J. Health Commun.*, 13, 5, 434–449, 2008.
7. Gupta, A., *et al.*, A Study on the Impact of Technology on Human Emotions. *Intelligence*, 3, 1, 2024.
8. White Hughto, J.M., *et al.*, "You can't just walk down the street and meet someone": The intersection of social–sexual networking technology, stigma, and health among gay and bisexual men in the small city. *Am. J. Men's Health*, 11, 3, 726–736, 2017.
9. Caporusso, N., Generative artificial intelligence and the emergence of creative displacement anxiety. *Res. Directs Psychol. Behav.*, 3, 1, 1–12, 2023.
10. Gardner, P., *The Consequences of and Factors Affecting Perceptions and Use of Technology*, Union College, Schenectady, New York, 2017.
11. Banga, C.A., *Developmental consequences of the digitally-mediated landscape: implications for empathic processing at the neural and behavioural levels-of-analysis during the early adolescent pubertal transition*, Department of Clinical & Health Psychology, School of Health in Social Science, University of Edinburgh, Scotland, UK, 2023.
12. Filice, E., *Distortions in the digital looking glass: Information and communication technologies and bodily self-conceptions in men seeking men*, Waterloo, Ontario, Canada, 2021.
13. Shiller, R.J., Narratives about technology-induced job degradation then and now. *J. Policy Model.*, 41, 3, 477–488, 2019.
14. Makridakis, S., The forthcoming Artificial Intelligence (AI) revolution: Its impact on society and firms. *Futures*, 90, 46–60, 2017.
15. Bessen, J., *AI and jobs: The role of demand*, National Bureau of Economic Research, Cambridge, MA, 2018.
16. Khalil, O.E., Artificial decision-making and artificial ethics: A management concern. *J. Bus. Ethics*, 12, 313–321, 1993.
17. Tajfel, H., Social identity and intergroup behaviour. *Soc. Sci. Inf.*, 13, 2, 65–93, 1974.
18. Bellwood, P., *Qualitative Study of Technology-Induced Errors in Healthcare Organizations*, School of Health Information Science, University of Victoria, Canada, 2013.
19. Jiang, H., Emmerton, L., McKauge, L., Academic integrity and plagiarism: a review of the influences and risk situations for health students. *Higher Educ. Res. Dev.*, 32, 3, 369–380, 2013.
20. Rajpurkar, P., *et al.*, AI in health and medicine. *Nat. Med.*, 28, 1, 31–38, 2022.
21. Khosrowabadi, N., Hoberg, K., Imdahl, C., Evaluating human behaviour in response to AI recommendations for judgemental forecasting. *Eur. J. Oper. Res.*, 303, 3, 1151–1167, 2022.

22. Vaingankar, J.A., *et al.*, Social media–driven routes to positive mental health among youth: Qualitative enquiry and concept mapping study. *JMIR Pediatr. Parenting*, 5, 1, e32758, 2022.
23. Tasnim, S., Hossain, M.M., Mazumder, H., Impact of rumors and misinformation on COVID-19 in social media. *J. Prev. Med. Public Health*, 53, 3, 171–174, 2020.
24. Bragazzi, N.L. and Garbarino, S., Assessing the accuracy of generative conversational artificial intelligence in debunking sleep health myths: mixed methods comparative study with expert analysis. *JMIR Form. Res.*, 8, 1, e55762, 2024.
25. Gunson, N., *et al.*, Coronabot: A conversational ai system for tackling misinformation, in: *Proceedings of the Conference on Information Technology for Social Good*, 2021.
26. Brynjolfsson, E. and Mcafee, A., Artificial intelligence, for real. *Harv. Business Rev.*, 1, 1–31, 2017.
27. Ybarra, M.L. and Suman, M., Help seeking behavior and the Internet: a national survey. *Int. J. Med. Inf.*, 75, 1, 29–41, 2006.
28. Qayyum, A., Student help-seeking attitudes and behaviors in a digital era. *Int. J. Educ. Technol. Higher Educ.*, 15, 1, 1–16, 2018.
29. Karabenick, S.A., Classroom and technology-supported help seeking: The need for converging research paradigms. *Learn. Instruction*, 21, 2, 290–296, 2011.
30. Kaess, M. and Bauer, S., Editorial promoting help-seeking using e-technology for ADolescents: the ProHEAD consortium. *Trials*, 20, 1, 72, 2019.
31. Er, E., *et al.*, Exploring college students' online help-seeking behavior in a flipped classroom with a web-based help-seeking tool. *Australas. J. Educ. Technol.*, 31, 5, 537–555, 2015.
32. Gere, B.O., Salimi, N., Anima-Korang, A., Social media use as self-therapy or alternative mental help-seeking behavior. *IAFOR J. Psychol. Behav. Sci.*, 5, 2, 21–36, 2020.
33. Karumbaiah, S., Ocumpaugh, J., Baker, R.S., Context matters: Differing implications of motivation and help-seeking in educational technology. *Int. J. Artif. Intell. Educ.*, 32, 3, 685–724, 2022.
34. Stockmann, D., Tech companies and the public interest: the role of the state in governing social media platforms. *Inf. Commun. Soc.*, 26, 1, 1–15, 2023.
35. Shane, S.A., *The illusions of entrepreneurship: The costly myths that entrepreneurs, investors, and policy makers live by*, Yale University Press, London, UK, 2008.
36. Mason, C. and Brown, R., Creating good public policy to support high-growth firms. *Small Bus. Econ.*, 40, 211–225, 2013.
37. King, A.V., Constitutionality of cyberbullying laws: Keeping the online playground safe for both teens and free speech. *Vand. L. Rev.*, 63, 845, 2010.

38. Rüsch, N., Angermeyer, M.C., Corrigan, P.W., Mental illness stigma: Concepts, consequences, and initiatives to reduce stigma. *Eur. Psychiatry*, 20, 8, 529–539, 2005.
39. Ben-Zeev, D., Drake, R.E., Brian, R.M., Technologies for people with serious mental illness, in: *Behavioral Health Care and Technology: Using Science-Based Innovations to Transform Practice*, pp. 70–80, 2015.
40. Naslund, J.A., *et al.*, Digital technology for treating and preventing mental disorders in low-income and middle-income countries: a narrative review of the literature. *Lancet Psychiatry*, 4, 6, 486–500, 2017.
41. Berrouiguet, S., *et al.*, Fundamentals for future mobile-health (mHealth): a systematic review of mobile phone and web-based text messaging in mental health. *J. Med. Internet Res.*, 18, 6, e135, 2016.
42. Cristol, S., *The Relationship of Delivery Modes, Self and Social Stigma, Treatment History, Familiarity with Technology, Age, and Likelihood to Engage in Behavioral Health Interventions*, William James College, Newton, USA, 2020.
43. Rains, S.A., The implications of stigma and anonymity for self-disclosure in health blogs. *Health Commun.*, 29, 1, 23–31, 2014.
44. Mitchell, K.M., Holtz, B.E., McCarroll, A.M., Assessing college students' perceptions of and intentions to use a mobile app for mental health. *Telemed. e-Health*, 28, 4, 566–574, 2022.
45. Bucci, S., Schwannauer, M., Berry, N., The digital revolution and its impact on mental health care. *Psychol. Psychotherapy Theory Res. Pract.*, 92, 2, 277–297, 2019.
46. Harvey, P.D., *et al.*, Technology and mental health: state of the art for assessment and treatment. *Am. J. Psychiatry*, 179, 12, 897–914, 2022.
47. Stein, D.J., *et al.*, Psychiatric diagnosis and treatment in the 21st century: paradigm shifts versus incremental integration. *World Psychiatry*, 21, 3, 393–414, 2022.
48. Savoy, R.L., History and future directions of human brain mapping and functional neuroimaging. *Acta Psychologica*, 107, 1–3, 9–42, 2001.
49. Malhi, G. and Lagopoulos, J., Making sense of neuroimaging in psychiatry. *Acta Psychiatrica Scand.*, 117, 2, 100–117, 2008.
50. García-Gutiérrez, M.S., *et al.*, Biomarkers in psychiatry: concept, definition, types and relevance to the clinical reality. *Front. Psychiatry*, 11, 432, 2020.
51. Orlowski, S., *et al.*, The promise and the reality: a mental health workforce perspective on technology-enhanced youth mental health service delivery. *BMC Health Serv. Res.*, 16, 1–12, 2016.
52. Malgaroli, M., *et al.*, Natural language processing for mental health interventions: a systematic review and research framework. *Transl. Psychiatry*, 13, 1, 309, 2023.
53. Scott, D.A., Valley, B., Simecka, B.A., Mental health concerns in the digital age. *Int. J. Ment. Health Addict.*, 15, 604–613, 2017.

54. Yang, Y.Y., *A Braive new world: How technology can transform access to mental health care*, University of Oslo, Problemveien, Oslo, Norway, 2020.
55. Di Carlo, F., *et al.*, Telepsychiatry and other cutting-edge technologies in COVID-19 pandemic: Bridging the distance in mental health assistance. *Int. J. Clin. Pract.*, 75, 1, 1–9, 2021.
56. Bondre, A., Pathare, S., Naslund, J.A., Protecting mental health data privacy in India: The case of data linkage with Aadhaar. *Global Health Sci. Pract.*, 9, 3, 467–480, 2021.
57. Kasula, B.Y., Ethical Considerations in the Adoption of Artificial Intelligence for Mental Health Diagnosis. *Int. J. Creative Res. In Comput. Technol. Des.*, 5, 5, 1–7, 2023.
58. Aboujaoude, E., Protecting privacy to protect mental health the new ethical imperative. *J. Med. Ethics*, 45, 9, 604–607, 2019.
59. Parker, L., *et al.*, How private is your mental health app data? An empirical study of mental health app privacy policies and practices. *Int. J. Law Psychiatry*, 64, 198–204, 2019.
60. Luxton, D.D., Recommendations for the ethical use and design of artificial intelligent care providers. *Artif. Intell. Med.*, 62, 1, 1–10, 2014.

9

ChatGPT (AI) vs. Standardized Psychological Testing: A Comparative Study on Anxiety Among Working Professionals in UAE

Maanasa Kirthivasan* **and Aradhana Balodi Bhardwaj**

Department of Psychology, School of Humanities, Arts and Applied Sciences, Amity University Dubai, Dubai, United Arab Emirates

Abstract

The pandemic has seen a rise in the growth of mental health disorders, and its effects are widespread, affecting communities at large. It has also seen significant developments in technology and artificial intelligence. As artificial intelligence gains momentum, the objectives of this study are (i) to explore the efficacy of a test of anxiety generated by artificial intelligence in comparison to a standardized test of anxiety, (ii) to assess the differences in levels of anxiety among male and female working professionals in the UAE, and (iii) to understand the levels of anxiety among working professionals across different age groups. The following objectives were studied using a standardized questionnaire, The State–Trait Anxiety Inventory, and one novel questionnaire, the Anxiety Assessment Scale. These were circulated among working professionals in the UAE *via* Google Forms, and ANOVA and *Z*-test were used to interpret the results. Findings supported the proposed hypothesis that artificial intelligence is not as developed to produce results equal to that of a standardized test of anxiety. Future recommendations are to make use of different artificial intelligence platforms to retest the efficacy of AI-generated psychological tests.

Keywords: Anxiety, artificial intelligence, ChatGPT, psychological testing, working professionals, United Arab Emirates

**Corresponding author*: maanasakirthivasan@gmail.com

Ridhima Sharma, Fazla Rabby, Rohit Bansal, Timcy Sachdeva and Jihene Mrabet (eds.) Confronting Mental Health Stigma with AI and Machine Learning, (203–238) © 2026 Scrivener Publishing LLC

9.1 Introduction

9.1.1 Anxiety

Anxiety is one of the most prevalent psychological disorders [1]. It affects almost 30% of individuals at least once across the span of their lives [2]. Anxiety can be described as a complex set of feelings and emotions that are marked by worry, apprehension, and disturbance in thoughts. Additionally, it can also be marked by certain physiological symptoms including sweating and a rise in blood pressure and heart rate. Anxiety is essentially the fear and worry concerning future outcomes and responses. It is a debilitating condition that causes individuals to react in ways that may cause them to avoid situations that trigger these thoughts [3].

Anxiety disorders are further classified as generalized anxiety, separation anxiety, social anxiety, phobias, and panic disorders. The most common symptoms of anxiety include feeling restless, apprehensive, worried, and irritable; experiencing physical symptoms such as back pain, muscle strain, tension headaches, stomach pains, and nausea; and experiencing difficulties in sleep, sweating, shivering, and greater heart rate [3]. Individuals with anxiety may find it extremely challenging to control these thoughts and function normally. Additionally, studies show that there are multiple factors that can lead to the development of anxiety, such as genetic predisposition, socio-cultural influences, and personality type.

Studies show that generalized anxiety, panic, and obsessive–compulsive disorders tend to carry within families. Additionally, some studies show that imbalances in chemical activities in the brain, such as gamma-aminobutyric acid (GABA), noradrenaline, and serotonin, can worsen the symptoms of anxiety [4]. There are multiple life events that may also affect the anxiety of an individual. Further, it was found that females are two times more prone to developing anxiety in comparison to males as mentioned in the DSM V [2].

The treatment of anxiety commonly follows a dual approach where both medication and therapy are used. Medications such as anti-anxiolytics, benzodiazepines, and anti-depressants are paired alongside different types of therapies, which may include cognitive–behavioral therapy, psychotherapy, and dialectic behavior therapy [5].

9.1.2 Increasing Prevalence of Anxiety in the United Arab Emirates Among Working Professionals

As discussed above, anxiety is one of the most prevalent psychiatric conditions known to affect individuals. Multiple studies have shown that working professionals living in the United Arab Emirates are at greater risk of anxiety. In the post-pandemic period, a significant rise in levels of anxiety has been observed, especially among working professionals. The reasons for this can be attributed to loss of jobs, job uncertainty, loss of loved ones, financial struggles, transition to online platforms for work, and rising competition.

Working professionals face struggles in work–life balance as they juggle between their professional duties and family life. The sudden disruption in the paradigm of traditional work may have caused extreme distress and apprehension, especially concerning future outcomes. The troubling uncertainty and lack of awareness of what could happen next, combined with the lack of stability, lead to rising rates of fear and worry. All of these factors point toward potential causes that have increased the levels of anxiety among working professionals. A study pointed out that over 55.7% of the participants had anxiety. These findings were attributed to employment and economic crises faced by these individuals [6].

Multiple other studies have highlighted the rising rates of anxiety among working professionals in the United Arab Emirates, and studies have reinforced the greater prevalence of anxiety in women; some factors that could explain the higher levels of anxiety among females include gender roles and socio-cultural factors that add responsibility and worry [6]. Some others have highlighted that the rising rates of anxiety are potentially tied to the increasing rates of loneliness and lack of social support [7].

9.1.3 Use of Artificial Intelligence in Psychological Assessment

Artificial intelligence, in essence, is the ability of technology and devices to mimic human intelligence [8]. Artificial intelligence has been the trending subject of research, especially within the scope of mental health. Multiple studies have shown the rising trend of making use of artificial intelligence in diagnosing various conditions or coming up with treatment methodologies [9]. Many researchers have pointed toward the capability of artificial intelligence in assisting with the prediction and identification of patterns and symptoms of high-risk individuals, and it can also pick up data and identify potential individuals who have a high or increased risk of developing abnormalities of mental health conditions in the future [10]. Although it is a new trend, some other studies have pointed toward potential strengths of artificial intelligence; other findings suggest that artificial intelligence has the ability to reduce various time-consuming processes in psychological testing, and it may help in the simplification of treatment and diagnosis.

At the moment, artificial intelligence has yet to be used independently in psychological testing due to a lack of standardization. Artificial intelligence as a tool is neither reliable nor valid and does not have any empirical evidence to support its usage. Artificial intelligence also has added limitations in that it lacks human touch; psychology as a field is bolstered by concepts of empathy, unconditional positive regard, and evidence-based approaches. Psychologists rely on soft skills and observation to notice abnormal or odd behaviors, which help enhance their diagnosis. Additionally, these observations help them gain a deeper understanding of the client and their persona, which is very helpful in personalizing treatment plans and counseling sessions. This human touch adds a sense of comfort and security, which facilitates trust and builds rapport, which is essential in the process of counseling [11].

Artificial intelligence is powered by data and does not have any form of personal relationship with the client, which can help prevent possible errors of bias and judgment; it helps in curbing these errors [12], but it still poses multiple questions pertaining to ethics. Artificial intelligence may have drawbacks concerning the confidentiality of data and other information and the privacy of such collected or stored data [13].

9.1.4 Interplay of Standardized Testing and Artificial Intelligence

The interplay of artificial intelligence and standardized psychological testing can help revolutionize the field of psychological testing. Standardized tests have various psychological properties, such as reliability and validity, which help ensure the accuracy and efficacy of the test. Additionally, these tests have empirical evidence, making them deeply rooted in literary and case evidence that support the test and the domains it attempts to measure. Standardized tests have always been the first choice for mental health professionals, psychometricians, and clinical psychologists as they help make diagnoses that aid psychologists in formulating counseling methodologies and techniques best suited for the client and their condition [14].

Artificial intelligence as a field has a wide plethora of applications as it is very convenient in terms of ease of access, feasibility, and wide scope of knowledge. Although it has the above-mentioned benefits, it does not possess any evidence of its applicability in the field of psychological testing. If the benefits of artificial intelligence are used in combination with traditional methods, psychological testing as a field could be amplified [15]. The aim of this research is to examine the potential applications of artificial intelligence in the field of psychological testing, especially in terms of its efficacy and accuracy. It can help reduce the possibilities of human error and bias and can make the process of testing more accurate and faster. It also allows psychologists to focus on the process of counseling and treatment as artificial intelligence would be able to gather data and make faster diagnoses.

9.2 Review of Literature

In this section, existing literature on topics concerning anxiety among working professionals, the prevalence of anxiety in the UAE, and the usage of artificial intelligence and ChatGPT in psychology were analyzed. These studies are vital in achieving a greater understanding of the objectives as they are substantially relevant to the current research statement. Additionally, this analysis of literature helps evaluate the existing gaps in the field and provides future direction and aid in research.

A United Arab Emirates-based study documented the levels of anxiety among the young and adult population. Standardized tests such as the Generalized Anxiety Disorder-7 Scale were used alongside other scales to assess anxiety and other psychological domains. The results showed that over 71% of the sample reported the highest levels of anxiety, wherein females and young adults scored 51.7% and 59.8%, respectively. The study highlighted some factors that could explain the higher levels of anxiety among females, including gender roles and socio-cultural factors that add responsibility and worry [6].

A study on working professionals living in the United Arab Emirates showed that they are at greater risk of mental health disorders due to increasing rates of loneliness and reduced social support. Studies highlighted that these individuals tend to face a lot of pressure concerning social norms, especially pressure from family, workplaces, and other settings. This increased anxiety is not only attributed to the above but also tends to give rise to increased health anxiety and health concerns. This study was conducted on a specific sample of Indian working professionals in the United Arab Emirates, thus implying that these demographic factors must be considered when offering psychological support [7].

The findings of a study on the possible applications of artificial intelligence on the various prospects and problems that are present in the field of treatment for patients with mental illness highlighted the huge gap present in mental health care and how alternatives are required to make treatment more accessible. The study examined the possible abilities of artificial intelligence, i.e., ChatGPT, in providing responses that are human-like and built on support and closeness. ChatGPT was proven superior in comparison to other artificial intelligence platforms as it proved to have a superior amount of knowledge in the field of psychological conditions. Although ChatGPT cannot diagnose conditions, it can assist in identifying patterns and symptoms, which can assist in the formulation of diagnosis [9].

Another study made use of artificial intelligence to help predict mental illness that could develop among workers in the healthcare setting during and after the coronavirus pandemic (COVID-19). The researchers carried out the study across various phases, during which data was collected and analyzed. Artificial intelligence was helpful in picking up quick changes and patterns to identify mental illness. This methodology can assist psychologists in making their diagnosis without the interference of any bias. Additionally, all these collected data can help in the early prediction and identification of mental illness caused by the pandemic. This can help early identification and quicker intervention for the treatment of these mental illnesses [10].

A study looked into the implementation of technology and artificial intelligence in improving the diagnosis of mental health conditions. The researchers highlighted that mental health care as a field has limitations that include bias, subjectivity, and time-consuming processes. The researchers emphasized tailor-made approaches used by therapists in their treatments and how using artificial intelligence-assisted technology can help in improving the detection of mental illness as it has the ability to gather data from various sources and make better assessments of the patient without allowing bias and subjectivity to interfere. They also highlighted that artificial intelligence could help monitor physiological factors and assist in determining the disorder and its severity while assisting the therapist to focus on the rapport building and therapy process while artificial intelligence assists with the other time-consuming processes such as making diagnosis and devising treatment plans [11].

The relationship between the stereotypical assumptions of ChatGPT as an artificial intelligence model with variables including self-esteem and well-being was studied using a cross-sectional analysis. The results of the study indicated that the absence of harmful stereotypes resulted in increased levels of self-esteem and well-being. The authors highlighted that improving attitudes toward artificial intelligence can significantly improve and create a positive relationship with software. The study additionally threw light on how ChatGPT, as an artificial intelligence platform, helps avoid biases that may result from human assessment. The results highlighted how positive perceptions of technology and artificial intelligence can also help decrease job anxiety. Essentially, the study highlighted the influence of ChatGPT and artificial intelligence in improving the mental well-being of users and how it can be used by psychologists to aid their services and provide unbiased outcomes [12].

A study on the prospective applications of artificial intelligence in improving the accuracy of psychological testing showed that artificial intelligence can provide objective outlooks and findings that are driven by data and its insights. The author suggested that artificial intelligence has the potential to analyze bigger sets of data, which can help in creating better predictions and results. The study also assessed the possibilities of automating the field of psychological testing by making use of artificial intelligence to study larger groups of clients with more efficiency and speed. Further, the author highlighted that despite the advantages artificial intelligence possesses, there could be potential drawbacks concerning the confidentiality of the data collected [13].

A study on the applicability of artificial intelligence in psycho-diagnostics and psychological interventions was carried out with the main aim of assessing future applications of technology in diagnosis. The authors of the study carried out a literature review to find studies that met their criteria. From the study, the researchers were able to deduce that deep learning technology could be useful in detecting various factors that might multiply the risk of an individual developing mental health concerns including depression and anxiety. It can also help in assessing groups of individuals who are at risk of developing mental illnesses. Further, the study showed that artificial intelligence could help in diagnosing mental illness by gathering data and analyzing databases to identify individuals displaying symptoms of mental illness. Additionally, artificial intelligence could assist in providing psychological interventions online. The study highlighted some limitations, including the problem of confidentiality and ethical considerations. Additional research on this area can help fill these gaps [15].

The use of ChatGPT in providing interventions and assessments of mental health was assessed to understand its capability as a collaborative tool in assisting mental health practitioners. The authors of the study created three imaginary conditions for patients and reported their mental health concerns to ChatGPT. ChatGPT was used as an online assistant to help provide treatment or recommendations. The study found that in one of the imaginary conditions presented, the suggestions offered by ChatGPT seemed somewhat appropriate and relevant and seemed to hold beneficial value to mental health professionals, but in the other two scenarios presented, the recommendations offered by ChatGPT were inappropriate and rather dangerous. It became evident that although ChatGPT could produce quick responses mimicking empathy, it could not interact with the users to gather deeper information or use clinical findings to foster patient management. This study reinforced the limitations of ChatGPT in not being the most accurate tool in mental health care practices [16].

A United Arab Emirates-based study analyzed the influence of COVID-19 on indicators of anxiety and depression among individuals. The researchers used standardized scales to assess the variables including the Patient Health Questionnaire-8 and Generalized Anxiety Disorder-7 scales for the purpose of this study. Findings suggested that 26.4% of the participants based in the United Arab Emirates had reported symptoms of anxiety. The study further showed that females had reported increased levels of depression and anxiety in comparison to males, and students had been assessed with greater levels of anxiety in comparison to working professionals. The study also highlighted an important demographic aspect, suggesting that young adults between the ages of 18 and 24 had the highest prevalence of anxiety in comparison to the rest of the population. Reasons for the same were attributed to the transition from study to employment [17].

In another UAE-based cross-sectional study, the researchers theorized that the prevalence of moderate or severe anxiety would be greater in students who are in the medical profession in comparison to those students who are not. The Generalized Anxiety Disorder-7 scale was administered, and results indicated that female medical students had statistically greater rates of anxiety in comparison to other students. Additionally, findings suggested that the students involved in this study viewed anxiety as normal and not as something that would cause dysfunctional behavior or debilitate them from carrying out their work. Overall, the study showcased the prevalence of anxiety among women and the importance of psychological support in mitigating these issues [18].

A cross-sectional study on anxiety, stress, and depression among students pursuing their undergraduate degree in the United Arab Emirates was conducted to understand the prevalence of these mental health issues. The authors used the Depression Anxiety Stress Scales and analyzed the results statistically. The findings of their results indicated that among the three mental health issues, anxiety was the most prevalent, with over 55% of the participants reporting symptoms of anxiety. The analysis of the results also highlighted that anxiety was more prevalent among females (61%) in comparison to males (47%). Thus, the study highlighted the widespread prevalence of anxiety among students in the UAE and further reinforced the prevalence of more excellent rates of anxiety among women. The reasons are that they require more profound research [19].

The usage of artificial intelligence in assessing mental health was studied by researchers who suggested that behavioral data can be collected from video games, GPS, location, and more, and these data could be analyzed to create a psychological profile of the person or user. The study suggested that the extraction of the user's expressions, voices, and actions can provide in-depth details of the person's mental health and can be evaluated by artificial intelligence to study the performance and psychological abilities of the user. The study also suggested that researchers could use devices that measure physiological changes to further study mental reactions. They proposed that monitoring brain waves, heart rate, and eye movement could indicate the user's mood and mental health. This study looks into the implementation of artificial intelligence in a new perspective in analyzing mental health and its efficacy in psychological testing using the assistance of physiological factors [20].

Another set of researchers reviewed the potential of a technology powered by artificial intelligence called the Mental Health Diagnostic Expert System in formulating diagnosis and treatment plans to promote the betterment of patients affected by mental illnesses. The authors inspected the availability of tailor-made approaches using this artificial intelligence-powered system. The study revealed that patients could use the technology to customize an intervention matching their budget and condition. The technology was developed after considering the expert opinions of psychologists to improve the accuracy of the diagnosis [21].

A cross-sectional study conducted by researchers in the UAE aimed to study the influence of the pandemic on anxiety and depression among working professionals in the healthcare setting. The researchers administered the Generalized Anxiety Disorder-7 and Patient Health Questionnaire scales. The findings of the study suggested that over 51.5% of the participants showed signs of anxiety, and the study suggested that female healthcare professionals reported greater rates of anxiety in comparison to male working professionals. Thus, this study was useful in analyzing the prevalence of anxiety among working professionals in the United Arab Emirates and also highlighted the levels of anxiety and their differences among the genders [22].

The efficacy of artificial intelligence in psychological testing was analyzed by Kim *et al.* (n.d.). For the purpose of this study, the authors specifically focused on the Minnesota Multiphasic Personality Inventory 2nd edition. The authors applied various machine learning algorithms to help identify gender identities. The findings of the study revealed a statistically significant response wherein over 97.06% of the predictions were accurate. These findings are useful in helping the field of psychological testing gain speed and accuracy in identifying patterns and scoring procedures [23].

In a randomized control trial, participants who presented with indicators of anxiety and depression were selected to engage in cognitive behavior therapy sessions with an automated chatbot. The participants engaged in approximately 12 sessions with the chatbot. The statistical analysis revealed that the participants engaged in the chatbot sessions had their symptoms of depression significantly reduced in comparison to the control group. This study thus found that conversational chatbots powered by artificial intelligence were a novel and interactive method for offering affordable, accessible, and effective treatment strategies based on cognitive and behavioral therapy [24].

One more study was conducted to assess depression, anxiety, and stress among doctors residing in the UAE, which showed that the prevalence of anxiety among them was over 57.4%, indicating high rates of anxiety. The anxiety reported by female doctors was 58.6% in comparison to male doctors, which was reported to be 50.6%, thus indicating higher rates of anxiety among females. Despite the gender differences, the widespread prevalence of mental health disorders among doctors was attributed to factors such as lack of social and financial support. Additionally, they also reported stress due to their working conditions and inability to balance their work life and personal life. These factors contributed to greater rates of anxiety among this population of healthcare workers [25].

The efficiency and practicability of using artificial intelligence to reduce symptoms of mental illness were analyzed in a randomized trial. The study considered college students who had self-reported symptoms of psychological issues such as anxiety and depression. The methodology employed utilized cognitive behavior therapy interventions, which were delivered by a chatbot powered by artificial intelligence. The findings showed that artificial intelligence offered an economically affordable and accessible method of intervention and was deemed more efficient when offered in addition to the traditional methods of therapy. Additionally, the study's symptoms of depression and anxiety were reduced after the use of the cognitive--behavior-therapy-based interventions, which were delivered by a chatbot powered by artificial intelligence [26].

A study on using a dialogue-based platform for mental health interventions inspected the applications of chatbots to help bridge the gap in mental health care. The research found that artificial intelligence offered a feasible method of providing a platform that provides support and facilitates better engagement among users. The study also highlighted that these digital interventions for mental health, when assessed by mental health professionals and used in combination, may have better outcomes. The authors highlighted that mental health professionals can help develop these platforms by updating data systems with patient preferences, symptoms, personality, and patterns. These data systems can help make these digital mental health intervention platforms create results and responses that are adaptive and personalized [27].

In research conducted by Dashwood *et al.* on using artificial intelligence as a tool to aid in formulating diagnosis for dementia, the authors have shown that techniques of artificial intelligence, when bolstered by patient records and other medical information, enable affordable and effective diagnosis. Artificial intelligence can also identify early risk factors that may predict the onset of dementia. However, some challenges concerning the quality of data and possible inconsistencies are present. Additionally, there could be some inconsistencies concerning the confidentiality of the data. The researchers suggested that artificial intelligence should never be used independently but only as a complementary aid to traditional methods of making diagnoses [28].

Mrabet and Studholme discovered the progressive importance of ChatGPT as an artificial intelligence (AI) model as a component of everyday life and its substantial influence on various fields of life, including personal, educational, professional, and health domains. The authors found that the incorporation of artificial intelligence into these domains can aid in enhancing quality of life [29].

Another study aimed at assessing the efficiency of providing mental health support using ChatGPT. The author of the study utilized a quasi-experimental design where participants diagnosed with mental health conditions such as anxiety and depression were recruited. The participants were instructed to make use of ChatGPT to take support for their condition for 15 minutes a day for 2 weeks. Following this, the participants were subjected to a semi-structured interview where their experiences using ChatGPT were explored. Post-thematic analysis, the study's results showed that ChatGPT was found to be very useful with regards to psychoeducation and in providing emotional support to the participants. One of the key limitations identified was that although the participants found the platform useful, they were reluctant to accept the information due to concerns about the reliability and validity of the information. Additionally, it was found that ChatGPT was not able to fully assess the severity or the complexity of the symptoms, thus raising concerns about the quality of support offered [30].

Another study looked at using ChatGPT as a tool to carry out suicide risk assessments. The authors tasked ChatGPT with evaluating a case of an assumed patient situation demonstrating a sense of hindered belongingness and burdensomeness. The authors compared the assessments created by ChatGPT with standard assessments usually carried out by certified mental health practitioners. They also compared the differences between earlier and later models of ChatGPT. The results of the study implied that the results produced by the more updated model of ChatGPT, i.e., ChatGPT-4, were somewhat parallel to the norms of mental health practitioners, yet a significant discrepancy was identified in the assessments generated by the ChatGPT-3.5 model. There were significant discrepancies in the prediction of potential suicide attempts by ChatGPT in comparison to mental health professionals. Additionally, another finding of the study showed that levels of resilience assessed by both the versions of ChatGPT were lower compared to the assessment findings carried out by mental health care providers. The findings of this study are somewhat ambiguous with regards to the efficacy of using ChatGPT in assessing suicide risk as it downplays the risk but demonstrates the capability to increase accuracy as seen in the difference in the updated versus the earlier model [31].

Through an in-depth analysis of existing literature on the chosen variables for the purpose of this study, the incidence of anxiety and the usage of artificial intelligence have been highlighted. However, a majority of this research does not take into consideration the employment of artificial intelligence within the scope of psychological testing and is limited to understanding the interplay of humans and technology and its role in mental health and other psychological domains. The following study has implemented specific variables that are associated with the objectives, and a quantitative approach has been implemented to assist further research.

9.3 Methodology

9.3.1 Problem Statement

The following study aims to understand the efficacy of a test of anxiety generated by ChatGPT (artificial intelligence) in comparison to a standardized test of anxiety.

9.3.2 Objectives

- To explore the efficacy of a test of anxiety generated by artificial intelligence in comparison to a standardized test of anxiety.
- To assess the differences in levels of anxiety among male and female working professionals in the UAE.
- To understand the levels of anxiety among working professionals across different age groups.

9.3.3 Hypothesis

H:1 The test generated by artificial intelligence will not be as effective in comparison to the standardized test of anxiety.
H:2 Female working professionals will have higher levels of anxiety in comparison to male working professionals in the UAE.
H:3 There will be a difference in levels of anxiety among working professionals across different age groups.

9.3.4 Variables

The following study examines the following three variables: anxiety, artificial intelligence, and standardized testing. The standardized anxiety scale analyzes anxiety on two levels: state and trait anxiety. The artificial intelligence scale of anxiety studies general anxiety.

9.3.5 Sample of the Study

Table 9.1 shows the sample of this study which comprised of 181 working professionals working in the United Arab Emirates. The sample consisted

Table 9.1 Demographic characteristics of the sample ($N = 181$).

Sample characteristics		N (%)
Age	Years	Mean = 41–50 (30%)
Sex	Male Female Prefer not to say	102 (56.7%) 78 (42.8%) 1 (0.6%)

of 102 men and 78 women. Only one individual chose not to identify with either category. The mean age group of the sample is between 41 and 50.

9.3.6 Sample Design

For the purpose of data collection in the following study, the purposive sampling method was used. Purposive sampling is essentially a form of non-probability sampling wherein the researcher uses their own judgment to select members of the population for the study. In this scenario, only the working professional category of individuals working in the UAE was chosen.

9.3.7 Research Design

The research design is an efficient method employed to find solutions to the problem at hand. It considers the different objectives, hypotheses, and variables of the study. Essentially, it serves as the blueprint of the research and consists of data collection and analysis. This study makes use of an exploratory research design. The exploratory research method is used when not much data is available regarding the study's variables. This methodology of research essentially attempts to identify links and possible connections between the variables and tests out different hypothesis in otherwise unspecified situations or circumstances.

9.3.8 Inclusion Criteria

The study included working professionals in the United Arab Emirates either employed or working as entrepreneurs above the age group of 20.

9.3.9 Instruments Used

For completing the objectives of this study, two scales were used to assess anxiety.

9.3.9.1 Anxiety Assessment Scale — AAS

The Anxiety Assessment Scale (AAS) is a test designed by ChatGPT to assess an individual's anxiety level [32]. The test has 20 statements, which are to be rated on a scale of 1 to 5, from Strongly Disagree to Strongly Agree. The test is scored on a 5-point Likert scale, with the options of Strongly Disagree, Disagree, Neutral, Agree, and Strongly Agree. This test has not been previously used before; thus, it cannot be said to be reliable or valid at the moment. This test does not cover all the symptoms and experiences as it is generated by artificial intelligence. This test was generated by the following prompt, "Generate a psychological test to test anxiety and provide the scoring and interpretation procedure."

9.3.9.2 State–Trait Anxiety Inventory — STAI

The State–Trait Anxiety Inventory is a test of anxiety developed by Charles D. Spielberger. This inventory includes two tests: the State inventory, i.e., STAI Form Y-1, which has a total of 20 statements that assess anxiety at the moment or how an individual feels at that moment. State anxiety can also be described as a situation that is marked by temporary or situational influences on mood. The Trait inventory, i.e., STAI Form Y-2, also has a total of 20 statements that assess an individual's general anxiety or how an individual's temperament is across situations and is considered to be more stable. The total scores obtained on the test range between 20 and 80; scores on the higher side are indicative of greater levels of anxiety. The test is a self-report inventory. The State–Trait Anxiety Inventory is both reliable and valid [14].

9.3.10 Scoring

9.3.10.1 Anxiety Assessment Scale — AAS

The test has both normal and reverse scoring. Table 9.2 depicts that statements 1, 3, 5, 7, 9, 11, 13, 15, 17, and 19 are scored normally, with 1 being Strongly Disagree and 5 being Strongly Agree. Conversely, Table 9.3 depicts that statements 2, 4, 6, 8, 10, 12, 14, 16, 18, and 20 are scored in reverse with 1 being Strongly Agree to 5 being Strongly Disagree.

Table 9.2 Depicting standard scoring for anxiety assessment scale.

Response options	Score
Strongly Disagree	1
Disagree	2
Neutral	3
Agree	4
Strongly Agree	5

Table 9.3 Depicting reversed scoring for anxiety assessment scale.

Response options	**Score**
Strongly Disagree	5
Disagree	4
Neutral	3
Agree	2
Strongly Agree	1

9.3.10.2 State–Trait Anxiety Inventory — STAI

The test has both normal and reverse scoring. In the State anxiety form, the 20 statements are marked on a scale of 1 to 4 with the options from 'Not at all,' 'Somewhat,' 'Moderately so,' and 'Very much so.' On the Trait anxiety form, the 20 statements are marked on a scale of 1 to 4 with the options ranging from 'Almost never,' 'Sometimes,' 'Often,' and 'Almost always.' Table 9.4 depicts the standard scoring of the state anxiety test and Table 9.5 depicts the reversed scoring of the state anxiety test. Table 9.6 depicts the standard scoring of the trait anxiety test and Table 9.7 depicts the reversed scoring of the trait anxiety test. The statements marked in reversed order for the anxiety forms are the following:

State Anxiety — 1, 2, 5, 8, 10, 11, 15, 16, 19, 20.
Trait Anxiety — 21, 23, 26, 27, 30, 33, 34, 36, 39.

Table 9.4 Depicting standard scoring for state anxiety test.

State anxiety Y1 — normal scoring	
Not at all	1
Somewhat	2
Moderately so	3
Very much so	4

Table 9.5 Depicting reversed scoring for state anxiety test.

State anxiety Y1 — reverse scoring	
Not at all	4
Somewhat	3
Moderately so	2
Very much so	1

Table 9.6 Depicting standard scoring for trait anxiety test.

Trait anxiety Y2 — normal scoring	
Almost never	1
Sometimes	2
Often	3
Almost always	4

Table 9.7 Depicting reversed scoring for the trait anxiety test.

Trait anxiety Y2 — reverse scoring	
Almost never	4
Sometimes	3
Often	2
Almost always	1

The scoring is done by adding all the raw scores obtained, including the reversed scores; the scoring for each test is done separately. Scores can be anywhere between 20 and 80.

9.3.11 Procedure of the Study

The participants who were chosen for this research were chosen on the basis of the given inclusion criteria. The method of sampling chosen was purposive sampling; working professionals in the United Arab Emirates were chosen as the sample. Instructions on how to participate in the research were made clear to all participants. The primary aim and objective of the study were kept hidden to prevent any form of bias. Additionally, all the participants consented to be a part of the study and were given the option to step down from the study at any point in time. All participants were asked to provide honest responses and choose statements that they related to and agreed with the most. The survey included demographic information-based questions and two questionnaires. Confidentiality of all participants was maintained. A clear list of instructions was also provided. After the collection of responses, all results were scored and tabulated. Additionally, statistical analysis was carried out on the data.

9.3.12 Data Collection

A total of two surveys, the Anxiety Assessment Scale and the State–Trait Anxiety Inventory, alongside some demographic detail-based questions, were put into the Google form for easy accessibility and convenience. Responses were collected from professionals and entrepreneurs in the United Arab Emirates. They were circulated on social networking platforms such as WhatsApp and LinkedIn.

9.3.13 Statistical Procedure

The study utilizes descriptive and inferential statistics to analyze the study's objectives. Descriptive analysis was conducted by determining the mean, standard deviation, and variance. The inferential analysis included measures such as the two-sample *Z*-test and ANOVA. All of the data was analyzed in Microsoft Excel using the Data Analysis ToolPak. All data was represented in graphical formats in the form of bar diagrams and histograms.

1. The comparison of anxiety among genders and age groups was carried out using an independent *Z*-test.
    - For both tests, the levels of anxiety were assessed by looking at the scores obtained for trait anxiety. The reasons for this selection are as follows.
        - Trait anxiety measures the general levels of anxiety of an individual, thus indicating the general disposition of the individual. This gives a better idea of the anxiety levels of an individual.
        - State anxiety only measures how anxious an individual feels at that moment and time, which may be affected by various factors. Hence, it cannot be considered for the purpose of the analysis.
        - The Anxiety Assessment Inventory generated by ChatGPT has not been validated against external criteria and is not reliable. It is a sample test generated for the purpose of this research; due to no empirical evidence supporting the efficacy of this test, it cannot be used for the purpose of data analysis.

    - Within the trait anxiety scores, individuals scoring above '45' were considered as it classifies as Moderate to Severe anxiety. Scores below '45' indicate no or low anxiety; hence, individuals with these scores were not considered to be a part of this sample.
    - Although the study sample's demographic data consisted of 4 age groups, "20–30," "31–40," "41–50," and "50+," the age groups were clubbed into "20–40" and "41 and above." This has classified the sample into two age groups: young adults and middle-aged working professionals.
    - Further, the study sample's demographic data consisted of their gender criterion, "Female," "Male," and "Prefer not to say"; only "Male" and "Female" were considered for the study.
    - For all tests, the alpha value was assumed to be 0.05.

2. The comparisons in the efficacy of artificial intelligence and the State–Trait Anxiety Inventory were made using single-factor ANOVA (analysis of variance).
    - ANOVA analysis was done three times to analyze the above objective.

- For all tests, the alpha value was assumed to be 0.05.
- The first test involved assessing anxiety scores obtained on the Anxiety Assessment Inventory (artificial intelligence) and both the sub-tests of the State–Trait Anxiety Inventory.
- The second test involved assessing anxiety scores obtained on the Anxiety Assessment Inventory (artificial intelligence) and the State Anxiety test on the State–Trait Anxiety Inventory.
- The third and final test involved assessing anxiety scores obtained on the Anxiety Assessment Inventory (artificial intelligence) and the Trait Anxiety test on the State–Trait Anxiety Inventory.

9.4 Result Analysis

This section of the study interprets the key findings obtained through the statistical analysis carried out in the previous section. These results present key observations regarding gender and age-related disparities in the scores of anxieties while simultaneously comparing the scores of anxieties across the different instruments used. The obtained findings have been displayed graphically through tables and graphs, along with their interpretations.

These results provide valuable insights regarding the efficacy of artificial-intelligence-generated psychological tests of anxiety and anxiety among working professionals in the United Arab Emirates, which can be further used to create policies and interventions to promote the well-being of employees at workplaces. Additionally, researchers can make use of these findings to help develop platforms of artificial intelligence, such as ChatGPT, with concepts of standardization to make psychological tests generated by artificial intelligence more reliable and valid.

Table 9.8 depicts the mean differences in levels of anxiety among male and female working professionals in the UAE. As observed in Table 9.8,

Table 9.8 Sample and mean differences in levels of anxiety among male and female working professionals in the UAE.

	Gender	Sample (*N*)	Mean
	Male	29	50.31
Levels of anxiety	Female	39	51.23

the number of female working professionals with anxiety is greater than the number of male working professionals. Additionally, from Table 9.8, it can be interpreted that a difference in the mean of scores of anxieties exists among males and females. The above results thus signify that female working professionals in the UAE have greater levels of anxiety in comparison to male working professionals in the UAE.

Figure 9.1 demonstrates the mean values of levels of anxiety among male and female working professionals in the UAE. The mean values depict that females have a significantly higher mean, which indicates that they have increased anxiety in comparison to males.

Table 9.9 depicts the differences in the means of the scores obtained on the trait anxiety test. The sample of the above test is taken as male and female working professionals in the UAE having moderate to high levels of anxiety. As observed in Table 9.9, there is a difference in the mean and variance of the two samples. The resulting test statistic value is −0.66, and the *p*-value is 0.51. As the test statistic value is less than the *p*-value, the alternate hypothesis is accepted, and the null hypothesis is rejected. Therefore, it can be established that there is a significant variation in anxiety among male and female working professionals in the UAE.

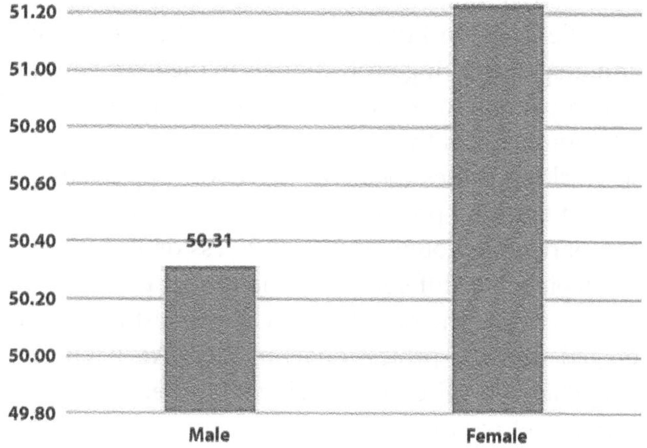

Figure 9.1 Mean differences in levels of anxiety among male and female working professionals in the UAE.

Table 9.9 *Z*-test depicting the differences in levels of anxiety among male and female working professionals in the UAE.

	Male	**Female**
Mean	50.31	51.23
Known variance	27.79	39.34
Observations	29	39
***Z*-statistic**	−0.66	
***P* ($Z \leq z$) two-tail**	0.51	
***z* Critical two-tail**	1.96	

Table 9.10 Sample and mean differences in levels of anxiety among young and middle-aged working professionals in the UAE.

	Age groups	**Sample (*N*)**	**Mean**
	Young adults	47	50.62
Levels of anxiety	**Middle-aged**	21	51.33

Table 9.10 depicts the mean differences in levels of anxiety among young and middle-aged working professionals in the UAE. From Table 9.10, it can be interpreted that there is a mean difference in the scores of anxious young and middle-aged working professionals. The above results thus signify that middle-aged working professionals in the UAE have greater levels of anxiety in comparison to young working professionals in the UAE.

Figure 9.2 demonstrates the mean values of anxiety among young and middle-aged working professionals in the UAE. The mean values depict that middle-aged working professionals in the UAE have greater levels of anxiety in comparison to young working professionals in the UAE.

Table 9.11 depicts the differences in the means of the scores obtained on the trait anxiety test. The sample of the above test is taken from young and middle-aged working professionals in the UAE having moderate to high levels of anxiety. As observed in Table 9.11, there is a difference in the mean and variance of the two samples.

The value of the obtained test statistic is −0.41, and the *p*-value is 0.67. The null hypothesis was rejected because the test statistic value is less than

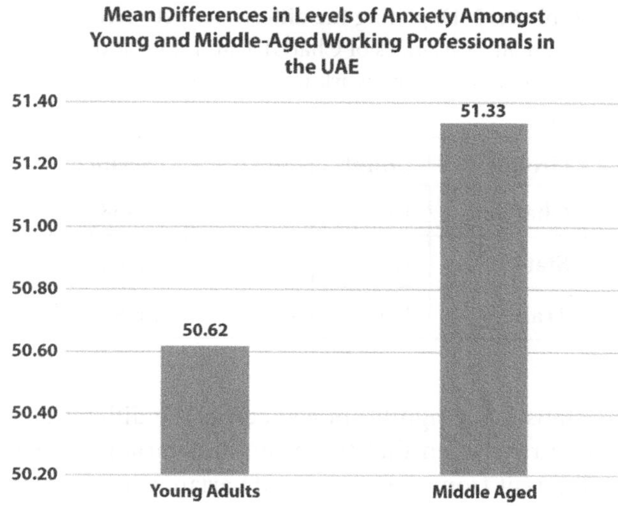

Figure 9.2 Mean differences in levels of anxiety among young and middle-aged working professionals in the UAE.

Table 9.11 *Z*-test depicting the differences in levels of anxiety among young and middle-aged working professionals in the UAE.

	Young adults (20–40 years)	Middle-aged adults (41 years and above)
Mean	50.62	51.33
Known variance	27.68	50.33
Observations	47	21
***Z*-statistic**	−0.4145589	
***P* (*Z*≤*z*) two-tail**	0.67846484	
***z* Critical two-tail**	1.959963985	

the *p*-value. Therefore, it can be determined that there is a considerable difference in anxiety among young and middle-aged working professionals in the UAE.

Table 9.12 depicts the mean differences in levels of anxiety measured by ChatGPT and the State–Trait Anxiety Inventory. From Table 9.12, it can be interpreted that there is a significant mean difference in the scores for anxiety. The above results thus indicate that the means are not equal,

Table 9.12 Depicting the differences between mean and variances of ChatGPT and state and trait anxiety among working professionals in the UAE.

Groups	Count	Mean	Variance
ChatGPT	181	61.144	12.468
State	181	38.481	132.029
Trait	181	40.729	106.910

showcasing a statistically significant gap across the different testing mediums. It can be further seen that the mean and variance of ChatGPT are significantly different from the means and variances of the State and Trait Anxiety Inventory.

Figure 9.3 demonstrates the differences in the mean and variance values of the anxiety scores on ChatGPT's Anxiety Assessment Scale and the State and Trait Anxiety Inventory. From Figure 9.3, it can be observed that there is a statistically significant difference in the mean scores of anxieties.

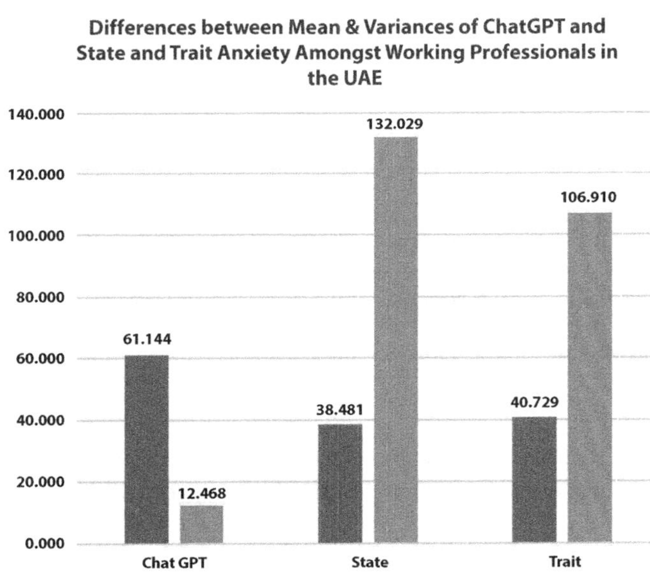

Figure 9.3 Graphical representation of the differences between mean and variances of ChatGPT and state and trait anxiety among working professionals in the UAE.

Table 9.13 Depicting the differences between ChatGPT and state and trait anxiety among working professionals in the UAE using ANOVA.

Source of variation	SS	df	MS	*F*	*p*-Value	*F* crit
Between groups	56,436.6	2	28,218.30	336.73	1.15E−95	3.01
Within groups	45,253.18	540	83.802			
Total	101,689.8	542				

Additionally, it can be observed that there is a drastic difference in the variances of the above three tests. Therefore, it can be concluded that anxiety scores measured by ChatGPT are not similar to the scores of anxieties as measured on the State and Trait Anxiety Inventory.

The ANOVA test was conducted to study the mean differences across the three tests. After the analysis was completed, the following scores were obtained as seen in Table 9.13. For this study, the H0 (null hypothesis) remained as if all means were equal. The obtained p-value is 1.15E−95, and the alpha value, i.e., significance level, is 0.05. Thus, as the p-value is less than the alpha value, the HA (alternate hypothesis) was accepted, thus indicating that the scores of anxieties as observed in the means are not the same.

Table 9.14 depicts the mean differences in levels of anxiety measured by ChatGPT and the State of Anxiety. From Table 9.14, it can be interpreted that there is a significant mean difference in the scores for anxiety. The above results thus indicate that the means are not equal, showcasing a statistically significant gap across the different testing mediums. It can be further seen that the mean and variance of ChatGPT are significantly different from the mean and variance of the State Anxiety Inventory.

Table 9.14 Depicting the differences between mean and variances of ChatGPT and state anxiety among working professionals in the UAE.

	Count	Mean	Variance
ChatGPT	181	61.14	12.47
State Anxiety	181	38.48	132.03

Figure 9.4 depicts the mean differences in levels of anxiety measured by ChatGPT and the State Anxiety Inventory. From Table 9.14, it can be interpreted that there is a significant mean difference in the scores for anxiety. The above results thus indicate that the means are not equal, showcasing a statistically significant gap across the different testing mediums. It can be further seen that the mean and variance of ChatGPT are significantly different from the means and variances of the State Anxiety Inventory.

The ANOVA test was done to study the differences in the means across the above two tests. After the analysis was completed, the following scores were obtained as seen in Table 9.15. For this study, the H0 (null hypothesis) remained as if all means were equal. The obtained p-value is 4E−82, and the alpha value, i.e., significance level, is 0.05. Thus, as the p-value is less than the value of alpha, the null hypothesis was rejected, and the HA (alternate hypothesis) was accepted, thus indicating that the scores of anxieties observed in ChatGPT and State Anxiety are not the same.

Table 9.16 depicts the mean differences in levels of anxiety measured by ChatGPT and the Trait Anxiety Inventory. From Table 9.16, it can be interpreted that there is a considerable mean difference in the scores for anxiety. The above results thus indicate that the means are not equal, showcasing a statistically significant gap across the different testing mediums. It can be further seen that the mean and variance of ChatGPT are significantly different from the means and variances of the Trait Anxiety Inventory.

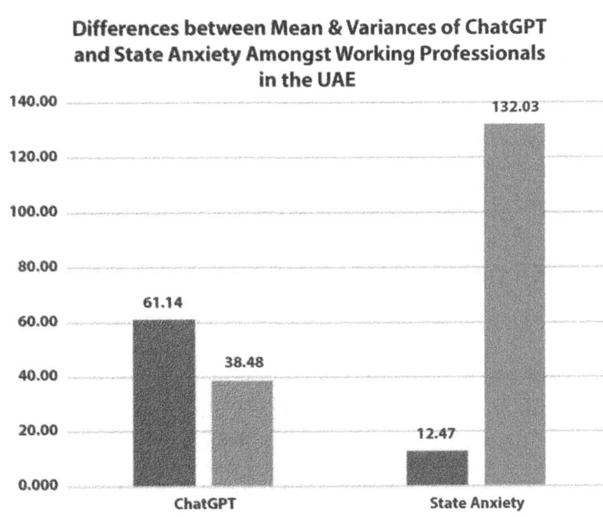

Figure 9.4 Graphical representation of differences between mean and variances of ChatGPT and state anxiety among working professionals in the UAE.

Table 9.15 Depicting the differences in scores of anxiety between ChatGPT and state anxiety among working professionals in the UAE using ANOVA.

Source of variation	SS	df	MS	*F*	*p*-Value	*F* crit
Between groups	46,481.78	1	46,481.78	643.36	4E–82	3.87
Within groups	26,009.45	360	72.25			
Total	72,491.23	361				

Table 9.16 Depicting the differences between mean and variances of ChatGPT and trait anxiety among working professionals in the UAE.

	Count	Average	Variance
ChatGPT	181	61.14	12.47
Trait Anxiety	181	40.73	106.91

Figure 9.5 depicts the mean differences in levels of anxiety measured by ChatGPT and the Trait Anxiety Inventory. From Table 9.16, it can be interpreted that there is a significant mean difference in the scores for anxiety. The above results thus indicate that the means are not equal, showcasing a

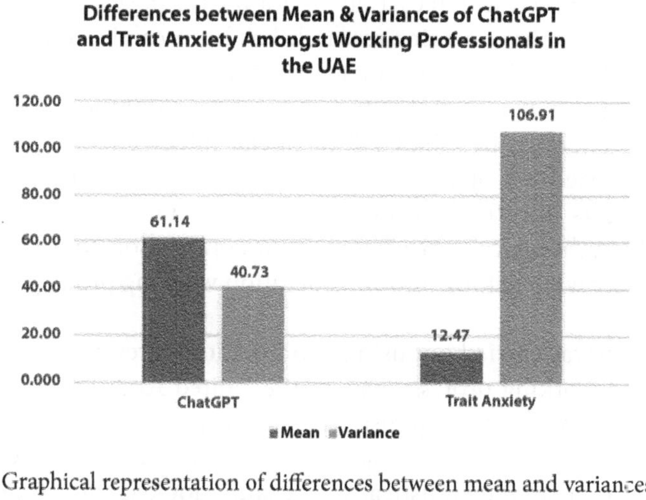

Figure 9.5 Graphical representation of differences between mean and variances of ChatGPT and trait anxiety among working professionals in the UAE.

Table 9.17 Depicting the differences in scores of anxiety between ChatGPT and trait anxiety among working professionals in the UAE using ANOVA.

Source of variation	SS	df	MS	*F*	*p*-Value	*F* crit
Between groups	37,715.5	1	37,715.54	631.87	3.11E–81	3.87
Within groups	21,488	360	59.69			
Total	59,203.5	361				

statistically significant gap across the different testing mediums. It can be further seen that the mean and variance of ChatGPT are significantly different from the means and variances of the Trait Anxiety Inventory.

The ANOVA test was conducted to study the differences in the means across the above two tests. After the analysis was completed, the following scores were obtained as seen in Table 9.17. For this study, the H0 (null hypothesis) remained as if all means were equal. The obtained *p*-value is 3.11E−81, and the alpha value, i.e., significance level, is 0.05. Thus, as the *p*-value is less than the alpha value, the HA (alternate hypothesis) was accepted, thus indicating that the scores of anxieties observed in ChatGPT and Trait Anxiety are not the same.

9.5 Discussion

From the elaborate research carried out for the purpose of this study, it has been made clear that no prior research has been carried out to compare standardized psychological testing with testing generated by artificial intelligence. The primary aim of the study is to understand the efficacy of a test of anxiety generated by ChatGPT (artificial intelligence) in comparison to a standardized test of anxiety. The findings have thrown light on some crucial insights into the efficacy of an artificial-intelligence (ChatGPT)-generated psychological test of anxiety in comparison to a standardized test of anxiety while taking into consideration working professionals in the UAE.

This study was carried out using two questionnaires, which were circulated among working professionals in the United Arab Emirates through social media platforms. Responses were collected from professionals and entrepreneurs in the United Arab Emirates. The data collected from the research were analyzed statistically. The study looked into three primary objectives: (i) to explore the efficacy of a test of anxiety generated by artificial intelligence in comparison to a standardized test of anxiety, (ii) to assess the differences in rates of anxiety among male and female working professionals in the UAE, and (iii) to understand the levels of anxiety among working professionals across different age groups.

The results implied that there is a substantial difference in anxiety among male and female working professionals in the UAE. Female working professionals have greater levels of anxiety in comparison to male working professionals in the UAE. This was identified using an independent *Z*-test. This finding is highly consistent with previous studies carried out, thus highlighting the gender disparities in the prevalence of anxiety in the UAE. Females were reported to show higher rates of depression and anxiety compared to males [17, 19].

Some factors that could explain the higher levels of anxiety among females include gender roles and socio-cultural factors that add responsibility and worry [18]. Lack of social and financial support, stress due to their working conditions, and inability to balance their work life and personal life are also some factors that point toward the greater rates of anxiety among females [25]. These studies highlight the pressing need to address these gender-specific issues in the workplace to help women manage and cope with their anxiety [22]. Implementation of policies to create a supportive environment at the workplace can also help enhance well-being.

Furthermore, this study also pointed out that there is a sizable difference in the levels of anxiety among young and middle-aged working professionals in the UAE. Middle-aged working professionals exhibit greater levels of anxiety in comparison to young working professionals in the UAE. This finding was not previously found in the research reviewed for the study, but they do imply that age as a factor may play an imperative role in the development of anxiety. Addressing concerns of the middle-aged pertaining to retirement, work-life balance, mid-life crisis, career advancement, and health factors may help mitigate the trend of rising anxiety and promote quality of life.

In addition to the above, the study also examined the effectiveness of an anxiety test generated by ChatGPT in comparison to the State–Trait Anxiety Inventory. The study found significant differences in the scores observed. The scores obtained on artificial intelligence were compared independently with the State–Trait Anxiety Inventory, the State Anxiety Inventory, and the Trait Anxiety Inventory. The results showed that anxiety scores measured by ChatGPT are not similar to the scores of anxieties as measured on the State–Trait Anxiety Inventory. Further, it also showed that scores of anxieties as observed in the means of ChatGPT and State Anxiety and ChatGPT and Trait Anxiety were significantly different. These findings from the above study suggest that artificial intelligence has not effectively understood the multiaxial nature of anxiety.

Through this study, it can be implied that artificial intelligence can prove to be a revolutionary tool that can be employed in psychological testing. ChatGPT holds potential as it is both an effective and a feasible platform, but it is not reliable enough to make use of its advantages to boost psychological testing [15]. Mental health experts and psychometricians can work together alongside artificial intelligence experts in integrating measures to make this artificial intelligence as a platform more reliable and valid to standardize it. Artificial intelligence can help identify patterns and symptoms, which can aid in the formulation of a diagnosis [9]. This can help provide a holistic and comprehensive understanding of anxiety and its diagnosis, which can assist in developing better treatment plans in a faster and more feasible manner.

Artificial intelligence can work alongside traditional methods to improve speed and accuracy [10] and can help mitigate potential errors that may be caused as a result of human error [11].

The above study has quite a few strengths due to its employment of a highly reliable and valid anxiety inventory (State–Trait Anxiety Inventory). The collected data was also analyzed using advanced statistical measures. Furthermore, the surveys were circulated on digital platforms, thus maintaining confidentiality and ensuring convenience.

Future recommendations focus on strategies to improve the efficacy of artificial-intelligence-generated tests of psychological illness. Using different platforms of artificial intelligence to study the efficacy of artificial-intelligence-generated psychological tests may also help provide a wider range of data, which can help understand its potential for standardization. It is also recommended to employ a wider sample to better understand the prevalence of anxiety among working professionals in the United Arab Emirates. By taking these above findings into consideration, mental health experts can help develop policies and strategies to promote more accurate diagnoses such as anxiety and its treatment; this can help facilitate a better quality of life and well-being of working professionals across the United Arab Emirates.

9.6 Limitations

The above study has the following few limitations, which may be taken into consideration for further research and development. The sample size could be higher in number to get a better understanding of the prevalence of anxiety among working professionals in the United Arab Emirates. Additionally, the test inventories used for the purpose of this research had multiple questions, summing up to a total of 60 questions, which may have caused a potential lack of interest in completing the survey or may have impacted the mood of the participants. The self-report methodology used may pose a risk of "Social Desirability," which is the tendency of the participant to choose a response that makes them feel socially accepted, and "Acquiescence," which is the inclination to choose responses irrespective of their content or meaning. Finally, the circulation of the questionnaire on social media platforms may have caused a limitation in achieving a greater number of participants due to the digital divide.

9.7 Conclusions and Implications

Anxiety is one of the most widespread mental health concerns; it tends to affect a wide population at least once across the span of their lives. It is a debilitating condition that causes individuals to react in ways that may cause them to avoid situations that trigger these thoughts. The post-pandemic period has seen a significant rise in levels of anxiety among working professionals. Loss of jobs, uncertainty, financial struggles, transition to online platforms for work, and rising competition are some of the reasons that cause struggles in the work–life balance of working professionals. All of these factors point toward potential causes that have increased the levels of anxiety among working professionals.

The study conducted analyzed anxiety across the population of working professionals in the United Arab Emirates. Multiple existing studies on similar areas were reviewed to help identify gaps. The study aimed to examine the efficacy of a ChatGPT (artificial intelligence)-generated test of anxiety in comparison to a standardized test of anxiety (State–Trait Anxiety Inventory) while observing the differences in the levels of anxiety across age groups and genders. According to the analysis conducted, multiple key findings were observed: female working professionals in the United Arab Emirates report higher levels of anxiety compared to males. Additionally, it was found that middle-aged working professionals in the UAE have greater levels of anxiety in comparison to young working professionals in the UAE.

The study further revealed that the novel test of anxiety generated by artificial intelligence (Anxiety Assessment Scale) did not prove to be as effective as the State–Trait Anxiety Inventory. This suggests that artificial intelligence does not take into consideration all the dimensions and nuances of anxiety as measured by standardized and traditional inventories. This study thus suggests that artificial intelligence should be used alongside standardized measures to produce maximum efficacy and benefits.

In conclusion, this study offers beneficial insights into the utilization of artificial intelligence in psychological testing. The study highlights the importance of refining these tools to match the reliability, validity, and other features of standardized tests. It also provides data that can be used by psychologists in formulating policies to help mitigate the rising levels of anxiety and promote well-being.

References

1. Thibaut, F., Full article: Anxiety disorders: A review of current literature, in: *Taylor & Francis Online*, 2022, April 1, https://www.tandfonlin.com/doi/full/10.31887/DCNS.2017.19.2/fthibaut.
2. American Psychiatric Association, Anxiety disorders, in: *Diagnostic and Statistical Manual of Mental Disorders*, 5th, 2013, https://doi.org/10.1176/appi.books.9780890425596.dsm05.
3. American Psychological Association, *Anxiety*, American Psychological Association, n.d, https://www.apa.org/topics/anxiety.
4. Kothari, Dr. V., Anxiety Disorders, Panic and Phobias, in: *Psychopathology*, pp. 71–83, Spring Season Publications, Navi Mumbai, 2020.
5. U.S. Department of Health and Human Services, *Anxiety Disorders*, National Institute of Mental Health, 2024, December, https://www.nimh.nih.gov/health/topics/anxiety-disorders.
6. Saddik, B., Hussein, A., Albanna, A., Elbarazi, I., Al-Shujairi, A., Temsah, M., Sharif-Askari, F.S., Stip, E., Hamid, Q., Halwani, R., The psychological impact of the COVID-19 pandemic on adults and children in the United Arab Emirates: a nationwide cross-sectional study. *BMC Psychiatry*, *21*, 1, 8, 2021. https://doi.org/10.1186/s12888-021-03213-2.
7. Mohan, H. and Lone, Z.A., Loneliness and mental health amongst Indians working in Abu Dhabi, UAE. *J. Crit. Rev.*, 8, 2, 559–572, 2021. https://doi.org/10.2139/ssrn.3841377.
8. Copeland, B.J., Artificial intelligence, in: *Encyclopedia Britannica*, 2024. https://www.britannica.com/technology/artificial-intelligence.
9. Singh, O.P., Artificial intelligence in the era of ChatGPT- Opportunities and challenges in mental health care. *Indian J. Psychiatry*, *65*, 3, 297, 2023. https://doi.org/10.4103/indianjpsychiatry.indianjpsychiatry_112_23.

10. Ćosić, K., Popović, S., Šarlija, M., Kesedžić, I., Jovanovic, T., Artificial Intelligence in the prediction of mental health disorders induced by the COVID-19 pandemic among healthcare workers. *Croatian Med. J.*, 61, 3, 279–288, 2020, July 5. https://www.ncbi.nlm.nih.gov/pmc/articles/PMC7358693/.
11. Graham, S., Depp, C., Lee, E.E., Nebeker, C., Tu, X., Kim, H., Jeste, D.V., Artificial Intelligence for Mental Health and Mental Illnesses: an Overview. *Curr. Psychiatry Rep.*, *21*, 11, 2019. https://doi.org/10.1007/s11920-019-1094-0.
12. Salah, M., Alhalbusi, H., Abdelfattah, F., Ismail, M.M., Chatting with ChatGPT: Investigating the Impact on Psychological Well-being and Self-esteem with a Focus on Harmful Stereotypes and Job Anxiety as Moderator. *Res. Square (Research Square)*, 2023. https://doi.org/10.21203/rs.3.rs-2610655/v1.
13. Uduafemhe, M., Exploring the potential of artificial intelligence to improve psychological testing accuracy, in: *Leverage Assessments Website*, 2023, January 13, https://www.leverageassessments.com/exploring-the-potential-of-artificial-intelligence-to-improve-psychological-testing-accuracy/.
14. Gregory, R.J., *Psychological testing: History, Principles, and Applications History, Principles and Applications*, Pearson Higher Ed, Boston, 2013.
15. Zhou, S., Zhao, J., Zhang, L., Application of Artificial Intelligence on Psychological Interventions and Diagnosis: An Overview. *Front. Psychiatry*, *13*, 5, 2022. https://doi.org/10.3389/fpsyt.2022.811665.
16. Dergaa, I., Fekih-Romdhane, F., Hallit, S., Loch, A.A., Glenn, J.M., Fessi, M.S., Aissa, M.B., Souissi, N., Guelmami, N., Swed, S., Omri, A.E., Bragazzi, N.L., Saad, H.B., ChatGPT is not ready yet for use in providing mental health assessment and interventions. *Front. Psychiatry*, *14*, 2024. https://doi.org/10.3389/fpsyt.2023.1277756.
17. Blooshi, M.A., Ameri, T.A., Marri, M.A., Ahmad, A., Leinberger-Jabari, A., Abdulle, A., Taimah, M., Zaabi, T.A., Remeithi, K.A., Hosani, A.A., Sherman, S., Ali, R., The impact of the COVID-19 pandemic on depression and anxiety symptoms: Findings from the United Arab Emirates Healthy Future (UAEHFS) cohort study. *PLoS One*, *17*, 11, e0277684, 2022. https://doi.org/10.1371/journal.pone.0277684.
18. Saddik, B., Hussein, A., Sharif-Askari, F.S., Kheder, W., Temsah, M.H., Koutaich, R.A., Haddad, E.S., Al-Roub, N.M., Marhoon, F.A., Hamid, Q., Halwani, R., Increased Levels of Anxiety Among Medical and Non-Medical University Students During the COVID-19 Pandemic in the United Arab Emirates. *Risk Manage. Healthcare Policy*, *13*, 2395–2406, 2020. https://doi.org/10.2147/RMHP.S273333.
19. Marzouqi, A.M.A., Otim, M.E., Alblooshi, A., Marzooqi, S.A., Talal, M., Wassim, F., Prevalence of Depression, Anxiety, and Stress Among Undergraduate Students in the Middle East: a Cross-sectional Survey in United Arab Emirates. *Res. Square (Research Square)*, 2021. https://doi.org/10.21203/rs.3.rs-577800/v1.

20. Jiang, L., Tian, X., Ren, P., Luo, F., A new type of mental health assessment using artificial intelligence technique. *Adv. Psychol. Sci.*, *30*, 1, 157–167, 2022. https://doi.org/10.3724/sp.j.1042.2022.00157.
21. Masri, R.Y. and Jani, H.M., Artificial intelligence techniques are employed in mental health diagnostic expert systems, in: *2012 International Conference on Computer & Information Science (ICCIS)*, vol. 1, IEEE, pp. 495–499, 2012, June.
22. Zarooni, A.A.R.A., Alghfeli, A.K., Alremeithi, H.M., Almadhaani, R.A., Alketbi, L.B., *Impact of COVID-19 on depression and anxiety among healthcare professionals in Abu Dhabi*, 18, 3, e0282198, 2023. https://doi.org/10.1371/journal.pone.0282198.
23. Kim, S.H., Rising, S., Green, R., Sin, C., Machine learning analysis of The mmpi -2 items For Gender Identity. *J. Asia Pac. Couns.*, 10, 2, 79–98, 2020. http://japconline.org/journal/article.php?code=75197.
24. Fitzpatrick, K.K., Darcy, A., Vierhile, M., Delivering cognitive behavior therapy to young adults with symptoms of depression and anxiety using a fully automated conversational agent (Woebot): a randomized controlled trial. *JMIR Ment. Health*, 4, 2, e7785, 2017.
25. Faisal, W.A., *Perceived depression, anxiety and stress among Dubai Health Authority residents*, Damasuniv, Dubai, UAE, 2022, https://www.academia.edu/70306381/Perceived_Depression_Anxiety_and_Stress_Among_Dubai_Health_Authority_Residents_Dubai_UAE.
26. Fulmer, R., Joerin, A., Gentile, B., Lakerink, L., Rauws, M., Using Psychological Artificial intelligence (TESS) to relieve symptoms of depression and anxiety: randomized controlled trial. *JMIR Mental Health*, *5*, 4, e64, 2018. https://doi.org/10.2196/mental.9782.
27. Boucher, E.M., Harake, N.R., Ward, H.E., Stoeckl, S.E., Vargas, J., Minkel, J., Zilca, R., Artificially intelligent chatbots in digital mental health interventions: a review. *Expert Rev. Med. Devices*, *18*, sup1, 37–49, 2021, https://doi.org/10.1080/17434440.2021.2013200.
28. Dashwood, M., Churchhouse, G., Young, M., Kuruvilla, T., *Artificial Intelligence as an aid to diagnosing dementia: An overview*, Wiley Online Library, 2021, https://wchh.onlinelibrary.wiley.com/doi/pdfdirect/10.1002/pnp.721.
29. Mrabet, J. and Studholme, R., ChatGPT: A friend or a foe?, in: *International Conference on Computational Intelligence and Knowledge Economy (ICCIKE)*, Dubai, United Arab Emirates, pp. 269–274, 20232023, doi: 10.1109/ICCIKE58312.2023.10131713.
30. Alanezi, F., Assessing the Effectiveness of ChatGPT in Delivering Mental Health Support: A Qualitative Study. *J. Multi. Healthcare*, *17*, 461–471, 2024. https://doi.org/10.2147/JMDH.S447368.

31. Levkovich, I. and Elyoseph, Z., Suicide risk assessments through the eyes of ChatGPT-3.5 versus ChatGPT-4: vignette study. *JMIR Ment. Health, 10,* e51232, 2023.
32. OpenAI, 2023. ChatGPT (Mar 14 version) [Large language model].

10

Predictive Analysis for Mental Health Stigma: Self-Awareness Alleviates Mental and Physical Illnesses

Prerna Chowdhary Siroya* **and Jihene Mrabet**

Amity University, Dubai, UAE

Abstract

Self-awareness is an innate skill, something that each one of us must learn to better develop over time to have good health, both mental and physical. Time and application of this self-awareness is key to one's healthy survival not just to cope but rather to enhance the experiences one faces in life. The simple yet complex journey every individual goes through is one of "self-discovery." It is a lifelong learning that one must unlearn and learn many times.

This qualitative research aims to show this correlation between conscious self-awareness and health and how people in general have different levels of self-awareness. It gathers how one consciously applies it depending upon the current situation of life and how this defines abilities to either enhance their experiences or well-being or to unconsciously embark on the longer struggle till the self-awareness journey is awakened. This was done using a two-method data collection using a 38-item Self-Awareness Outcomes Questionnaire (SAOQ) that evaluates one's Perceived Self-Development, Accountability, Proactivity at Work, and Emotional Costs to define the control and focus groups, followed by a 19-question interview to understand how people in different situations and with different challenges faced in their lives use this self-awareness.

The results reveal that the Focus Group had a tough time trying to navigate life's challenges related to but not limited to mental and physical health in comparison to the Control Group, which showed a deeper understanding of the challenges by learning and implementing those lessons in their daily lives.

**Corresponding author*: pchowdhary@amityuniversity.ae

Ridhima Sharma, Fazla Rabby, Rohit Bansal, Timcy Sachdeva and Jihene Mrabet (eds.) Confronting Mental Health Stigma with AI and Machine Learning, (239–282) ©2026 Scrivener Publishing LLC

Keywords: Mental health and self-awareness, mental health and physical health relationship, self-awareness impact on mental health, self-awareness impact on physical health

10.1 Introduction

Self-awareness has been a subject of interest for numerous psychologists, and more light is being shed on the benefits of this self-awareness. The Seminal theory [60] of self-awareness pertains to the act of directing one's attention toward oneself and possessing a conscious understanding of attitudes and dispositions. The concept of mindful understanding encompasses the recognition and acknowledgement of various aspects such as bodily sensations, emotional states, cognitive processes, interpersonal connections, and their interplay [1].

They further added that people can direct their attention at any time to themselves or the external environment, thus allowing for self-evaluation. Comparing oneself to standards might cause people to behave differently and experience both pride and dissatisfaction with themselves. Self-awareness is an important process of self-control [2]. Surprisingly, studies have found that when people are not self-focused, their behaviors are frequently unconnected to their personal standards—self-awareness is required for people to lessen differences between their acts and goals [3]. During the latter part of the 19th century, William James introduced the differentiation between the subjective and objective self.

The ongoing pursuit to establish the precise moment at which the self emerges, its significance, and its implications for our developmental trajectory remains a subject of scholarly inquiry [4, 61]. In our current research, we are aiming to find if self-awareness could alleviate mental and physical illnesses, for which we did find that self-awareness can in fact achieve the desired results.

10.2 Review of Literature

10.2.1 Definition of Self-Awareness

Self-awareness is one's ability to perceive and comprehend the aspects of their identity, including personality, actions, values, beliefs, emotions, and ideas. It is a psychological state where the ego is the center of attention [5]. Research indicates that when one has a distinct image of themselves, they are confident, creative, make better decisions, reinforce relationships, and communicate effectively. It is less likely that one will deceive, cheat, or steal. They are superior employees who receive more promotions and are more effective leaders with happier workers and more profitable businesses [6]. According to the American Psychological Association, self-awareness is defined as "the consequences of focusing attention on the self" [7].

Contemporary research and literature frequently differentiate between two distinct forms of self-awareness, which are subjective and objective. The concept of "subjective self-awareness" posits that individuals are the creators of their own perceptions, thoughts, and actions. Our observations and experiences shape our perception that the world revolves around us [8]. The American Psychological Association defines "objective self-awareness" as a reflective state of self-focused attention. When we compare ourselves to others and change our behaviors and ideas to fit the outside view of acceptance and validation, unease arises as our ideal and actual selves vary [9].

10.2.2 Theories of Self-Awareness

10.2.2.1 Philippe Rochat: The Five Levels of Self-Awareness in Childhood

According to this theory, children typically attain self-awareness at approximately 18 months of age. This stage signifies the onset of the commonly known "terrible twos" experienced by numerous parents. The child displays an increased level of independence in their behavior. Individuals perceive themselves as distinct from others and demonstrate self-awareness by exhibiting recognition of their own reflection in mirrors. The individual's recently preferred term is 'no' — this statement exemplifies "subjective awareness" [10].

- Level 0 — Confusion: Child exhibits a lack of ability to distinguish between their own physical presence and the image of their physical presence reflected on a surface.
- Level 1 — Differentiation: Child develops an awareness that the mirror serves as a representation of the surrounding environment; they perceive a variance in the observed phenomenon.

- Level 2 — Situation: Child demonstrates an understanding that the reflection exists externally in relation to their physical body.
- Level 3 — Identification: Acknowledgement of the reflection as a representation of oneself becomes increasingly evident.
- Level 4 — Permanence: Child demonstrates the ability to recognize their own image in visual media even when the depicted self is at a younger age.
- Level 5 — Self-consciousness or "meta": Child demonstrates an understanding of social perception [11].

10.2.2.2 Dan Goleman: Emotional Self-Awareness and Emotional Intelligence

According to Goleman [67], self-awareness skills encompass the ability to comprehend one's emotions and underlying causes. The aforementioned factors serve as the foundation for sound intuition and effective decision making. Self-awareness serves as a guiding principle for ethical decision making. The theory outlines three competencies that are integral to self-awareness.

- Emotional self-awareness — Ability to identify and acknowledge our own emotions and their impacts.
- Accurate self-assessment — Acquiring an understanding of one's own capabilities and limitations.
- Self-confidence — Possessing a robust perception of our inherent value and aptitudes.

Self-confidence refers to an individual's belief in their own abilities and inherent value. According to Goleman, the acquisition of emotional intelligence is contingent upon the mastery of three essential skills that operate on self-awareness. It is widely acknowledged that humans possess an innate inclination toward socialization, indicating their status as social animals. According to Mlodinow [68], it is common for communication to take place on an unconscious level. The level of familiarity between individuals is inconsequential. Typically, individuals possess a high level of proficiency in discerning nonverbal cues. Enhancing one's self-awareness has the potential to result in improved interpersonal achievements across diverse social groups [12].

10.2.3 Different Types of Self-Awareness

The concept of *Internal Self-Awareness* is an individual's ability to accurately perceive their own thoughts, emotions, and values, to know how these internal factors impact their behavior and decision making. As per Dr. Eurich's assertion, the concept of internal self-awareness is an individual's ability to identify their own values, passions, aspirations, and responses — within their surroundings (encompassing thoughts, emotions, actions, strengths, and limitations). The attainment of internal self-awareness is vital for an individual's psychological well-being, as it enables them to identify or anticipate any potential triggers that may impact their mental health. In the context of substance use disorder recovery, self-awareness of personal behaviors and vulnerabilities can facilitate the acquisition of coping mechanisms that promote adherence to the recovery process.

External Self-Awareness is an individual's ability to observe and comprehend how others perceive them. External self-awareness pertains to comprehending how individuals perceive oneself on factors including values, ambitions, feelings, behaviors, strengths, weaknesses, and the influence one has on another. Furthermore, individuals who possess external self-awareness exhibit elevated levels of empathy and robust social norms. It is imperative for individuals to acquire the skill of balancing both internal and external self-awareness to prevent excessive preoccupation with external opinions, which may result in social anxiety, rumination, and hyper-analysis [13, 14].

The concept of self-awareness is broken down into four distinct dimensions.

1. Awareness of another's opinion
Even if one may not realize it, other people's judgments and opinions have weight. The truth of the matter is that people's ideas and impressions of our persona are a direct reflection of the impact we have on them. We have no power to change people's responses; all we can do is control the impact we have on them. A key indicator of our impact on the environment is the reaction that our actions cause. With the use of empathy, we may better understand who we are and change the way we behave. It should be emphasized that some people's emotions could not be indicative of anything.

2. Awareness of the thoughts and feelings about oneself
The second facet of self-awareness pertains to comprehending the underlying factors that give rise to our cognitive and affective responses directed toward our own selves. If due caution is not exercised, one's thoughts and

emotions can potentially cause harm to their spiritual essence. The negativity bias of the human brain results in a greater weightage being assigned to negative experiences, leading to a higher likelihood of recollection of disparaging remarks made by a parent or former partner as compared to compliments received from a coach. Consequently, individuals tend to establish their self-concept based on adverse encounters.

However, one's personal history may also encompass instances of positivity and emotional sensitivity, necessitating a greater effort to unearth such recollections. It is imperative to acknowledge and retain the recollections of those who have provided us with affection and motivation.

3. Awareness of self-perception

The third dimension of self-awareness pertains to the introspective evaluation of one's actions, motivations, and emotions as a reflection of their true self. According to Stephen M.R. Covey in his publication titled The Speed of Trust, individuals tend to evaluate themselves based on their own intentions, while assessing others based on their actions. This is a phenomenon of individuals possessing a certain identity but exhibiting behaviors that are incongruent with said identity. This inconsistency is attributed to a limited awareness of one's actions as opposed to one's intentions.

4. Awareness of future self

The fourth dimension of self-awareness pertains to the comprehension of one's future self and the desired identity one aspires to attain. It is imperative to engage in periodic introspection regarding our desired personal growth trajectory as we advance in age and experience. This necessitates relinquishing (1) external perceptions of oneself, (2) internal self-perceptions, and (3) current societal conventions, actions, and routines. It is imperative to shift our cognitive focus from historical events and current circumstances toward prospective endeavors [15].

10.2.4 External Research on the Impact of Self-Awareness in Life

Self-Awareness and Mental and Physical Health

Self-awareness has been seen by practitioners and researchers as a fundamental strategy of reducing mental discomfort and the track to self-development for mentally healthy individuals. This is discussed by Anna Sutton, the founder of the Self-Awareness Outcomes Questionnaire, which we have used in this study.

Self-Awareness and Psychopathology

In psychiatric disorders, the pathophysiology is rooted in the brain. In this context, neuropsychology presents a potentially useful strategy [59]. An example of a specific psychological dysfunction domain is self-reflection, which satisfies three criteria: (1) is measurable using performance-based tests and self-report scales; (2) is frequently disrupted in psychiatric illness; and (3) can be dimensionally linked to activity within a specific neural circuit.

In this paper, we review pertinent literature, highlight open research issues, and suggest a research agenda that would facilitate the use of neuropsychological self-reflection measures in conjunction with neuroimaging as a model for developing a neuro-psycho-pathophysiological foundation for mental health services.

Self-Awareness and Personality

Aiming for and achieving goals is a constant process in life [69]. It's a reality that most human behavior, whether it be in relationships, sports, the workplace, or health, is thought to be goal driven. Goal-related obstacles, or things that get in the way of a goal that has been set [62], are recognized as a necessary condition for successfully achieving goals [63, 70]. Goal pursuit, however, is not always without difficulties. Using a personality–psychological approach, the research examines individual variations in self-awareness as well as a person's propensity to focus on themselves as a possible precursor to the identification of difficulties. By analyzing self-awareness in the context of daily goal pursuit, they expanded on studies highlighting the importance of personality processes for studying self-regulatory processes (Hoyle, 2010). Then, they clarify the importance of obstacle identification in the goal-pursuit process and go over how self-awareness should make it easier to identify goal-related difficulties, which is how they demonstrate how self-awareness plays an essential part in self-regulation.

Self-Awareness and Performance

The constant modifications in our environment require training that incorporates technical knowledge in the areas of mental health and awareness. Demand is strong, especially in industries like engineering, which can harm students' mental health by elevating stress and psychological pain, which reduces self-efficacy and detracts from academic achievement. Healthier environments emphasize embodied learning and put a strong emphasis on stress reduction, self-awareness, and self-knowledge. For this population group, creative therapies may serve as an effective means of promoting health problem prevention. For example, dance movement therapy has shown promise in both clinical and non-clinical contexts for enhancing health. In this study, engineering students participate in the development and application of a body awareness program based on dance movement therapy. Its impact was assessed using a mixed pre-post methodology. Data sources include reflective diaries, physiological indicators, and psychometric exams. The findings indicate that the experimental group experienced lower stress levels and higher degrees of body awareness and connectedness, well-being, and life satisfaction than the control group. Measures of cortisol confirmed the results. Additionally, the students recognized that their levels of self-awareness and self-knowledge had risen and that these bodily techniques needed to be included in higher education.

10.3 Methodology

This study aims at clarifying the role of self-awareness on mental and physical health. It explains whether awareness allows one to take control of 'life' and how the stressors of life are better regulated. It addresses an important area of research with significant implications for understanding, prevention, and intervention efforts, ultimately resulting in improved outcomes for this population's mental and physical health. Past research and present studies focusing more on patients have been used to underline the rapport among self-awareness and mental plus physical health. Moreover, the potential strategies to become more in control, which may help the patients, are also discussed. Furthermore, the study aims to fill the gaps in the literature and understand the factors that influence the lack of self-awareness in the population. The sample of this study comprised 12 participants with a mean age of 35, working in the United Arab Emirates and India. The research design is an effective strategy used to address the main problem and logically integrate the different variables of the study. This study employs the Self-Awareness Outcomes Questionnaire (SAOQ) — a self-report 38-item questionnaire designed to assess the frequency with which respondents experience outcomes related to the development of self-awareness. It measures 4 subscales of Perceived Self-Development, Acceptance, Proactivity at Work, and Emotional Costs. The reflective self-development subscale (RSD, 11 items) contains items representing the development of continuous attention to the self, with a focus on conscious, reflective, and balanced learning. The acceptance of self and others subscale (Acceptance, 11 items) represents outcomes including a positive self-image and confidence as well as a deeper understanding of others. The proactive at work subscale (Proactive at Work, 9 items) consists of items specifically related to the outcomes of self-awareness in the workplace and represents an objective and proactive approach to dealing with work. The final subscale represents the emotional costs of self-awareness (Emotional Costs, 7 items) and includes items representing the potential negative emotional impacts of being more aware of oneself, such as guilt, vulnerability, and fear. The first three subscale scores are added as they have a positive impact on a person's self-awareness, and the score of the last subscale of Emotional Costs is subtracted from the sum of the first three subscales as it has a negative impact on one's self-awareness.

A 20-question interview was conducted, which was inspired by different literature review studies. It went through an inter-judge validity process where the questions were shared with other experts who agreed that these questions were able to measure our aim of research.

The questions were as follows:

- Do you suffer from any mental/physical illnesses? May I ask what it is?
- Does it hamper your life or daily activities?
- How would you describe your work atmosphere?
- Do you have a good working relationship with your boss/manager/colleagues?
- How do you describe your relationship with your family?
- How do you describe your relationship with your friends?
- Do you often feel angry?
- What makes you angry?
- What does 'having fun' mean to you?
- What do you think about your future?
- How do you see yourself in your future?
- Do you have any goals that you are working toward? What are they?
- As a kid, was 'healthy living' given importance to? Physical and mental
- Growing up, were you taught about mental/physical health? Who — home/school?
- Did your parents insist on this healthy lifestyle?
- Did they talk to you about mental health?
- Was it a taboo/open conversation?
- How did your parents handle stress?

- Did they have open dialogue with you about the meaning of certain concepts (confidence/stress/emotions/self-awareness)?

10.4 Results for SAOQ Scale

The Self-Awareness Outcomes Questionnaire (SAOQ) — a 38-item questionnaire — has 4 subscales of Perceived Self-Development (RSD), Acceptance (ACC), Proactivity at Work (PRO), and Emotional Costs (EMO). The first three subscale scores are added as they have a positive impact on a person's self-awareness, and the score of the last subscale of Emotional Costs is subtracted from the sum of the first three subscales as it has a negative impact on one's self-awareness. The final number helped categorize participants into the Focus Group and the Control Group.

Focus Group:

	[RSD + ACC + PRO] – [EMO]			
	RSD	ACC	PRO	EMO
	4.09	3.09	4.22	3.85
Participant no. 1	[4.09 + 3.09 + 4.22] – [3.85] = 7.55			

The result of participant 1 for Perceived Self-Development (RSD) was 4.09, Acceptance (ACC) was 3.09, Proactivity at Work (PRO) was 4.22, and Emotional Costs (EMO) was 3.85. The result of EMO was then subtracted from the sum of RSD + ACC + PRO to arrive at a final score of 7.55.

	[RSD + ACC + PRO] – [EMO]			
	RSD	ACC	PRO	EMO
	4	4.09	3.55	4.14
Participant no. 2	[4 + 34.09 + 3.55] – [4.14] = 7.50			

The result of participant 2 for Perceived Self-Development (RSD) was 4, Acceptance (ACC) was 4.09, Proactivity at Work (PRO) was 3.55, and

Emotional Costs (EMO) was 4.14. The result of EMO was then subtracted from the sum of RSD + ACC + PRO to arrive at the final score of 7.50.

	[RSD + ACC + PRO] – [EMO]			
	RSD	ACC	PRO	EMO
	3.09	3.18	3.77	3.57
Participant no. 3	[3.09 + 3.18 + 3.77] – [3.57] = 7.28			

The result of participant 3 for Perceived Self-Development (RSD) was 3.09, Acceptance (ACC) was 3.18, Proactivity at Work (PRO) was 3.77, and Emotional Costs (EMO) was 3.57. The result of EMO was then subtracted from the sum of RSD + ACC + PRO to arrive at the final score of 7.28.

	[RSD + ACC + PRO] – [EMO]			
	RSD	ACC	PRO	EMO
	3.45	3.54	3.66	3.42
Participant no. 4	[3.45 + 3.54 + 3.66] – [3.42] = 7.23			

The result of participant 4 for Perceived Self-Development (RSD) was 3.45, Acceptance (ACC) was 3.54, Proactivity at Work (PRO) was 3.66, and Emotional Costs (EMO) was 3.42. The result of EMO was then subtracted from the sum of RSD + ACC + PRO to arrive at the final score of 7.23.

	[RSD + ACC + PRO] – [EMO]			
	RSD	ACC	PRO	EMO
	3.45	3	4.55	4.28
Participant no. 5	[3.45 + 3 + 4.55] – [4.28] = 6.72			

The result of participant 5 for Perceived Self-Development (RSD) was 3.45, Acceptance (ACC) was 3, Proactivity at Work (PRO) was 4.55, and Emotional Costs (EMO) was 4.28. The result of EMO was then subtracted from the sum of RSD + ACC + PRO to arrive at a final score of 6.72.

	[RSD + ACC + PRO] – [EMO]			
	RSD	ACC	PRO	EMO
	3.27	3	3.22	3.24
Participant no. 6	[3.27 + 3 + 3.22] – [3.42] = 6.07			

The result of participant 6 for Perceived Self-Development (RSD) was 3.27, Acceptance (ACC) was 3, Proactivity at Work (PRO) was 3.22, and Emotional Costs (EMO) was 3.24. The result of EMO was then subtracted from the sum of RSD + ACC + PRO to arrive at a final score of 6.07.

Control Group:

	[RSD + ACC + PRO] – [EMO]			
	RSD	ACC	PRO	EMO
	4.62	3.90	3.66	1.85
Participant no. 7	[4.62 + 3.90 + 3.66] – [1.85] = 10.34			

The result of participant 7 for Perceived Self-Development (RSD) was 4.62, Acceptance (ACC) was 3.90, Proactivity at Work (PRO) was 3.66, and Emotional Costs (EMO) was 1.85. The result of EMO was then subtracted from the sum of RSD + ACC + PRO to arrive at the final score of 10.34.

	[RSD + ACC + PRO] – [EMO]			
	RSD	ACC	PRO	EMO
	4.18	4.09	4	2.57
Participant no. 8	[4.18 + 4.09 + 4] – [2.57] = 9.70			

The result of participant 8 for Perceived Self-Development (RSD) was 4.18, Acceptance (ACC) was 4.09, Proactivity at Work (PRO) was 4, and Emotional Costs (EMO) was 2.57. The result of EMO was then subtracted from the sum of RSD + ACC + PRO to arrive at the final score of 9.70.

	[RSD + ACC + PRO] – [EMO]			
	RSD	ACC	PRO	EMO
	4	4.18	4.33	3.14
Participant no. 9	[4 + 4.18 + 4.33] – [3.14] = 9.37			

The result of participant 9 for Perceived Self-Development (RSD) was 4, Acceptance (ACC) was 4.18, Proactivity at Work (PRO) was 4.33, and Emotional Costs (EMO) was 3.14. The result of EMO was then subtracted from the sum of RSD + ACC + PRO to arrive at the final score of 9.37.

	[RSD + ACC + PRO] – [EMO]			
	RSD	ACC	PRO	EMO
	3.72	4	3.88	2.57
Participant no. 10	[3.72 + 4 + 3.88] – [2.57] = 9.03			

The result of participant 10 for Perceived Self-Development (RSD) was 3.72, Acceptance (ACC) was 4, Proactivity at Work (PRO) was 3.88, and Emotional Costs (EMO) was 2.57. The result of EMO was then subtracted from the sum of RSD + ACC + PRO to arrive at the final score of 9.03.

	[RSD + ACC + PRO] – [EMO]			
	RSD	ACC	PRO	EMO
	3.27	3.81	4.22	2.85
Participant no. 11	[3.27 + 3.81 + 4.22] – [2.85] = 8.45			

The result of participant 11 for Perceived Self-Development (RSD) was 3.27, Acceptance (ACC) was 3.81, Proactivity at Work (PRO) was 4.22, and Emotional Costs (EMO) was 2.85. The result of EMO was then subtracted from the sum of RSD + ACC + PRO to arrive at the final score of 8.45.

	[RSD + ACC + PRO] – [EMO]			
	RSD	ACC	PRO	EMO
	4.18	3.90	3.77	3.71
Participant no. 12	[4.18 + 3.90 + 3.77] – [3.71] = 8.14			

The result of participant 12 for Perceived Self-Development (RSD) was 4.18, Acceptance (ACC) was 3.90, Proactivity at Work (PRO) was 3.77, and Emotional Costs (EMO) was 3.71. The result of EMO was then subtracted from the sum of RSD + ACC + PRO to arrive at the final score of 8.14.

We aimed at comparing two groups: the Focus Group, which had a low cumulative result, and the Control Group, which in comparison had a higher cumulative result when it comes to self-awareness.

10.5 Data Analysis for Interview

Table 10.1 shows the gender of the participants.
Gender

Table 10.1 Gender of participants.

Gender	Frequency
Male	4
Female	8

Table 10.2 shows the age of the participants.
Age

Table 10.2 Age of participants.

Age	Frequency
30–35	6
35–40	6

Table 10.3 shows the groups of participants.
Groups

Table 10.3 Groups of participants.

Group	Frequency
Focus Group	6
Control Group	6

The two groups of Focus and Control Groups were identified based on the SAOQ questionnaire to identify how each group uses awareness to deal with mental and physical illnesses. The Focus Groups have a lower threshold than the Control Group when it came to challenges faced, the impact of those challenges on their daily life activities, their relationship status, future planning, relationship with their family, history of their family and how they dealt with stress or spoke to the participants about mental health, and whether or not they were taught about mental and physical health in school or at home.

10.6 Findings

Q1. Do You Suffer from Any Physical Illnesses? May I Ask What It Is?

Table 10.4 Physical illnesses.

Focus group	Control group
Yes	**Yes**
2 participants (frequency): sorosis, acid reflux	5 participants (frequency): migraines (3), heart palpitations, insomnia, anxiety (1), acid reflux (2), thyroid, low blood pressure, GERD (gastrointestinal reflux disease)
No	**No**
4 participants	1 participant

Table 10.4 displays the question of how physical illnesses/disturbances was asked to bring light to the awareness one shows toward their current condition and how openly one can speak of it. It can be seen that the Focus Group's two participants described their physical health constraints, while four participants answered saying they had no physical illnesses or disturbances. In the Control Group, five participants expressed their daily physical constraints spanning from Migraines to GERD (Gastrointestinal Reflux Disease), and one participant answered that nothing bothered them.

Q2. Do You Suffer from Any Mental Illnesses? May I Ask What It Is?

Table 10.5 Mental illnesses.

Focus group	Control group
Yes	**Yes**
5 participants: stress (2), anxiety (5), PMS, depression, sensitive — quick to respond to people negatively	4 participants: anxiety (3), stress (2), overreacting, negative thoughts, fear, phobia
No/not aware	**No/not aware**
1 participant	2 participants

Table 10.5 displays the question that brings to light the awareness one has toward their mental health and how openly they choose to speak of it. The understanding of these two categories shows one's acceptance of self. From the Focus Group, five participants described their mental health or mental disturbances from Stress and Anxiety with the frequency of times mentioned to Premenstrual Syndrome. One participant from this group answered that they had no mental health issues or they were not aware if they had any. From the Control Group, four participants described their mental health disturbances from Anxiety to Phobia with the frequencies mentioned and two participants answered saying no/not aware.

Q3. Does It Hamper Your Life or Daily Activities? May I Ask How?

Table 10.6 Daily activity hindrances.

Focus group	Control group
Yes	**Yes**
5 participants: effect mood (3), decision-making ability, immobility, discomfort, affects happiness level, anxiety to function (2), drained, exhausted, comfort, isolated, inability to function	4 participants: burnouts (2), social anxiety (2), difficulty in forming and maintaining relationships, phobia restricts free movement
No	**No**
1 participant	2 participants

Table 10.6 displays how this questions highlights how one either takes control of one's state or allows it to overtake one's life. From the Focus Group, five participants answered that their physical and/or mental health illnesses hamper their daily activities by affecting their mood to decision making, immobility due to the depression and anxiety, discomfort and effects of their happiness level leading to isolation, to becoming drained, exhausted, and unable to function. One participant said that nothing hampered their daily routine. From the Focus Group, four participants described their lives being affected by burnout due to the added illnesses of Anxiety and Stress with the frequency mentioned, to forming and maintaining relationships, and one participant has a phobia that does not allow them to meet animals. Two participants from this group said that nothing affected their daily activities as they had learnt tools to better cope with their stressors.

Q4. How Would You Describe Your Work Atmosphere?

Table 10.7 Work atmosphere.

Focus group		**Control group**	
Positive	Happy, comfortable, chilled, challenging, good team, enjoy it, understand responsibilities well	**Positive**	Faced paced (2), chilled, positive, collaborative, own boss, free and frequent discussions, open-door policy, trust, relaxed, opportunistic, challenging
Negative	Hard, too much responsibility, don't feel like performing, don't love my work, challenging, own boss, stressful, hectic, unpredictable, politics	**Negative**	Competitive, high pressure (2), traditional setting, seek validation, deadlines (2), requires adapting
Positive and negative	Work from home – flexibility, alienating, comfortable, no boundaries, no structure, challenging	**Positive and negative**	Competitive, best and worst place to be. Work from home – ownership, lack structure

Table 10.7 displays how the question is meant to deep dive into one's daily life activity and how they receive their strengths and weaknesses, the confidence attached to the answers, and the awareness articulated toward the negative mentions. Looking into the answers given for describing one's work atmosphere, the Focus Group highlighted positive traits like they were happy and comfortable at work, it is challenging, and participants mentioned having good teams to work with, understanding their responsibilities well while enjoying the work. The negative traits mentioned the work being hard which led to not wanting to perform, politics in the workplace, too much responsibility, didn't love the work, was sometimes too challenging, being one's own boss was stressful, work for some was hectic, and unpredictable. Some participants from the same group mentioned that some traits that were meant to be both positive and negative were working from home, which was flexible yet alienating, comfortable but with no boundaries, and no structure, which made it even more challenging. Whereas the Control Group highlights positive traits like work atmosphere being faced paced yet chilled, positive and collaborative, being one's own boss they gave importance to free and frequent discussions, having an open-door policy, trusting their employees and being trusted in return, some mentioned that the environment was relaxed, and opportunistic yet challenging enough to incorporate growth. The negative traits mentioned were that some participants' work environment was too competitive, high pressure, some had a traditional setting where decision making took longer, some admitted to seeking too much validation, and a few mentioned that the deadlines were high pressure, which required constant adapting. The positive and negative traits were that even though the atmosphere was competitive, it was sometimes the best and worst place to be, for some work from home provided ownership but lacked structure.

Q5. Do You Have a Good Working Relationship With Your Boss/ Colleagues?

Table 10.8 Relationship with co-workers.

Focus group	Control group
Yes	**Yes**
3 participants	6 participants
No	**No**
-	-
Yes and no	**Yes and no**
3 participants	

Table 10.8 displays the question that shows the efforts participants choose to put into their daily stressors or the perception of it. When asked about participant relationships with bosses and colleagues, from the Focus Group, three participants answered that they had a good relationship with their work relationships, and three participants said they had good and bad relationships at work. However, all six participants from the Control Group answered saying that they have good working relationships with their bosses and colleagues.

Q6. How Do You Describe Your Relationship with Your Family?

Table 10.9 Relationship with family.

Focus group		Control group	
Positive	Calm, relaxed, supportive, helpful, comfortable, caring	**Positive**	Loving (2), evolving, healthy, respectful, peaceful, open
Negative	Restricted, lack of communication, dictated, aggressive, intrusive, overly dependent, don't accept/understand me, don't want this relationship	**Negative**	Dominant alphas, lack emotions
Positive and negative	Too involved, overwhelming, can be better (2), ups and downs	**Positive and negative**	Too involved, can be better (2)

Table 10.9 displays how the question brings to light the effect family has on participants, the awareness attached to their well-being, whether they have had a healthy vision of their surroundings and upbringings, and the value they attach to those experiences. When asked about the relationship with participant families, the Focus Group mentioned positive traits like their relationship being calm, relaxed, supportive, helpful, comfortable, and caring. The negative traits mentioned were restricted and thus lacked healthy communication or no communication, dictated due to authoritative and highly intrusive parenting style, were aggressive, overly dependent due to cultural parenting style, and some participants didn't want to

continue having a relationship with their family at all as they felt misunderstood and unaccepted. However, some participants did acknowledge that their relationships with their families could be better. The Focus Group mentioned positive traits like their home relations to be loving, evolving, healthy, respectful, peaceful, and open. The negative trait highlighted by one participant was that they had dominant alphas in their homes who lacked emotions. They also mentioned that they could work on having better relationships with their families.

Q7. How Do You Describe Your Relationship with Your Friends?

Table 10.10 Relationship with friends.

Focus group		**Control group**	
Positive	Good (2), easy, dependable, accepting, don't need many as have family (2), friends like family	**Positive**	Friends like family (2), supportive, loving, good times, no judgment, happy, evolving, healthy
Negative	Not available, don't want many, not deep connections (2)	**Negative**	Don't understand me sometimes
Positive and negative	Cannot depend on them (2), need to work hard to keep, need more (2), could be better (3)	**Positive and negative**	Could be better (2)

Table 10.10 displays how the question is to understand the sense of belonging, purpose, and support that participants exhibit and what they expect in return from their social relationships. When asked about participant relationships with friends, the Focus Group mentioned that it was good, easy, dependable, and accepting: two participants mentioned that they didn't need many friends as they had large families, and one participant mentioned that their friends were more than their family. The negative traits mentioned by two participants were that they themselves or their friends were not available for them when needed and so they didn't want many friends, and two participants mentioned that their relationships were to just have fun and not for deep connections. The Control Group mentioned positive traits like their friends being like family, supportive, loving, having

good times with them as there is no judgement, happy feelings, it's evolving, and healthy. The negative trait mentioned by one participant was that they sometimes didn't understand them. Three participants mentioned that their relationships could be better if they had more time or lived closer to their friends.

Q8. Do You Often Feel Angry?

Table 10.11 Anger timeframe.

Focus group	Control group
Yes	**Yes**
1 participant: everyday 2 participants: once a week	3 participants: once a week
Annoyed/irritated	**Annoyed/irritated**
1 participant: everyday 2 participants: once a week	3 participant: once a week

Table 10.11 displays how the question is asked about anger to comprehend how often participants perceived pain/threat and what they did with that information. The Focus Group mentioned one participant getting angry daily; two participants getting angry once a week, whereas getting annoyed or irritated was concerned; one participant getting irritated daily; and two participants getting irritated once a week. In the Control Group, three members get angry once a week, and three members get annoyed or irritated once a week.

Q9. What Makes You Angry?

Table 10.12 Reasons for getting angry.

Focus group					
Stupidity	**Incompetence**	**Being unfair**	**Mistreatment of self/ others**	**Crossing boundaries**	**Being misunderstood/ misunderstandings**
1	2	1	1	3	3
Control group					
Stupidity	**Incompetence**	**Mistreatment of self/ others**	**Not being in control**	**Ethics**	
2	4	4	3	8	

Table 10.12 displays how the question answers the understanding of what makes one angry, the intensity felt toward the situation, and the perception of control over it. For the Focus Group were people's stupidity, work incompetence, being unfair to self or others, getting mistreated or others mistreating others, people crossing boundaries, and being misunderstood. For the Control Group, there was also mention of people's stupidity, work incompetence, mistreating of self or others, participants not being in control of the situation, and unethical means adopted all caused anger.

Q10. What Does 'Having Fun' Mean to You?

Table 10.13 Meaning of having fun.

Focus group							
Relaxing	**Good food**	**TV/movies/ art/ music**	**No thinking/no stress/no worries**	**Going to parties**	**Hanging with friends/ family**	**Being alone**	**Travelling/new experiences**
6	3	5	7	1	2	2	2
Control group							
Being outdoors	**Overcoming challenges**	**No stress/ no worries**	**Being around positive people**	**Being in the moment**	**Travelling/new experiences**	**Self-care**	**Uplifting myself and other/ charity**
2	2	3	3	3	7	2	2

Table 10.13 displays how the question encapsulates the awareness of one's physical and mental needs to stay positive. The idea of having fun and letting loose is to understand participant capacity attached to viewing life as serious or light. The Focus Group mentioned the frequency of highlighting their perception of fun as relaxing, good food and entertainment, not having any stressful decisions to make or thoughts, going to parties by one participant, hanging out with friends and family, being alone and doing nothing, and having new experiences through traveling. The Control Group talked about being outdoors, overcoming challenges, having no stress and worries as being in a fun state, being around positive people, being in the moment to enjoy what's in front of them, new experiences through travel, self-care for two participants, and one participant was uplifting themselves and others through charity and compassion.

Q11. Do You Think About Your Future?

Table 10.14 Future thinking.

	Focus group	Control group
Yes	5 participants	4 participants
No		
Sometimes	1 participant	2 participants

Table 10.14 displays how the question about the future is to better understand optimistic or pessimistic attitudes toward life and future plans to determine this current self-perception. In the Focus Group, five participants said yes to thinking about their future, and one participant said sometimes, as it stressed them out. From the Control Group, four participants said yes to thinking of their future, and two participants said sometimes, as it either stressed them out or they liked living in the moment and not worrying much.

Q12. How Do You See Yourself in Your Future?

Table 10.15 View of self in the future.

Focus group						
Financial stability	**Better life/ lifestyle**	**Successful**	**Marriage/ children**	**The same**	**Better version of myself**	**More control of life**
4	3	5	3	1	9	2
Control group						
Long life	**New experiences**	**Successful**	**Married**	**More independence**	**Better version of myself**	**Healthier**
2	5	4	1	5	6	7

Table 10.15 displays how the question was to understand self-perception and views on how participant life could be made better with willingness. From the Focus Group, most participants mentioned financial stability, having a better lifestyle for some, being successful, being married, or having

children; one participant mentioned that they didn't see their life change at all. All six participants mentioned they want to be a better version of themselves, like being more confident or outgoing, and some mentioned having more control of life. The Control Group mentioned having long lives, wanting new experiences, and being successful; one mentioned of being married; five mentioned of wanting more independence; six mentioned a better version of themselves; and seven mentioned wanting a healthier life.

Q13. Do You Have Any Goals That You Are Working Toward Currently? What Are They?

Table 10.16 Future goals.

Focus group	Control group
Positive	**Positive**
Work (3), financial stability (4), personal well-being (3), mental well-being (2), easier life (2)	New experiences (5), healthier (3), making better decisions (1), financial freedom (4), more work opportunities (4), better work–life balance (2), more positive thinking, worry less (3)
Negative	**Negative**
Waiting for the right time, need to take more initiative (2), no goals	Overcoming: paranoia, anxiety

Table 10.16 displays how the question on goals was to better understand the proactiveness and eagerness of participants toward their life. The Focus Group participants talked about the positive traits of work, financial stability, personal well-being, and an easier life, all with higher mentions of each. Some of the participants mentioned waiting for the right time to be able to achieve goals and the need to take more initiative, and one participant mentioned that they had no goals at all.

The next seven questions understand the background of the participants and how it helped shape perceptions of self, of life, and its challenges; the role of caretaker, the importance attached to it, and the learnings from school and home; their strengths and weaknesses; insight on the outcomes related to the past today; the view of self in these older years; external/internal attachment of blame; and view of illnesses as manageable or challenging.

Q14. As a Kid Was 'Healthy Living' Given Importance to? Physical and Mental Health

Table 10.17 Healthy living.

Focus group		
	Physical	**Mental**
Yes	4 participants	1 participant
No	2 participants	4 participants
They didn't know themselves		1 participant
Control group		
	Physical	**Mental**
Yes	4 participants	4 participants
No	2 participants	1 participant
They didn't know themselves		1 participant

Table 10.17 displays how the question is to better understand the participants' childhood perception of 'health.' For both Focus and Control Groups, physical health was given importance to; however, mental health was not given importance to or mentions of parents not knowing themselves of mental health was mentioned.

Q15. Growing Up, Were You Taught About Mental/Physical Health? Home/School?

Table 10.18 Healthy lifestyles taught in school/home.

Focus group		
	Physical — school	**Mental — school**
Yes	4 participants	
No	2 participants	6 participants
	Physical — home	**Mental — home**
Yes	2 participants	1 participant
No	4 participants	5 participants
Control group		
	Physical — school	**Mental — school**
Yes	6 participants	
No		6 participants
	Physical — home	**Mental — home**
Yes	6 participants	1 participant
No		5 participants

Table 10.18 displays how the question explores if the participants were taught growing up about the importance of self and health. All participants of both groups mentioned that mental health was never taught in school, or was it taught at home for most participants. One participant in each group vaguely mentioned indirect conversations at home about mental health. Both groups mentioned physical health being taught at home and school but in indirect means.

Q16. Did Your Parents Insist on This Healthy Lifestyle?

Table 10.19 Parents' role in healthy lifestyle.

Focus group		
	Physical	**Mental**
Yes	4 participants	1 participant
No	2 participants	4 participants
Control group		
	Physical	**Mental**
Yes	3 participants	1 participant
No	4 participants	3 participants

Table 10.19 displays how the question explores participants adult comprehension of what was perceived as 'healthy habits' vs. 'unhealthy habits.' For both Focus and Control Groups, physical health was insisted upon, but mental health was not.

Q17. Did They Talk to You About Mental Health?

Table 10.20 Parents' role in mental health talks.

	Focus group	**Control group**
Yes		3 participants
No	6 participants	3 participants

Table 10.20 displays how the question explores whether parents spoke about mental health at home identifies the level of acceptance or negligence of mental health conversations and thus the level of acceptance or rejection of one's own health. In the Focus Group, all six participants answered no, whereas three participants in the Control Group answered yes and three answered no.

Q18. Was It Taboo or Open Conversation or Do You Think They Didn't Know Themselves?

Table 10.21 Mental health, a taboo or not.

	Focus group	Control group
Taboo	1 participant	1 participant
Open conversation		2 participants
They didn't know themselves/indirectly	5 participants	3 participants

Table 10.21 displays how the question talks about taboo vs. open dialogue shows participants' childhood perception of mental health and the level of acceptance or blame of it today. For both Focus and Control Groups, two participants said it was a taboo topic, eight participants from both said that their parents probably didn't know themselves or spoke of it indirectly, and three participants said that their families spoke about mental health openly.

Q19. How Did Your Parents Handle Stress?

Table 10.22 How parents handled stress.

	Focus group	Control group
Well		
Badly	4 participants	2 participants
Kept to themselves	2 participants	4 participants

Table 10.22 displays how the question helps understand how participants have implemented their idea of awareness from their past. Four participants from the Focus Group answered badly, and two participants from the Control Groups answered badly. Two participants from the Focus Group and four participants from the Control Group mentioned that their parents kept their stress to themselves.

Q20. Did They Have Open Dialogue with You about the Meaning of Certain Concepts Like Confidence/Stress/Emotions/Self-Awareness?

Table 10.23 Open dialogue with parents.

Focus group				
	Confidence	**Stress**	**Emotions**	**Self-awareness**
Yes	2 participants (indirectly)		1 participant (indirectly)	2 participants (indirectly)
No	4 participants	6 participants	5 participants	4 participants
Control group				
	Confidence	**Stress**	**Emotions**	**Self-awareness**
Yes	1 participant (indirectly)	1 participant (indirectly)	1 participant (indirectly)	3 participants (indirectly)
No	5 participants	5 participants	5 participants	3 participants

Table 10.23 displays how the question explores participants adult comprehension of certain concepts that may or may not have been discussed in the past and their level of acceptance of it. It dives into the relationship participants have made with their past and the lessons learnt or rejected and the view of the caretaker. From the Focus Group, two participants mentioned indirect conversations about confidence, no conversation for all six about stress, one participant mentioned indirect conversations about emotions, and two participants mentioned indirect conversations about self-awareness. From the Control Group, one participant mentioned indirect conversation about confidence, one mentioned of indirect conversation about stress, one mentioned of indirect conversation about emotions, and three mentioned indirect conversations about self-awareness. The remaining all mentioned a firm no when asked this question.

10.7 Discussion

The research attempted to gain a deeper understanding how self-awareness can help alleviate mental and physical illnesses. The formulated hypothesis was that self-awareness can in fact reduce the impact of illnesses. In addition, it is seen that when self-awareness acts from the present conscious, people can mitigate challenges with better strength and capabilities.

According to the results, self-awareness has a huge impact on one's self-worth and perception toward their abilities. Having unconscious awareness or low self-awareness can be a major threat to one's healthy survival and tools needed to face threatening situations.

The research data shows that the two identified Focus and Control Groups both exhibit self-awareness in different situations. The difference in the data highlights the outcome of this self-awareness used to handle challenging situations throughout life and its impact reduced or maintained. However, the difference in the groups stood to test when subtle changes in the responses were noted.

It was noted that when asked about whether the Focus Group were aware of their physical illnesses, they were less keen on exploring hindrances to their daily life and eager to dismiss the topic as opposed to the Control Group who were keen on exploring even the smallest issues that cause a disturbance to their life. According to research by Panoma Valley Health Center, individuals typically seek medical attention solely in the event of illness or impending mortality. Presently, the adoption of preventive healthcare is increasingly prevalent as individuals become more knowledgeable and self-determined regarding their personal health [16]. There exists a significant correlation between physical health issues and the likelihood of developing mental health issues, as well as a reciprocal relationship between the two. Approximately 33% of individuals with a chronic physical health ailment concurrently experience a mental health disorder, predominantly manifesting as depression or anxiety [17].

The next question brings to light the awareness one has toward their mental health and how openly they choose to speak of it. The understanding of these two categories shows one's acceptance of self. According to the National Alliance on Mental Illness, about 18.5% of all adults in the US experience some kind of mental illness in any given year, and of those, about 4.2% are subject to an illness or disorder that significantly constraints at least one major life activity. During the interview, the insight shared by the Control Group showed a higher level of acceptance and openness to talk about their daily 'stressors.' The simplicity of awareness attached to this helps this group to further talk freely later into the interview.

The inquiry about the work atmosphere was to dive deep into one's daily life activity and how they receive their strengths and weaknesses, the confidence attached to the answers, and the awareness articulated toward the negative mentions. According to the American Psychological Association, workplace stress results in a loss of over $500 billion from the U.S. economy and causes the loss of 550 million workdays annually. Stress has been identified as a significant contributor to workplace accidents, accounting for a range of 60% to 80%. Additionally, stress is believed to be the underlying cause for over 80% of medical consultations. Research has established a correlation between workplace stress and a variety of health issues, including metabolic syndrome, cardiovascular disease, and mortality [18].

When asked about the participant's relationship with boss and colleagues, the question was an extension to the previous one to see the efforts participants choose to put into their daily stressors or the perception of it. According to a meta-analysis published in the Personality and Social Psychology Review, individuals who experience a greater sense of camaraderie with their colleagues and a stronger connection to their organization exhibit improved levels of health and well-being and are less susceptible to experiencing burnout. Individuals who exhibited a higher degree of identification with their co-workers and organizational affiliations experienced enhanced psychological well-being as well as improved physical health [19]. Being aware of one's strengths and places required to be built, the Control Group had more control over their challenges and relationships as they were better able to describe their surroundings and what was required of them. This includes having to adapt, change, or even work on their shortcomings to better fit their future goals.

The question asked to describe participant relationship with family brings to light the affects family may have on well-being, the awareness attached to this well-being, whether they have had a healthy vision of their surroundings and upbringings, and the value they attach to those experiences. The JAMA Paediatrics conducted a study on a sample of 18,185 individuals, comprising 9,233 females and 8,952 males. The study revealed that individuals who had positive family relationships during their adolescence exhibited significantly lower levels of depressive symptoms from early adolescence to midlife (late 30s to early 40s) compared to those who had less positive family relationships. The results indicate that favorable familial relationships during adolescence are linked to improved psychological well-being in both genders, spanning from the onset of adolescence to middle adulthood. It appears that interventions implemented during the early stages of family life hold significance in promoting sound mental development that can persist throughout an individual's lifespan [20]. The Control Group's responses used words that attached a more positive and growth mindset, like evolving, healthy, and peaceful, which shows a certain degree of self as well as others acceptance attached to it. This allows one to grow out of the blame game, to take on life on their own, to essentially grow up, and to take responsibility for one's own life.

The question asking about the relationship with friends was to understand the sense of belonging, purpose, and support that participants exhibit themselves, and what they expect in return. According to research conducted by Gallup, individuals who maintain positive interpersonal connections in their professional environment are more inclined to exhibit a heightened level of engagement in their work. Positive work relationships have been found to be positively associated with enhanced profitability and heightened productivity [21]. However, this, in turn, leads to satisfactory life habits which are inculcated into personal life, including family, relationships, and finally, mental and physical health. Holt-Lunstad conducted a meta-analysis study at Brigham Young University, which revealed that the presence of a few intimate friends had a greater impact on health outcomes such as high blood pressure, heart disease, depression, and cancer, compared to dietary and exercise habits. The study also found that the impact of having close friends on health outcomes was equivalent to that of smoking. Furthermore, Santini's research conducted at the University of Barcelona has established a correlation between friendship and a decrease in depression and mortality rates. The longitudinal study revealed that individuals who experienced a reduced sense of disconnection and loneliness and an increased sense of social connectedness were less prone to depression or anxiety. Remarkably, companions appear to hold greater significance than kin. According to research conducted by Chopik at Michigan State University, involving a sample size of 280,000 individuals, it was found that the presence of friendships is a significant indicator of an individual's well-being and contentment. Particularly for the elderly population, the positive effects are more strongly associated with friendships as compared to familial relationships [22]. Here, the Focus Group had a harder time with their friendships as they did not see much value attached to the idea. The Control Group was able to vocalize their friendships with a higher positive note, which shows a larger acceptance of life and self. The ability to extend oneself into the world and form relationships with others also shows confidence and self-esteem. The benefits of friendships are on the lower side with the Focus Group.

When asked about the frequency of getting angry, it was to comprehend how often participants perceived threat and what they did with that information. We further dove deep into the following questions, asking what makes one angry and what is done to answer the comprehension of anger, the intensity felt toward the situation, the perception of control over it, and whether they can regulate their emotions or not. The scientific literature has established a correlation between anger, hostility, and aggressiveness and a range of health hazards. Consequently, interventions aimed at preventing or treating these ailments should encompass not only pharmacological approaches but also psychological ones. Psychotherapists should prioritize strategies for managing these behaviors to mitigate the potential risks and diseases associated with them [23]. Both groups here had insight into what made them angry.

The next three questions asking about the future were to better understand optimistic or pessimistic attitudes toward life and future plans to determine this current self-perception. Haley Neidich, LCSW, a mental health professional, says, "Individuals who naturally have vivid imaginations and are optimistic tend to have better skills in managing life's stressors and dealing with triggering events." She says, "When people are in positive future thinking mode, their body is relaxed. Therefore, a stressor simply will not register as a massive issue" [24].

The next seven questions better understand the background of the participants and how it helped shape perceptions of themselves, of life, and its challenges; the role of caretaker, the importance attached to it, and the learnings from school and home; their strengths and weaknesses; the insight toward the outcomes today related to the past; the view of themselves in these older years; external or internal attachment of blame; and their view of illnesses as manageable or challenging.

The promotion of mental health during childhood and adolescence is of utmost importance, given that over 50% of mental health issues originate during these developmental stages, with a significant proportion persisting into adulthood [71]. Presently, addressing mental health concerns in childhood and adolescence has gained significant importance due to global statistics indicating a rise in their prevalence [72]. The percentage of individuals affected by these issues has reached nearly 20% [44]. The predicament is compounded by the reality that a considerable number of minors and young adults are not obtaining the specific treatment that is necessary, as evidenced by various studies [42, 73, 74].

As a result, significant endeavors have been made to consolidate the most reliable evidence pertaining to mental health, thereby highlighting the need to reach a consensus on fundamental aspects of the discipline, including the definition of mental health and associated concepts [64]. The World Health Organization (WHO) defines mental health as a state of well-being that encompasses more than just the absence of illness. It involves individuals developing their abilities, coping with daily stressors, engaging in productive work, and contributing to the betterment of their community [43]. The definition in question formed the foundation for the WHO Mental Health Action Plan, 2013–2020, which encompasses the principles of promoting mental health, preventing and treating mental illness, and facilitating rehabilitation. The plan places significant emphasis on addressing critical facets of mental health interventions, particularly the developmental aspects of children and young people that include the ability to manage thoughts and emotions, build social relationships, and the aptitude to learn [25].

According to this study, the importance of mental health regulation for children seems to be of imperative importance. The research data of this paper found that the awareness attached to mental health information from a younger age was low in both groups. The parents were indirect in their approach in talking about mental health as most participants say that they themselves were unaware of such topics for various reasons and very few mentions of it being a taboo. Friends or social groups of this generation in their childhood days spoke of health as opposed to the times today. The process of social and cognitive development is facilitated by social interactions that occur within a specific cultural and social milieu [41, 75]. Utilizing Vygotsky's cognitive development model, it can be posited that learning is augmented through human interaction within social and cultural environments, thereby serving as a crucial component for psychological functioning. The acquisition and advancement of cultural knowledge and skills are facilitated through social interactions with both peers and individuals with greater expertise, such as teachers, as described by [65] and Cole [76]. It is noteworthy that specialized tools have been developed to document effective modes of communication within educational settings, as reported by [66].

It is seen in the research data that teacher–student relationships ceased to exist when it came to this topic. The educational system suffered the gaps where teachers were themselves unable to fulfil. We do not talk about community here as at the grassroots level of family and school, the topic seems void, so we did not extend the search to community.

The data shows that most participants from both groups were raised in households where physical health was given importance, which was not limited to but included eating right, exercising, playing sports, staying active, learning instruments, and dancing, to include a few. This extends to how parents handle stress as well. However, when it comes to parental focus on mental health or handling stress, the Focus Group had more negative responses, stating that they had not spoken about mental health or stress or seen their parents handle stress very well in their homes while growing up. The Control Group respondents, however, did acknowledge that mental health and stress were indirectly spoken about with their parents growing up. The takeaway from this data is more 'how' participants answered these questions as opposed to 'what' they answered. The self-reflection and articulation of the past experiences and how the Control Group chose to answer goes to show that self-awareness is also about introspecting upon lessons taught and recalibrating them into life to fit the situation. This extends to the question about parent and participant conversations about topics like confidence, stress, emotions, and self-awareness. Though the number for all groups is relatively low, the stories shared by the Control Group reflect a low level of blame and a higher level of forgiveness, understanding, and learning from their environments.

Self-awareness has a wide range of positive effects on a person's life, including personal development, improved emotional regulation, improved mental health, the building of relationships, and living a happier life. Personal development is seen widely. As people mature, change, and acquire new skills, their personal development broadens during the course of their lives. The changes a person will go through on a mental, physical, social, emotional, and spiritual level are all included when we talk about personal growth, which also enables one to make better decisions and solve problems.

Self-discipline and emotion regulation are facilitated by self-awareness, which also fosters emotional awareness, thus enabling people to govern their emotions. For example, if a person is conscious of a certain emotion, like rage, they can calm it down with tried coping techniques. It enhances relationships as self-awareness helps one recognize harmful patterns, which helps build enduring bonds with family and friends. People can learn from their errors and discover solutions to go forward with self-compassion and improved communication if an issue occurs in a relationship. Being self-aware also helps with a happier life as people understand what makes them happy and, as a result, live happier lives by being inwardly and externally aware of their values, aspirations, emotions, behaviors, strengths, and impact on others. And most importantly, all these factors make life more blissful and more in control, as it improves mental health. Self-awareness enables one to recognize negative feelings and take action that will help them feel better. This is especially helpful when negative feelings are brought on by a mental health issue. Once it is in someone's conscious awareness or internal awareness, the confidence, strength, and power to deal with any disturbances in life becomes more tolerable and easier to handle, endure, and overcome [26].

All this self-awareness cannot benefit anyone if they don't implement it or put it into action. Self-awareness is a healthy trait to cultivate because it enables one to respond more effectively to situations or individuals that could provoke a reaction. When one is aware of emotions and how to manage them, one can be equipped to process and overcome them, thereby avoiding needless conflict. It can help set a positive example for team members, friends, and family and encourage them to approach situations with questions and concerns.

Presented below are some recommendations for enhancing one's self-awareness:

- Maintain a receptive attitude. The capacity to self-regulate one's emotional state enables an individual to be more perceptive and responsive to the emotional experiences of others. This demonstrates the ability to effectively participate as a team member without requiring individual recognition as the primary goal. Entrepreneurs who exhibit greater openness toward others tend to demonstrate higher levels of creativity.
- It is important to be cognizant of one's personal strengths and weaknesses. Individuals who possess self-awareness are cognizant of their personal strengths and limitations and are capable of utilizing this knowledge to their advantage. Exhibiting mindfulness entails recognizing the appropriate time to seek aid and when to independently manage a given circumstance.
- Establishing connections is a crucial aspect of leadership; however, this task may be impeded by distractions. To enhance productivity, it is advisable to cultivate the habit of sustained concentration without succumbing to diversions such as social media, emails, or other minor interruptions.
- Establishing boundaries is crucial. It is imperative for a leader to establish robust boundaries. Demonstrate warmth and kindness toward individuals while also asserting boundaries and declining requests when necessary. It is imperative to approach one's work and passions with a serious demeanor

while maintaining steadfast boundaries to uphold the integrity of one's objectives and the effort invested in them.

- It is important to be aware of one's emotional triggers. Individuals who possess self-awareness have the ability to recognize and acknowledge their emotional states in real time. It is advisable to avoid suppressing or negating one's emotions and their underlying reasons. Rather, it is recommended to adapt and accommodate them and thoroughly analyze them prior to engaging in interpersonal communication.
- It is advisable to acknowledge and trust one's intuition. Individuals who achieve success have developed the ability to rely on their intuition when making decisions and are willing to take calculated risks in pursuit of their goals. One's instincts are rooted in the principle of survival of the fittest and the drive to achieve success. Effective leaders exhibit a propensity for self-discipline of their personal as well as professional lives.
- It is imperative to contemplate the influence of one's actions on others. Impulsive behavior is characterized by people who prioritize their own desires over those of others without giving them any thought. These individuals must become self-aware in order to identify their coping mechanisms, emotions, and the consequences of their actions on other people. Being more considerate to others can help deal with difficult situations more skillfully.
- It is advisable to express regret or remorse when the situation calls for it. Errors are an inevitable part of human behavior; however, possessing self-awareness can aid in identifying instances where one's mistakes necessitate the offering of apologies. It is possible that there has been an instance of lashing out but expressing genuine remorse and subsequently modifying one's conduct is the most effective approach to progress past any errors made.
- Providing feedback is crucial. Self-awareness allows one to comprehend oneself without external influence. However, soliciting candid feedback from employees necessitates both bravery and self-awareness. Engaging in this practice acknowledges one's inherent biases toward oneself, a universal phenomenon, and facilitates the attainment of a more impartial perspective [27].

10.8 Conclusion

The aim of this research was to see if self-awareness can reduce the impact of physical and mental illnesses on people. It addresses the importance of self-awareness required to live life and face challenges that we may encounter on a daily basis. It aims to help people realize that without the right attitude of wanting to awaken ourselves, disturbances of life can take over, rendering us merely an object of that fate.

The data shows that most participants weren't taught about emotions, self-awareness, or mental health in school, nor were these addressed at home. As mental health remains a taboo in many cultures, it is of utmost importance to spread this information despite the cultural differences. It is important to shed light on the stigma of counselling in the cultural families of India and UAE and spread awareness about the importance of counselling services. Through the practice of self-awareness, people can learn how to bring their unconsciousness to the present moment and get back in control of their thoughts and emotions. People can also learn how to further enhance their self-awareness to lessen physical and mental illnesses.

Results show that most participants from both groups were raised in households where physical health was given importance to, and it extends to how parents handled stress as well. However, when it comes to parental focus on mental health or handling stress, the Focus Group had more negative responses, stating that they had not spoken about mental health or stress, nor seen their parents handle stress very well in their homes while growing up. The Control Group respondents, however, did acknowledge that mental health and stress were indirectly spoken about with their parents growing up. The takeaway from this data is more 'how' participants answered these questions as opposed to 'what' they answered. The self-reflection and articulation of the past experiences and how the Control Group chose to answer goes to show that self-awareness is also about introspecting upon lessons taught and recalibrating them into life to fit the situation. This extends to the question about parent and participant conversations about topics like confidence, stress, emotions, and self-awareness. Though the number for all groups is relatively low, the stories shared by the Control Group reflect a low level of blame and a higher level of forgiveness, understanding, and learning from their environments.

Self-awareness has a wide range of positive effects on a person's life, including personal development, improved emotional regulation, improved mental health, the building of relationships, and living a happier life. Personal development is seen widely. As people mature, change, and acquire new skills, their personal development broadens during the course of their lives. The changes a person will go through on a mental, physical, social, emotional, and spiritual level are all included when we talk about personal growth. The key to personal growth is self-awareness as it enables us to make aware decisions and resolve problems while also identifying ways to get better.

Based on the results of this study, firstly, we would recommend that self-awareness be implemented in the school curriculum from literature review stating the importance of it in daily life, to help people understand thoughts and emotions, enhance the procedure of expressing and releasing emotions in a healthy matter, and then learn the tools required to execute this self-awareness when making decisions in life. It was seen in the research data that teacher–student relationships ceased to exist when it came to this topic. The educational system suffered the gaps where teachers were themselves unable to fulfil.

Secondly, self-awareness has a huge impact on one's self-worth and perception toward their abilities. Having unconscious awareness or low self-awareness can be a major threat to one's healthy survival and tools needed to face threatening situations, and therefore, continued exposure through government initiative, media, and educational sources should be incorporated. We did not talk about community in the research at grassroots level of family and school; the topic seemed void, so we did not extend the search to community.

Lastly, by conducting this research, it was found that participants are willing to open up and talk about self-reflection and improvement toward their lives. Continuing to fight against the taboo of mental health seems like the best way forward. Opening channels of communication about mental health awareness, self-awareness, and counselling could help teach adults the tools required to navigate the daily challenges they face instead of them accumulating and becoming an illness later in life.

Bibliography

1. Miller, K.D., *Using self-awareness theory and skills in psychology*, PositivePsychology.com, 2023, https://positivepsychology.com/self-awareness-theory-skills/.
2. Cherry, K., *Self-awareness: How it develops and why it matters*, Verywell Mind, 2023, Available at: https://www.verywellmind.com/what-is-self-awareness-2795023.

3. Eurich, T., *What self-awareness really is (and how to cultivate it)*, Harvard Business Review, 2023.
4. Silvia, P.J., *International encyclopaedia of the social sciences*, 2023, https://www.encyclopedia.com/social-sciences/applied-and-social-sciences-magazines/self-awareness-theory.
5. Courtney E. Ackerman, M.A., *What is self-awareness? (+5 ways to be more self-aware)*, PositivePsychology.com, 2023, https://positivepsychology.com/self-awareness-matters-how-you-can-be-more-self-aware/.
6. Pvhcdev, P., *The importance of regular check-ups*, Pomona Valley Health Centers, 2023, February 1, https://mypvhc.com/importance-regular-check-ups/.
7. Roebuck, S., *Why is building great work relationships important? - employsure*, Employsure AU, 2023, February 8, https://employsure.com.au/blog/why-is-building-great-work-relationships-important/#:~:text=Effective%20working%20relationships%20can%20consequently,increased%20profit%20and%20improved%20productivity.
8. Brower, T., *Maximize mental health with a few good friends: Here's how*, 2023, March 8.
9. Peek, S., *10 tips for leaders to improve their self-awareness*, Business News Daily, 2023, February 21, https://www.businessnewsdaily.com/6097-self-awareness-in-leadership.html.
10. Manwaring, J., *Why is being self-aware important for your mental health?*, API, Alvarado Parkway Institute, San Diego, 2022, https://apibhs.com/2022/10/03/why-is-being-self-aware-important-for-your-mental-health#:~:text=Improving%20mental%20health%3A%20When%20any,helps%20them%20improve%20their%20mood.
11. Cherry, K., *What are the signs of healthy or low self-esteem?*, Verywell Mind, 2022, November 7, https://www.verywellmind.com/what-is-self-esteem-2795868.
12. Geary, D.C. and Xu, K.M., *Evolution of self-awareness and the cultural emergence of academic and non-academic self-concepts - educational psychology review*, SpringerLink, 2022, https://link.springer.com/article/10.1007/s10648-022-09669-2.
13. Foundation, M., *Physical Health and Mental Health*, Mental Health Foundation, 2022, February 18, https://www.mentalhealth.org.uk/explore-mental-health/a-z-topics/physical-health-and-mental-health.
14. Manwaring, J., *Why is being self-aware important for your mental health?*, API. Alvarado Parkway Institute, San Diego, 2022, October 3, https://apibhs.com/2022/10/03/why-is-being-self-aware-important-for-your-mental-health#:~:text=Improving%20mental%20health%3A%20When%20any,helps%20them%20improve%20their%20mood.
15. Goleman, D., *What is emotional self-awareness?*, Korn Ferry, 2021, Available at: https://www.kornferry.com/insights/this-week-in-leadership/what-is-emotional-self-awareness.

16. Ninivaggi, F.J., *Self-awareness, Self-Awareness- an overview*, ScienceDirect Topics, 2017, https://www.sciencedirect.com/topics/psychology/self-awareness.
17. https://hbr.org/2018/01/what-self-awareness-really-is-and-how-to-cultivate-it.
18. XS, A., *Apa Dictionary of Psychology*, American Psychological Association, 2016, https://dictionary.apa.org/self-awareness.
19. Rochat, P., *Five levels of self-awareness as they unfold early in life*, 2003, Available at: http://psychology.emory.edu/cognition/rochat/Rochat5levels.pdf.
20. Bem, D.J., Self-perception: An alternative interpretation of cognitive dissonance phenomena. *Psychol. Rev.*, 74, 3, 183, 1967.
21. Fazio, R.H., Zanna, M.P., Cooper, J., Dissonance and self-perception: An integrative view of each theory's proper domain of application. *J. Exp. Social Psychol.*, 13, 5, 464–479, 1977.
22. Sternthal, B., Scott, C.A., Dholakia, R.R., *Self-Perception as a Means of Personal Influence: The Foot-in-the-Door Technique*, ACR North American Advances, 1976.
23. Robak, R.W., Self-definition in psychotherapy: is it time to revisit self-perception theory? *North Am. J. Psychol.*, 3, 3, 2001.
24. Montgomery, R.L. and Haemmerlie, F.M., Self-perception theory and the reduction of heterosocial anxiety. *J. Soc. Clin. Psychol.*, 4, 4, 503–512, 1986.
25. Burger, J.M., The foot-in-the-door compliance procedure: A multiple-process analysis and review. *Personality Soc. Psychol. Rev.*, 3, 4, 303–325, 1999.
26. Spitzley, K., *The 4 dimensions of self-awareness you didn't know about*, 2019, April 20, https://www.linkedin.com/pulse/4-dimensions-self-awareness-you-didnt-know-kyle-spitzley.
27. Enamorado, Y., *Mental Health Check-up and its importance*, Msmc.com, 2017, January 21, https://www.msmc.com/mental-health-check-up-and-its-importance/.
28. Seppälä, E., *Proof that positive work cultures are more productive*, Harvard Business Review, 2017, May 8, https://hbr.org/2015/12/proof-that-positive-work-cultures-are-more-productive.
29. Walton, A.G., *Why work relationships affect our mental and physical health*, Forbes, 2016, October 14, https://www.forbes.com/sites/alicegwalton/2016/10/13/why-work-relationships-affect-our-mental-and-physical-health-so-strongly/?sh=27efaca92075.
30. Chen, P., *Positive family relationships and Mental Health from adolescence to midlife*, JAMA Pediatrics, 2019, December 2, https://jamanetwork.com/journals/jamapediatrics/fullarticle/2752557.
31. https://www.forbes.com/sites/tracybrower/2023/03/07/maximize-mental-health-with-a-few-good-friends-heres-how/?sh=13c5503e62fd

32. Staicu, M.-L. and Cuţov, M., Anger and health risk behaviors. *J. Med. Life*, 2010, November 25. https://www.ncbi.nlm.nih.gov/pmc/articles/PMC3019061/.
33. Field, B., Verywell Mind, 2021, June 8, https://www.verywellmind.com/the-power-of-future-thinking-5114362.
34. García-Carrión, R., Villarejo-Carballido, B., Villardón-Gallego, L., Children and adolescents mental health: A systematic review of interaction-based interventions in schools and communities. *Front. Psychol.*, 2019, April 24. https://pubmed.ncbi.nlm.nih.gov/31068881/.
35. Allen, S.A.S., *How thinking about the future makes life more meaningful*, Greater Good, 2019, May 1, https://greatergood.berkeley.edu/article/item/how_thinking_about_the_future_makes_life_more_meaningful.
36. Rogoff, B., *The Cultural Nature of Human Development*, Oxford University Press, New York, NY, 2003.
37. Seikkula, J. and Arnkil, T.E., *Dialogical Meetings in Social Networks*, Karnac, London, 2006.
38. Suldo, S.M., Gormley, M.J., DuPaul, G.J., Anderson-Butcher, D., The impact of school mental health on student and school-level academic outcomes: current status of the research and future directions. *Sch. Mental Health*, 6, 84–98, 2014. 10.1007/s12310-013-9116-2.
39. Valls, R. and Kyriakides, L., The power of interactive groups: how diversity of adults volunteering in classroom groups can promote inclusion and success for children of vulnerable minority ethnic populations. *Camb. J. Educ.*, 43, 17–33, 2013. 10.1080/0305764X.2012.749213.
40. Villardón-Gallego, L., García-Carrión, R., Yáñez-Marquina, L., Estévez, A., Impact of the interactive learning environments in children's prosocial behavior. *Sustainability*, 10, 2138, 2018. 10.3390/su10072138.
41. Vygotsky, L.S., *Mind in Society: The Development of Higher Mental Process*, Harvard University Press, Cambridge, MA, 1978.
42. Weist, M.D. and Murray, M., Advancing school mental health promotion globally. *Adv. Sch. Mental Health Promot.*, 1, 2–12, 2008. 10.1080/1754730X.2008.9715740.
43. WHO, *Promoting Mental Health: Concepts, Emerging Evidence, Practice: Summary Report*, World Health Organization, Geneva, 2004, Retrieved, http://www.who.int/mental_health/evidence/en/promoting_mhh.pdf.
44. WHO, *WHO| Child and Adolescent Mental Health*, WHO. World Health Organization, 2016, http://www.who.int/mental_health/maternal-child/child_adolescent/en/.
45. WHO, *WHO| "Depression: Let's Talk" Says WHO, as Depression Tops List of Causes of Ill Health*, WHO. World Health Organization, 2017, http://www.who.int/mediacentre/news/releases/2017/world-health-day/en/.
46. Chida, Y. and Steptoe, A., The Association of Anger and Hostility with Future Coronary Heart Disease, A Meta-Analytic Review of Prospective Evidence. *J. Am. Coll. Cardiol.*, 53, 936–946, 2009.

47. Onyike, C.U. and Liketsos, C.G., *Textbook of Psychosomatic medicine*, pp. 171–192, Amer. Psychiatric Publish, London, 2005, Aggression and Violence.
48. Reif, A., REsler, M., Freitag, C.M., Nature and Nurture Predispose to Violent Behavior: Serotonergic Genes and Adverse Childhood Environment. *Neuropsychopharmacology*, 32, 2375–2383, 2007.
49. Golden, S.H., Williams, J.E., Ford, D.E., Anger temperament is modestly associated with the risk of type 2 diabetes mellitus, The atheroslcerosis risk in communities study. *Psychoneuroendocrinology*, 31, 3, 325–332, 2006.
50. Davidson, K.W. and Mostovsky, E., Anger expression and risk of coronary heart disease: Evidence from the Nova Scotia Health Survey. *Am. Heart J.*, 2, 199–206, 2010.
51. Laszlo, K., Janszky, I., Ahnve, S., Anger expression and prognosis after a coronary event in women. *Int. J. Cardiology*, 40, 60–65, 2010.
52. Vella, E. and Friedman, B.H., Hostility and anger. *Int. J. Psychophysiol.*, 72, 253–259, 2009.
53. Angerer, P., Siebert, U., Kothny, W., Muhlbauer, D., Impact of Social Support, Cynical Hostility and Anger. Expression on Progression of Coronary Atherosclerosis. *J. Am. Coll. Cardiol.*, 36, 1781–1788, 2000.
54. Larkin, K.T. and Zayfert, C., Anger expression and essential hypertension, Behavioral response to confrontation. *J. Psychosomatic Res.*, 56, 113–118, 2004.
55. Engel, S.G. and Boseck, J.J., The relationship of momentary anger and impulsivity to bulimic behavior. *Behav. Res. Therapy*, 45, 437–447, 2007.
56. Sullman, M.J.M., Gras, E., Cunill, M., Driving anger in Spain. *Pers. Individ. Differ.*, 42, 701–713, 2007.
57. Musante, L. and Treiber, F.A., The relationship between anger coping styles and lifestyle behaviors teenagers. *J. Adolesc. Health*, 27, 63–68, 2000.
58. Julkunen, J. and Ahlstrom, R., Hostility, anger, and sense of coherence as predictors of health-related quality of life. Results of an ASCOT substudy. *J. Psychosomatic Res.*, 61, 33–39, 2006.
59. Insel, T., Cuthbert, B., Garvey, M., Heinssen, R., Pine, D.S., Quinn, K., Sanislow, C., Wang, P., Research domain criteria (RDoC): toward a new classification framework for research on mental disorders. *Am. J. Psychiatry*, 167, 748–751, 2010. doi: 10.1176/appi.ajp.2010.09091379.
60. Duval, S. and Wicklund, R.A., A theory of objective self awareness. Academic Press, 1972
61. Brownell, C.A., Zerwas, S., Ramani, G.B., "So Big": The Development of Body Self-Awareness in Toddlers. *Child Dev.*, 78, 1426–1440, 2007.
62. Oettingen, G. and Stephens, E.J., Fantasies and motivationally intelligent goal setting, in: G. B. Moskowitz and H. Grant (Eds.), *The psychology of goals*, pp. 153–178, The Guilford Press, 2009.
63. Marguc, J., Förster, J., Van Kleef, G.A., Stepping back to see the big picture: When obstacles elicit global processing. *J. Pers. Soc. Psychol.*, 101, 5, 883–901, 2011.

64. Mehta, N., Clement, S., Marcus, E., Stona, A.C., Bezborodovs, N., Evans-Lacko, S., Palacios, J., Docherty, M., Barley, E., Rose, D., Koschorke, M., Shidhaye, R., Henderson, C., Thornicroft, G.N., Evidence for effective interventions to reduce mental health-related stigma and discrimination in the medium and long term: Systematic Review. The British journal of psychiatry : the journal of mental science, 2015. https://pubmed.ncbi.nlm.nih.gov/26527664/.
65. Rogoff, B., Apprenticeship in thinking: Cognitive development in social context, Oxford academic. 1990. https://academic.oup.com/book/53473.
66. Hennessy, S., Howe, C., Mercer, N., Vrikki, M., Coding classroom dialogue: Methodological considerations for researchers, Learning, Culture and Social Interaction, 25, 100404, ISSN 2210-6561, 2020.
67. Goleman, D., *Emotional Intelligence: Why It Can Matter More Than IQ*. Bantam Books, 1995.
68. Mlodinow, L., *Subliminal: How your unconscious mind rules your behavior*. Pantheon Books, 2012.
69. Kruglanski, A. W., Shah, J. Y., Fishbach, A., Friedman, R., Chun, W. Y., Sleeth-Keppler, D., A theory of goal systems. *Adv. Exp. Soc. Psychol.*, 32, 331–378, 2000, https://doi.org/10.1016/S0065-2601(00)80008-9.
70. Baumeister, R. F., Vohs, K. D., Tice, D. M., The Strength Model of Self-Control. *Curr. Dir. Psychol. Sci.*, 16, 6, 351–355, 2007, https://doi.org/10.1111/j.1467-8721.2007.00534.x.
71. Kessler, R. C., Berglund, P., Demler, O., Jin, R., Merikangas, K. R., Walters, E. E., Lifetime prevalence and age-of-onset distributions of DSM-IV disorders in the National Comorbidity Survey Replication. *Arch. Gen. Psychiatry*, 62, 6, 593–602, 2005.
72. de la Barra, M. F., Epidemiología de trastornos psiquiátricos en niños y adolescentes: estudios de prevalencia [Epidemiology of psychiatric disorders in children and adolescents: prevalence studies]. *Revista Chilena de Neuro-Psiquiatría*, 47, 4, 303–314, 2009.
73. Mills, R., Scott, J., Alati, R., O'Callaghan, M., Najman, J. M., Strathearn, L., Child maltreatment and adolescent mental health problems in a large birth cohort. *Child Abuse Neglect*, 30, 7, 813–822, 2006.
74. Green, J. G., McLaughlin, K. A., Berglund, P. A., Gruber, M. J., Sampson, N. A., Zaslavsky, A. M., Kessler, R. C., Childhood adversities and adult psychiatric disorders in the National Comorbidity Survey Replication I: Associations with first onset of DSM-IV disorders. *Arch. Gen. Psychiatry*, 70, 2, 115–125, 2013.
75. Bronfenbrenner, U., *The ecology of human development: Experiments by nature and design*. Harvard University Press, 1979.
76. Cole, M., *Cultural psychology: A once and future discipline*. Harvard University Press, 1996.

11

Navigating Mental Health Stigma in the Age of AI: Benefits and Risks

Mahshid Manouchehri[1]*, Aaras Y. Kraidi[2] and Aradhana Balodi Bhardwaj[1]

[1]*Psychology Department, Amity University Dubai Campus, Dubai International Academic City, Dubai, United Arab Emirates*
[2]*Engineering Department, University of Technology and Applied Science, Shinas, Sultanate of Oman*

Abstract
The inclusion of artificial intelligence (AI) in mental health treatment has the potential to bring about transformative changes, reshaping perceptions of mental health stigma. This in-depth analysis investigates how AI influences mental health stigma, exploring both its beneficial and adverse effects. It encompasses various AI techniques, such as natural language processing and machine learning, digital phenotyping, and virtual reality, and assesses their impact on mental health care. The study also addresses critical ethical issues, including informed consent, bias, privacy, and the need for a balance between technological innovation and human-centered care. Through comprehensive case studies and theoretical frameworks, the analysis reveals how AI can both mitigate and reinforce stigma. It underscores the necessity for culturally sensitive and ethically robust AI implementations. It encompasses various AI techniques, such as natural language processing and machine learning, aiming to harness AI's potential to enhance mental health care while effectively reducing stigma.

Keywords: Artificial intelligence (AI), mental health, stigma, machine learning

11.1 Introduction

Artificial intelligence (AI) has become a transformative force in many sectors, including mental health care. AI encompasses a variety of technologies

**Corresponding author*: Mmanouchehri@amityuniversity.ae

Ridhima Sharma, Fazla Rabby, Rohit Bansal, Timcy Sachdeva and Jihene Mrabet (eds.) Confronting Mental Health Stigma with AI and Machine Learning, (283–312) © 2026 Scrivener Publishing LLC

that mimic human intelligence, such as machine learning and natural language processing (NLP and robotics). In mental health, AI is increasingly used for diagnostic purposes, treatment recommendations, and therapeutic interventions. AI-driven tools like chatbots, predictive analytics, and virtual reality applications are revolutionizing mental health care delivery, offering new ways to enhance accessibility and personalize care.

The incorporation of AI into mental health care offers the potential for substantial advancements in early detection and intervention, personalized treatment plans, and efficient management of mental health conditions. For instance, AI-powered chatbots provide real-time support and cognitive behavioral therapy (CBT), while predictive analytics identify individuals at risk of severe mental health crises, enabling timely intervention [1, 2]. The increasing presence of AI in mental health gives rise to significant concerns about privacy, bias, and the potential reinforcement of stigma.

Mental health stigma has long been a barrier to seeking help and receiving appropriate care. Historically, individuals with mental health conditions have faced discrimination and social exclusion rooted in misconceptions and cultural beliefs about mental illness. Erving Goffman's seminal work on stigma highlights how societal labeling and stereotyping contribute to the marginalization of individuals with mental health issues [3]. Stigma can manifest as public stigma, where society holds negative views about mental illness and self-stigma, where individuals internalize these negative views, leading to self-doubt and reluctance to seek help.

Efforts to address mental health stigma have included public education campaigns, anti-stigma initiatives, and the promotion of mental health awareness. Despite these efforts, stigma persists, influencing how individuals perceive and manage their mental health. The incorporation of AI into mental health services offers both possibilities and difficulties in combating stigma, as it has the potential to either lessen or worsen negative perceptions.

Understanding the impact of AI on mental health stigma is crucial for several reasons. First, AI has the potential to revolutionize mental health care by making it more accessible and efficient. However, if not implemented thoughtfully, AI technologies may inadvertently reinforce existing stigmas or introduce new forms of discrimination. Examining AI's effects on stigma can help identify the best practices and strategies for leveraging AI to reduce stigma while addressing ethical concerns.

Second, as AI technologies become more integrated into mental health care, it is essential to consider how these technologies interact with societal attitudes and beliefs about mental illness. AI-driven tools perceived as impersonal or intrusive may exacerbate stigma, whereas those offering empathetic and supportive interactions may reduce stigma.

Finally, studying AI's impact on mental health stigma can inform policy and practice, "Leading the advancement of AI technologies that are morally upright and considerate of different cultures." By understanding the potential risks and benefits, stakeholders can make informed decisions about AI implementation in mental health care.

In the introduction, it was noted that integrating AI into mental health care has the potential to bring significant changes and challenges in addressing the stigma associated with mental illness. Understanding the underlying theories of stigma is crucial to comprehending how AI might impact these perceptions. The following section will explore foundational theories, such as Goffman's conceptualization of stigma and Link and Phelan's framework, and examine how these theories can be applied to the context of AI-driven mental health care. By examining these theoretical perspectives, we can better understand AI's dual role in reinforcing or mitigating mental health stigma.

11.2 Theories of Stigma and their Application to AI

To understand the impact of AI on mental health stigma, we must explore stigma's fundamental theories. This section examines how AI technologies intersect with societal attitudes towards mental illness, highlighting their potential to either reinforce harmful stereotypes or promote social inclusion. By referencing Goffman's theory of stigma and Link and Phelan's model, along with additional concepts like Social Identity Theory and Labelling Theory, we gain insights into AI's role in reshaping mental health stigma.

11.2.1 Goffman's Theory of Stigma

Erving Goffman's influential publication, "Stigma: Notes on the Management of Spoiled Identity" [3], offers a foundational comprehension of stigma as a societal occurrence. Goffman described stigma as a profoundly discrediting trait that diminishes an individual from a complete and typical person to someone tarnished and devalued. He identified three primary categories of stigma: physical abnormalities, personal imperfections, and cultural stigmas linked to race, nationality, or religion. Within the realm of mental health, personal imperfections often come into play, where mental illness is viewed as a moral shortcoming or individual frailty.

Goffman's theory is particularly relevant in AI applications in mental health care. AI technologies, such as chatbots and diagnostic algorithms, have the potential to either reinforce or challenge the stigma associated with mental illness. For example, AI tools that prioritize clinical objectivity and data-driven decision making may inadvertently contribute to dehumanizing individuals with mental health conditions. On the other hand, AI systems designed to offer empathetic support and personalized care could help diminish stigma by normalizing discussions about mental health and enhancing access to care.

11.2.2 Link and Phelan's Conceptualization of Stigma

Link and Phelan [4] provide a comprehensive framework for understanding stigma that moves beyond simplistic definitions of labeling and stereotyping. Their model emphasizes that stigma is a social process involving the interplay of power dynamics, societal structures, and discrimination. They identify five interrelated components that collectively shape the experience and consequences of stigma:

Labeling: This involves identifying individuals with mental health conditions as different or deviant from societal norms. Labels can lead to a fixed identity that overshadows other personal attributes, reducing individuals to their mental health condition rather than recognizing them as multifaceted individuals.

Stereotyping: Once labeled, individuals often become associated with negative attributes or stereotypes. For example, those diagnosed with depression may be unfairly perceived as weak or incapable, reinforcing harmful societal perceptions about mental health conditions.

Separation: This component reflects the social distance created between those who are labeled and the rest of society. By viewing individuals with mental health conditions as "other," societal norms reinforce exclusion and marginalization, perpetuating stigma and reducing opportunities for meaningful inclusion.

Status Loss: Stigma often leads to a diminishment of societal status for those with mental health conditions. This can manifest in reduced access to opportunities, such as employment or education, and a general devaluation of individuals' contributions to society.

Discrimination: Discrimination is the tangible enactment of stigma, where individuals face unfair treatment based on their mental health condition. This can include social, institutional, and systemic barriers that limit access to resources and perpetuate inequities.

AI has the potential to both reinforce and mitigate stigma, as conceptualized by Link and Phelan. On one hand, AI technologies like predictive analytics and diagnostic algorithms, if developed using biased or unrepresentative data, can perpetuate stereotypes and harmful categorizations. For instance, if training data overemphasizes certain symptoms within specific demographic groups, AI tools may reinforce discriminatory assumptions, leading to increased labeling, stereotyping, and status loss for marginalized populations.

Conversely, AI also offers opportunities to reduce stigma by fostering social inclusion and understanding. Virtual support groups powered by AI can connect individuals with shared experiences, breaking down the barriers of separation and promoting empathy. AI-driven educational tools can challenge stereotypes by providing accurate, culturally sensitive information about mental health, reducing misunderstandings and promoting acceptance. Additionally, AI can support early intervention and treatment personalization, empowering individuals and counteracting the notion that mental health conditions are insurmountable.

By aligning AI development with Link and Phelan's framework, we can better understand its dual role in stigma. Ethical considerations, culturally diverse data, and collaborative input from stakeholders are essential to ensuring that AI's potential to reduce stigma is realized while mitigating its risks. Such alignment can foster a transformative approach to mental health care that addresses the root causes of stigma and promotes equitable, stigma-free support systems.

11.2.3 Application of Theories: Public Stigma vs. Self-Stigma in AI-Driven Mental Health Care

Public stigma pertains to the adverse societal perceptions of individuals with mental health conditions, while self-stigma involves these negative attitudes being internalized by the affected individuals themselves. AI technologies can influence both forms of stigma in diverse ways:

- Public Stigma:
  - AI Tools for Awareness and Education: AI-driven applications that promote mental health education and awareness can help reduce public stigma by providing accurate information and challenging misconceptions. For example, AI-powered platforms that disseminate educational

content and share positive stories about mental health can shift societal attitudes [5].
  - Risk of Reinforcing Stereotypes: If AI systems use biased data or lack transparency, they may perpetuate stereotypes and reinforce public stigma. It is essential to develop AI tools with a focus on mitigating bias and addressing ethical considerations.

- Self-Stigma:
  - AI-Powered Support and Therapy: AI applications that offer private support and therapy can assist individuals in handling their mental health without worrying about being judged, potentially reducing self-stigma. For instance, AI-driven chatbots providing CBT can provide a non-judgmental environment for individuals to explore their mental health issues [1].
  - Concerns about Privacy: Despite the benefits, privacy and data security concerns may exacerbate self-stigma if individuals worry about misusing or exposing their personal information. Ensuring robust privacy protections and transparent data practices is essential for mitigating these concerns.

11.2.4 Additional Theories and their Relevance to AI and Mental Health

Several other theories contribute to understanding the relationship between AI and mental health stigma:

- Social Identity Theory indicates that individuals form their self-concept based on their group memberships [6]. AI tools like virtual support communities can strengthen social identity and reduce feelings of isolation for those with mental health conditions, fostering belonging and helping to combat stigma.
- Labeling Theory: Based on Goffman's work, labeling theory suggests that the labels assigned to individuals can shape their self-identity and social interactions [7]. AI applications that use supportive, non-judgmental language can help reduce the negative effects of labeling on self-concept.

- Theories of Social Change, like the Diffusion of Innovations [8] and the Theory of Planned Behavior [9], shed light on how AI technologies can influence societal attitudes. These theories help explain how AI-driven mental health interventions can promote positive attitudes and reduce stigma over time.

The exploration of stigma theories reveals how artificial intelligence (AI) interacts with societal perceptions of mental illness, both challenging and reinforcing existing attitudes. Understanding this connection offers insights into AI's role in shaping and potentially transforming stigma.

The next section will focus on AI methods in mental health care, including natural language processing (NLP), machine learning, predictive analytics, and virtual/augmented reality (VR/AR). We will assess their applications, effects on stigma, and ethical considerations. This analysis will highlight the practical impact of AI on mental health and identify strategies to maximize its benefits while addressing potential drawbacks.

11.3 AI Techniques in Mental Health Care

Artificial intelligence (AI) is rapidly transforming mental health care through advanced techniques. This section examines key AI methods, including natural language processing (NLP), machine learning, predictive analytics, digital phenotyping, and virtual and augmented reality (VR/AR). It highlights their applications, effects on mental health stigma, and ethical considerations. Ultimately, the section emphasizes AI's potential to improve mental health care while addressing the challenges of its implementation.

11.3.1 Natural Language Processing (NLP)

Natural language processing (NLP), a specialized area of artificial intelligence (AI), focuses on comprehending and processing human language in a way that computers can interpret meaningfully. NLP employs various techniques, such as sentiment analysis, to assess the emotional undertone of words and discern individuals' mental states. It also includes named entity recognition, which identifies and categorizes significant entities within text, such as names of people, locations, or conditions. Additionally, text classification categorizes text into predefined groups, making it useful for identifying mental health symptoms.

In mental health care, NLP is widely applied. AI-powered chatbots like Woebot and Wysa use NLP to engage in therapeutic conversations and provide cognitive-behavioral therapy (CBT). These chatbots process users' input to deliver tailored responses based on therapeutic principles [1]. Furthermore, NLP algorithms analyze text data from sources like social media or personal journals to track symptoms and detect mental health issues early.

NLP applications significantly contribute to reducing mental health stigma. Tools powered by NLP offer anonymity and round-the-clock accessibility, alleviating the fear of judgment. According to Vayena [10], individuals might feel more comfortable discussing sensitive topics with a chatbot than with a human therapist. Additionally, NLP tools facilitate open discussions about mental health, helping to normalize these conversations and reduce internalized stigma. Their ease of interaction encourages users to seek help and discuss their issues more openly.

Despite its benefits, NLP poses challenges and raises ethical considerations. The accuracy and reliability of NLP tools depend on the quality of the algorithms and training data. Misinterpretations or errors could result in unsuitable responses, potentially worsening mental health issues [11]. Moreover, maintaining privacy and confidentiality is crucial. NLP applications must incorporate robust security protocols to safeguard sensitive information and prevent misuse [12].

11.3.2 Machine Learning and Predictive Analytics

Machine learning (ML), a subset of AI, involves systems learning from data to make predictions or decisions based on patterns. Predictive analytics, a specialized application of ML, leverages historical data to forecast future outcomes. In mental health care, ML and predictive analytics are applied in various ways. For instance, ML models analyze data from diverse sources, such as electronic health records and social media, to detect individuals who may be at risk of mental health conditions or crises [2]. Additionally, ML algorithms enhance personalized treatment by customizing plans based on individual data, improving both efficacy and patient engagement.

The impact of ML on stigma is notable, particularly in fostering early intervention and normalization of mental health care. By identifying at-risk individuals before a crisis occurs, ML facilitates proactive care, helping to normalize seeking support and reducing the stigma associated with waiting until conditions become severe.

However, challenges and ethical considerations must be addressed to maximize the benefits of ML in mental health care. Bias and fairness are critical concerns, as ML models may reinforce biases present in their training data, leading to unequal treatment of certain groups. Prioritizing fairness and reducing bias is essential to ensure equitable care. Furthermore, transparency and accountability in ML decision-making processes are crucial. Users and clinicians need to understand how predictions are made to trust and effectively utilize these tools in mental health settings.

11.3.3 Digital Phenotyping

Digital phenotyping involves collecting and analyzing data from digital devices to understand and monitor mental health. Key methods include analyzing smartphone data, such as app usage and communication patterns, to provide insights into mental health and behavioral trends. Wearable devices that track physiological data like heart rate and sleep patterns can also be employed to monitor symptoms of mental health conditions and stress levels.

However, ethical considerations are critical in implementing digital phenotyping. Users must be informed about the information being gathered and its intended use, ensuring transparent consent processes that respect user autonomy and privacy [14]. Additionally, protecting the security of health data is paramount, requiring digital phenotyping systems to employ strong measures to prevent unauthorized access and misuse [10].

Digital phenotyping has significant implications for stigma. Providing objective data can help reduce stigma by supporting individuals in understanding their conditions without relying solely on subjective self-reports [1]. At the same time, privacy concerns remain a challenge, as responsible handling of data collection and usage is essential to maintaining user trust and mitigating stigma associated with mental health monitoring.

11.3.4 Virtual and Augmented Reality (VR/AR)

Virtual reality (VR) and augmented reality (AR) technologies generate immersive environments suitable for therapeutic applications. VR is particularly effective in exposure therapy, helping individuals confront anxiety-inducing situations in a controlled setting, allowing them to manage their fears. For instance, it can simulate social interactions to treat social anxiety [15]. Additionally, AR and VR facilitate skills training and therapeutic exercises by creating interactive and engaging experiences that enhance learning and practice.

These technologies also have a significant impact on stigma. VR provides safe and controlled environments for therapy, offering a private and supportive space for mental health work, which helps reduce stigma. Furthermore, VR experiences that simulate the challenges of mental health conditions can foster empathy and challenge stereotypes, promoting a more nuanced understanding of mental health and reducing public stigma.

However, there are challenges and ethical considerations associated with these technologies. VR therapy must be carefully designed to avoid causing distress or re-traumatization, with customized experiences tailored to individual needs being essential for effective and safe therapy [15]. Additionally, the accessibility and cost of VR therapy remain significant barriers, as the high expense of VR technology could limit its widespread availability. Addressing these obstacles is crucial to ensure that the benefits of VR therapy reach a broader demographic.

The exploration of AI methods like natural language processing (NLP), machine learning, and virtual/augmented reality (VR/AR) highlights their significant potential to enhance mental health care. These technologies provide innovative approaches to diagnosis, treatment, and support, fostering more personalized and effective care. The next section will examine the intersection of these AI advancements with mental health stigma, evaluating their potential to reduce stigma while also addressing new ethical and practical challenges. This analysis is vital for maximizing AI's benefits in evolving mental health care compassionately and effectively.

11.4 Impact of AI on Mental Health Stigma

The emergence of artificial intelligence (AI) in mental healthcare offers both progress and challenges. This section examines how AI can both reduce and worsen mental health stigma. On the positive side, AI enhances accessibility, promotes awareness, and supports early intervention and personalized care [1, 16]. However, the integration of AI also brings potential risks, including the reinforcement of biases, a reduction in human interaction and empathy, and privacy concerns that can lead to self-stigma [10, 13]. This section offers a detailed examination of how AI influences attitudes and approaches in the field of mental health care by delving into these elements.

11.4.1 Positive Impacts of AI in Reducing Stigma

AI technology can improve access to mental health services for those hesitant to seek help due to stigma. It provides confidential support through AI-powered chatbots and online platforms, allowing individuals to address their concerns without fear of judgment. For instance, apps like Woebot offer cognitive behavioral therapy (CBT) *via* a chatbot, which is helpful for those uncomfortable discussing mental health with a human therapist [1]. AI can help normalize seeking mental health support by allowing users to interact with services anonymously. This is vital in cultures where mental health issues are stigmatized, as it offers a safe space for individuals to seek help without societal pressure.

Additionally, AI can greatly improve mental health awareness and education, which are essential for reducing stigma. AI-driven platforms spread accurate information, challenge misconceptions, and provide resources for learning about mental health. For example, AI can analyze social media trends to create targeted campaigns that address specific stigmatizing beliefs in communities [5]. Artificial intelligence can also create interactive educational tools, like virtual reality (VR) simulations, that help users understand the challenges faced by those with mental health conditions. These immersive experiences foster empathy and reduce stigma by challenging stereotypes and providing a deeper perspective on mental illness.

Early intervention is another critical area where AI plays a significant role. By analyzing data from sources like social media, wearable devices, and electronic health records using predictive analytics and machine learning, AI can help identify at-risk individuals and provide tailored interventions [12]. Early intervention has the potential to prevent the exacerbation of mental health issues and diminish the stigma associated with serious or persistent mental illnesses. Furthermore, AI improves mental health treatment by creating personalized plans that cater to individual needs and preferences. This approach challenges the misconception of a uniform treatment model, empowering individuals to take control of their mental well-being and reducing the stigma associated with mental health issues [16].

11.4.2 Negative Impacts and Potential Risks

A major concern about AI in mental health care is its potential to reinforce existing biases and stereotypes. AI systems learn from large datasets, and if these datasets contain biased information, the AI may perpetuate those biases. For example, if trained on data that misrepresents certain demographic groups or links specific mental health conditions to negative traits, the AI could produce biased predictions that contribute to stigma [13]. This issue is critical in predictive analytics, where biased models may unfairly label certain populations as high risk, leading to stigmatization and unequal access to care. Addressing these biases requires careful consideration of data sources, fairness testing, and diverse perspectives in AI development.

While artificial intelligence can improve the efficiency and accessibility of mental health services, excessive reliance on it might reduce essential human interaction and empathy. Human therapists provide crucial emotional support and understanding, which are key to effective mental health treatment. AI-driven tools like chatbots and virtual therapists may not provide the nuanced emotional support of human therapists. This could make mental health care seem more impersonal, potentially worsening stigma by suggesting that those with mental health conditions don't deserve human care [10].

Privacy issues further complicate the use of AI in mental health care. Fear of information misuse can deter individuals from seeking help, increasing self-stigma regarding their mental health. To combat this, strong privacy protections and transparent data practices are essential. AI developers and mental health professionals must ethically handle sensitive information and clearly communicate how data will be used, stored, and protected. Addressing these concerns can help reduce self-stigma and encourage more people to access AI-powered mental health services [10].

The exploration of AI in mental health care reveals its potential to enhance accessibility, raise awareness, and provide personalized support, while also posing risks like reinforcing biases and reducing human interaction. This sets the stage for the next section, which will examine case studies of AI in mental health and their impact on stigma. By analyzing real-world applications, the section will illustrate how these technologies affect mental health stigma and assess their effectiveness in everyday situations.

11.5 Case Studies of AI in Mental Health and their Implications for Stigma

In the evolving landscape of mental health care, AI technologies are increasingly making their mark. This section delves into a series of case studies that showcase the real-world applications of AI in mental health care. By scrutinizing these examples, the section aims to uncover how AI solutions impact mental health stigma in both positive and negative ways. Each case study provides a lens through which to explore the practical effects of AI, highlighting successes and challenges in the journey towards transforming mental health support. Additionally, the section addresses the ethical considerations intertwined with these innovations, offering a comprehensive view of how AI is reshaping mental health care and its implications for stigma.

11.5.1 AI-Driven Chatbots in Mental Health Support

AI-driven chatbots, such as Woebot, Wysa, and Replika, have gained popularity as tools for providing mental health support, utilizing natural language processing (NLP) and machine learning algorithms; these chatbots engage in conversations with users about their mental well-being. They offer cognitive behavioral therapy (CBT), mindfulness exercises, and tools for tracking moods. These chatbots deliver prompt responses and guidance based on user input [1].

AI chatbots can help reduce stigma by providing anonymous, 24/7 support for individuals reluctant to seek help from human therapists. Their anonymity allows users to discuss sensitive topics without fear of judgment, which is especially beneficial in stigmatized communities. For example, a study on Woebot showed that users appreciated its confidential nature, encouraging them to share their mental health struggles. This indicates that AI chatbots can play a vital role in normalizing mental health conversations and reducing the shame that prevents people from seeking help.

11.5.1.1 Woebot — AI-Powered CBT and Stigma Reduction

Woebot is an AI-driven chatbot that provides cognitive behavioral therapy (CBT) through conversation. A study found that users reported significant reductions in symptoms of depression and anxiety after interacting with Woebot, highlighting its potential for effective mental health support.

Notably, Woebot's anonymous and non-judgmental nature helped reduce self-stigma, allowing users to discuss their mental health openly. This case study shows how AI tools can offer accessible and stigma-free mental health assistance.

The adoption of AI chatbots also gives rise to ethical issues, specifically concerning the possibility of these tools offering insufficient or unsuitable assistance in intricate situations. Unlike human therapists, AI chatbots may struggle to interpret nuanced emotions or recognize when a user is in crisis, leading to suboptimal care. This could exacerbate stigma if users perceive AI-driven mental health support as inferior or impersonal [10]. Furthermore, privacy concerns are paramount, as users may hesitate to share sensitive information with a machine, fearing data breaches or misuse. Ensuring robust data security and transparent privacy policies is essential to maintaining trust and mitigating self-stigma.

11.5.2 AI in Suicide Prevention

AI is increasingly utilized in suicide prevention, with predictive analytics being crucial in identifying individuals at high risk. By analyzing data from electronic health records, social media activity, and other sources, AI models can identify patterns and indicators linked to suicidal behavior. These insights allow healthcare providers to intervene early and offer targeted support to those most at risk [2].

Using AI in suicide prevention can help reduce stigma by shifting the focus from reactive to proactive mental health care. By identifying at-risk individuals early, AI encourages help-seeking behavior and normalizes early intervention, challenging the notion that mental health issues should only be addressed in crises. However, there are concerns that AI may unintentionally reinforce stigma if people feel labeled by predictive models. It is vital to present AI-driven interventions in a supportive way that emphasizes care and prevention rather than surveillance [12].

11.5.2.1 AI and Predictive Analytics in Suicide Prevention

Predictive analytics has been utilized to detect individuals at risk of suicide by analyzing electronic health records, social media activity, and other data sources. A study by Franklin *et al.* [2] showcased the potential of AI-powered predictive models to accurately pinpoint individuals at high risk of suicide, enabling timely interventions and potentially saving lives. However, the study also highlighted concerns about the possibility of these models' reinforcing stigma. If the algorithms are not meticulously developed and tested, they may unfairly identify certain groups as high risk, resulting in stigmatization and discrimination. This real-life example emphasizes the significance of addressing bias in AI models to prevent the amplification of stigma in mental health care.

The moral dilemmas involved in employing AI for suicide prevention encompass issues related to consent, privacy, and the risk of algorithmic bias. For example, predictive models may disproportionately flag certain demographic groups as high risk, leading to stigmatization and unequal access to care. Ensuring that AI models are transparent, fair, and subject to regular auditing is essential to addressing these challenges and promoting ethical AI use in mental health [13].

11.5.3 Virtual Reality (VR) in Exposure Therapy

The use of virtual reality (VR) is on the rise in the field of mental health treatment, especially for disorders like PTSD, phobias, and social anxiety.

VR enables individuals to participate in controlled exposure therapy, providing a secure and immersive setting for them to address and handle their fears. Through simulating real-life situations, VR assists individuals in rehearsing coping mechanisms and developing resilience [15].

Virtual reality (VR) in mental health treatment can help reduce stigma by offering a personalized and private therapeutic experience. It allows individuals to engage in treatment without fear of judgment while fostering a deeper understanding of mental health conditions. For instance, VR simulations that let users experience challenges faced by individuals with schizophrenia or depression can dispel stereotypes and promote empathy, ultimately decreasing the stigma around these conditions.

11.5.3.1 Virtual Reality (VR) for Social Anxiety Treatment

Virtual reality (VR) is used to treat social anxiety by creating simulated environments for practicing social interactions. A study by Fodor showed that combining VR with cognitive behavioral therapy (CBT) effectively reduced social anxiety symptoms and increased participants' confidence in real-life situations. The immersive aspect of VR helped minimize the stigma by providing a safe space to confront fears. However, the study emphasized the need for inclusive and non-stigmatizing VR designs, as poorly crafted simulations could reinforce negative stereotypes.

Challenges and Ethical Considerations

The implementation of virtual reality (VR) in mental health, despite its potential advantages, raises ethical concerns. A significant worry is the possibility of re-traumatization, especially in exposure therapy for PTSD, which involves exposing individuals to distressing stimuli. It is crucial to carefully design and customize VR experiences to meet the specific needs of each individual in order to prevent causing harm [15]. Additionally, the high cost of VR technology may limit access to this form of therapy, potentially exacerbating health disparities and stigma for those who cannot afford it. Addressing these barriers to access is crucial for ensuring that the benefits of VR in mental health are equitably distributed.

11.5.4 AI in Diagnosing Mental Health Conditions

AI is increasingly utilized to aid in the detection of mental health disorders. By analyzing patterns in speech, text, and behavior, AI algorithms can help recognize early indications of conditions such as depression, bipolar disorder, and schizophrenia. These tools offer valuable assistance to healthcare professionals, improving diagnostic precision and facilitating earlier intervention [17]. The use of AI in diagnosing mental health conditions could also help diminish stigma by providing impartial, data-based assessments that challenge personal biases. For instance, AI algorithms that examine speech patterns for indications of depression could present a non-intrusive and non-judgmental method to identify mental health issues, potentially reducing the stigma linked with traditional diagnostic techniques. Moreover, AI-driven diagnostic tools could demystify mental health conditions by offering straightforward and accessible explanations of how these conditions manifest. This could enhance public understanding and acceptance, ultimately reducing the stigma associated with mental illness.

However, the use of AI in diagnosis raises ethical challenges, particularly regarding potential misdiagnosis and the reduction of complex human experiences to algorithmic outputs. There is concern that excessive reliance on AI tools may oversimplify mental health conditions, potentially reinforcing stigma rather than reducing it [17]. To address these issues, it is crucial to ensure that AI diagnostic tools are used as a supplement to, rather than a replacement for, human clinical judgment. Furthermore, ongoing research and validation are necessary to guarantee these tools' accuracy, reliability, and fairness.

Examining AI case studies in mental health care offers valuable insights into these ethical dimensions, paving the way for a deeper exploration of related challenges. The next section will focus on ethical considerations in AI and mental health, delving into dilemmas, privacy concerns, and transparency. This discussion will aim to clarify how to navigate the ethical challenges of AI in mental health care and its role in reducing stigma.

11.6 Ethical Considerations in AI and Mental Health

As AI technologies become increasingly integrated into mental health care, addressing the ethical implications becomes essential. The combination of artificial intelligence and mental healthcare gives rise to important concerns regarding privacy, data security, bias, fairness, and human supervision. Understanding these ethical dimensions is crucial to ensuring that AI advancements contribute positively to mental health support while safeguarding individuals' rights and maintaining trust. This section explores these ethical considerations in depth, focusing on privacy and data security, informed consent and transparency, bias and fairness in AI models, the role of human oversight, and the future of ethical AI in mental health.

11.6.1 Privacy and Data Security

1. The sensitivity of mental health information is significant, as it contains personal and private details about an individual's psychological and emotional well-being. There is a risk of misuse, including discrimination and breaches of confidentiality. Effective protection methods include strong encryption, secure storage, and compliance with strict data protection laws like the General Data Protection Regulation (GDPR). These measures are essential for maintaining user trust and safeguarding personal information against unauthorized access or misuse [10].
2. Informed Consent and Transparency: Informed consent is a fundamental ethical principle that requires individuals to understand how their data will be used and the associated risks. The intricate nature of AI technologies can pose difficulties in obtaining unambiguous and thorough consent. To tackle this issue, AI systems should prioritize transparency, presenting users with clear details about data collection, processing, and sharing practices. By offering users the choice to manage their data, such as opting in or out of different levels of data sharing, individuals are empowered and can make informed decisions [10].

11.6.2 Bias and Fairness in AI Models

Algorithmic bias occurs when AI systems replicate or exacerbate existing social prejudices, often due to biased training data or flawed model design. In mental health care, such biases can result in unequal treatment, misdiagnosis, or reinforcement of stigma, particularly impacting marginalized populations. For instance, if an AI model is trained on data that fails to adequately represent certain demographic groups or disproportionately emphasizes specific symptoms, it may produce biased outcomes that perpetuate health disparities [13].

Addressing algorithmic bias requires implementing various strategies. Ensuring that training data is inclusive and reflective of all demographic groups is critical, encompassing a wide range of mental health conditions and responses to treatment [12]. Testing and auditing AI models for bias are also essential to identify and rectify disparities. This process involves evaluating model performance across different demographic groups and making necessary algorithmic adjustments to achieve fairer outcomes.

Additionally, engaging a diverse group of stakeholders, including mental health professionals, ethicists, and representatives from marginalized communities, ensures that AI technologies are equitable and inclusive. These collaborative efforts can help create AI systems that support all users effectively and responsibly.

11.6.3 The Role of Human Oversight

Striking a balance between automation and human insight is essential in the application of AI to mental health services. AI's ability to process vast amounts of data and identify patterns that might elude human recognition holds significant promise. However, effective mental health care often requires a nuanced understanding, empathy, and awareness of an individual's unique context—qualities that AI lacks. As a result, AI should function as a supportive tool rather than a replacement for human judgment. Mental health professionals play a crucial role in analyzing AI-derived information and making clinical decisions that consider the patient's full situation and preferences [10].

Ensuring accountability is another critical aspect of AI-driven mental health care. Clear lines of responsibility must be established for the decisions and actions of AI systems, particularly when incorrect predictions or recommendations impact patient care. Addressing this requires collaboration between AI developers, healthcare providers, and regulatory bodies to establish guidelines and standards for accountability. Measures such as forming oversight committees, creating processes for handling grievances, and ensuring transparency in AI systems can help. By making AI tools clear and understandable, clinicians and patients can examine and comprehend the basis of decisions, fostering trust and enabling responsible use [13].

11.6.4 The Future of AI Ethics in Mental Health

The future of AI in mental health care hinges on the establishment of ethical frameworks that prioritize the well-being and rights of individuals. Achieving this requires ongoing efforts to strengthen data privacy, minimize bias, and ensure transparency, accountability, and fairness. One effective method is "Ethics by Design," which integrates ethical considerations throughout every phase of AI development, from data collection and model training to deployment and monitoring. By embedding ethics into AI systems, developers can create technologies that are not only effective but also aligned with societal values [18].

Collaboration in governance is equally crucial for addressing the complex ethical challenges associated with AI in mental health care. This approach involves uniting technology developers, healthcare providers, policymakers, patients, and ethicists to jointly shape the development and regulation of AI technologies. Collaborative governance ensures that AI systems reflect the needs and values of all stakeholders, especially those most affected by mental health stigma. It also creates a platform for addressing emerging ethical dilemmas, fostering socially responsible and beneficial evolution of AI technologies [10].

Understanding the ethical dimensions of AI in mental health care is essential for ensuring that these technologies enhance mental health support while safeguarding individual rights and fostering trust. As AI continues to advance, addressing these ethical issues will be critical for maximizing benefits and minimizing potential risks. The following section will explore the future of AI in mental health care, focusing on predictions and emerging trends. It will examine how increasing personalization in AI-driven interventions and the integration of AI with other emerging technologies could shape the landscape of mental health support and influence stigma. This analysis will provide insights into how future advancements may further transform mental health care while addressing challenges and opportunities ahead.

11.7 AI and the Future of Mental Health Stigma

As AI technology advances, its influence on mental health care is changing, offering both opportunities to reduce stigma and potential risks of reinforcing it. This section explores the future of AI in mental health, emphasizing important trends such as enhanced personalization, the integration of AI with new technologies, and AI's role in public health initiatives. It also discusses the necessary policy considerations and recommendations to ensure that AI-based mental health interventions are implemented ethically and fairly. By looking to the future, we can gain a better understanding of how AI may transform mental health care and address the persistent issues of stigma.

11.7.1 Predictions and Emerging Trends in AI

Advances in AI for mental health care are driving significant emerging trends, one of which is the shift towards increasingly personalized interventions. Machine learning and data analytics are enabling AI systems to provide tailored support based on an individual's unique needs, preferences, and circumstances. This personalization is expected to improve further, with AI tools becoming increasingly adept at addressing the specific mental health challenges of diverse individuals and populations [19]. For instance, future AI systems could predict when an individual is at risk of a mental health crisis by analyzing subtle behavioral or physiological changes. These systems could then deliver personalized interventions, such as mindfulness exercises or connecting the individual with a human therapist, potentially reducing the risk of a crisis and associated stigma.

Another significant trend is the integration of AI with other emerging technologies, such as virtual reality (VR) and augmented reality (AR). Combining AI with these immersive technologies can enhance the effectiveness of mental health treatments by creating tailored, interactive experiences. For example, VR environments can help individuals with anxiety or PTSD confront and manage their fears in a safe and controlled setting [15]. Additionally, the integration of AI with wearable technology is likely to become more prevalent. Wearable devices can continuously monitor physiological and behavioral indicators, enabling AI systems to analyze real-time data and provide personalized mental health support. This seamless monitoring and intervention can help normalize mental health care, making it a routine and stigma-free part of daily life.

AI is also set to play a transformative role in public health campaigns aimed at reducing mental health stigma. By analyzing large datasets from sources such as social media and public health records, AI can identify trends in mental health stigma and design tailored public health messages that resonate with specific populations. This targeted approach can promote inclusivity and reduce stigma [20]. Furthermore, AI systems can measure the effectiveness of these campaigns in real time, allowing for rapid adjustments and improvements. This data-driven strategy ensures that public health initiatives are practical, efficient, and impactful in addressing mental health stigma on a broader scale.

11.7.2 Policy Implications and Recommendations for the Future

As AI becomes increasingly integrated into mental health care, implementing comprehensive regulations is vital to ensure ethical and effective use. Policymakers must establish clear guidelines and standards for AI applications in mental health, covering critical aspects such as data privacy, algorithm transparency, and informed consent. These regulations should also address potential biases in AI systems by setting stringent standards for training data and mandating regular audits to identify and mitigate biases over time. By embedding inclusivity and equity into regulatory frameworks, policymakers can help create AI tools that are both reliable and fair.

Equitable access to AI-driven mental health care is another critical policy priority. Bridging the digital divide requires investing in digital infrastructure, particularly in underserved communities, to ensure that everyone has access to the necessary technology, such as smartphones and reliable internet connectivity [13]. In addition to infrastructure, affordability must be addressed through policies such as subsidizing AI-driven mental health tools for low-income individuals or providing training and support to help users effectively navigate these tools. These efforts can help ensure that AI-based mental health interventions reach and benefit all populations.

Encouraging collaboration among stakeholders is equally important for the successful integration of AI into mental health services. Governments, healthcare providers, technology firms, and patient advocacy organizations must work together to create solutions that address diverse individual needs. Public-private partnerships and interdisciplinary collaboration can ensure that AI-driven mental health tools are continually refined and updated based on user feedback and the latest research. This collective approach also helps tackle the stigma surrounding mental illness, fostering a more inclusive environment for mental health care.

As AI advances in mental health care, striking a balance between innovation and ethical, equitable practices is crucial to fully harness its transformative potential while safeguarding individual rights. Addressing these challenges will ensure that AI enhances mental health support in ways that are inclusive, just, and impactful.

The following section will delve into the socio-cultural implications of AI in mental health, focusing on how cultural sensitivity in AI design is essential for creating effective and inclusive systems. This exploration will consider the importance of incorporating cultural perspectives, the challenges of developing culturally sensitive AI, and strategies to improve AI's responsiveness to diverse needs. Understanding these factors is key to ensuring that AI positively contributes to mental health care across varying cultural contexts.

11.8 Socio-Cultural Implications of AI in Mental Health

Acknowledging the socio-cultural factors related to AI in mental health care is vital for designing effective and inclusive interventions. This section delves into how culturally sensitive AI design can address diverse needs, the impact of AI on marginalized communities, and the importance of global collaboration and policy in shaping equitable mental health solutions. By investigating these elements, we can gain a clearer understanding of how AI can help reduce stigma and improve mental health care in diverse cultural environments.

11.8.1 Cultural Sensitivity in AI Design

Incorporating cultural sensitivity into AI design is essential for developing effective mental health tools. AI systems that account for cultural differences can better understand and address the specific needs of individuals from various backgrounds. This includes considerations of language, cultural norms, values, and mental health challenges unique to specific communities. For instance, an AI tool designed for mental health intervention in the U.S. may not perform effectively in another cultural context if it does not consider local customs or the stigma surrounding mental illness.

To achieve cultural sensitivity, developers must collaborate with mental health experts, sociologists, and representatives from diverse cultural groups. This collaborative approach ensures that AI tools are both effective and respectful of the populations they aim to serve. Ignoring cultural differences can lead to systems that not only fail to deliver appropriate care but also exacerbate mental health stigma or result in misdiagnosis and unsuitable interventions.

Creating culturally aware AI poses significant challenges, particularly regarding algorithmic bias. AI systems are often trained using datasets that fail to reflect the full diversity of the population. If the training data predominantly represents one cultural group, the AI may struggle to interpret mental health symptoms accurately for others, leading to inappropriate recommendations [12]. Another challenge lies in understanding cultural nuances, as mental health is deeply intertwined with beliefs, practices, and stigma that vary widely between societies. Developing AI systems that navigate these complexities effectively requires substantial effort and a commitment to regular updates to align with evolving societal norms and values.

To enhance cultural sensitivity in AI, developers should prioritize building diverse datasets that mitigate algorithmic bias and improve the accuracy of AI-driven mental health interventions. Involving culturally diverse teams in the development process can offer critical insights into the nuances that must be addressed. Additionally, incorporating user feedback from different cultural groups is crucial. AI systems should be designed to gather and integrate this feedback through iterative updates, ensuring that the tools remain relevant, adaptive, and effective across various cultural contexts. These strategies can help create AI tools that not only support mental health care but also promote inclusivity and cultural respect.

11.8.2 Impact on Marginalized Communities

AI's impact on marginalized communities is multifaceted, offering both challenges and opportunities in addressing mental health disparities. While AI has the potential to improve mental health care, it also risks exacerbating existing health inequalities. Marginalized communities often face barriers such as stigma, limited resources, and discrimination in accessing mental health services. If AI tools are not designed with these challenges in mind, they could reinforce or worsen disparities [21]. For example, individuals in these communities may lack access to the technology required for AI-driven interventions, such as smartphones or reliable internet connectivity. Additionally, AI systems trained on data that do not adequately represent these populations may provide less accurate or relevant recommendations, further disadvantaging those who are already underserved.

Despite these challenges, AI holds a significant promise for empowering marginalized communities. By developing low-cost, scalable mental health interventions, AI can reach individuals in remote or underserved areas. AI-driven chatbots, for instance, can offer mental health support in regions with limited access to human therapists. These tools can be designed to function in multiple languages and incorporate cultural nuances, ensuring accessibility for a broader audience. Moreover, AI can analyze patterns in data to uncover specific mental health needs within marginalized communities, leading to targeted and effective interventions that address their unique challenges.

Ethical considerations are crucial when introducing AI to marginalized communities. Developers and policymakers must ensure that AI tools do not unintentionally perpetuate existing biases or inequalities. Transparency in the development and use of these systems is essential, as is involving community members in the design process to ensure that their needs are adequately addressed. Regular assessments of AI interventions are necessary to confirm their fairness and effectiveness. Additionally, policies aimed at bridging the digital divide, such as improving digital infrastructure, providing training on AI tools, and ensuring affordability, are vital to ensuring that all communities benefit from AI-driven mental health services. Such initiatives can help create an equitable and inclusive approach to leveraging AI for mental health care.

11.8.3 Global Perspectives on AI and Mental Health Stigma

Mental health stigma varies significantly across cultures, influencing how AI-driven mental health tools are perceived and utilized. In some cultures, mental health issues are highly stigmatized, leading individuals to avoid seeking help. In such contexts, AI tools that offer anonymous or discreet support can play a critical role in reducing stigma and encouraging individuals to access care [22]. Conversely, in cultures where mental health issues are less stigmatized, AI tools may be more readily accepted and integrated into existing healthcare systems. Recognizing these cultural variations is essential for designing AI systems that effectively combat stigma and enhance mental health globally.

To address the diverse needs of people worldwide, international collaboration in AI development is increasingly recognized as essential. This involves the sharing of data, best practices, and resources among nations to create AI systems capable of functioning effectively in various cultural settings. Such global collaboration can also ensure that AI tools are inclusive and accessible, regardless of geographic location or financial circumstances [18]. Initiatives like AI4D (Artificial Intelligence for Development) exemplify this approach by bringing together stakeholders from different countries to develop AI solutions tailored to challenges faced by low- and middle-income nations. These collaborative efforts can help produce culturally sensitive, affordable, and scalable AI-driven mental health tools, reducing stigma on a global scale.

Global policy plays a pivotal role in shaping the future of AI in mental health. Organizations such as the World Health Organization (WHO) are increasingly establishing guidelines and standards for the ethical application of AI in healthcare. These policies ensure that AI technologies are developed and deployed in ways that uphold human rights, promote fairness, and mitigate stigma. Moreover, global policy initiatives can help create equitable access to AI-driven mental health resources by advocating for investments in digital infrastructure, fostering data-sharing agreements, and encouraging the development of AI tools that address the diverse needs of communities worldwide.

The exploration of cultural sensitivity in AI design highlights its importance in fostering inclusivity and addressing the unique needs of marginalized communities. By embracing diverse cultural perspectives and tackling ethical challenges, AI tools can advance mental health care while contributing to the global reduction of stigma. The next section will delve into AI's transformative potential in mental health care, synthesizing key insights and offering strategic recommendations to harness its advantages. By navigating the associated ethical and practical issues, these efforts aim to enhance mental health support universally.

11.9 Conclusion and Recommendations

The adoption of AI in mental health services offers groundbreaking possibilities along with considerable challenges. This section summarizes key findings on how AI can revolutionize mental health interventions, emphasizing the need for careful consideration of ethical, cultural, and practical aspects. It outlines detailed recommendations for developers, policymakers, healthcare providers, and researchers to guide future efforts and address potential pitfalls. By adopting these recommendations, stakeholders can utilize AI to enhance mental health services and reduce stigma, striving for a more inclusive and effective approach to support individuals with mental health issues.

The incorporation of AI into mental health care brings both significant opportunities and notable challenges. It has the potential to transform the field by offering personalized, scalable, and accessible interventions that can help reduce stigma and enhance outcomes for those with mental health issues. However, to achieve this potential, it is essential to carefully address the ethical, cultural, and practical challenges related to AI.

Key insights from this analysis point to the necessity of cultural awareness in AI development. While AI can provide empowerment to marginalized groups, it also risks putting them at a disadvantage. Thus, comprehensive regulations are crucial for the ethical application of AI in mental health care.

Furthermore, the analysis identifies emerging trends in AI-driven mental health, including greater personalization, the fusion of AI with other technologies, and the use of AI in public health initiatives.

11.9.1 Recommendations for Stakeholders

- For Developers:

Prioritize the inclusion of diverse datasets in AI development to reduce bias and improve cultural sensitivity. Involve culturally diverse teams in the design and testing of AI-driven mental health tools. Incorporate user feedback to continuously improve AI systems and ensure they remain relevant and effective.

- For Policymakers:

Create thorough guidelines for the application of AI in mental health care, with an emphasis on standards for data privacy, transparency in algorithms, and ensuring informed consent. Promote equity in AI-driven mental health care access by investing in digital infrastructure and ensuring affordability. Promote cooperation among stakeholders to improve the creation and deployment of AI-based mental health tools.

- For Healthcare Providers:

Guide patients in understanding the advantages and limitations of AI-based mental health tools, enabling them to make informed choices regarding their care.

Collaborate with AI developers to provide insights into the clinical needs and challenges individuals with mental health conditions face.

Monitor the impact of AI-driven interventions on patient outcomes and provide feedback to developers and policymakers.

- For Researchers:

Carry out a study on how effective AI-driven mental health interventions are within various populations and cultural settings. Explore the ethical implications of AI in mental health care, including the potential for bias and the impact on patient autonomy. Investigate emerging trends in AI and mental health, such as the integration of AI with other technologies and its role in public health campaigns.

11.9.2 Advancing AI in Mental Health: Balancing Challenges and Opportunities

The future of AI in mental health care presents a critical intersection of challenges and opportunities, demanding a nuanced and interdisciplinary approach to fully realize its potential. Key challenges include addressing algorithmic bias, which can perpetuate existing inequities if AI systems are trained on unrepresentative or biased datasets. Ensuring cultural sensitivity is equally vital, as mental health care practices and stigma vary significantly across cultures. Ethical concerns, such as privacy, transparency, and accountability in AI-driven interventions, further emphasize the need for robust frameworks that safeguard individual rights and promote equitable outcomes.

Conversely, AI offers transformative opportunities to reshape mental health care. Advances in machine learning and data analytics enable personalized interventions tailored to individual needs, preferences, and contexts. The integration of AI with technologies like virtual reality and wearable devices enhances the delivery of real-time, immersive, and interactive mental health support. These advancements can contribute to destigmatizing mental health care by normalizing its integration into everyday life and making support more accessible to underserved populations.

Future research must adopt a holistic perspective, exploring how AI can not only optimize mental health outcomes but also reduce stigma at both societal and individual levels. This involves examining the long-term impact of AI on mental health literacy and access to care. Collaborative efforts among researchers, policymakers, technologists, and mental health professionals are essential to ensure that AI systems align with ethical principles and societal values. Such interdisciplinary collaboration can foster innovation while addressing the complexities and inequities inherent in mental health care.

By navigating these challenges and leveraging the opportunities presented by AI, mental health care has the potential to become more inclusive, accessible, and effective. Ultimately, the goal is to integrate AI technologies in a manner that upholds dignity, promotes equity, and transforms mental health care into a stigma-free and universally accessible domain.

References

1. Fitzpatrick, K.K., Darcy, A., Vierhile, M., Delivering mental health care *via* iPhone: A review of the Woebot application. *Biomed. Inf. Insights*, 9, 1–7, 2017. https://doi.org/10.1177/1178222617730063.
2. Franklin, J.C., Ribeiro, J.D., Fox, K.R., Bentley, K.H., Kleiman, E.M., Huang, X., Nock, M.K., Risk factors for suicidal thoughts and behaviors: A meta-analysis of 50 years of research. *Psychol. Bull.*, 143, 2, 187–232, 2017. https://doi.org/10.1037/bul0000084.
3. Goffman, E., *Stigma: Notes on the management of spoiled identity*, Prentice-Hall, New Jersy, USA, 1963.
4. Link, B.G. and Phelan, J.C., Conceptualizing stigma. *Annu. Rev. Sociol.*, 27, 363–385, 2001. https://doi.org/10.1146/annurev.soc.27.1.363
5. Pescosolido, B.A., Martin, J.K., Lang, A., Olafsdottir, S., , Rethinking theoretical approaches to stigma: A framework integrating normative influences on stigma (Fitzpatrick 2017). *Am. J. Sociol.*, 115, 1, 234–260, 2010. https://doi.org/10.1086/648366.
6. Tajfel, H. and Turner, J.C., An integrative theory of intergroup conflict, in: *The social psychology of intergroup relations*, W.G. Austin and S. Worchel (Eds.), pp. 33–47, Brooks/Cole, Monterey, California, USA, 1979.

7. Becker, H.S., *Outsiders: Studies in the sociology of deviance*, Free Press, Glencoe, Illinois, USA, 1963.
8. Rogers, E.M., *Diffusion of innovations*, 5th, Free Press, New York, USA, 2003.
9. Ajzen, I., The theory of planned behavior. *Organizational Behav. Hum. Decis. Processes*, 50, 2, 179–211, 1991. https://doi.org/10.1016/0749-5978(91)90020-T.
10. Vayena, E., Blasimme, A., Cohen, I.G., Machine learning in medicine: Addressing ethical challenges. *PLoS Med.*, 15, 11, e1002689, 2018. https://doi.org/10.1371/journal.pmed.1002689.
11. Bettencourt, A., Ostermann, C., Barros, J., Addressing the challenges of digital health in a global context. *Health Policy*, 124, 7, 765–774, 2020. https://doi.org/10.1016/j.healthpol.2020.04.01.
12. Obermeyer, Z., Powers, B., Vogeli, C., Mullainathan, S., Dissecting racial bias in an algorithm used to manage the health of populations. *Science*, 366, 6464, 447–453, 2019. https://doi.org/10.1126/science.aax2342.
13. Morley, J., Machado, C.C., Burr, C., Cowls, J., Joshi, I., Taddeo, M., Floridi, L., The ethics of AI in health care: A mapping review. *Soc. Sci. Med.*, 260, 113172, 2020. https://doi.org/10.1016/j.socscimed.2020.113172.
14. Felzmann, H., Villaronga, E.F., Lutz, C., Tamò-Larrieux, A., Transparency you can trust: Transparency requirements for artificial intelligence between legal norms and contextual concerns. *Big Data Soc.*, *6*, 1, 2053951719860542, 2019.
15. Fodor, L.A., Coteț, C.D., Cuijpers, P., Szamoskozi, Ș., David, D., Cristea, I.A., The effectiveness of virtual reality-based interventions for symptoms of anxiety and depression: A meta-analysis. *Sci. Rep.*, 10, 1, 1–13, 2020. https://doi.org/10.1038/s41598-020-68223-1.
16. Thornicroft, G., Mehta, S., Clement, S., Williams, P., Evidence for effective interventions to reduce mental health-related stigma and discrimination. *Lancet Psychiatry*, 3, 5, 346–354, 2016. https://doi.org/10.1016/S2215-0366(15)00525-0.
17. Cummins, N., Schuller, B.W., Krajewski, J., A review of depression detection in speech, in: *2015 International Conference on Affective Computing and Intelligent Interaction (ACII)*, pp. 7–11, 2015, https://doi.org/10.1109/ACII.2015.7344575.
18. Floridi, L., Cowls, J., Beltrametti, M., Chatila, R., Chazerand, P., Dupre, S., Taddeo, M., AI4People—An ethical framework for a good AI society: Opportunities, risks, principles, and recommendations. *Mines Mach.*, 28, 4, 689–707, 2018. https://doi.org/10.1007/s11023-018-9482.
19. Kumar, S., Grama, A., Ravindranath, S.S., Toward AI-enhanced mental health treatment: Challenges, methods, and recommendations. *Commun. ACM*, 64, 5, 44–51, 2021. https://doi.org/10.1145/344238.
20. Torous, J., Bucci, S., Bell, I.H., Kessing, L.V., Faurholt-Jepsen, M., Whelan, P., Firth, J., The growing field of digital psychiatry: Current evidence and the

future of apps, social media, chatbots, and virtual reality. *World Psychiatry*, 20, 3, 318–335, 2021. https://doi.org/10.1002/wps.20880.

21. Barnett, B.S., Torous, J., Staples, P., Sandoval, L., Keshavan, M., Digital phenotyping in severe mental illness: Two illustrative case reports. *Schizophr. Res.*, 197, 1–3, 2018. https://doi.org/10.1016/j.schres.2018.01.031.
22. Jorm, A.F. and Reavley, N.J., The stigma of mental disorders: A review of the literature and implications for mental health services. *J. Mental Health*, 23, 1, 3–12, 2014. https://doi.org/10.3109/09638237.2013.853037.

12

Breaking Barriers — Understanding Mental Health Stigma — Concepts, Challenges, and Intervention Strategies

Pankhuri Sharma and Meenakshi Gandhi*

Vivekananda Institute of Professional Studies-TC, Pitampura, Delhi, India

Abstract

Stigma that revolves around mental health is a global challenge that persists worldwide, which creates a hindrance in access to mental health service to individuals dealing with such challenges. This stigma tends to create isolation, discrimination, and a barrier toward inclusivity among individuals struggling with such conditions. This chapter explores the multifaced challenges that are associated with mental health and stigma, sliding its root toward different dimensions. Different measurements and tools that aim to understand the prevalence of stigma toward mental health have also been widely discussed. Additionally, it highlights different interventions that aim at reducing the stigmatization. Effective strategies in every sector, including mental health awareness camps, policy reform, community engagement, and digital tools to measure and combat the stigma, have also been emphasized. By addressing the root cause and refining measurement tools, this chapter underscores the need for a collaborative and multisectoral approach to foster a culture of acceptance and understanding. Also, there is a need for the development of innovative and scalable tools for stigma reduction and accessibility for mental health services to improve the mental health outcomes globally.

Keywords: Mental health care, mental health stigma, stigma measurement tools, mental health interventions, policy reforms, barriers to mental health care

**Corresponding author*: meenakshi.gandhi@vips.edu

Ridhima Sharma, Fazla Rabby, Rohit Bansal, Timcy Sachdeva and Jihene Mrabet (eds.) Confronting Mental Health Stigma with AI and Machine Learning, (313–334) © 2026 Scrivener Publishing LLC

12.1 Introduction

Mental health disorders present many challenges to sufferers, often exacerbated by stigma due to the lack of awareness across the globe. The chapter explores the multifaceted identity of stigma that resolves around the mental health of an individual, its effects on both individuals and the communities, and measures for its reduction. The stigma undoubtedly contributes to the underutilization of mental health resources and the isolation of affected individuals. This stigma manifests in three primary dimensions: public stigma, self-stigma, and structural stigma. These interconnected facets create a complex web of challenges for those experiencing mental health issues, hindering their access to care and overall well-being.

The conceptualization of stigma has evolved over time, shaped by societal attitudes, cultural beliefs, social media, and misinformation. This evolution has accelerated stereotypes and discrimination against people with mental illnesses, necessitating a comprehensive approach to address its root causes and manifestations. One of the core challenges in combating mental health stigma lies in its accurate measurement. Current tools and scales for stigma assessment have both advantages and disadvantages. The chapter advocates for a multidimensional approach to stigma measurement that accounts for intersectionality, considering factors such as race, gender, socioeconomic status, and other identity axes that may compound stigma experiences.

Strategies for stigma reduction encompass a range of evidence-based practices, including contact-based interventions, psychoeducation, and media campaigns. These approaches target public, self, and structural stigma, aiming to create a more supportive environment for people experiencing mental health challenges. Emerging trends in stigma reduction include participatory approaches that engage individuals with lived experience in co-designing interventions. These strategies not only help affected individuals to feel accepted, but also create more authentic solutions for addressing stigma at both community and institutional levels. The role of policy reform is crucial in this context, emphasizing the need for legislative changes that address structural barriers and discriminatory practices in healthcare systems, workplaces, and educational institutions. The path to reducing mental health stigma requires a synergistic approach, combining accurate measurement tools with innovative, evidence-based interventions. By fostering collaboration across sectors, involving people with lived experience, and promoting systemic change, we can begin to dismantle the pervasive stigma that continues to hinder mental health advocacy and care.

This chapter also serves as a call to action for mental health professionals, researchers, and policymakers to intensify efforts in stigma measurement and reduction, especially in the formulation of structural stigma. It emphasizes the importance of fostering knowledge, understanding, acceptance, and effective intervention methods in society at large. By addressing the complexities of mental health stigma through a multidimensional approach, we can work toward establishing an inclusive and supportive environment for people experiencing mental health conditions, improving access to care, resources, services, and quality of life for those affected by mental health issues.

12.1.1 Defining Mental Illness Stigma

Mental health refers to the overall emotional, psychological, and social well-being of individuals, affecting how individuals think, feel, and behave. Additionally, it influences how an individual copes with stress, makes everyday decisions, and interacts with others. In the fast-paced modern world, where there are constant demands from the environment, maintaining mental health is very essential. However, mental health is often overlooked, especially when compared to physical health, leading to widespread misunderstanding, neglect, and lack of acknowledgment by society.

Mental health disorders contribute a significant amount, approximately 20–25% of the overall global diseases [2]. Overlooking mental health can be due to mental illness stigma, which refers to the negative attitude, beliefs, and typical stereotypes that still exist and surround mental health conditions. There is an involvement of social exclusions, established discrimination, and marginalization in groups experienced by individuals who are diagnosed with mental illnesses or those who seek mental health treatment. This usually creates a barrier for the individuals who suffer from such conditions [7].

Factors that actually shape mental illness stigma are genetics, early life experiences, trauma, environmental stressors, physical health, interpersonal relationships, crime, and violence [9]. There has been an emphasis on elements that unfold the stigma, which are labeling, stereotyping, separations, status loss, discrimination, and power influence [13]. Yet, despite its importance, these elements can lead to creating an environment where individuals with mental health conditions not only face personal suffering but also can also get manifested through feelings of shame, blame, secrecy, and isolation. The sufferers can also be viewed as weak, which fuels underutilization of mental health resources and creates a tough barrier toward recovery, particularly in India, where cultural beliefs and social norms continue to create a barrier toward the mental health conditions.

12.1.2 Evolution of Mental Illness Stigma

Over the decades, mental illness has been misunderstood in many ways, feared, and often demonized. In ancient times, individuals with mental health conditions were frequently believed to be possessed by evil spirits or suffering from divine punishment and could be only treated with the help of ojhas or tantriks. Such views led to brutal treatment and isolation.

In medieval Europe, for example, people with mental illness were often confined to asylums or subjected to inhumane treatments in an attempt to "cure" them of their afflictions. Similar stigmatizing attitudes were prevalent in many parts of the world, including India, where traditional beliefs sometimes attributed mental illness to supernatural causes such as possession, curses, spirits, or karma.

With the advent of modern psychiatry in the 19th and 20th centuries, with modern psychology playing its benefited role, the understanding of mental illness began to shift toward medical and scientific explanations, which are valid and reliable. However, despite its development, the stigma persisted, as mental illness was still seen as a personal failing or a sign of weakness. In India, for example, people with mental health conditions were often kept hidden from society, and families would sometimes avoid seeking treatment due to fear of social isolation.

In recent decades, efforts to reduce stigma have intensified, with global initiatives focusing on raising awareness, promoting mental health literacy, and encouraging help-seeking behaviors. The rise of social media has played a dual role in this evolution. On one hand, it has contributed to the spread of misinformation and harmful stereotypes, but on the other hand, it has also provided a platform for mental health advocates to challenge stigma and share their stories. India, like many other countries, has witnessed a gradual shift in attitudes toward mental health. The Mental Healthcare Act of 2017, National Mental Health Programme (NMHP) marked a significant step forward by promoting the rights of individuals with mental health conditions and recognizing mental health as a fundamental part of existence.

12.1.3 Mental Illness Stigma in India

In India, mental illness is often seen as a taboo subject, making individuals hesitant to seek treatment due to the fear of judgment and societal repercussions. The cultural emphasis on maintaining family honor plays a significant role in this stigma. A mental health condition within a family can be viewed as a reflection of the family's failure to uphold social and moral values. This often leads to families hiding or ignoring the condition to protect their reputation. Consequently, individuals experiencing mental health challenges are either forced into isolation or prevented from accessing the care they need. Families may also discourage members from discussing mental illness publicly, contributing to an environment where mental health issues are swept under the rug.

In rural areas, the involvement of traditional beliefs and the idea of "*izzat*" are deeply entrenched, and mental illness is often misunderstood and misinterpreted. Many people believe that mental disorders are primarily created by supernatural forces such as black magic, curses, or possession by spirits. This leads families to seek solutions from religious or spiritual healers rather than mental health professionals. Such views can delay or prevent individuals from accessing appropriate psychological or medical treatment, as traditional healers offer methods that may not address the underlying causes of mental health disorders. This belief in supernatural causes is also prevalent in certain urban areas, especially among communities with limited mental health literacy. This has led to a lack of belief in evidence-based care.

12.1.4 Types of Stigma

Stigma that is related to mental illness is a phenomenon that can be categorized into several types [5]. Understanding these types is important for addressing the various ways stigma manifests in society and impacts individuals:

12.1.4.1 Public Stigma

This type of stigma refers to the attitudes and negative beliefs held by the broader community toward individuals suffering with mental illness.

12.1.4.2 Self-Stigma

This refers to the internalization of negative societal beliefs and attitudes formed for individuals with mental health conditions. When people with mental illness adopt these stigmatizing views, they may feel ashamed, powerless, or inadequate, which can lead to reluctance to get professional help.

12.1.4.3 Structural Stigma

Unlike public stigma (which comes from individuals or social groups) and self-stigma (which is internalized by individuals), structural stigma is embedded in societal structures, norms, policies, and laws, often leading to the exclusion of marginalized groups. Table 12.1 shows the different types of mental health stigma and their impact.

Table 12.1 Different types of stigma related to mental health.

Category	Public stigma	Self-stigma	Structural stigma
Stereotypes and prejudices	People with mental illness are dangerous, incompetent, unpredictable, and to blame for their disorder	*"I am dangerous, incompetent, and to blame for my mental illness"*	Stereotypes are embodied in laws, policies, and institutional norms that reinforce stigma
Discrimination	Employers may not hire them, landlords may not rent to them, and health systems may offer substandard care	These thoughts lower self-esteem and self-efficacy: *"Why try? I am not worthy or able to work or live independently"*	Discrimination is reflected in both intended and unintended loss of opportunities in employment, housing, and healthcare systems

Adapted from Corrigan et al. [5].

12.1.5 Prevalence of Mental Health Stigma

World Health Organization (WHO) [23] reports that approximately one quarter of the world's population has dealt with a mental disorder during their lifetime. This leads to serving as a reminder to what the individuals dealing with mental issues must be going through, especially in terms of availability of support resources and services that are being offered.

Studies have also shown that negative outlooks, stereotypes, and discriminatory attitudes toward individuals dealing with mental issues exist not only to the general public but to the healthcare professionals, employers, and even with their family members [20].

12.1.6 Causes of Mental Health Stigma and Its Impact

12.1.6.1 Portrayal of Accurate Information

One of the major factors that contribute to mental health issues and its related stigma is lack of accuracy of information that has been widespread; this generally creates a sensationalized viewpoint toward creating misunderstandings and eventually leads to arise of stereotypical and discriminatory practices which can further lead to fear, in person going through such difficult times and general public as well [9].

12.1.6.2 Social Media Representation

Social media has been a core part of the everyday lives of each individual and plays an impactful and fierce role in shaping attitudes toward mental health portrayal over big platforms. However, social media's representation is very different and limited to understanding the deeper aspects of mental illnesses. Many of the things on the screen are glamorized to satisfy the audience's perceptions and also give a bend toward entertainment. Rather than depicting through a more sensitive approach, it sometimes can lead to arise in violent cases [22].

12.1.6.3 Labeling Practices and Use of Unethical Diagnostic Criteria

Certain labeling words like "*crazy*," "*weak*," and "*incapable*" are viewed to be used, which can lead to further isolation and societal divide. When diagnoses are made quicker, or based on incomplete assessments, or by a person who is not licensed to make the diagnosis, this can lead individuals to start viewing themselves through the lens of that diagnosis and limit their potential, which may also create a sense of shame and prevent them from actually seeking help from a licensed practitioner.

12.1.6.4 Institutional Practices and Policies

Structural policies also affect the individual dealing with mental health issues. A study reported that institutional practices and policies also increase stigma in individuals dealing with mental illness [12]. Thus, it's important for the establishment of comprehensive practices and policies to ensure that mental health services are accessible to each individual of society.

12.1.6.5 Cultural Beliefs

The stigma toward mental illness also arises through cultural beliefs and practices. For instance, a study by Chen and M [4] argued that few Asian cultures view mental issues as a sign of weakness. Additionally, mental illness is often associated to causal factors, which include interpersonal connections like family conflicts, which can also lead to blame within the family, increasing further notions around stigma and the individual's mental illness.

12.1.7 Mental Health Stigma in Different Settings

Stigma concerned with mental health is related to every setting in society, be it educational institutions or any work settings. Worldwide, 14% of youth deal with mental health illness. A study by Salam *et al.* [1] concluded that individuals view mental health conditions as comparable to other types of diseases. However, a significant portion also believed that treatment availability for such can lead to addiction eventually, which was depicted as a barrier that surrounds mental health as they are not vocal about their illness and may affect their job later. In work settings, many of the employees and employers feel a stigma around mental health in work-related environments [24].

12.2 Research Methodology

This study employs a review approach to explore the complexities of mental health stigma and the strategies used to understand its impact. Key tools and scales were reviewed to evaluate how stigma is assessed in various contexts. The chapter also examines the evolution of stigma, especially a surge in stigma linked to mental health issues, as individuals faced societal pressure and judgment for their coping mechanisms during the pandemic. Peer-reviewed articles, global mental health studies, and reports were analyzed to identify relevant interventions. Additionally, this chapter highlights the growing role of digital mental health tools and community-driven initiatives in reducing stigma post-pandemic.

12.3 Measurement of Mental Health Stigma

Many theories and measurements have been established to understand the framework that revolves around mental health stigma [3].

Theories like Corrigan's Attribution Theory posit that stigma arises from attributions about the cause of mental illness, leading to feelings of fear, anger, or pity. The theory suggests that when mental illness is seen as controllable, stigma is increased due to the belief that individuals are responsible for their condition. Conversely, when mental illness is seen as a result of factors that can't be controlled (like genetics), the stigma is more likely to be reduced. This theory is often used to explain public stigma and self-stigma, as it connects stigma to emotional reactions and results in such behavior [6].

Additionally, Erving Goffman's work on stigma, particularly in his seminal 1963 text, has profoundly shaped the understanding of how society perceives and reacts to individuals with certain attributes. He defines stigma as an attribute that significantly discredits a person, transforming them from a "whole and usual person" to one who is "tainted" and "discounted" [8]. This foundational definition highlights the social dynamics at play in stigma formation and the resulting consequences for those who are stigmatized.

Goffman distinguishes between two categories of stigmatized individuals: the "discredited," whose stigma is visible and known, and the "discreditable," who can conceal their stigma. This distinction has led to further explorations in stigma research, particularly in terms of visibility and secrecy as coping mechanisms [10].

Additionally, Goffman introduces the concepts of the "own," individuals who share the same stigma, and the "wise," those who understand and accept the stigma, which has been influential in subsequent stigma research.

Building upon Goffman's insights, Jones *et al.* [10] introduced a multidimensional framework for understanding stigma, delineating six key dimensions:

1. Concealability — Refers to how easily a stigmatizing attribute can be hidden.
2. Course — Indicates whether the stigmatizing condition is reversible over time.
3. Disruptiveness — Assesses how much a stigma affects social interactions.

4. Aesthetics — Relates to the visceral reactions (often negative) that a stigmatized mark might evoke.
5. Origin — Concerns how a stigmatized condition comes to be perceived and the perceived responsibility of the individual for it.
6. Peril — Captures feelings of threat or danger that the stigmatizing mark might provoke in others.

These dimensions help elucidate the complex nature of stigma and how it manifests in social contexts, influencing both individual experiences and broader societal attitudes.

12.3.1 Quantitative Measurement of Mental Health Stigma

Quantitative instruments for measuring mental health stigma provide structured data that can be statistically measured. These scales typically have various dimensions of stigma, including public stigma, self-stigma, perceived discrimination, and attitudes toward mental illness. While various quantitative and qualitative measures exist, several critical gaps remain in the assessment of mental health stigma, particularly regarding structural stigma — the societal-level factors that perpetuate discrimination and hinder access to mental health care. Current measurements tend to focus on individual attitudes and self-reported experiences, often neglecting the systemic issues that contribute to stigma. Structural stigma encompasses institutional policies, cultural norms, and societal attitudes that devalue individuals with mental health conditions.

12.3.1.1 The Stigma Scale for Mental Illness (SSMI)

The SSMI comprises 24 items rated on a 5-point Likert scale, measuring dimensions of public stigma, self-stigma, and social distance. High internal consistency is confirmed with a Cronbach's alpha exceeding 0.90. Factor analysis has revealed three distinct dimensions, affirming the scale's construct validity [8]. The SSMI has been employed in various populations, including students, healthcare professionals, and individuals with lived experiences of mental illness. However, its cultural applicability may vary, necessitating adaptations for diverse contexts.

12.3.1.2 The Internalized Stigma of Mental Illness Scale (ISMI)

The ISMI, containing 29 items, assesses self-stigma, focusing on how individuals with mental health conditions internalize negative societal attitudes. The scale has demonstrated good reliability, with Cronbach's alpha values ranging from 0.80 to 0.90 [15].

It effectively measures feelings of alienation, stereotype endorsement, discrimination experience, and social withdrawal. The ISMI is particularly useful in clinical settings to understand how internalized stigma affects treatment engagement. Its length, however, may be a barrier in contexts requiring brief assessments.

12.3.1.3 The Perceived Devaluation-Discrimination Scale (PDDS)

The PDDS includes 12 items focusing on perceived public stigma and the discrimination individuals believe they might encounter. With a Cronbach's alpha above 0.85, it demonstrates solid construct validity [13]. The PDDS captures the fear of discrimination, influencing help-seeking behaviors. Its brevity and focus on perceived stigma make it suitable for community surveys and educational interventions, though it may not encompass broader attitudes toward mental illness [13].

12.3.1.4 The Mental Illness Stigma Scale (MISS)

The MISS is a 30-item scale designed to measure attitudes toward mental illness among the general public. It assesses various dimensions, including benevolence, stigmatization, and coercion. The scale has shown strong psychometric properties, with Cronbach's alpha values consistently above 0.80 [21]. The MISS is valuable for identifying public attitudes toward mental illness and informing stigma-reduction initiatives. However, its application may be limited in clinical settings where individual experiences of stigma are more relevant.

12.3.1.5 The Modified Labeling Theory (MLT) Scale

The MLT scale assesses the consequences of labeling and stigma on individuals with mental health conditions. It consists of items that evaluate perceived labeling by others and the impact on self-esteem and help-seeking behaviors. Studies have reported good reliability, with Cronbach's alpha values ranging from 0.70 to 0.85 [18]. The MLT scale emphasizes the social processes involved in stigma, making it a valuable tool for understanding the dynamics between labeling and personal experiences of mental health. Swan and Wainwright [18] emphasized how labelling contributes significantly to internalized stigma.

12.3.1.6 The Mental Health Stigma Scale (MHSS)

The MHSS is a culturally adapted tool designed to assess stigma in Indian populations. It evaluates various dimensions, including social distance, attitudes, and beliefs regarding mental illness [14]. The scale demonstrated good psychometric properties, with Cronbach's alpha values ranging from 0.80 to 0.85, making it a reliable instrument for assessing mental health stigma in India [14].

12.3.1.7 The Perceived Stigma Scale (PSS)

The PSS focuses on perceived stigma among individuals with mental health conditions in India. This scale measures beliefs about being stigmatized by society and its impact on help-seeking behaviors. It has shown strong internal consistency and validity, providing valuable insights into the stigma experienced by individuals in the Indian context [17].

12.3.2 Qualitative Measurements of Mental Health Stigma

Qualitative research methods offer nuanced insights into individuals' experiences and perceptions of mental health stigma, capturing the complexities often overlooked by quantitative measures. These methods are particularly effective for exploring the lived experiences of individuals, understanding the contextual factors influencing stigma, and identifying barriers to care [7]. A study by Tanaka *et al.* [20] found that socioeconomic factors affect mental health and stigma.

12.3.2.1 In-Depth Interviews

In-depth interviews allow researchers to explore stigma in a flexible, open-ended manner. By facilitating conversations, researchers can gather detailed personal narratives, capturing participants' feelings, thoughts, and experiences related to stigma. This method fosters a trusting environment, encouraging individuals to share their stories and reflections candidly.

12.3.2.2 Focus Groups

Focus groups are effective for exploring collective experiences and societal attitudes toward mental health stigma. By facilitating guided discussions among a small group of participants, researchers can capture diverse perspectives and uncover shared experiences. This method provides a platform for participants to engage with one another, often leading to rich discussions about stigma, discrimination, and barriers to seeking help.

For example, a study by Corrigan *et al.* [6] employed focus groups to investigate community attitudes toward mental illness, revealing the impact of media portrayals on stigma. Participants discussed their perceptions of mental health conditions and shared personal experiences, illustrating how group dynamics can enrich the understanding of stigma.

12.3.2.3 Narrative Analysis

Narrative analysis involves examining personal stories and experiences to understand how individuals construct their identities in relation to mental health stigma. This approach allows researchers to explore how stigma shapes individuals' narratives and influences their coping mechanisms. By analyzing the narratives of individuals with mental health conditions, researchers can identify recurring themes and patterns related to stigma.

12.3.2.4 Photovoice

Photovoice is a participatory research method that empowers individuals to document their experiences through photography. Participants take photographs representing their perceptions of mental health stigma and then discuss their meanings within a group setting. This method allows for the exploration of stigma through a creative and engaging medium, highlighting the lived experiences of individuals in a visual format.

For example, a study using photovoice with individuals diagnosed with schizophrenia revealed themes of isolation, misunderstanding, and resilience. Participants expressed how their photographs conveyed the stigma they faced and their desire for greater acceptance and understanding from society.

12.4 Strategies to Reduce Mental Illness Stigma

Reducing the negative outlook or attitudes that surround mental illness is a critical public health issue that requires a multifaceted approach. The stigma often manifests as negative attitudes, discrimination, and social isolation, which can significantly hinder individuals from seeking the help they need. To effectively combat this stigma, it is vital to implement comprehensive strategies that educate the public, advocate for policy changes, and promote open dialogue around mental health issues [16].

12.4.1 Raising Mental Health Awareness and Psychoeducation

One of the foundational strategies in reducing stigma is raising mental health awareness through psychoeducation. This involves the effort to inform the public about mental health conditions, their prevalence, and the challenges faced by individuals who experience these issues. Public campaigns that utilize various media—such as print, television, and online platforms—can be instrumental in disseminating accurate information. These campaigns should highlight the fact that mental illnesses are medical conditions, much like physical illnesses, requiring appropriate treatment and support.

For instance, campaigns can include testimonials from individuals who have experienced mental health challenges, detailing their journeys toward recovery. These narratives can humanize mental health issues, making them relatable to a broader audience. Psychoeducation can also extend into the workplace, where organizations can start with workshops and seminars to educate employees about mental health, reduce workplace-related stigma, and encourage supportive behaviors among colleagues.

12.4.2 Educational Resources and School Curriculums

The integration of mental health education into school curriculums is another crucial aspect of combating stigma. By teaching students about mental health from an early age, we can equip them with the right knowledge and skills important to recognize and address mental health issues in themselves and others. Curriculum design can include modules on emotional intelligence, coping mechanisms, and the importance of seeking help. Integrating mental health education into the primary and secondary school curricula can lay a strong foundation for reducing stigma from a young age. Teaching children about mental health, emotional regulation, and coping strategies can equip them with the knowledge to understand their own mental health and that of their peers. By normalizing discussions around feelings and mental health in school settings, students can learn empathy, compassion, and support for one another, thereby reducing stigma early in life. Also, incorporating mental health education into subjects such as biology or social studies can also enhance students' understanding of the biological and societal factors contributing to mental health conditions. Interactive activities, such as role-playing scenarios or group discussions, can foster a more profound understanding of mental health issues and promote empathy among students. Schools can also establish peer support programs where trained students offer guidance and support to their classmates, creating a safe space for open conversations about mental health.

12.4.3 Leveraging Social Media for Awareness

Social media has emerged as a powerful tool for influencing public perceptions and promoting mental health awareness. Platforms like Instagram, Twitter, and TikTok can be used to create engaging and informative content that resonates with younger audiences. This content may include infographics that simplify complex mental health concepts, videos that discuss coping strategies, or posts that share uplifting quotes and messages of support.

Furthermore, mental health organizations can collaborate with social media influencers and public figures who are willing to share their experiences with mental health issues. By leveraging their reach and credibility, these influencers can help normalize conversations about mental health and encourage their followers to seek help when needed. Campaigns that utilize specific hashtags can also facilitate community-building, allowing individuals to share their stories and connect with others who have similar experiences.

However, while social media can be a double-edged sword—sometimes spreading misinformation or negative portrayals of mental illness—it's essential to curate content that is factual and supportive. Digital literacy campaigns can educate users about discerning reliable information from harmful stereotypes or myths about mental health.

12.4.4 The Power of Social Contact and Celebrity Disclosures

Social contact remains one of the most effective strategies for reducing stigma. When individuals with lived experiences share their stories in public forums, they help break down barriers of misunderstanding and fear. Personal narratives can provide insights into the daily realities of living with a mental illness, showcasing resilience and the possibility of recovery.

Celebrity disclosures can have a particularly profound impact. When well-known figures share their struggles with mental health, they reach wide audiences and demonstrate that mental illness can affect anyone, regardless of their status or success. For example, when prominent celebrities like Selena Gomez and Dwayne "The Rock" Johnson openly discuss their mental health battles, they not only inspire others but also validate the experiences of individuals facing similar challenges. These disclosures can motivate fans to prioritize their mental health and seek support.

12.4.5 Advocacy for Mental Health by Influential Groups

Advocacy plays a crucial role in driving societal change regarding mental health. Influential groups, including non-profit organizations, mental health coalitions, and grassroots movements, can unite to promote awareness and push for policy changes that prioritize mental health care. These organizations can conduct research to provide data-driven insights into the prevalence and impact of mental health issues, which can be instrumental in advocacy efforts. Additionally, they can mobilize community members to participate in campaigns that encourage the normalization of mental health conversations. For example, awareness days, such as World Mental Health Day, can be leveraged to promote community events, workshops, and activities that raise awareness and reduce stigma [19].

Influential groups can also engage in lobbying efforts to influence legislation related to mental health. By working closely with policymakers, they can advocate for increased funding for mental health services, improved access to care, and the implementation of supportive policies that protect the rights of individuals with mental health conditions.

12.4.6 Workplace Mental Health Programs

Implementing workplace mental health programs can significantly impact stigma reduction. Organizations can create supportive environments by offering mental health resources, counseling services, and employee training programs focused on mental health awareness. Training managers and supervisors to recognize signs of mental distress and to respond appropriately can help foster an atmosphere where employees feel comfortable and safe to discuss their mental health challenges. Furthermore, promoting work–life balance and mental wellness initiatives can normalize conversations about mental health within corporate culture.

12.5 Policy Formation

12.5.1 Global Initiatives

Globally, there has been a growing recognition of mental health as a critical component of public health. The World Health Organization (WHO) [23] has emphasized the importance of integrating mental health into primary healthcare systems. This initiative encourages countries to develop policies that support mental health awareness, education, and accessible services.

WHO's "Mental Health Action Plan 2013–2020" outlined strategies aimed at reducing stigma, improving mental health services, and ensuring that mental health is prioritized alongside physical health.

12.5.2 National Mental Health Policy in India

In India, the National Mental Health Policy, launched in 2014, aims to provide a comprehensive framework for improving mental health care and reducing stigma. This policy emphasizes the need for a rights-based approach to mental health care and promotes the integration of mental health services into general healthcare. It seeks to ensure that mental health care is accessible, affordable, and available to all segments of the population, particularly marginalized communities.

12.5.3 Mental Health Care Act, 2017

The Mental Health Care Act of 2017 is a landmark piece of legislation in India that has made significant strides toward recognizing and protecting the rights of individuals with mental health conditions. This act decriminalizes mental illness and emphasizes the need for humane treatment, promoting a shift from institutional care to community-based care. Some key provisions include the following:

- Right to Access Care: The act ensures that every individual has the right to access mental health care and treatment. This is crucial for combating stigma, as it acknowledges mental health as a fundamental aspect of health.
- Advance Directives: The legislation allows individuals to create advanced directives regarding their treatment preferences, empowering them to make informed choices about their mental health care. This approach fosters a sense of agency and dignity for those living with mental illness.
- Mental Health Facilities: The act mandates the establishment of mental health facilities in every district to ensure accessibility. This decentralization of care is vital in reducing stigma, as it brings mental health services closer to communities and normalizes seeking help.
- Awareness and Education: The act emphasizes the need for public awareness campaigns to educate the populace about mental health, thereby aiming to dismantle stereotypes and promote understanding.

12.5.4 National Mental Health Programme (NMHP)

The National Mental Health Programme (NMHP) aims to provide comprehensive mental health care through a network of services at the community, district, and state levels. The NMHP promotes the training of healthcare professionals to recognize and treat mental health conditions effectively. It also focuses on the integration of mental health services into the general healthcare system, making treatment more accessible and reducing the stigma associated with seeking help. The program's community-based approach encourages local involvement, which can help shift public perceptions of mental illness.

12.5.5 Initiatives for Youth Mental Health

Recognizing that youth are particularly vulnerable to mental health issues, several initiatives target this demographic. Programs like the "School Mental Health Program" promote mental health education in schools and provide counseling services for students. These initiatives not only help in identifying and addressing mental health concerns early but also foster an environment where mental health discussions are normalized among young people. By equipping students with the knowledge and tools to understand mental health, we can help reduce stigma from a young age.

12.5.6 Telemedicine and Digital Health Initiatives

The COVID-19 pandemic has accelerated the adoption of telemedicine and digital health solutions toward mental health care. These initiatives have proven beneficial, particularly in rural and underserved areas where access to mental health professionals is limited. Digital platforms enable individuals to seek help discreetly and conveniently, which can be especially important in cultures where stigma is prevalent. Moreover, the anonymity offered by online counseling can encourage individuals to reach out who might otherwise hesitate due to fear of judgment.

12.5.7 Collaboration with NGOs and Community-Based Organizations

Many non-governmental organizations (NGOs) and community-based organizations play a critical role in advocating for mental health policy changes and providing services to individuals with mental health conditions. By partnering with these organizations, governments can leverage their expertise and reach to promote mental health awareness and support. Initiatives like "Manas — The Mind" and the "Vandrevala Foundation" in India focus on community outreach, public education campaigns, and training local healthcare providers to address mental health issues effectively. Collaborating with these organizations can enhance the effectiveness of policy implementations and promote community engagement.

12.5.8 Focus on Research and Data Collection

For effective policy formulation, it is essential to gather reliable data on mental health issues, prevalence rates, and the effectiveness of existing programs. Research initiatives aimed at understanding the societal impact of mental health stigma can inform future policies. Investment in mental health research can uncover insights into how best to educate the public, design effective interventions, and evaluate the success of various programs in reducing stigma.

Integration of Mental Health into the Universal Health Coverage (UHC)
In alignment with WHO's goals, integrating mental health into the UHC agenda is a critical step toward reducing stigma. By ensuring that mental health services are part of the broader health system, we can promote the message that mental health is as important as physical health. This integration can facilitate better resource allocation, enhance training for healthcare providers, and improve overall health outcomes.

12.6 AI in Mental Health Stigma Intervention

AI is helping the mental health stigma in enabling the integration of technology, machine learning, and designing of algorithms in conducting brain mapping in resting state while identifying the early signs of various mental health disorders.

Cases related to depression, stress-related disorders, schizophrenia, obsessive-compulsive disorders (OCD), anxiety disorders, mood disorders, and post-traumatic stress disorder (PTSD) are some of the mental health disorders that are enabled for early-stage detection through AI. Voice frequency graphs and mapping of voice using patented software are being done by some start-ups like Manodayam and BrainSightAI [11].

However, it is important to understand that after the diagnosis, the road to recovery is through well-planned, mental health professional-supported counseling. Technology definitely acts as a useful tool to strengthen the diagnostic capability of an individual. Therapy *via* an online therapist or a voice-enabled assistant that uses artificial intelligence and machine learning is still on its way before it can be called successful. Counseling *via* an online counselor without a photo-sharing device remains the choice of the person receiving the counseling. Individuals dealing with mental health disorders need the right support and resources, especially the presence of a support group that can definitely accelerate the recovery rate.

12.7 Future Directions in Combating Mental Health Stigma

In order to reduce the stigma, it is important to work at different levels that include training mental health professionals in a more cultural response manner and evolving social norms. Mental health advocacy across different areas can be practiced, including campaigning and raising awareness. Most importantly, structurally based strategies, including policy frameworks, can give rights and a sense of direction to individuals with mental health conditions. Additionally, seeking teletherapy can also reduce the visibility of taking treatments right through their homes, which can be convenient and private for the individual to feel safe in their own space. Also, programs that promote mental health strategies to equip individuals, whether employee or student, to regulate their emotions thoroughly and promote wellness can result in positive changes. Lastly, collaboration within the sectors can lead to a more holistic approach to promote mental health wellness, approach mental health with care, reduce barriers, and accelerate accurate portrayals of mental health.

12.8 Conclusion

Summarizing, mental health-related stigma still continues to be a barrier to both treatment and utilization of resources, globally. It is important to address the stigma as it not only influences personal perception but also helps to shape the structural framework for those who are in need of the same and may lead to more inclusive and supportive communities in every sphere, worldwide. Thus, a collective effort from policymakers, professionals, and especially the general public is a need of the hour. This may ensure that viewing and seeking help with mental health-related illnesses is a sign of strength and not a sign of weakness.

References

1. Abd El Salam, A.E., AbdAllah, A.M., El Maghawry, H.A., Effect of health education program on improving knowledge and attitude towards mental health stigma and professional help-seeking among adolescents. *Middle East Curr. Psychiatry*, 30, 32, 2023. https://doi.org/10.1186/s43045-023-00298-1.
2. Ahmedani, B.K., Mental health stigma: Society, individuals, and the profession. *J. Soc. Work Values Ethics*, 8, 2, 41–416, 2011. PMCID: PMC3248273.
3. Angermeyer, M.C., Beck, M., Dietrich, S., & Holzinger, A. The stigma of mental illness: An empirical test of the modified labelling theory. *Psychiatric Serv.*, 52, 12, 1671–1676, 2001. DOI: 10.1034/j.1600-0447.2003.00150.x.
4. Chen, S.X. and Mak, W.W., Seeking professional help: Etiology beliefs about mental illness across cultures. *J. Couns. Psychol.*, 55, 4, 442–450, 2008. https://doi.org/10.1037/a0012898.
5. Corrigan, P. and Kosyluk, K., Mental illness stigma: Types, constructs, and vehicles for change. *Clin. Psychol. Rev.*, 34, 5, 378–388, 2014. DOI:10.1037/14297-003.
6. Corrigan, P., Markowitz, F.E., Watson, A., Rowan, D., Kubiak, M.A., An attribution model of public discrimination towards persons with mental illness. *J. Health Soc. Behav.*, 44, 2, 162–179, 2003. https://doi.org/10.2307/1519806.
7. Fox, A.B., Earnshaw, V.A., Taverna, E.C., Vogt, D., Conceptualizing and measuring mental illness stigma: The mental illness stigma framework and critical review of measures. *Stigma Health*, 3, 4, 348–376, 2018. https://doi.org/10.1037/sah0000104.
8. Goffman, E., *Stigma: Notes on the management of spoiled identity*, Prentice-Hall, Englewood Cliffs, NJ, USA, 1963, https://doi.org/10.1093/sf/43.1.127.
9. Javed, A., Public mental health: An agenda for action. *J. Pak. Psychiatric Soc.*, 20, 01, 01–06, 2023. https://doi.org/10.17816/CP156.
10. Jones, E.E., Farina, A., Hastorf, A.H., Marcus, H., Miller, D T., Scott, R.A., *Social stigma: The psychology of marked relationships*, Freeman and Company, New York, USA, 1984, DOI:10.1037/h0092827.
11. Kalmady, S.V., Greiner, R., Agrawal, R., Shivakumar, V., Narayanaswamy, J.C., Brown, M.R., Venkatasubramanian, G., Towards artificial intelligence in mental health by improving schizophrenia prediction with multiple brain parcellation ensemble-learning. *npj Schizophr.*, 5, 1, 2, 2019. DOI: 10.1038/s41537-018-0070-8.
12. Klein, P., Fair-weather, A.K., Lawn, S., Stallman, H.M., Cammell, P., Structural stigma and its impact on healthcare for consumers with borderline personality disorder: Protocol for a scoping review. *Syst. Rev.*, 10, 1, 1–7, 2021. DOI: 10.1186/s13643-021-01580-1.
13. Link, B.G., Yang, L.H., Phelan, J.C., Collins, P.Y., Measuring mental illness stigma. *Schizophr. Bull.*, 30, 3, 511–541, 2004. https://doi.org/10.1093/oxfordjournals.schbul.a007098.

14. Rathod, S., Pinninti, N., Irfan, M., Gorczynski, P., Mental health stigma scale: Development and validation of a culturally adapted scale for Indian populations. *BMC Psychiatry*, 19, 1, 139, 2019.
15. Rüsch, N., Todd, A.R., Bodenhausen, G.V., The internalized stigma of mental illness: Psychometric properties of a new measure. *Psychol. Med.*, 36, 2, 211–221, 2006. DOI: 10.1016/j.psychres.2003.08.008.
16. Shahwan, S., Goh, C.M.J., Tan, G.T.H., Ong, W.J., Chong, S.A., Subramaniam, M., Strategies to reduce mental illness stigma: Perspectives of people with lived experience and caregivers. *Int. J. Environ. Res. Public Health*, 19, 3, 1632, 2022. https://doi.org/10.3390/ijerph19031632.
17. Sharma, P., Gopalkrishnan, N., Singh, A., Perceived stigma scale: Development and validation in an Indian context. *Asian J. Psychiatry*, 54, 102355, 2020. doi: 10.1093/abm/kaad015.
18. Swan, R. and Wainwright, L., Modified labelling theory: Consequences of stigma on mental illness. *Int. J. Soc. Psychiatry*, 56, 1, 43–53, 2010. DOI: 10.1002/9781118410868.wbehibs328.
19. Taghva, A., Farsi, Z., Javanmard, Y., *et al.*, Strategies to reduce the stigma toward people with mental disorders in Iran: Stakeholders' perspectives. *BMC Psychiatry*, 17, 17, 2017. DOI: 10.1186/s12888-016-1169-y.
20. Tanaka, C., Tuliao, M.T.R., Tanaka, E., Yamashita, T., Matsuo, H., A qualitative study on the stigma experienced by people with mental health problems and epilepsy in the Philippines. *BMC Psychiatry*, 18, 1–13, 2018. DOI: 10.1186/s12888-018-1902-9.
21. Angermeyer, M.C., Beck, M., Dietrich, S., Holzinger, A., The stigma of mental illness: An empirical test of the modified labelling theory. *Psychiatric Serv.*, 52, 12, 1671–1676, 2001. DOI: 10.1177/0020764004043115.
22. Wahl, O.F., News media portrayal of mental illness: Implications for public policy. *Am. Behav. Sci.*, 46, 12, 1594–1600, 2003. https://doi.org/10.1177/0002764203254615.
23. World Health Organization, *Voice, agency, empowerment-handbook on social participation for universal health coverage*, World Health Organization, Geneva, 2021, Available *via* https://apps.who.int/iris/handle/10665/342704.
24. McKinsey & Company, *National surveys reveal disconnect between employees and employers around mental health need*, McKinsey & Company, New York, USA, April 21, 2021.

13

Mental Health and Artificial Intelligence: A Case of Tourism Industry

Jatin Vaid

Vivekananda School of Business Studies, Vivekananda Institute of Professional Studies – TC, New Delhi, India

Abstract

The chapter describes in detail the concept of mental health and its importance. It further delves into the facts related to mental health disorders by classifying and discussing the various types of it along with their symptoms and possible causes. The chapter further highlights the impact of mental health disorders on one's psychological and physical well-being and suggests a strategic game plan at the policy level with curated action points to deal with such disorders. The chapter comprehensively discusses the evolution of artificial intelligence (AI) and machine learning (ML) and its varied applications in businesses and mental health care. The challenges and risks associated with AI and its application in the tourism industry are also discussed. Finally, it deliberates on the concerns of tourists suffering from mental health disorders and lists avenues for future research-based work in this domain area.

Keywords: Artificial intelligence, tourism, mental health, WHO, marketing

13.1 Mental Health

The phenomenon of mental health may be described as a psychological state of well-being that enables people to amicably deal with the pressures of life, recognize their abilities to enhance their learning, and work seamlessly to make significant and positive contributions to the communities they live in [26]. Mental health is a vital component of overall health that determines our capacity to make decisions, helps us nurture relationships,

Email: jatin.vaid@vips.edu

Ridhima Sharma, Fazla Rabby, Rohit Bansal, Timcy Sachdeva and Jihene Mrabet (eds.) Confronting Mental Health Stigma with AI and Machine Learning, (335–352) © 2026 Scrivener Publishing LLC

and shapes our lives. In contrast to physical health, people seem to be less literate about mental health, which means they do not understand how to take care of their mental health or seek professional help when required [27]. Mental health broadly reflects a person's psychological health that helps them manage their thoughts and behavior in a constructively positive manner, as defined by the World Health Organization [21]. As noted by WHO [26], it's a fundamental part of one's health and influences one's quality of life and their abilities to work under various situations and circumstances [21]. There is no single construct that defines mental health; rather, it has various components, viz., brain, nervous system, sensations, attention, memory, decision making, and emotions [4].

13.1.1 Mental Health Disorders

According to WHO Mental Disorders Factsheet [25], one out of every eighth person globally has some mental disorder; these people are observed to cause significant disturbances in their thought process, regulating emotions, and their overall behavior. A mental disorder disturbs a person's cognitive faculties and is generally associated with distress and impairment in their functioning. It is also noted that though preventive options exist, most of the people suffering from mental disorders do not have access to preventive care or effective treatment facilities [26]. The National Mental Health Program of the Government of India also recognizes that about 7 percent of the country's population suffers from mental disorders and that its disability-adjusted life year (DALY) loss is substantially more than that caused by malaria and tuberculosis [19].

13.1.2 Classification of Mental Disorders

Disorders related to mental health, majorly comprise of mental chaos, psychological disabilities, and mental states, closely associated with distress, relationship issues with family and friends, problems at work, and risk of self-harm. It is seen that people with mental health disorders usually die earlier than the general population and have higher suicidal tendencies and probabilities of experiencing human rights violations [26].

Some of the more common types of mental disorders, as noted by NICE Clinical Guidelines [20] and WHO Mental Disorders Factsheet [25], are as follows:

i. Anxiety disorders:
Anxiety-related disorders are usually illustrated by extreme fear and deep concerns causing behavioral disturbances [25]. People with this

disorder excessively worry, causing them early fatigue, low concentration on important matters, irritation, disturbed sleep, and restlessness [20]. The consequences of this disorder are that those suffering from it feel demoralized, discouraged, ashamed, and worthless about their inability to carry out their routine chores. It may eventually lead to depression.

ii. Depression:

Depression causes a person to experience long episodes of depressed mood, including feelings of sadness, irritation, or purposelessness, continuously for at least 2 weeks. Other vital symptoms of depression are low concentration, guilty conscience, hopelessness, and suicidal tendencies [25]. As a result of depression, a person develops self-harming feelings that originate from social withdrawal, diminishing interest in activities, and resurfacing of pre-existing pains [20]. Medical research has shown that depression may vary in forms and types, and clinical depression is its most severe type [13]. It's one of the most crucial of the issues faced by employees in the workplace, making it a leading cause of suicide [13].

iii. Bipolar disorder:

Persons with bipolar disorders often experience alternative depressive episodes with agitated symptoms. Depressive mood episodes may be marked with sadness, irritation, and suicidal tendencies, whereas manic episodes are often marked by increased energy levels of hyperactivity, racing thoughts, increased self-esteem, and impulsive, reckless behavior [25]. Also, as explained by National Health Mission, GoI [19], manic episodes may be characterized by excessive appetite for food or sex, and depressive episodes may be characterized by slow talking, forgetfulness, and indecisiveness and have the potential to affect one's brain function.

iv. Post-traumatic stress disorder (PTSD):

The prevalence of PTSD is observed particularly in high-conflict environments. It usually develops after a person is exposed to extremely threatening and horrific events in their life. Some of the defining symptoms of PTSD are visualizing flashbacks or memories of that event, regular nightmares, or continuous perception of threat [25]. People who are at risk are war survivors or survivors of severe accidents, riots, or sexual crimes. People with PTSD involuntarily re-experience those traumatic events vividly, causing intense distress and emotional numbing [20].

v. Obsessive-compulsive disorders (OCD):

The World Health Organization in its flagship report of the Eastern Mediterranean Region describes OCD as a mental health condition that may affect people of all ages and walks of life. The affected people suffer from obsessive thoughts, feelings, or fears that they realize are wrong but are unable to stop. Such thoughts are intrusive and may cause high distress and functional impairment. These feelings are repetitive and compulsorily drive the person to perform, temporarily to reduce anxiety and derive pleasure [28]. These symptoms can consume significant time and cause a lot of distress to the people suffering from it [20]. Some of the common-placed obsessions include fear of contamination by germs, arranging things symmetrically and in order, disturbing thoughts about losing control, and unwanted taboos involving religious practices [28]. Such obsessions are often met with the following compulsions like repeated hand washing, cleaning utensils, repeatedly checking locked doors and gas stoves, counting in a certain pattern, and ensuring orderliness by arranging things in a defined pattern [28]. OCD is caused as a result of genetics, personal experiences, traumatic experiences in childhood, and temperament [28].

13.1.3 Impact of Mental Health Disorders

The impact of the above-mentioned mental health disorders is far reaching and is characterized by cross-cutting issues [18]. These are discussed as follows:

i. Stigma:
People with mental health disorders often face public disgrace and humiliation. Their families, in most cases, are unwilling to recognize their illness or are reluctant to provide them with professional medical help to deal with their problems.

ii. Honoring fundamental rights:
In the light of the lack of suitable design and enforcement of public policy, most people suffering from mental health disorders find their rights violated, causing discriminatory behavior in their public life.

iii. Vulnerable population:
The segments of the vulnerable population highly likely to face public wrath and extreme discriminatory behavior are young children, people of economically weaker sections, women, senior citizens, and persons with additional physical disabilities.

iv. Poverty:
There exists a vicious circle between poverty and mental health disorders. People belonging to economically weaker sections are firstly more prone

to mental illness, and secondly, spending money out of their own pockets (majorly, in cases of lack of government support or public policy implementation) leads them to even severe poverty, given the high cost of medical care and consultancy fee.

v. Homelessness:
An adverse consequence of mental health problems is homelessness, as they can be abandoned by their families. This may happen as families are constraint on resources, feel helpless, or may be uncaring about their special needs.

13.1.4 Action Plan and Strategic Recourse

The medical and healthcare systems are currently inadequate to respond to the needs of people suffering from mental health disorders. The current systems are under-resourced and often observed to be of an inferior quality, especially at the time of resource delivery. Addressing these issues is of vital importance as people suffering from such disorders require social support and care in helping them maintain their social relationships [27]. The World Health Organization (WHO), in its flagship initiative dealing with mental health, prescribes an action plan that focuses on a strategic level and recommends the following [25]:

i. Strengthening and forging effective leadership and governance for mental health;
ii. Providing robust and comprehensive mental health services;
iii. Implementing large-scale strategies to ensure prevention and early treatment;
iv. Strengthening data systems, empirical evidences, and research capabilities.

Moreover, at the country or micro level, the DGHS, Health and Family Welfare Ministry, and GoI have proposed their intention to introduce the 'National Mental Health Program,' with the objective of ensuring availability and accessibility of mental health services and promoting community participation in development of mental health services [6]. This briefly includes the following:

i. District mental health program with OPD facilities
ii. PPP model activities with financial support to model activities

iii. Day care centers with financial support
iv. Residential centers with financial support
v. Mental health lifeline

Some strategic directions and action plans, as highlighted by Ministry of Health & Family Welfare, GoI [18], are as follows:

i. *Effective governance* and delivery mechanism for mental health including development of relevant policies and programs with adequate budgetary provisions for effective implementation of mental health plans and actions.
ii. *Promotion of mental health* by redesigning Anganwadi Centers to cater to early child care and timely organizing training programs for Anganwadi staff and school teachers in helping build self-confidence for parents.
iii. *Prevention of mental illness* and reduction of suicide rates by addressing stigma, discrimination, and reduction in suicide rates.
iv. *Universal access to mental health services* by increased availability of daycare centers, hospitals, and other stay facilities to promote recovery with support from regional bodies.
v. *Community participation for mental health* and development by removing political and policy barriers to protect rights of persons with mental illness. This includes increased availability of appropriate housing with necessary support for the homeless and economically weaker sections of the society.
vi. *Improved availability of adequately trained human resources* to address the mental health needs of the community. This shall ensure a reduced gap between requirement and availability of mental health professionals like psychiatrists, psychologists, counselors, and doctors. There's also a pressing need to integrate modules of mental health in other allied fields.
vii. *Research and development* to ensure formulation and implementation of a robust research agenda for mental health. This will practically be feasible with the commitment of equitable funds for promoting mental health research and building research capacities in mental health both through existing institutions and building new institutions focusing on niche areas and conducting solid

research to evaluate the potential of traditional knowledge and alternate therapies to address mental health programs.

13.2 Artificial Intelligence (AI)

Intelligence is often referred to as the skill to learn and execute appropriate techniques of problem solving and achieving objectives appropriately in a world full of uncertainties [16]. The historical roots of AI stem from the early 1950s, an era characterized by machines with an intelligence of humans [23]. The expression 'artificial intelligence' or AI was first given by Prof. John McCarthy in the year 1955, as "the science and engineering of developing intelligent machines" [16]. Artificial intelligence connotes a machine's capacity to carry out some cognitive tasks, which usually are related to the functions of a human mind [17]. "It is an array of technologies that help computers and machines to carry out various complex functions, which include seeing, comprehending and translating languages, studying data, and making suitable suggestions" [8]. It may be defined as "an area of science dealing with developing computers and machines that are apt in cognitive reasoning, learning through inputs, and behaving as if with human intelligence or solving complex cases that involve data analysis of a magnitude that exceeds human abilities" [8]. IBM too describes AI as a technological breakthrough that makes computers replicate human learning and comprehension with complex problem solving and decision making with originality [12]. As mentioned in Harvard Business Review, technological innovations have been driving economic growth globally for more than 250 years, and the most important general-purpose technology of the present era being artificial intelligence, and in particular machine learning (ML), i.e., machine's ability to keep improving its performance without human intervention [3]. Machine learning is a niche branch of artificial intelligence which is primarily involved in complex algorithm development that facilitates decision making and predicts consumer behavior by recognizing meaningful patterns in data [7]. Various definitions and explanations of AI seem to converge on some common points, broadly describing it as a science involving software and machines to develop tasks and work with big data to optimize decision making [22].

13.2.1 Applications of AI

AI is observed to have a transformational impact on businesses by showcasing super-human performances in areas like fraud detection, disease diagnosis, manufacturing, retail, and healthcare; its magnified effects in altering business models are yet to be seen in the times to come [3]. Some of the important areas where AI is applied [12] are as follows:

i. *Enhancing customer experience with superior service and support* by implementing virtual assistants and chatbots enabled by AI to satisfactorily answer customer queries and provide real-time customer support.
ii. *Fraud detection* by analyzing customer's transaction patterns and raising concerns with a red flag on sensing anything unusual like unusual spending and login locations that may indicate probabilities of a potential fraud.
iii. *Personalized marketing*, often used by online shopping forums, food delivery apps, and banks to create personalized customer experiences and social media campaigns based on consumer behavior and purchase history to improve sales and reduce customer churn rates.
iv. *Managing human resources* becomes easy with AI-driven HR platforms that can streamline the HRM process by assisting in screening of candidate's resumes, aligning candidate's profiles and applications with respective job descriptions (JDs), and carrying out the process of carrying out preliminary interviews, usually with the help of video analysis techniques, thereby significantly reducing the administrative paperwork and enhancing recruitment experience for candidates.
v. *Predictive maintenance* needs can be assessed from ML models analyzing data from sensors, Internet of Things (IoT) devices, and forecast maintenance needs and predict equipment failure before it occurs.
vi. *Mental health care* and vital information about mental disorders can be dealt with by modern AI through advanced prediction, detection, and treatment solutions that help mental health practitioners to define and treat the disorders effectively [23]. The integration of AI into mainstream healthcare, especially in the domain of mental health, gives possibilities of better diagnosis, monitoring, and treatment to positively enhance health outcomes for patients [15].

The advent of AI in mainstream businesses has empowered strategists with better and informed decision making based on insights powered by real-time data [23]. It is observed that the use of sentiment analysis, augmented reality, robotics, and natural language processing helps in recommendations and delivering personalized experiences to the clients in the hospitality and tourism industry [14]. AI seeks to assist businesses, especially tourism organizations, in performing online and enhancing their customer relationships with the help of developing technical solutions like Blockchain and Internet of Things [24].

13.2.2 Challenges and Risks of AI

An increasing number of research papers in the past have highlighted a lot of benefits that organizations reap with the use of AI; notable among them are convenient access to customer data, an easy booking process, and efficient services [22]. However, there are challenges that are also associated with its use; prominently concerns about data security and overdependence on technology are mentioned [22]. As rightly mentioned by Benitez and Martinez [2], an inherent disadvantage of AI adoption is that it makes use of customers' personal and, often, sensitive data to draw inferences and carve out niche marketing strategies, which may be unethical [2]. This phase of AI and ML brings with it its own set of challenges and risks. AI- and ML-based systems, in general, have low interpretability; that is, people can find it difficult to find out how these machines make decisions [3]. This is possibly a result of the fact that machines have hidden biases, are based on statistical truths, and make errors that are difficult to diagnose and correct. A few prominent challenges and risks [12] associated with AI are as follows:

i. *Data risks* as over-relying on data sets that may be tampered, biased, or prone to cyberattacks and data breaches.
ii. *Model risks* with high vulnerability of manipulation, reverse engineering, and theft of data models that may compromise the model's functionality.
iii. *Operational risks* like complete breakdown of the model or inculcating biases that may lead to system failures and cybersecurity threats.
iv. *Ethical and legal risks*, including customer privacy violations, generating biased outcomes like reinforcing gender/racial stereotypes that can lead to serious ramifications for the organization.

In addition to the above-mentioned challenges, some of the challenges in adoption of AI have been listed by Kirtil and Askun [14], such as affirming the applicability of AI to the specific business model, ensuring complete and relevant data to be fed to the systems, need of skilled AI programmers and AI experts to drive the business model, ensuring transparency in the process to make systems ethical and unbiased, and finally ensuring adoption and seamless integration of existing business model with the novels of AI-based technological systems [14]. Moreover, fake news and manipulated data have the propensity to negatively impact strategy formulation through AI; thus, it is pivotal to do away with the said biases to enhance the overall efficiency of the AI process [2]. Some of the other challenges and intricate issues associated with the implementation of AI in tourism organizations include high fixed costs of implementation, overdependence on automation, and the risks of cyberattacks and data theft impacting all the concerned stakeholders [2]. Personalized data pertaining to an individual's mental health is highly sensitive, and any case of its unsolicited or unlawful disclosure can lead to stigma and public discrimination for them [15]. There is a pressing need to maintain equilibrium between the potential of AI-enabled technologies and its ethical and social concerns in this ever-transforming technological world [23].

13.3 AI and Tourism

In the era of digital transformation and innovations in technology, especially in the areas of artificial intelligence and machine learning, tourism is an important area where its applications have generated a noteworthy impact [1]. However, research studies understanding the role of AI on sustainable tourism are still evolving and are in their early stages of development, with most of the studies being conducted on the European continent and the Far East [24]. With the increasing developments in the field of technology, especially in the domain of AI adoption in behavioral analysis, fresh opportunities to decipher consumer behavior and enhance consumer satisfaction have surfaced for the highly complex tourism industry [7]. The convergence of artificial intelligence, augmented reality, virtual reality, metaverse, and simulation techniques has a profound impact on the tourism industry [1]. AI is used by tourism organizations to create innovative business models and formulate marketing strategies to boost sales, improve the bottom line, and positively influence customer experience and value creation [2]. Figure 13.1 illustrates how tourism organizations like hotels, resorts, destination management organizations, and

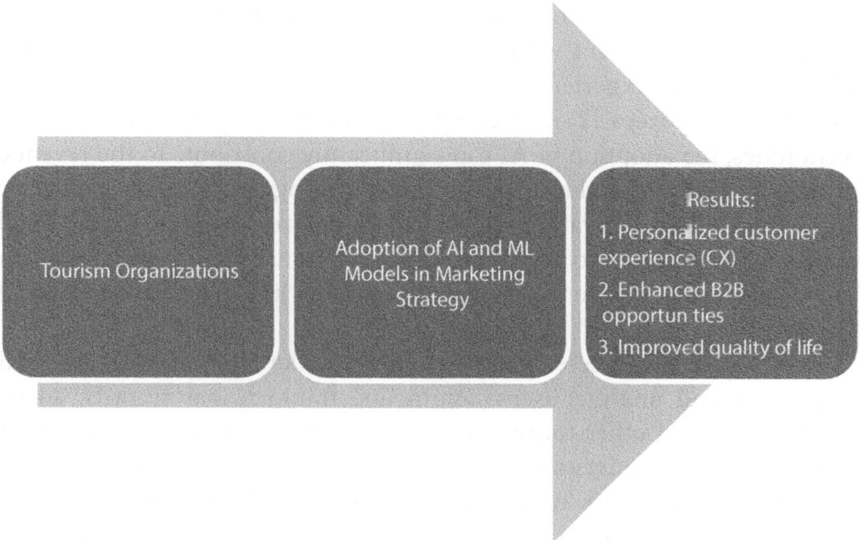

Figure 13.1 Impact of AI adoption in tourism (source: author's own).

convention centers deploy AI in their marketing campaigns to generate positive experiences for their clients, generate business opportunities for other allied businesses, and improve the quality of life of the local citizens by generating employment and income opportunities. A few of the notable applications of AI and its related streams like virtual reality (VR) in the travel and tourism industry, especially the hotels and accommodation sector of it, are virtual tours of hotel's facilities, virtual travel experiences highlighting the USPs of the hotel in three-dimensional formats, and virtual booking interfaces, helping the prospective tourists to explore their travel itinerary and make informed travel decisions [22]. Biometric data of tourists, especially their fingerprints and facial recognition systems, are widely used to verify the digital entity of people and detect their emotional variance, thereby providing useful insights to understand tourist behavior and assisting in improving customer experience with inducing efficiencies in booking systems with personalized interactions [22]. Ye and Huang [29] in their research go a mile ahead in proposing applications of AI in tourism and hospitality industry by way of an HBR algorithm that analyzes the impact of tourist psychology and consumer behavior, finding applications by judging the shopping intentions of tourists by deeply analyzing their shopping behavior and psychology, and making personalized recommendations by a robot [29]. Technologies based on AI in the realms of sustainable tourism seek to enhance work processes and work toward enhancing job-related satisfaction and performance by way of task automation and facilitating management with efficiencies in resource allocation, personalizing customer experiences, and eventually contributing to the satisfaction of employees [24]. In comparison to applying age-old analytical techniques, the adoption of AI can significantly contribute to the revenue growth of the travel and tourism industry, making it its largest beneficiary [14], and assist in generating relevant content at reasonable costs for hotel marketing campaigns to revive customer relationships and foster growth in business with the use of AI-enabled chatbots like Trip Planner AI and Vacay [2].

Artificial-intelligence-enabled technologies like NLP and ML are used to process and analyze user's comments, transactional records, social media posts, and other tourism data to uncover deep insights to predict tourist behavior, understand their choices more precisely, and reflect on their broad decision-making process [7]. A few of the important applications of adopting AI in understanding the buying behavior of tourists [7] may be listed as follows:

i. Understanding behavioral changes in tourist's historical data to predict their preferences and provide tailored recommendations.
ii. Using sentimental analysis and natural language processing techniques to depict tourists' emotional predispositions by analyzing their social media posts and comments.
iii. Examining market trends and prototyping patterns of tourist behavior to forecast demand for tourism services.
iv. Aggregating tourists' behavioral data using AI-enabled algorithms to deliver customized and personalized recommendations to enhance the satisfaction of tourists.
v. Analyzing consumer behavior of tourists on travel-related applications and websites and working toward providing them a seamless online experience.

The above-mentioned applications of AI-enabled technologies in tourism behavior have truly empowered the tourism industry to be better equipped to provide exceptional customer experience with the help of a data-driven mindset, optimized resource allocation, and a customized approach to design tourism services [7].

13.4 Mental Health and Tourism

Tourism is one of the crucial contributors to the world economy for foreign exchange and employment generation [24]. The vulnerability of tourists with mental health disorders poses unique challenges as it impacts their physical functioning, leading to difficulties in mobility and accessibility [10]. Mental health disorders are known to drastically impact one's cognitive, emotional, and social capabilities, making the entire tourism experience stressful and traumatic for them, worsening existing conditions, or triggering mood swings and manic episodes [10]. There is a lot of scope in academic literature to explore the impact of mental health on tourism activities. Researchers have shown that outdoor tourism and recreation can have a therapeutic impact on the mental health of tourists and assist in healing an existing disorder [5]. The respondents suffering from depressive disorders, when exposed to outdoor tourism, reported having improved health conditions and positive emotional well-being with feelings of gratitude and joy, feeling relaxed, and getting a renewed sense of clarity in accomplishing their jobs [5]. Well-being tourism with a focus on yoga, pranayamas, spas, and meditation retreats is increasingly considered to provide relief to tourists with mental health disorders. Mental health issues and psychological well-being are crucial subject matters of the hospitality and tourism industry and should be included in the mainstream curriculum for students to make them aware and sensitive to the cause [21]. Thus, it is imperative to design a mental health framework that seamlessly connects policy making related to mental health with broad economic outlook [4]. It is often seen that depression stemming from workplace-related stress and specifically due to the fear of losing one's job is one of the leading causes of suicide among the working population [13]. However, the fear that the adoption of AI will reduce job opportunities rather than enhance them is not true [14]. No doubt that AI adoption will impact automation and rule-based jobs, but if AI integration is done in a thoughtful and organized way, it will enhance business opportunities and will create more jobs, as the human workforce is extremely important and indispensable in creating a robust AI adoption and integration strategy [14]. In the academic realm of mental health care, the amalgamation of artificial-intelligence-based predictive and prescriptive analytics opens the possibilities in the following ways [23]:

i. Deploying sentiment analysis, data mining, and AI-based NLP to create awareness and promote engaging conversations about mental health issues and constructing impactful campaigns.

ii. AI-driven client engagement strategies that work closely with certain mobile applications can support the recovery of individuals struggling with mental health problems by atomizing their medicine timetable, monitoring recovery, tracking their progress, providing real-time response on the progress, and helping connect with medical practitioners to support faster recovery.

iii. AI-based machine learning with its interventionist approach can evaluate an individual's probability of developing a mental health issue based on their genetics, scanning environmental variables, and their personal profile, thereby enabling early detection and providing invention with customized treatments.

These applications of artificial-intelligence-enabled technologies in the domain of mental health care are pictorially illustrated in Figure 13.2.

AI-enabled technologies have truly automated cognitive appraisal inducing objectivity, early detection, and timely intervention by medical professionals in dealing with various kinds of intellectual disorders (autism, Down syndrome, cerebral palsy), neurodegenerative disorders (Parkinson, Alzheimer's disease), and seizures [23]. While considering all

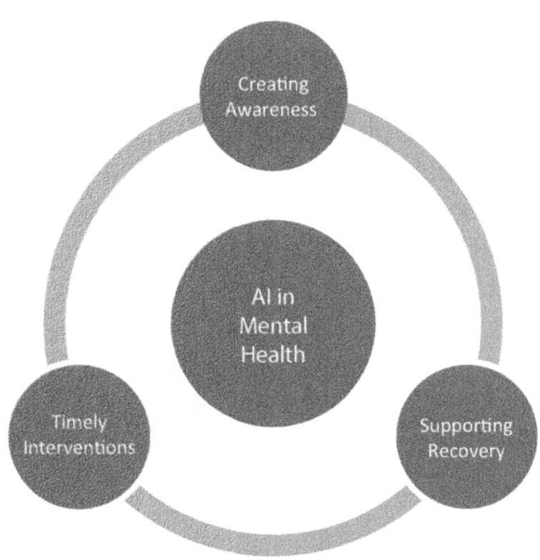

Figure 13.2 Applications of AI-enabled technologies in mental health (source: author's own).

the positive impacts, there is a pressing need to address the issues of ensuring protection and security of personal medical data, guaranteeing people's informed consent, and pursuing transparency with reduced bias to ensure effective implementation of AI in the domain of medical health care [23]. Mental health is very closely related to tourism, and its direction and intensity are largely a function of the destination in question, tourism services under consideration, and the personality of the tourist [4]. There are some prominent mental health disorders, namely, monophobia, anxiety, depression, and fear of missing out, that are closely linked with excessive usage of technological gadgets at tourism destinations and can be controlled with an upcoming concept of digital-free tourism which involves traveling or holidaying without the use of Internet or any electronic or digital gadget [9]. However, the novel concept of digital-free tourism may be in the direction of curbing mental health issues among tourists, but its adoption in real life is very challenging as digital withdrawal symptoms are not simple for tourists [9]. Tourists with mental health issues have distinctive distresses that can significantly impact their abilities to function and take care of themselves, thus not only inducing problems in their hassle-free mobility and accessibility access, but also impacting their emotional and cognitive abilities [11]. There is an urgent need for the tourism industry to work toward designing travel itineraries, travel packages, and design accommodation tailored to their specific needs, given the wide gamut of mental disorders and their symptoms [11]. Providing cost-effective and reachable tourism options coupled with a congenial social environment and a sense of close community goes a long way in providing feelings of happiness and rejuvenation to tourists plagued by mental health issues [5]. At the broad policy—formulation level and to form a culture in the tourism economy to efficiently deal with such cases of tourists grappling with mental health issues, it is suggested that mental health education should be included in the higher education curriculum, especially in courses related to management and hospitality management, to better prepare professionals of tomorrow [21].

References

1. Baggio, R. and Ruggieri, G., Metaverse in the tourism domain - introduction to the special issue. *Inf. Technol. Tourism*, 25, 263–264, 2023.
2. Benitez, L.F. and Martínez, B., How Artificial Intelligence (AI) Is Powering New Tourism Marketing and the Future Agenda for Smart Tourist Destinations. *Electronics*, 13, 1–20, 2024.

3. Brynjolfsson, E. and McAfee, A., The Business of Artificial Intelligence, in: *Harvard Business Review*, 2017.
4. Buckley, R., Tourism and Mental Health: Foundations, Frameworks, and Futures. *J. Travel Res.*, *62*, 1, 3–20, 2023.
5. Buckley, R. and Westaway, D., Mental health rescue effects of women's outdoor tourism: A role in COVID-19 Recovery. *Ann. Tourism Res.*, 85, 1–12, 2020.
6. Directorate General of Health Services, *National Mental Health Programme*, 2024, DGHS, GoI, India, Retrieved 2024, from DGHS Ministry of Health & Family Welfare Website: https://dghs.gov.in/content/1350_3_NationalMentalHealthProgramme.aspx#:~:text=To%20address%20the%20huge%20burden,to%20the%20Program%20in%201996.
7. Duan, J., Identification and Influence of Tourism Consumption Behavior Based on Artificial Intelligence. *Informatica*, *48*, 135–150, 2024.
8. Google Cloud, *What is Artificial Intelligence (AI)?*, Google Inc, US, 2024, Retrieved 2024, from Google Cloud Website: https://cloud.google.com/learn/what-is-artificial-intelligence.
9. Hassan, T.H., Salem, A.E., Saleh, M., II, Digital-Free Tourism Holiday as a New Approach for Tourism Well-Being: Tourists' Attributional Approach. *Int. J. Environ. Res. Public Health*, 19, 1–14, 2022.
10. Hu, F., Wen, J., Kozak, M., Mental health research in tourism and hospitality: a horizon 2050 paper, in: *Tourism Review*, 2024.
11. Hu, F., Wen, J., Lim, W.M., Hou, H., Wang, W., Mental Health on the Go: Navigating Travel and Travel Eligibility. *J. Travel Res.*, *63*, 4, 1029–1040, 2024.
12. IBM, *What is AI?*, 2024, Retrieved 11 11, IBM, U.S., 2024, from IBM Website: https://www.ibm.com/topics/artificial-intelligence.
13. Kalargyrou, V., Sundar, V., Jahani, S., Managers' attitudes toward employees with depression and organizational citizenship behaviors in the hospitality industry: assessing the mediating role of personality. *Int. J. Contemp. Hosp. Manage.*, *35*, 2, 602–629, 2023.
14. Kirtil, I.G. and Askun, V., Artificial Intelligence In Tourism: A Review And Bibliometrics Research. *Adv. Hosp. Tour. Res. (AHTR) An Int. J. Akdeniz Univ. Tour. Fac.*, *9*, 1, 205–233, 2021.
15. Lovejoy, C.A. and Buch, V., Technology and mental health: The role of artificial intelligence. *Eur. Psychiatry*, 55, 1–3, 2019.
16. Manning, C., *HAi Stanford University - AI Definitions*, 2020, September, Retrieved 11 11, Stanford University, U.S., 2024, from Human-Centered Artificial Intelligence HAI Stanford University: https://hai.stanford.edu/sites/default/files/2020-09/AI-Definitions-HAI.pdf.
17. Mckinsey & Company, *What is AI?*, McKinsey & Co.,U.S., 2024, Retrieved 11 13, 2024, from Mckinsey & Company Website: https://www.mckinsey.com/featured-insights/mckinsey-explainers/what-is-ai#/.
18. Ministry of Health & Family Welfare, GoI, *New Pathways New Hope*, Government of India, New Delhi, 2014.

19. National Health Mission, GoI, *National Mental Health Programme*, NMHP, GoI, India, 2024, Retrieved 2024, from NHM Website: https://nhm.gov.in/index1.php?lang=1&level=2&sublinkid=1043&lid=359.
20. NICE Clinical Guidelines, *Common Mental Health Disorders: Identification and Pathways to Care*, NIHCE, U.K., 2011, Retrieved November 11, 2024, from NIH National Library of Medicine: https://www.ncbi.nlm.nih.gov/books/NBK92254/.
21. Sisson, A.D., Peele, M., Sisson, Z., Teaching hospitality and tourism students' strategies for recognizing and supporting mental health conditions and crises in industry: an exploratory study. *J. Teach. Travel Tour.*, 24, 53–70, 2024.
22. Sousa, A.E., Cardoso, P., Dias, F., The Use of Artificial Intelligence Systems in Tourism and Hospitality: The Tourists' Perspective. *Administrative Sci.*, 14, 1–23, 2024.
23. Thakkar, A., Gupta, A., Sousa, A.D., Artificial intelligence in positive mental health: a narrative review. *Front. Digit. Health*, 6, 01–11, 2024.
24. Vasto, P.M. and Castro, M.L., Artificial Intelligence (AI) In Sustainable Tourism: Bibliometric Analysis. *Cuadernos de Turismo*, 53, 157–185, 2024.
25. WHO Mental Disorders Factsheet, *Mental Disorders*, WHO, Geneva, Switzerland, 2022, June 8, Retrieved November 11, 2024, from WHO Newsroom Factsheets: https://www.who.int/news-room/fact-sheets/detail/mental-disorders.
26. WHO, *Mental Health*, WHO, Geneva, Switzerland 2022, June 22, Retrieved November 11, 2024, from WHO Website: https://www.who.int/news-room/fact-sheets/detail/mental-health-strengthening-our-response.
27. WHO Mental Health Report, *Who European Framework For Action On Mental Health 2021–2025*, World Health Organization, Copenhagen, 2022.
28. WHO, *Obsessive compulsive disorder (OCD)*, World Health Organization, Eastern Mediteranian Region, 2023.
29. Ye, Z. and Huang, X., Adoption of a deep learning-based neural network model in the psychological behavior analysis of resident tourism consumption. *Front. Public Health*, 10, 1–12, 2022.

14

AI-Driven Educational Resources for Mental Health Promotion: Reducing Stigma and Empowering Individuals

Abhinav Sharma[1], Ankur Kumar[1]*, Gunjan Shuklaa[2] and Surita Maini[1]

[1]Department of Electrical and Instrumentation Engineering, Sant Longowal Institute of Engineering and Technology, Longowal, Sangrur, Punjab, India
[2]SICA College, Indore, India

Abstract
This paper examines AI's potential to revolutionize mental health education. AI offers personalized, accessible, and interactive resources aimed at promoting mental well-being and combating stigma. By leveraging AI's capabilities in data analysis, personalized content delivery, and interactive learning, mental health education can become more engaging, effective, and inclusive. AI-powered tools can reduce stigma, empower individuals, and provide early detection of mental health challenges. While AI presents significant opportunities, challenges such as privacy concerns, bias in algorithms, and ethical considerations must be carefully addressed to ensure its responsible and beneficial use in mental health care.

Keywords: Artificial intelligence, mental health, Internet of Things, machine learning, education

14.1 Introduction

People of various ages and social backgrounds are affected by mental health issues, which are a serious worldwide concern. Even with advancements in mental health knowledge, stigma remains a major barrier that frequently discourages people from getting help [1, 2]. Artificial intelligence (AI) has become a powerful tool in mental health education in recent years [3].

**Corresponding author*: khatriankur007@yahoo.com

Ridhima Sharma, Fazla Rabby, Rohit Bansal, Timcy Sachdeva and Jihene Mrabet (eds.) Confronting Mental Health Stigma with AI and Machine Learning, (353–382) © 2026 Scrivener Publishing LLC

It provides interactive, simply available, and customized resources to support mental health and fight stigma [4]. By offering individualized mental health education, changing public perceptions, and transforming methods of addressing these issues, AI-powered solutions play a crucial role in empowering people [5]. In the field of mental health treatment, the quick development of technology has brought both benefits and obstacles. In addition to creating new complications, it has opened the door for creative treatments meant to support, maintain, and improve mental health. Efforts to address negative behaviors related to mobile internet technology are part of this [6]. However, as the World Health Organization (WHO) noted in their guidelines for the 11th revision of the International Classification of Disorders [7], identifying and studying these behaviors has proven to be a challenging undertaking. However, there are a lot of promises to resolve these problems with online and mobile technology. Promising approaches for investigating, identifying, and addressing harmful online behaviors are presented by tools like ecological momentary assessment (EMA) and intervention (EMI) [8].

A complicated and multidimensional issue, stigma can negatively impact people, families, and society. When it comes to mental health, stigma has been found to occasionally be more upsetting and incapacitating than the condition itself. The majority of the evidence comes from high-income nations, despite the fact that much research has examined the varieties of stigma, their nature, and successful remedies. Few studies have been done in low- and middle-income nations, according to reviews of interventions aimed at reducing stigma around mental health [2]. AI-driven mental health education: interactive tools, data insights, and personalized learning are depicted in Figure 14.1.

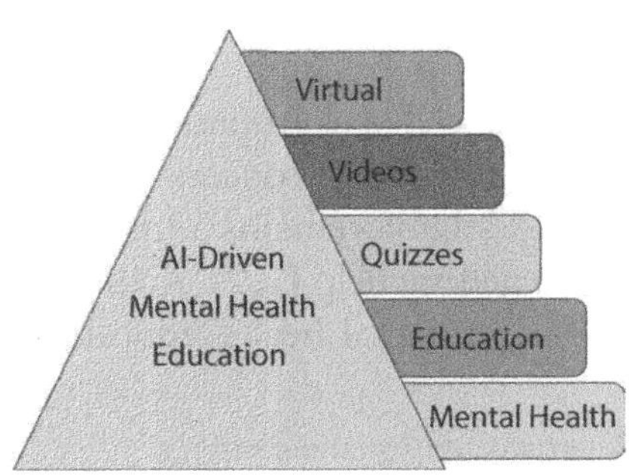

Figure 14.1 Framework of AI-driven mental health education: personalized learning, interactive tools, and data insights.

This discussion emphasizes how important AI-powered learning materials can be in fostering mental health by lowering stigma and giving people the tools they need to take charge of their mental health.

14.2 The Role of AI in Mental Health Education

Figure 14.2 illustrates the wide range of uses for artificial intelligence (AI) in healthcare. By utilizing AI's strengths in data analysis, personalized content distribution, and interactive learning, mental health education could undergo a significant transformation [9]. These characteristics allow AI systems to simplify difficult mental health ideas and make them more approachable and understandable. This is essential for increasing awareness, encouraging mental health literacy, and giving people the tools they need to take better care of their mental health [10]. The main roles AI plays in mental health education are as follows [11]:

14.2.1 Personalized Learning

Personalized learning is one of the most significant ways AI improves mental health education. In order to develop individualized learning experiences, AI algorithms can assess user behavior, including how they engage with instructional materials, their emotional reactions, and even their social media activity [12]. A person's particular learning preferences, mental health needs, and even psychological condition can all be met with this tailored approach. For instance, AI is able to identify when a person is experiencing stress or anxiety and then offer tailored resources, such as mindfulness exercises, relaxation

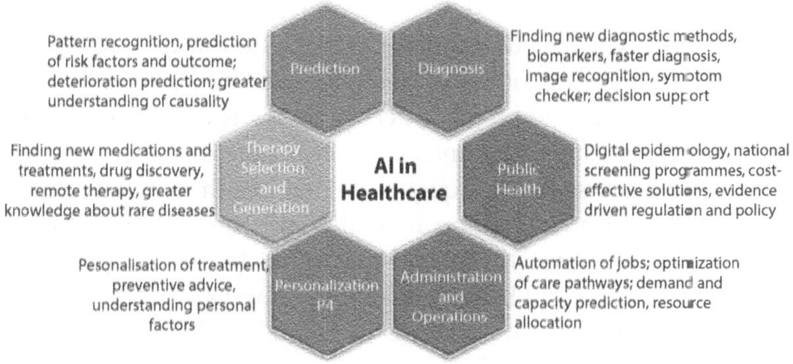

Figure 14.2 Potential applications of AI in healthcare [5].

methods, or educational materials that specifically target their mental health issues [13].

14.2.2 Interactive Tools and Simulations

Chatbots, virtual simulations, and gamified learning environments are just a few examples of the extremely dynamic and captivating educational technologies made possible by AI. These resources give consumers engaging experiences that can help them comprehend mental health ideas more thoroughly. For example, in a safe virtual setting, users can practice mindfulness, participate in stress management scenarios, or investigate real-life coping mechanisms through virtual simulations. In addition to making education more interesting, this experiential learning method gives people the useful skills they need to maintain their mental health in everyday circumstances [14].

14.2.3 Data-Driven Insights

AI can find trends, patterns, and real-time insights on mental health because of its enormous data processing capacity. AI can help create more relevant and efficient targeted instructional materials by assessing massive datasets from user behavior, medical records, or public health surveys. Furthermore, by spotting minute variations in user conduct or language use, AI can spot early indicators of mental health issues and enable prompt interventions. This feature aids in improving instructional materials by making sure they are suited to new developments in mental health and the requirements of various demographic groups [15].

14.2.4 Accessibility and Availability

The potential of AI to make resources available to a wide audience is one of the biggest benefits it offers to mental health education. AI-powered educational resources can be made accessible *via* text messaging systems, websites, or mobile apps, guaranteeing that people in underprivileged or rural areas have access to high-quality mental health material. This eliminates geographic restrictions on mental health support and education. Additionally, these AI systems can provide round-the-clock, real-time support, ensuring that mental health education is always accessible. For those who might not otherwise have access to mental health specialists, this is especially helpful because it allows them to get prompt care and direction when they need it [11].

14.2.5 Early Detection and Intervention

By tracking minute behavioral changes and trends in writing, voice, and internet activity, artificial intelligence (AI) can aid in the early detection of mental health problems. For example, using language usage, tone, and emotional context, natural language processing (NLP) computers may analyze text and detect symptoms of anxiety or depression. AI can notify users of possible mental health issues before they become more serious by incorporating this capability into educational platforms and offering them resources, instructional materials, or guidance for early intervention [16].

14.2.6 Tailored Feedback and Progress Tracking

AI is able to track a person's learning progress and mental health development over time in addition to personalizing instructional content. AI-powered platforms that have ongoing feedback loops might modify the content's focus or level of difficulty according to the user's progress. This guarantees that people obtain educational resources and mental health assistance that change based on their requirements, encouraging ongoing participation and long-term advantages [17].

14.2.7 Multilingual and Culturally Adaptive Content

By providing multilingual and culturally appropriate mental health education, AI can aid in bridging linguistic and cultural divides. It is possible to make mental health education more accessible by utilizing natural language translation and artificial intelligence's capacity to comprehend and modify content for various cultural contexts. Reaching non-native speakers, immigrants, and culturally varied groups—who could have particular mental health issues and need culturally relevant resources—is particularly crucial [18].

14.2.8 Virtual Mental Health Coaches and Therapists

Virtual therapists or coaches with AI capabilities can be easily available resources for users. Through AI-powered dialogues, these virtual assistants can give emotional support, cognitive behavioral therapy (CBT) activities, and psychoeducation. By providing a confidential, judgment-free environment for people to learn about mental health and practice self-care techniques, these virtual coaches can lessen the stigma attached to asking for help [19].

14.2.9 Adaptive Learning for Different Mental Health Conditions

AI is capable of producing teaching materials that are specifically tailored to address mental health issues like PTSD, bipolar disorder, depression, or anxiety. AI technologies can offer condition-specific instructional resources, coping mechanisms, and symptom management procedures that are most pertinent to the needs of the individual by utilizing adaptive learning algorithms. This degree of personalization increases the efficacy and individualization of mental health education [15].

14.2.10 Incorporating Biofeedback for Emotional Regulation

Wearable technology that monitors breathing patterns, pulse rate variability, or sleep data are examples of biofeedback instruments that AI systems can incorporate. Based on the data, these systems can suggest instructional materials or relaxation techniques and provide real-time feedback on a person's physiological condition. For instance, the AI system may instantly offer instructional materials on stress-reduction methods or breathing exercises if biofeedback data indicates elevated tension, assisting people in controlling their emotions and stress levels [20].

14.2.11 Peer Support Networks Powered by AI

AI can connect people with comparable mental health experiences or educational objectives, facilitating peer-to-peer learning and support networks. Users can communicate, exchange stories, and offer support to one another in a monitored and secure setting by using chatbots, online forums, or AI-powered social media platforms. In addition to improving the educational process, community-based learning makes people feel less alone on their path to mental wellness [11].

14.2.12 Mental Health Literacy through Gamification

AI can use gamification strategies to improve the fun and engagement of mental health education. AI-powered platforms can increase mental health literacy while retaining users by transforming instructional content into engaging games, challenges, or quizzes. Complex psychological ideas can be simplified into enjoyable, manageable activities through gamified learning experiences, which improve comprehension and memory [21].

14.2.13 AI-Enhanced Emotional Intelligence Training

By providing interactive lessons and simulations that educate users on how to recognize, comprehend, and control their emotions, artificial intelligence (AI) can aid in the development of emotional intelligence (EQ). Artificial intelligence (AI) systems may evaluate a user's emotional reactions to various situations and offer tailored advice on how to enhance empathy, communication, and emotional control. This aids people in strengthening their emotional stability and mental toughness [18].

14.2.14 AI-Assisted Personalized Coping Strategies

Artificial intelligence (AI) solutions can offer highly customized coping mechanisms to handle stress, anxiety, or other mental health issues by learning from user behavior. Based on real-time user data, including mood tracking and daily routines, these AI systems can suggest certain mindfulness exercises, cognitive reframing strategies, or relaxation approaches [11].

14.2.15 Scalable Mental Health Education for Institutions

Platforms for AI-driven mental health education can grow to offer thorough instruction for communities, businesses, and educational institutions. AI can assist in creating a culture of mental health awareness, lowering stigma in a variety of settings, and advancing mental health literacy widely by automating mental health training programs and customizing them for various organizations [11].

14.3 Reducing Mental Health Stigma with AI-Driven Resources

One of the most difficult obstacles to treatment is still the stigma around mental health, which is driven by misunderstandings, preconceptions, and a general lack of knowledge. As illustrated in Figure 14.3, AI-driven instructional materials have enormous potential to fight this stigma by addressing it in innovative, approachable, and customized ways.

Below are some detailed strategies through which AI can help reduce mental health stigma:

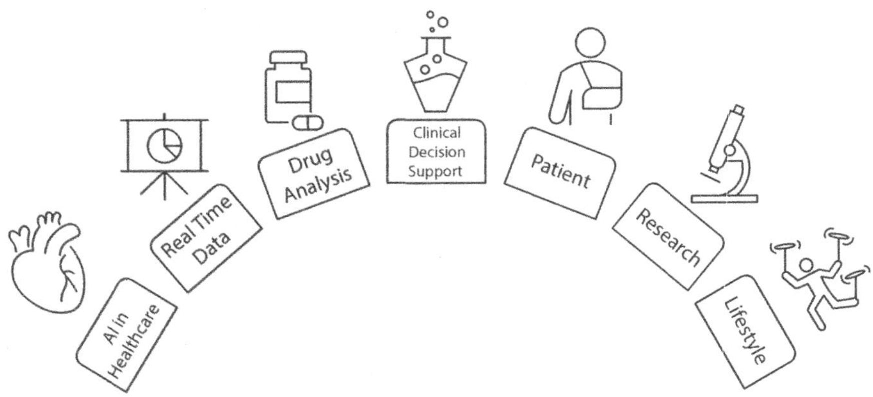

Figure 14.3 AI in mental health education [22].

14.3.1 Anonymous and Private Learning Platforms

Many people are afraid of being judged or ashamed, which makes them reluctant to seek mental health treatment. A solution is provided by AI-powered apps, websites, and virtual platforms, which offer private, anonymous areas where people can learn about mental health without social pressure. Users can study mental health subjects at their own speed without fear of criticism because of this privacy, which promotes learning in a secure setting. These platforms can include coping mechanisms, self-assessment tools, and instructional modules that people might not feel comfortable obtaining from conventional sources, allowing them to get help without worrying about stigma [23].

14.3.2 Myth-Busting Algorithms

By providing correct, fact-based information, AI can be trained to dispel widespread misconceptions and preconceptions about mental health. AI chatbots and virtual assistants, for instance, can answer user questions with accurate information, debunking myths like "depression is just sadness" or "people with mental health disorders are dangerous." AI systems can contribute to changing the public's perception of mental health concerns by actively dispelling these beliefs and providing accurate answers to widespread misconceptions that reinforce stigma. These myth-busting algorithms can also produce interactive infographics or educational quizzes that assist people in distinguishing between myths and facts, advancing mental health literacy [11].

14.3.3 Inclusive and Diverse Content

AI may evaluate and improve educational resources to guarantee diversity and representation of various cultures. Cultural, ethnic, and socioeconomic groups all experience different levels of stigma around mental health, and AI can customize educational materials to meet their particular needs. AI can, for example, curate content that recognizes regional or cultural difficulties that may contribute to stigma in particular groups. AI makes mental health education more approachable and culturally aware by making sure that the content speaks to people from various backgrounds. In minority groups, where mental health concerns may be more taboo or poorly understood, this inclusivity is crucial to lowering stigma.

14.3.4 Empowering through Storytelling

By utilizing the power of storytelling, AI can significantly contribute to the reduction of stigma associated with mental health. Hearing firsthand accounts from others who have effectively dealt with mental health challenges might normalize them and lessen their sense of alienation. AI can select which personal tales have the greatest influence on lowering stigma by curating a variety of them using data-driven insights. These narratives can be adapted to fit the needs of many audiences and presented in a variety of media, including written testimonies, podcasts, and videos. AI might, for instance, choose stories about conquering depression for young adults and highlight information about anxiety management for professionals working in high-stress settings. AI promotes empathy and more candid conversations about mental health by showcasing individual journeys.

14.3.5 Real-Time Stigma Monitoring and Adaptation

AI can analyze social media, news stories, and online forums to track changes in public perceptions of mental health. This enables real-time detection of damaging trends or new stigmatizing words by AI-driven platforms. AI can quickly modify instructional materials to meet new problems based on this data, guaranteeing that the curriculum is effective and current. AI-driven resources can stay up to speed with changing discussions regarding mental health thanks to their real-time reactivity, offering current material that counters new waves of false information or damaging narratives.

14.3.6 Personalized Stigma Reduction Campaigns

AI can also be used to create customized campaigns to lessen stigma. AI can suggest specialized educational resources that are most likely to change a person's perceptions by studying their behavior, preferences, and interactions with mental health information. Someone with particular preconceived notions about therapy, for example, would be shown success stories of people who have benefited from counseling, while another user might be shown customized infographics that describe the science underlying prevalent mental health issues. Users are more likely to connect with these tailored ads and be inspired to reconsider their perspectives on mental health.

14.3.7 AI-Driven Support Communities

AI can help build secure, encouraging online communities where people can talk about their experiences with mental health without worrying about being judged. These networks can be moderated by AI algorithms, guaranteeing that conversations stay civil and stigma-free [24]. AI can also facilitate peer support and shared learning by bringing people together who have had comparable experiences. By helping people understand that mental health problems are widespread and curable, these groups are an essential resource for lowering the stigma associated with getting treatment.

14.3.8 Gamification for Stigma Reduction

While gently tackling stigmatizing notions, gamified AI tools can make learning about mental health interesting and enjoyable. AI can create interactive challenges or games that use role-playing, trivia, or problem-solving techniques to encourage mental health education. For instance, gamers can encounter scenarios in which they assist virtual characters in coping with stress or provide assistance to an individual who is suffering from anxiety. By placing gamers in scenarios that mimic actual mental health issues, these interactive experiences not only educate users but also foster empathy and aid in the destruction of stigmatizing ideas.

14.3.9 Continuous Learning Algorithms for Long-Term Impact

It takes constant work to reduce stigma, and AI-powered tools can give consumers the opportunity for continual education. Over time, AI can track a person's development and suggest new tasks or content that progressively change perspectives and broaden comprehension. In order to promote a long-term shift of viewpoint, a user who first interacts with basic mental health literacy content might thereafter be exposed to more complicated subjects, such as the significance of therapy or medicines. This continual learning makes sure that initiatives to lessen stigma are a part of a continuing educational process rather than being one-time fixes.

14.3.10 Breaking the Cycle of Stigmatizing Language

This proactive approach ensures that conversations about mental health become more respectful and compassionate, further reducing stigma. AI-driven language processing tools can analyze written or spoken content to identify stigmatizing language in real time. On platforms such as social media, AI can flag harmful terms and suggest alternative, non-stigmatizing language instead. By giving users real-time corrections, AI helps people become more mindful of their words, reducing the unintentional perpetuation of stigma.

AI-driven mental health tools can greatly lessen stigma, promote empathy, and enable people to seek treatment without worrying about being judged by others by addressing these different facets. Stories, real-time adaption, personalized material, and anonymous learning all work together to normalize mental health and progressively eliminate stigma [11].

14.4 Applications of AI to Mental Health Status

There are some applications of AI to mental health status, as shown in Figure 14.4.

14.4.1 Monitoring and Diagnosing Mental Health

- **Chatbots and Virtual Therapists Driven by AI:**
  - Natural language processing (NLP) is used by programs like Woebot and Wysa to communicate with users, gauge their mood, and offer coping mechanisms.
  - 24/7 support is available, which lessens the stigma associated with asking for assistance.

Figure 14.4 Applications of AI to mental health status [25].

- **Symptom Recognition:**
  - AI is able to identify symptoms of bipolar disorder, PTSD, anxiety, and sadness by analyzing speech, text, and facial expressions.
  - For instance, patients' utterances can be processed by sentiment analysis technologies to reveal underlying mental health issues.
- **Systems for Early Warning:**
  - AI systems use smartphones or wearable technology to track behavioral changes and notify medical professionals or carers of potential emergencies (such as suicidal thoughts).

14.4.2 Tailored Therapy Programs

- AI systems examine genetic data, lifestyle, and medical history to suggest individualized treatments.
- As an illustration, determine which drugs work best for each person based on their particular response profiles.

- AI-driven mental health applications are able to dynamically modify therapy sessions in response to user input and progress.

14.4.3 Delivery of Cognitive Behavioral Therapy (CBT)

- Through interactive apps, AI systems provide cognitive behavioral therapy (CBT) programs that teach users how to manage stress, anxiety, or depression.
- By making therapy rewarding and interactive, gamified cognitive behavioral therapy applications increase adherence and engagement.

14.4.4 Risk Prediction for Mental Health

- AI models forecast who is likely to experience mental health problems based on:
  - Social media activity (such as negative sentiment or language patterns) among people at risk of mental health problems is predicted by AI models based on:
  - Information from wearable technology, such as heart rate variability and sleep habits.
- Used to find vulnerable groups, like veterans, frontline workers, and students.

14.4.5 Intervention for Crises

- **Using AI to Prevent Suicide:**
  - AI examines conversation data to identify suicidal thoughts and notify emergency contacts or professionals.
  - Using text analysis, AI is used by organizations such as Crisis Text Line to triage high-risk individuals.
- During a mental health crisis, AI-powered virtual assistants offer real-time support.

14.4.6 Assistance for Mental Health in Distant Places

- AI technologies and applications help those who don't have easy access to mental health specialists.
- Offers language-specific and culturally appropriate interventions.

14.4.7 AI for Managing Stress and Emotions

- Wearable technology powered by artificial intelligence (AI), such as smartwatches, tracks physiological indicators like skin temperature and heart rate to determine stress levels.
- Stress management is aided by real-time feedback and relaxation techniques (such as breathing techniques).

14.4.8 Research and Data Analysis in Mental Health

- By examining big datasets from surveys, clinical trials, or electronic medical records to find trends and treatment results, AI speeds up research.
- Finding links between social determinants (such loneliness and money) and mental health is one example.

14.4.9 Enhancing Clinicians and Therapists

- AI tools help professionals by automating repetitive processes like follow-ups and patient paperwork.
- Give therapists information on their patients' development over time so they can improve their treatment plans.

14.5 Empowering People with AI-Powered Mental Health Resources

Beyond merely imparting knowledge, AI-powered educational materials enable people to take charge of their mental health by providing them with helpful, individualized, and easily accessible tools. Users can take proactive measures towards well-being, feel less alone in their mental health journey, and gain a better understanding of their mental health disorders thanks to these features. The following are the main enabling aspects of AI in mental health:

14.5.1 Self-Assessment and Early Detection

Self-assessment and early mental health issue identification are two of the most potent ways AI tools empower people. Questionnaires, symptom checkers, and behavioral tracking tools based on machine learning models are common examples of AI-driven platforms. These models are able to identify emotional reactions, mood swings, or trends in user behavior that could indicate disorders like PTSD, anxiety, or depression. Early symptom detection encourages users to get treatment sooner, which lessens the severity of their diseases and enhances long-term results. Additionally, early detection empowers people to take charge of their mental health without waiting for outside validation from medical professionals [26].

14.5.2 Personalized Action Plans

By creating individualized mental health action plans according to each person's unique needs, AI improves empowerment. Depending on the user's mental health profile, these plans may incorporate a mix of self-care routines, treatment approaches, and lifestyle advice. An AI system might, for example, evaluate a user's stress levels, sleep habits, and emotional triggers before recommending a stress-reduction plan that includes exercise, meditation, or cognitive behavioral therapy (CBT). By developing a customized mental health management roadmap, AI gives people concrete actions they can take to enhance their well-being, making the process seem more doable and in line with their unique objectives.

14.5.3 Continuous Support and Motivation

AI-powered applications keep users involved in their mental health journey, providing ongoing support and encouragement. For example, AI chatbots can ask users how they're feeling, remind them to take care of themselves, and conduct daily check-ins. When users perform healthy behaviors, such as practicing mindfulness or sticking to a regular sleep schedule, these chatbots can offer support and positive reinforcement. People who receive this ongoing assistance feel less alone and more like they have a friend on their path to mental wellness. Additionally, users are kept accountable and motivated by the real-time nature of AI support, which guarantees that they accomplish their mental health objectives [11].

14.5.4 Access to Resources

AI-powered solutions provide users with carefully selected access to a variety of mental health resources, including self-help manuals, educational articles, therapeutic alternatives, and community support groups. Because these resources are customized to each user's unique mental health requirements, people are guaranteed to obtain pertinent and helpful information. AI can also suggest online treatment platforms or local mental health providers, which makes it simpler for people to get the support they require. Furthermore, these platforms might offer a variety of learning formats to suit various learning preferences, such as interactive activities, podcasts, and videos. AI enables people to actively participate in learning about and managing their mental health by making such information easily accessible.

14.5.5 Language and Communication Assistance

The natural language processing (NLP) capabilities of AI make mental health materials available in a variety of languages, removing barriers for those from different cultural backgrounds or non-native speakers. Artificial intelligence (AI) techniques can reduce medical jargon and complex mental health terms for people who might find it difficult to understand, making mental health education more approachable and intelligible. Because the material is given in an understandable manner, users who want mental health education or support feel more confident and knowledgeable. AI guarantees that mental health education reaches a wider audience by eliminating language and communication barriers, enabling people who might otherwise encounter difficulties to get the information they require.

14.5.6 Anonymity and Privacy

AI-powered mental health solutions frequently offer a high degree of privacy and anonymity, which might empower people who are hesitant to talk about their mental health in public or at work. Because mental health is stigmatized, many people put off getting treatment, but AI technologies provide a safe, accepting environment for learning and self-evaluation. Because they don't have to worry about being judged or embarrassed, people are encouraged to explore their mental health issues more freely and at their own pace. Without outside pressure, anonymity enables people to begin the process of comprehending and regulating their mental health.

14.5.7 Crisis Management and Immediate Assistance

By recognizing warning indicators and providing crisis management resources, AI-powered solutions can help people in emergency circumstances right away. For instance, an AI system can immediately suggest crisis helplines, emergency contacts, or mental health hotlines if it determines from a user's interactions that the user is experiencing significant anxiety or suicidal thoughts. AI-powered platforms might occasionally be able to put users in touch with emergency services or mental health specialists directly. When people are most in need of assistance, this prompt action can save their lives and enable them to get it.

14.5.8 User Empowerment through Self-Reflection Tools

Users can better comprehend their ideas, feelings, and behaviors by using AI technologies to facilitate self-reflection. AI apps that include journaling tools, mood monitoring, and self-reflection prompts might inspire people to consider their everyday lives and spot trends that might have an impact on their mental health. People who engage in this practice over time may become more self-aware and emotionally intelligent, which will empower them to manage their well-being more actively.

14.5.9 Remote and On-Demand Access

AI-powered mental health solutions give consumers round-the-clock access to mental health assistance, enabling them to ask for guidance or instruction whenever they need it. For those who might not have instant access to mental health specialists or who would rather study and get help in the comfort of their own homes, this is especially empowering. People may take control of their mental health whenever they need it thanks to on-demand access, which eliminates the need for fixed appointments or a shortage of medical professionals.

14.5.10 Gamified Mental Health Engagement

To keep users interested in their mental health objectives, AI platforms frequently incorporate gamification features, including challenges, reward systems, and progress tracking. By making mental health management more engaging and fun, these gamified experiences motivate people to maintain their routines and experience a sense of achievement as they advance. Younger users can benefit greatly from gamification since it makes learning about mental health and forming healthy habits enjoyable and rewarding.

Artificial-intelligence (AI)-driven solutions enable people to take charge of their mental health in ways that were previously challenging or unattainable by providing real-time resources, ongoing interaction, and personalized assistance. These resources encourage self-awareness, facilitate early intervention, and guarantee that everyone, anywhere, at any time, has access to mental health education [15].

14.6 Challenges and Considerations

Although AI-powered mental health teaching materials have a lot of promises, there are drawbacks as well.

14.6.1 Bias in AI Algorithms

Large datasets are used to train AI models, and if these datasets are not representative of all demographics or varied, the resulting AI systems may reinforce preexisting prejudices. An AI product that was trained exclusively on data from a single geographic, ethnic, or socioeconomic group, for example, might not be able to appropriately meet the needs of users from diverse backgrounds. As a result, some populations may receive guidance from AI systems that is less helpful or even dangerous. AI models must be routinely checked for bias, and efforts must be taken to guarantee that the training data is varied. This problem can be resolved, and more fair results for various user groups can be guaranteed with ongoing model upgrades and improvements.

14.6.2 Privacy Concerns

Because mental health data is sensitive, privacy is of utmost importance. Artificial intelligence (AI) platforms gather personal data, such as user behavior, emotional states, and even specifics from private chats or social media activities. To avoid unwanted access or data breaches, it is essential to make sure that strong data protection measures are in place, such as encryption and adherence to privacy laws (like the GDPR). Users must have control over their information and be able to see how their data is gathered, saved, and used. Users may lose trust in and be reluctant to use AI-driven mental health resources if their privacy is not protected.

14.6.3 Accuracy and Ethical Use

Ensuring the accuracy of assessments and recommendations is a significant difficulty in AI-driven mental health education. Advice that is too vague or inaccurate could make someone's mental health condition worse. When using AI in healthcare, ethical considerations are crucial since consumers could be harmed if they receive inaccurate or inappropriate advice. Before AI products are made available to the general public, mental health practitioners must thoroughly evaluate and validate them. Furthermore, including human oversight in AI systems—for example, by having a medical expert evaluate insights produced by AI—can help reduce the possibility of inaccurate diagnoses or recommendations.

14.6.4 Over-Reliance on AI

AI should not be used in place of human intervention, especially for those with severe mental health disorders, even though it can be a useful and accessible tool for mental health education. Over-reliance on AI for mental health support may result in lost opportunities for people to seek professional assistance or delayed treatment. When needed, users should be encouraged to seek advice from mental health specialists through AI systems, and these platforms should be created to enhance rather than replace conventional therapy. AI tools with explicit disclaimers and instructions can assist users in determining when it is acceptable to refer mental health issues to a qualified expert.

14.6.5 Technical Limitations and Misinterpretation

Though it is far from flawless, AI is getting better at processing and interpreting human emotions, language, and behavior. AI systems still run the danger of misinterpreting emotional cues or failing to identify more complex mental health issues. For instance, AI may fail to recognize significant mental health symptoms that don't fall into predetermined patterns or incorrectly identify some behaviors as indicators of anxiety or depression when they are not. To overcome these technological constraints and guarantee that AI systems correctly understand human emotions and behaviors, constant algorithmic improvement and cooperation with mental health specialists are needed [27].

14.6.6 Accessibility and Digital Divide

Although AI-powered resources can increase access to mental health education, they frequently depend on digital skills, cell phones, and internet connectivity. People who live in rural or low-income areas or have limited access to these services can be left behind. Existing health disparities may be made worse by this digital gap. The development of AI-powered mental health products that work with low-tech platforms, like entry-level smartphones, and provide content in numerous languages and formats is essential to guaranteeing equal access.

14.6.7 Regulatory and Legal Challenges

There are legal and regulatory issues with the use of AI in healthcare, especially in mental health education. Regulating AI systems, especially when they offer health-related advice, is still a challenge for governments and health authorities. Liability concerns are still unanswered, especially when an AI tool gives bad advice or misses significant mental health problems. To guarantee that AI-driven mental health products meet healthcare standards and that users have legal options in the event that AI recommendations malfunction or cause harm, clear regulatory frameworks must be put in place.

14.6.8 Emotional Disconnect

Despite their progress, AI systems still lack the emotional intelligence and empathy provided by human mental health specialists. When using AI tools, users may experience emotional detachment, particularly when they are emotionally vulnerable. AI is capable of offering factual knowledge and coping mechanisms, but it is unable to replace a human therapist's compassion, empathy, and support. The efficacy of AI solutions in fostering user comfort and trust may be constrained by this emotional gap. As a result, human mental health experts continue to play a crucial role, particularly for those looking for compassionate, understanding care.

14.6.9 Continuous Monitoring and Updates

To keep up with developments in both AI technology and mental health research, AI-driven mental health solutions need to be updated on a frequent basis. However, it can be difficult to continuously monitor and update these technologies, particularly for smaller organizations that do not have the means to keep their systems up to date. Advice that is out of date or ineffectual may result from algorithms that are not updated. To guarantee that AI technologies continue to be useful and relevant, developers must make a commitment to continuous research, updates, and cooperation with mental health specialists.

14.6.10 Trust and Adoption

A lack of trust may prevent AI-driven mental health education tools from being widely adopted. People may be reluctant to give AI platforms sensitive information about their mental health, particularly if they don't understand how the technology operates or are worried about data misuse.

Gaining users' trust is crucial to these products' success. To boost user confidence, developers and healthcare providers must establish transparent privacy policies, involve mental health professionals in the design and monitoring of AI systems, and clearly explain the advantages and limitations of AI tools.

In order to guarantee the efficacy, morality, and accessibility of AI-driven mental health education resources, these issues must be resolved. AI has the ability to completely transform mental health education and support globally by identifying and addressing these problems [15]. Table 14.1 depicts the challenges and solutions for AI-powered mental health.

Table 14.1 Challenges and solutions for AI-powered mental health.

Challenge	Description	Proposed solution
Bias in AI algorithms	Not all demographics may be represented in the training data, which could result in damaging or biased recommendations for under-represented groups.	Make use of a variety of training datasets and conduct frequent bias tests. Make constant improvements to algorithms to increase accuracy and fairness.
Privacy concerns	Strong protection is necessary for sensitive mental health data to prevent misuse and illegal access. Issues with trust may arise from a lack of openness and data protection.	Put strong encryption into place, abide by privacy laws (like the GDPR), and give people control over their data. Make sure that data storage and consumption are transparent.
Accuracy and ethical use	Ethical issues occur when AI systems offer incorrect or generalized mental health guidance. Users can be harmed by inaccurate advice or assessments.	Before releasing AI systems, validate them with mental health specialists. Ensure thorough testing and updates and incorporate human oversight.
Over-reliance on AI	Over-reliance on AI could postpone seeking professional help, particularly in cases of severe mental illness.	Create AI tools that support conventional care while including explicit caveats urging users to get expert assistance when necessary.

(*Continued*)

Table 14.1 Challenges and solutions for AI-powered mental health. (*Continued*)

Challenge	Description	Proposed solution
Technical limitations	Misclassifications could result from AI misinterpreting delicate emotional cues or failing to identify complex mental health issues.	Work with mental health professionals and continuously update algorithms to increase the precision of identifying human emotions and behaviors.
Accessibility and digital divide	Because AI technologies sometimes require sophisticated equipment, low-income or rural populations cannot use them.	Deliver offline access, provide tools that work with simple devices, and deliver material in a variety of languages and formats.
Regulatory and legal challenges	Liability in cases of harm or failure is a concern due to the absence of established legal frameworks for AI in healthcare.	Specify legal requirements for AI-powered mental health resources. Describe who is responsible for damages brought on by AI recommendations.
Emotional disconnect	Because AI lacks human therapists' empathy and emotional intelligence, it may be less trustworthy and consoling in times of vulnerability.	To provide compassionate care, combine AI technologies with human intervention. While humans take care of emotional assistance, use AI to deliver factual knowledge.
Continuous monitoring and updates	AI solutions must be updated frequently to remain effective, but smaller businesses can find it difficult to meet their resource needs.	Make a commitment to ongoing research and cooperation with mental health specialists. Set aside funds for routine monitoring and updates.
Trust and adoption	Because they are inexperienced with the technology and have worries about data security, users may be reluctant to embrace AI solutions.	Establish trust by involving mental health professionals in system design, educating users about the advantages and limitations, and having clear policies.

14.7 How Does AI Reduce Stigma

By educating people, encouraging candid discussions, ensuring anonymity, and dispelling negative perceptions, artificial intelligence (AI) significantly contributes to the reduction of the stigma associated with mental health. Here are some ways that AI lessens stigma:

14.7.1 Access to Mental Health Resources in an Anonymous Manner

Fear of stigma or condemnation is a major deterrent to getting mental health treatment. Chatbots and smartphone apps are examples of AI-driven technologies that enable private, anonymous access to mental health resources. As a result, more people are inspired to learn about mental health, get treatment, and begin their path without worrying about being stigmatized.

Example: Apps with AI capabilities, such as Wysa and Woebot, offer users private mental health education and support, easing stigma-related anxiety. These resources provide a secure environment for talking about emotions, working through coping mechanisms, and getting information.

14.7.2 Dispelling Myths and False Information

By providing consumers with accurate and true information, AI can be utilized to dispel stereotypes about mental health. For example, chatbots can dispel myths and offer fact-based responses to frequently asked enquiries concerning mental health issues. This aids in the fight against false information, which frequently feeds stigma.

Example: Artificial intelligence (AI) systems are able to recognize prevalent fallacies (such as "mental illness is a sign of weakness") and offer fact-based justifications that refute these detrimental notions.

14.7.3 Promoting Honest Discussions

Artificial intelligence (AI) solutions, such as chatbots for mental health and virtual assistants, encourage users to talk about mental health and help normalize talks about mental health issues. The stigma associated with mental health concerns is lessened when people feel at ease talking about it using AI tools than when they do with friends and family.

Example: Youper and Ginger, two AI chatbots, encourage users to discuss their feelings and mental health issues. This promotes an environment of openness and support by normalizing conversations about mental health.

14.7.4 Individualized Instruction and Knowledge

AI-powered systems are able to tailor mental health instruction according to a person's symptoms, experiences, or inquiries. AI makes sure that people get the correct information by providing them with content that is pertinent and customized for them, which helps them comprehend mental health concerns and the significance of getting treatment.

Example: AI has the ability to customize instructional materials for particular populations, making sure that it appeals to various age, gender, and cultural groups. This helps dispel stigmas in cultures where mental health topics may be viewed as sensitive by making mental health education more approachable and relatable.

14.7.5 Dispelling Preconceptions with Data-Driven Understanding

AI is able to evaluate enormous volumes of data and spot trends that go against popular perceptions of mental health. AI assists in changing the emphasis from unfavorable stereotypes to a data-driven comprehension of mental health concerns by providing objective insights.

Example: AI-powered mental health platforms can dispel the myth that only a select group of "weak" or "unstable" people deal with mental health by sharing data demonstrating how common mental health problems are.

14.7.6 Diverse and Inclusive Representation

AI can guarantee that content about mental health is inclusive and represents a variety of experiences. AI can fight stigma in populations where cultural norms prevent or restrict mental health conversations by customizing educational materials for different cultures.

Example: In order to lessen stigma in marginalized communities, such as racial minorities or LGBTQ+ people, AI tools can produce teaching materials that highlight the particular mental health issues they confront.

14.7.7 Continually Offering Assistance

AI solutions provide users with ongoing, non-judgmental support, enabling them to deal with mental health issues without worrying about criticism. People feel less alone and more empowered to ask for assistance when they receive this ongoing support.

Example: Woebot and other AI chatbots offer round-the-clock mental health support, enabling users to discuss their feelings and receive the assistance they require in a setting free from stigma.

14.7.8 Prevention and Early Detection

AI-powered technologies are able to spot mental health issues early on before they worsen. This proactive approach teaches people that asking for help when they need it is a show of strength rather than weakness. AI lessens the stigma attached to waiting until mental health problems worsen by normalizing early intervention.

Example: Apps using AI capabilities, such as Mindstrong, monitor user behavior, including smartphone usage patterns, to identify early indicators of anxiety or depression. By encouraging users to act quickly, these tools lessen the stigma and stop symptoms from getting worse.

14.7.9 AI Conversations Driven by Empathy

Certain AI chatbots are made to react empathetically, imitating human conversations in ways that help users feel supported and understood. This lessens the stigma by enabling users to talk openly about their mental health without worrying about being misinterpreted or condemned.

Example: Replika and other AI-based chatbots for mental health engage users in emotionally supportive dialogues so they can explore their feelings and thoughts without worrying about being judged.

14.7.10 Encouraging Success Narratives and Positive Stories

AI programs are able to compile and disseminate success tales of people who have effectively dealt with mental health issues. These tales have the capacity to upend harmful stereotypes about mental health issues and empower others.

Example: By showcasing the experiences of individuals from a variety of backgrounds conquering mental health obstacles, AI-powered content platforms can dispel stigma by fostering the notion that mental health issues are widespread and treatable.

By providing accurate, individualized, and anonymous mental health education, AI lessens the stigma associated with mental illness. It offers users safe places to investigate their mental health, dispels myths, encourages candid communication, and offers judgment-free support. AI has the ability to further de-stigmatize mental health conditions and motivate people to get the care they require as it develops [15].

14.8 Conclusion

AI has the ability to completely transform mental health education by offering interactive, individualized, and easily available resources. AI can greatly enhance mental health outcomes by reducing stigma, empowering people, and promoting early detection. However, issues like algorithmic bias, privacy concerns, and the requirement for human oversight must be addressed. AI has the potential to be a useful tool for fostering mental health and aiding people on their path to mental health recovery if these variables are carefully taken into account. This chapter discusses the difficulties and potential solutions, provides a detailed explanation of how to empower people with AI-powered mental health resources, and suggests a method for using AI to reduce stigma.

References

1. Sharma, A., Dhanka, S., Bansal, R., Kumar, A., Maini, S., *Industry 5.0 with Sustainable Development*, vol. 0 pp. 347–370, Cham, Springer Nature Switzerland, 2024, doi: 10.1007/978-3-031-70996-8_17.
2. Gurung, D., *et al.*, Stigma against mental health disorders in Nepal conceptualised with a 'what matters most' framework: A scoping review. *Epidemiol.*

Psychiatr. Sci., 32, e16, Cambridge University Press, Cambridge, UK, 2023. https://doi.org/10.1017/S2045796022000844.

3. Sharma, A., Dhanka, S., Kumar, A., Maini, S., A comparative study of heterogeneous machine learning algorithms for arrhythmia classification using feature selection technique and multi-dimensional datasets. *Eng. Res. Express*, 6, 3, 035209, Sep. 2024. doi: 10.1088/2631-8695/ad5d51.
4. Kumar, A., *et al.*, Smart Crop Selection: Harnessing Machine Learning for Sustainable Agriculture in the Era of Industry 5.0. Industry 5.0 and Emerging Technologies: *Transformation Through Technology and Innovations*, pp. 111–134, Cham, Springer Nature Switzerland, 2024.
5. Dawoodbhoy, F.M., *et al.*, AI in patient flow: Applications of artificial intelligence to improve patient flow in NHS acute mental health inpatient units. *Heliyon*, 7, 5, e06993. Elsevier Ltd., 2021. https://doi.org/10.1016/j.heliyon.2021.e06993.
6. Roth, C.B., Papassotiropoulos, A., Brühl, A.B., Lang, U.E., Huber, C.G., Psychiatry in the digital age: A blessing or a curse? *Int. J. Environ. Res. Public Health*, 18, 16, 8302, MDPI, 2021. doi: 10.3390/ijerph18168302.
7. Stein, D.J., Szatmari, P., Gaebel, W., Berk, M., Mental, behavioral and neurodevelopmental disorders in the ICD-11: An international perspective on key changes and controversies. *J. fur Neurol. Neurochir. und Psychiatr.*, 21, 1, 30–32, 2020.
8. Beres, L.K., *et al.*, Mobile ecological momentary assessment and intervention and health behavior change among adults in Rakai, Uganda: Pilot randomized controlled trial. *JMIR Form. Res.*, 5, 7, 1–12, 2021. doi: 10.2196/22693.
9. Palta, P. and Kumar, A., Effect of vermicompost additive on physical, chemical and dielectric properties of soil and its modeling. *J. Microw. Power Electromagn. Energy*, 58, 3, 186–206, 2024. doi: 10.1080/08327823.2024.2378668.
10. Palta, P. and Kumar, A., Soil dielectric response to chemical fertilizers in Northern India's key agricultural areas. *Phys. Chem. Earth.*, 137, May 2024, 103806, 2025. doi: 10.1016/j.pce.2024.103806.
11. Alhuwaydi, A.M., Exploring the Role of Artificial Intelligence in Mental Healthcare: Current Trends and Future Directions – A Narrative Review for a Comprehensive Insight. *Risk Manag. Healthc. Policy*, 17, May, 1339–1348, 2024. doi: 10.2147/RMHP.S461562.
12. Singh, J., Pandey, B., Karna, S., Arora, A.S., Kumar, A., Enhancing the thermographic diagnosis of maxillary sinusitis using deep learning approach. *Quant. InfraRed Thermogr. J.*, 00, 00, 1–15, 2024. doi: 10.1080/17686733.2024.2349976.
13. Mallik, S. and Gangopadhyay, A., Proactive and reactive engagement of artificial intelligence methods for education: a review. *Front. Artif. Intell.*, 6, 1151391, Frontiers Media S.A., 2023. doi: 10.3389/frai.2023.1151391.
14. Mitsea, E., Drigas, A., Skianis, C., Digitally Assisted Mindfulness in Training Self-Regulation Skills for Sustainable Mental Health: A Systematic Review. *Behav. Sci. (Basel)*, 13, 12, 1008, MDPI, 2023. doi: 10.3390/bs13121008.

15. Gutierrez, G., Stephenson, C., Eadie, J., Asadpour, K., & Alavi, N., Examining the role of AI technology in online mental healthcare: Opportunities, challenges, and implications, a mixed-methods review. *Front. Psychiatry,* 15, 1356773, Frontiers Media S.A., Lausanne, Switzerland, 2024. https://doi.org/10.3389/fpsyt.2024.1356773.
16. He, T., *et al.*, *Towards a Psychological Generalist AI: A Survey of Current Applications of Large Language Models and Future Prospects*, pp. 1–22, Cornell University Library, Ithaca, New York, USA, 2023, [Online]. Available: http://arxiv.org/abs/2312.04578.
17. Schiff, D., Out of the laboratory and into the classroom: the future of artificial intelligence in education. *AI Soc.*, 36, 1, 331–348, 2021. doi: 10.1007/s00146-020-01033-8.
18. Thakkar, A., Gupta, A., De Sousa, A., *Artificial intelligence in positive mental health: a narrative review*, no. March, pp. 1–11, Frontiers Media S.A., Lausanne, Switzerland, 2024, doi: 10.3389/fdgth.2024.1280235.
19. Gupta, P., Muneshwar, K.N., Juganavar, A., Shegekar, T., Beyond the Asylum Walls: Tracing the Tapestry of Mental Health Interventions Across Eras and Cultures. *Cureus*, 15, 11, e48251, Cureus, Inc., 2023. doi: 10.7759/cureus.48251.
20. Woodward, K., *et al.*, Beyond Mobile Apps: A Survey of Technologies for Mental Well-Being. *IEEE Trans. Affect. Comput.*, 13, 3, 1216–1235, 2022. doi: 10.1109/TAFFC.2020.3015018.
21. Cho, Y.M., Rai, S., Ungar, L., Sedoc, J., Guntuku, S.C., An Integrative Survey on Mental Health Conversational Agents to Bridge Computer Science and Medical Perspectives, in: *EMNLP 2023-2023 Conf. Empir. Methods Nat. Lang. Process. Proc*, pp. 11346–11369, 2023, doi: 10.18653/v1/2023.emnlp-main.698.
22. Anand, N., Pant, L.M., Alam, T., Pundir, S., Thomas, L., Rakshith, U.R., Artificial Intelligence's Contribution To Mental Health Education, in: *2023 Int. Conf. Sustain. Comput. Data Commun. Syst*, no. August, pp. 462–467, 2023, doi: 10.1109/ICSCDS56580.2023.10104905.
23. Lem, W.G., Dos, K.H., Kawata, S., Oyama, H., Exploring the impact of immersive virtual reality on depression knowledge and stigma reduction: a cross-over RCT fMRI study. *Sci. Rep.*, 14, 1, 1–14, 2024. doi: 10.1038/s41598-024-55797-w.
24. Singh, V., Kumar, A., Kaur, S., Bansal, A., Singla, A.K., Enhancing cavitation erosion resistance of VC+TiC coatings with PTFE in marine environments *via* lasso regression optimization. *Tribol. Int.*, 196, April, 109697, 2024. doi: 10.1016/j.triboint.2024.109697.

25. Liu, H., Applications of Artificial Intelligence to Popularize Legal Knowledge and Publicize the Impact on Adolescents' Mental Health Status. *Front. Psychiatry*, 13, 902456, Frontiers Media S.A., May, 2022. doi: 10.3389/fpsyt.2022.902456.
26. Bickman, L., Improving mental health services: A 50-year journey from randomized experiments to artificial intelligence and precision mental health. *Administration and Policy in Mental Health and Mental Health Services Research*, 47, 5, 731–745, Springer US, 2020. https://doi.org/10.1007/s10488-020-01065-8.
27. Kumar, A., Singh, J., Khan, A.A., A comprehensive machine learning framework with particle swarm optimization for improved polycystic ovary syndrome (PCOS) diagnosis. *Eng. Res. Express*, 2024. doi: 10.1088/2631-8695/ad76f9.

15

Stigma, Society, and Systems: Integrating AI with Mental Health Interventions

Priya Chetty[1], Gayatri Chopra[2*] and Mamta Gupta[3]

[1]Department of Operations, Project Guru, Gurugram, Hayana, India
[2]Department of Management, Bhagwan Parshuram Institute of Technology, New Delhi, Delhi, India
[3]Department of Management, Maharaja Surajmal Institute, New Delhi, Delhi, India

Abstract

Mental health is defined as an important component of the well-being and health of an individual. The rapid development of artificial intelligence (AI) in healthcare has brought about changes in mental health stigma by providing various new tools for assessing mental health status and offering better mental health care. Among these benefits, the presence of barriers that prevent the patients from seeking help and deriving appropriate care holds a significant value. This chapter will explore how AI technologies influence the mental health stigma, positively as well as negatively, by examining different AI-driven systems, algorithms, and interventions that are used currently.

The capability of AI to use a large amount of data and assess patterns has been used for understanding the language used in clinical settings as well as social media platforms. AI tools help determine these stigmatizing behaviors, thus helping reduce societal stigma. Moreover, AI tools like virtual assistants and chatbots are enabling the creation of a safe space for individuals to seek help without having any fear of judgment. In this respect, this chapter will focus on assessing the role of different AI technologies in supporting the individual by reducing the impact of societal stigma.

Although the usage of AI is beneficial for mental health care, there persist some challenges. The existence of biases in AI algorithms as well as the data on which these algorithms are trained could result in reinforcing existing stereotypes about mental health. This chapter will dig deeper into these associated complexities with

**Corresponding author*: gayatrichopra@bpitindia.com

Ridhima Sharma, Fazla Rabby, Rohit Bansal, Timcy Sachdeva and Jihene Mrabet (eds.) Confronting Mental Health Stigma with AI and Machine Learning, (383–404) © 2026 Scrivener Publishing LLC

AI usage in mental healthcare. The focus would be on examining the relevant strategies like transparency needs or ethical considerations for ensuring that the contribution of AI is toward reducing the mental health stigma and not exacerbating it. This chapter thus examines the importance of responsible AI development, emphasizing the need for ongoing research and a robust framework for deriving the positive impact of AI on mental health stigma.

Keywords: Mental health, mental health stigma, Artificial Intelligence, machine learning

15.1 Introduction

A large percentage of the world population is experiencing a decline in their mental health conditions. Society is also taking proactive steps to address the different needs of people for effective management of mental health conditions. Nevertheless, the stigma around mental illness persists as it is [1]. Mental health stigma can be understood from here as the negative perception of a group of people regarding some mental health issues or illnesses. It is a deeply discrediting perception. In the backdrop of this stigma regarding mental health issues are the distinguishing characteristics or personal traits of people suffering from mental health issues. This perception influences people to think that these characteristics or traits are the disadvantages of patients with mental health illnesses. This perception eventually influences the development of negative attitudes and beliefs toward these patients.

15.2 Significance of Addressing Mental Health Stigma

Various reasons exhibit that addressing mental health stigma is as important as identifying and treating mental health illness. Some of these reasons are as presented in Figure 15.1 prevention of discrimination and ostracization, decrease in concealability and increase in controllability, decrease in disruptiveness, increase in patients' quality of life, and better recovery from ailments.

15.2.1 Prevents Discrimination and Ostracization

Mental health stigma related to specific mental health issues often develops prejudiced opinions, attitudes, and behaviors about people suffering from

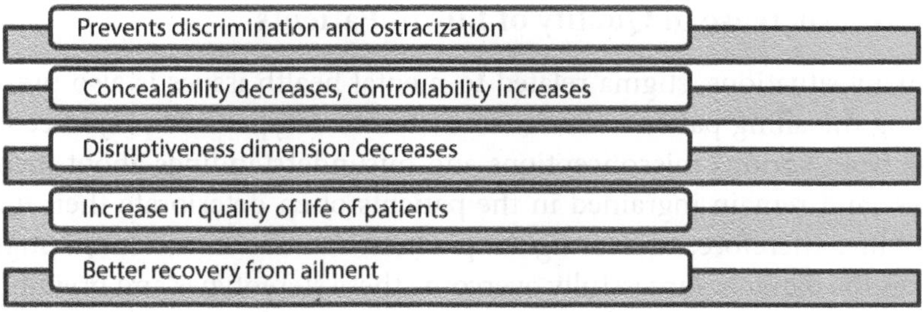

Figure 15.1 Reasons for mental health stigma.

such diseases. Eventually, they are subjected to discrimination, neglect, and ostracization [2]. So, addressing the stigma associated with mental health illness helps in eliminating this discriminating attitude.

15.2.2 Concealability Decreases, Controllability Increases

The stigmatized outlook of the greater part of society toward mentally ill patients often discourages patients from revealing their problems and seeking medical assistance. If this stigma is eliminated, the patients will not experience any shakiness or embarrassment in reporting their conditions and getting proper treatment [3, 4]. Hence, when there is no stigma of any kind regarding any mental health ailment, the tendency to conceal mental health problems will decrease. Eventually, the controllability of mental health issues will increase.

15.2.3 Disruptiveness Dimension Decreases

The disruptiveness dimension is an obvious outcome of mental health stigma, which determines the extent to which mental disorders might impact the relationship of patients with society. Detection of mental health problems often makes the patients face negative consequences like job loss, increased poverty, and decreased socioeconomic status due to the stigmatized outlook of society [5]. When the stigma associated with mental health is properly addressed and overcome, such socioeconomic issues are eliminated. The patients can continue their jobs successfully and engage in healthy relationships even during the detection and treatment of mental health illness. Thus, the *disruptiveness* dimension decreases if mental health stigma is overcome.

15.2.4 Increase in Quality of Life of Patients

In many situations, stigma related to mental health issues is also present among the ailing patients themselves. The stereotypes and prejudice that arise from various misconceptions and misunderstandings about mental illness and remain ingrained in the patients often deteriorate their quality of life. Therefore, addressing the phenomena related to this self-stigma makes the patients successfully overcome these stereotypes and prejudices. As a result, the quality of their life and recovery of the patients increase.

15.2.5 Better Recovery from Ailment

Where awareness of the various symptoms of mental health is the key to better recovery, stigma related to mental health issues leads to a gross lack of awareness. The patients start believing that the obvious signs of mental ailment might be mere signs of physical weakness or mania. They also start believing that they can overcome the problem themselves without going for any counseling or treatment. This hampers their mental health further. Addressing mental health stigma becomes very significant here in making these patients aware of their mental conditions so that they can identify the symptoms of ailment and seek counseling/treatment whenever it becomes necessary. This improves the recovery rate of the patients too [3, 6].

15.3 AI and Machine Learning and Mental Health Stigma

AI or artificial intelligence is a technology that is capable of mimicking human intelligence [7, 8]. Machine learning is a subset of AI that takes a data-driven approach and collects relevant data to enable AI computer systems to simulate human intelligence and attributes. The integration of AI and machine learning has shown remarkable results in enabling positive transformations in the healthcare industry. However, AI and machine learning have shown remarkable performance in areas where the pervasive stigma regarding mental health worsens mental health-related issues. For instance, AI technology successfully meets challenges like ethical concerns by safeguarding patient information and accurately diagnosing symptoms. AI is also capable of making patients suffering from mental health concerns feel empowered by helping them overcome misconceptions with the supply of accurate medical data on their mental health conditions [9]. AI plays a cardinal role in increasing awareness about mental health issues throughout society by disseminating accurate information about various mental health problems and encouraging the exchange of dialogues surrounding mental health. This helps in combating mental health stigma by debunking myths about various medical health problems that are the root of various medical health stigmas. In situations where societal perception about mental health issues creates self-stigma among mental health patients, AI plays an important role in removing these stigmas. This innovative technology helps in positive emotional regulation by providing insight into the emotional patterns of these patients so that they can identify and understand the emotional triggers accurately and timely. Simultaneously, these technologies equip the patients with information on developing relevant skills so that they can effectively manage these emotional triggers and handle their mental health on their own.

15.4 Types of Mental Health Stigma

Mental health stigma is a condition that doubly challenges patients. On the one hand, they struggle with the symptoms of the mental disease they suffer from. On the other hand, they struggle to accommodate the misconceptions and prejudices about their mental health conditions. There are multiple types or dimensions of mental health stigma based on the impact created by these stigmas. These include self-stigma, public stigma,

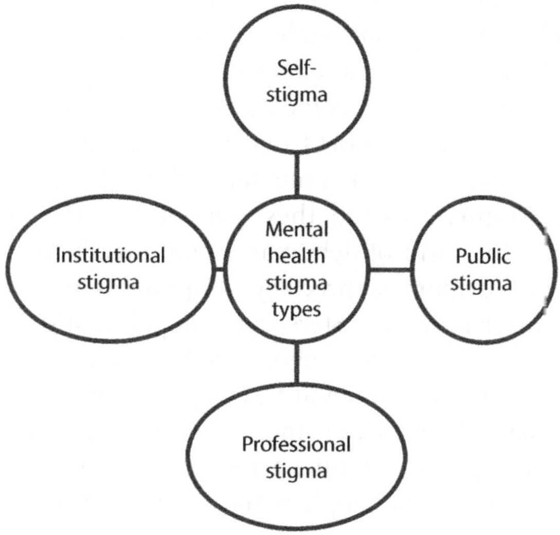

Figure 15.2 Types of mental health stigma.

professional stigma, and institutional stigma as represented in Figure 15.2 [10]. These have been discussed below:

15.4.1 Self-Stigma

Self-stigma is a mental situation in which people develop prejudices against themselves. Self-stigma is a form of internalized mental mechanism in which people start feeling ashamed of themselves due to their mental health conditions [11]. Self-stigma is generally the outcome of factors such as poor access to mental health treatment services, disempowerment, reduced quality of life, and diminished self-confidence. Self-stigma has three vital components, namely, stereotypes, prejudice, and discrimination. Stereotypes are certain negativities that people suffering from mental health issues associate themselves with. Patients with mental health problems often have a negative self-notion that they have a weak character. Prejudices are certain pre-conceived ideas or assumptions that do not have any real standing. In self-stigma, discrimination is the unequal treatment toward different people based on their mental health conditions [12]. Thus, self-stigma is equated with a personal feeling that people hold certain prejudices against these individuals due to their mental state, which makes them vulnerable to discrimination.

15.4.2 Public Stigma

Public stigma in the context of mental health can be interpreted as the societal attitude toward people suffering from mental health issues and diseases [13]. Mental health patients face public stigma in a more intensified form in comparison to people with physical deformities [14]. They do not get the necessary support from their community members, their peers, or other social groups that mental health patients strongly need to overcome their stigmas. Instead, these patients face the consequences of public stigma in the form of dehumanization, insult, and ostracization. Public stigma also comprises three key components, namely, stereotypes, prejudice, and discrimination. Stereotypes in public stigma about mental health are preconceived notions about the behavior, nature, and mental conditions of patients with mental health problems. For instance, some people might have the idea that these patients are dangerous, violent, or harmful to the general public. Such prejudiced perspectives cause discrimination where such people with mental health issues are treated unequally.

15.4.3 Professional Stigma

Professional stigma in the context of mental health stigma is the development of certain prejudices about the mental health condition of a person in a professional setting. Professional stigma usually manifests in the form of negative attitudes, social disapproval, and biases toward patients with mental health issues [15]. Professional peers develop a judgmental attitude toward the person suffering from mental health issues. Usually, factors such as fear, misunderstanding regarding the causes and symptoms of mental illness, and the impact of the association of general professionals with the person suffering from mental health concerns lead to the development of professional stigma. This professional stigma usually makes the suffering person shaky and embarrassed. Despite knowing about their mental health conditions, they show reluctance to access proper treatment. Eventually, the treatment gets delayed.

15.4.4 Institutional Stigma

Institutional stigma is the type of systemic stigma about mental health illnesses and people suffering from mental health issues. This stigma arises and emerges in governments, corporations, and other institutions. Institutional stigma is expressed by these organizations using the development of a culture of negative attitudes and beliefs toward persons suffering from mental health problems. Such stigmas are reinforced through legal frameworks, public policy, and professional practices [10, 16] Thus, driven by the stigmatized notions surrounding mental health, these institutions often develop policies and guidelines that restrict the rights of people suffering from mental health problems and discriminate against them. These patients with mental health problems are subjected to unequal treatment and denied opportunities that are granted to the general public. These institutions practice discrimination through activities such as poor fund allotment for the development of mental health resources and fewer work and housing facilities for such patients. With time, the institutional stigma gets deeply embedded within the fabric of society.

15.5 Consequences of Mental Health Stigma on Individuals and Society

Mental health stigma can bring deleterious consequences to individuals as well as society if not addressed and managed properly.

15.5.1 Impact on the Individual Level

15.5.1.1 Diminishing of Self-Confidence

Low self-confidence is usually the result of poor treatment by others [17]. Different types of stigma persist in society regarding mental health problems. The impact of the stigmatized view of the professional sphere, society, and institutional organizations surrounding patients with mental health problems is so strong that it gradually results in self-stigma among the patients. Gradually, this self-stigma makes these patients with mental health problems skeptical about their abilities and potential.

15.5.1.2 Feeling of Ostracization

Public, professional, and institutional stigma regarding the behavior and attitude of people suffering from mental health problems creates a gap between these patients. The patients are often deprived of the opportunities and scopes that the greater part of the population generally enjoys. This manifests in the form of a feeling of ostracization among the affected population and worsens their mental conditions further [18].

15.5.1.3 Deterioration in Quality of Life

There is a direct link between the mental health condition of people and their quality of life where stigma regarding the issue operates as a catalyst [19]. Perceived stigma among the patients as well as their friends and relatives regarding the outcome of mental health illnesses increases stress, depressive symptoms, and anxiety. Often, these patients develop various negative feelings about their conditions, which causes deterioration in their quality of life. Their sense of security and support and subjective well-being deteriorates. Their social relationships get affected as stigmatized approaches toward these patients increase their distance from their families, peers, and friends. The interest in functioning objectively in various social roles also gets hampered.

15.5.1.4 Worsening of Economic Well-Being

Societal and institutional stigmatization of patients with mental health problems robs the opportunity for economic progress to a large extent. The income and employability of these patients decrease due to the persistent misconceptions and misunderstandings of society. They face adverse economic impacts in the form of promotion denial, unemployment, and poverty due to discrimination and biases that result from stigmatization [2, 20].

15.5.1.5 Social Victimization

The victimization of patients with mental health problems as criminals is common due to the biased opinions of society about them. Specifically, patients with severe mental health complications like schizophrenia, alcoholism, and drug addiction are seen as criminals even if evidence proving their criminal acts might not be very strong. Since they are unaware of their actions, they perform crimes without knowing what they are doing. As a result, the stigmatized standpoint of society presents them as dangerous for society [21, 22].

15.5.2 Impact on the Societal Level

15.5.2.1 Development of Systemic Barriers

Facing mental health stigma is often viewed as an individual problem that only a particular person or a small sliver of the population faces. People often forget that they can become victims of stigmatization due to misconceptions regarding mental health issues. So, they unknowingly encourage this stigmatization and, in the process, build a systemic barrier in society that keeps this discrimination and inequality alive [23].

15.5.2.2 Enormous Economic Costs

The consequences of mental health problems are not restricted to the patients and their families only. Instead, the mental health issue is a global crisis that is associated with enormous economic costs [24]. In a report published by Arias *et al.* [25] in 2016, it was presented that the global economic value associated with mental health problems was approximately USD 5 trillion. Mental health stigmatization is a cardinal factor that often compels patients to conceal their problems. As their mental health issues do not get proper treatment, the burden of enormous economic costs on society increases. This not only includes the expenses incurred by the society for providing care facilities but also covers other indirect costs like financial downturn due to unemployment and income loss of the population affected by mental health problems, expenses for providing social support, and cost of confinement of critically ill mental health patients.

15.5.2.3 Negative Effect on the Labor Market

The impact of stigma among the institutions about mental health is felt by the labor market, too. Discrimination against stigmatized employees with mental health problems often leads to unemployment and underemployment [2]. The social distance created between the employer and employee due to this stigmatized perspective usually does not lead to the callback of skilled employees with mental health issues. The impact of this scenario on the labor market is reflected in society in the form of social unrest, reduced productivity, and loss of human capital.

15.5.2.4 Negative Status Quo Set by the Media

This stigmatized societal outlook toward patients with mental health problems is passed on to the media too [22]. Sometimes, the media takes a lead role in setting the status quo of these patients negatively. In the media, criminals are equated with these patients and pointlessly portrayed as 'crazy' people having mental disorders. Sometimes, the media presents exaggerated, erroneous, and comical images of the nature and behavior of these mental health patients to the audience. The influence of mass media is pervasive in the lives of the mass population. Media also takes part in shaping the outlook of society. Hence, this stigmatized representation of people with mental health problems in the media permanently establishes their negative public image by swaying popular opinion and making these patients as a harmful group that is separate from mainstream society.

15.5.2.5 Biases in the Criminal Justice System

The stigmatization of patients with mental health problems impacts the criminal justice system too [22]. Since the media has a persistent tendency to present these people as dangerous and not fit for socialization, the criminal justice system is also influenced. Various instances of this exist in the criminal justice system, where cases of psychiatric patients getting arrested at a higher rate are also seen. Sometimes, perceived stigma regarding the mental health problems of convicted persons also influences the criminal justice system. They are perceived as having poor community adjustment, exhibiting mild to severe mental health symptoms, substance dependence, and prone to recidivism. Here, recidivism can be understood as a key concept in the criminal justice system, which explains the tendency of criminals to relapse into criminal behavior [26]. Nonetheless, the criminal justice system often fails to acknowledge that these perceived stigmas cannot make accurate predictions of recidivism, substance dependence symptoms, or mental health symptoms of any person.

15.6 Traditional Strategies to Combat Stigma: Strengths and Limitations

From the discussion so far, it is clear that the discrimination that results from mental health stigma not only affects the patient but also impacts society negatively. Various strategies are used to cope with this stigma. Some of the traditional strategies are as presented in Figure 15.3 below: educational, contact policy, and peer support interventions.

15.6.1 Educational Intervention

Educational interventions in which campaigns are arranged to support anti-stigma in mental health are often arranged by various support groups and governmental and non-governmental organizations as a fundamental strategy to combat stigma [27]. Mental health literacy programs and campaigns are conducted as part of this strategy. The strength of this strategy is that it provides fact-based information to debunk various misconceptions regarding mental health stigma that are verifiable. However, the drawback of this strategy is that it focuses on biological or genetic causal attributions that lead to stress and does not cover the imperative role of psychosocial attributions in this phenomenon. Therefore, there are debates regarding the complete effectiveness of educational interventions [28].

15.6.2 Contact Interventions

The strategy of contact intervention centers on the stigmas, discomfort, and miscommunications that arise from a lack of contact with people suffering

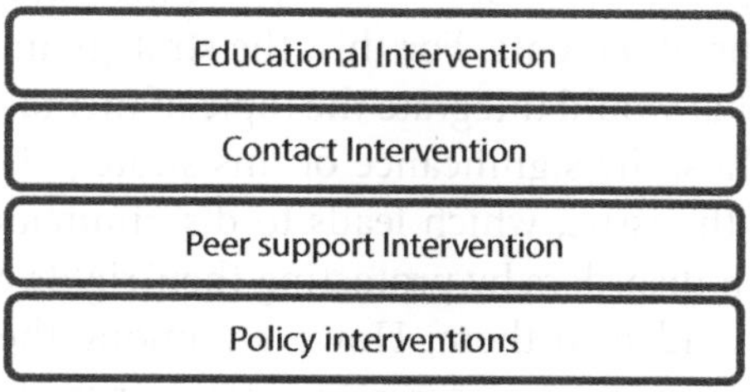

Figure 15.3 Strategies to combat mental health stigma.

from mental health issues [27, 29]. The significance of this strategy is that it works effectively in the management of public stigma by establishing contact with patients having lived experience of mental illness who share their experiences and success stories. Simultaneously, this strategy eliminates self-stigma about mental health problems by boosting the self-confidence of patients and generating a sense of empowerment in them. The drawback of this strategy is that these contacts with mental health patients are very brief and quite different from naturally occurring contacts in real-life situations. Moreover, this contact is more theoretical in nature, which combines education, unlike real-life contact where education is absent [30].

15.6.3 Peer Support Intervention

Peer support intervention is a strategy to tackle mental health stigma more practically. So, it emphasizes the application of the contact intervention simultaneous with the development of practices using which an anti-stigmatization approach can be applied to day-to-day activities through the use of use of peer services [27]. The major significance of this strategy is that it is more practical-oriented and involves the peer service providers' lived experiences of challenges, discrimination, rejection, and isolation encountered by patients with mental health issues. This strategy proves advantageous in helping patients overcome self-stigma and improve self-efficacy. Nevertheless, the drawback of this strategy is that it does not prove effective in helping mental health patients and the public overcome the stigma associated with clinical symptoms and withdrawal symptoms [31].

15.6.4 Policy Interventions

Policy interventions are legalized strategies in which the government, educational institutions, and other statutory bodies take the key role in safeguarding the rights of the stigmatized population suffering from mental health problems [27]. The purpose of this strategy is to improve the knowledge, awareness, perspective, and approach of the public about the mental health problems of patients. For this, the strategy intends to develop a legal framework that would integrate the topic of mental health into public health policies. Thus, the significance of this strategy is that it intends to reach the root of the issue, which leads to discrimination against people with mental health disorders by protecting their rights and advancing the quality of care provided to them. However, among the disadvantages of this strategy is a shortage of research facilities appropriate for new policy implementation and existing policy reform. Similarly, the lack of skilled personnel in different countries across the world who would be able to execute and enforce legislation on mental health effectively is also a problem in the case of the successful implementation of this strategy [32].

15.7 AI and Machine Learning Applications in Mental Health Stigma

15.7.1 AI in Diagnosis and Treatment of Mental Health Stigma

AI has taken a permanent place in healthcare services in the past few years. However, the arena of AI and machine learning has not remained limited to diagnosis, clinical prediction, and phenotyping of intricate disease states only. The scope of this state-of-the-art technology now includes the detection of self-stigma and public stigma associated with medical health issues [33].

The stigmas related to mental health issues manifest in the form of association of incorrect stereotypes to the patients and considering them as 'scary,' 'weak,' or 'incompetent' [34]. These stereotypes often develop self-stigma in the patients themselves. This creates a situation in which these mental health patients develop low self-efficacy and a lack of confidence and skepticism about their abilities [35]. Here, AI and machine learning have shown proven results in recent times. Underreporting and undercoding are recurrent issues in the mental health care sector. Both self-stigma and public stigma lead to the silencing of patients with mental health problems. This leads to underreporting due to stigma. The patients usually do this due to the fear of getting stigmatized, socially sanctioned, and disgraced and hide the behavior that is normal during that specific phase of mental health disorder [36]. Again, coding is the recording of accurately capturing the medical condition and diagnosis procedure of a patient [37, 38]. However, public stigma regarding mental health conditions often leads to a situation in which clinicians mostly claim and code chronic conditions of patients with both mental illness and a chronic condition. The diagnosis is lightened with the use of words such as "likely" or "suspected" because the clinicians fear that coding severe mental health symptoms accurately might generate institutional stigma [33]. Since the solution to such stigma-related comorbidities or severe mental illness is not undercoding but early detection, prognosis, and treatment, the clinicians are taking the help of AI to access and assess mental health conditions anonymously and confidentially and provide necessary support to the patients.

The work of AI and machine learning in this context is to focus on these instances of underreporting and undercoding to detect mental health stigma. AI uses tools such as brain imaging data, electronic health records (EHRs), novel monitoring systems, and mood rating scales to detect, classify, and subgroup different types of mental health issues like depression, schizophrenia, or suicide ideation with high precision [39]. Through brain imaging data, the brain activity of the patients is analyzed and changes in thinking, feelings, or behavior due to persisting mental health conditions are tracked. EHRs are a machine learning technology through which mental health conditions are constantly monitored over a period of time to precisely identify mental health crises at any given point in time [40]. Similarly, AI is integrated with machine learning technology, named novel monitoring systems, to attain more precision in mental health monitoring [41]. Again, mood rating scales closely track the changes in the mood of people with mental health problems. Through this, the clinicians can gauge if these people are facing any sort of stigma in the form of experienced *stigma*, anticipated *stigma*, and internalized *stigma.*

Machine learning tools can also predict the usual behavioral symptoms a person would exhibit while suffering from a specific form of mental health illness. So, in situations where patients conceal symptoms of mental health problems during clinical reporting, AI helps medical practitioners in the proper detection and re-defining of clinical diagnosis [39]. Another instance of mental health stigma is the case of undercoding mental health conditions. This is seen mostly in the cases of multiple comorbidities. Hence, the use of AI helps in the timely detection of mental health problems that stigmatized patients usually do not report and end up aggravating their illness and experiencing severe stages of mental health issues.

15.7.2 Machine Learning Models for Mental Health Prediction and Risk Assessment

The growing importance of public health has facilitated the need to evaluate the alteration in mental health stigma over a while. The use of machine learning has been growing fast as a result as a reliable tool for ascertaining the patterns of social stigma related to mental health problems [42]. Simultaneously, some machine learning models have also been popularized for accurate mental health prediction and risk assessment so that underreporting mental health problems due to stigma can be prevented. Some of these include the following:

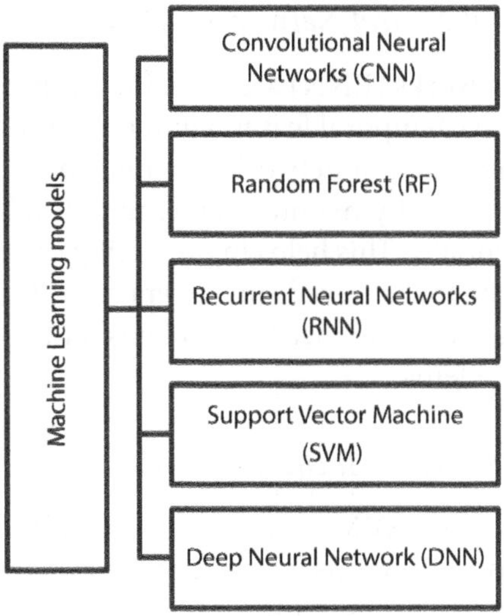

Figure 15.4 Machine learning models used in combating mental health stigma. Source: Authors' own elaboration.

15.7.2.1 Convolutional Neural Networks (CNN)

Convolutional neural network (CNN) is a type of machine learning model that is based on a deep learning algorithm. This form of AI has become popular in various computer vision tasks [43]. CNN has become an equally significant deep learning technology model because it can accurately detect mental health conditions through clinical images and expression data of the patients. Specifically, in the field of psychiatry, this model uses medical image analysis and facial recognition techniques for precisely detecting mental disorders.

15.7.2.2 Random Forest (RF)

Random forest (RF) is a machine learning model based on the ensemble learning method. The supervised algorithms used by this model create a 'forest' from the group of decision trees that are trained by the 'bagging' method in which multiple learning models are combined to improve the overall phenomenon prediction capacity [44]. In a nutshell, the output of multiple decision trees is combined in this model and analyzed before reaching a conclusion. This model of machine learning operates by identifying *mental health* conditions by detecting and analyzing the different factors determining different types of mental health problems.

15.7.2.3 Recurrent Neural Networks (RNN)

Recurrent neural networks (RNN) are machine learning tools that operate by using data that have temporal features and remain valid for a temporary period [45]. Recurrent neural networks operate an important deep learning algorithm that works by maintaining temporal relationships between data that flow sequentially. This helps in predicting the next outcome based on analysis of the data that succeeds in current data. This tool is effective in detecting symptoms of mental health problems and predicting the nature of mental health problems.

15.7.2.4 Support Vector Machine (SVM)

Support vector machine (SVM) is a type of machine learning algorithm that uses data to find applications in various sectors such as spam detection, classification of textual data, and image classification. The major advantage offered by this tool is that it can precisely detect depression, which often leads to underreporting of mental health issues.

15.7.2.5 Deep Neural Networks

Deep neural network is a form of resource-intensive network, and it comprises multiple hidden layers between the input and output layers. This category of machine learning can perform tasks such as classification, regression, and representation learning [46]. In deep learning, the computer is made to imitate the human brain; process data in the form of images, sounds, or texts; and then recognize, analyze, and classify these data accordingly. In mental healthcare, the deep neural network model is widely used for detecting and understanding mental health problems. The model operates by detecting the physiological signals given by patients with mental health problems in a passive and non-invasive manner.

Besides these models, there are other models of machine learning, such as extreme learning machines (ELM) and generative networks. The core purpose of these tools is to address mental health stigma by making mental health predictions and conducting risk assessment.

15.8 Data Privacy and Ethical Considerations in AI for Mental Health

AI and machine learning have brought revolutions in the detection of mental health illnesses and assisted in recusing the incidence of self-stigma, public stigma, and institutional stigma associated with it. Nevertheless, the issue of ethical concerns arising from the use of AI persists simultaneously, too [47]. Specifically, in the field of mental health, the use of AI generates ethical issues in the form of privacy-related concerns, consent-related issues, lack of transparency, accountability issues, bias, and the potential for unintentional harm. Along with these, there are other ethical challenges, too, like data security and algorithmic bias. Ethical issues are also generated from the impact created by automation on the mental health patient and healthcare service provider relationship. AI opacity is also an ethical issue that may hinder the comprehensive decision-making process due to its irresponsible use [47]. Ethical issues also arise in the development and use of AI in the absence of proper clinical validation to check if the technology is delivering correct, reliable, and clinically applicable results.

15.9 Chatbot's Role in Reducing Mental Health Stigma

So far, the role of AI and machine learning in the detection of mental health issues and risk assessment has been discussed to show that this helps in removing the stigma that leads to underreporting and undercoding. In this context, the role of virtual support systems and chatbots is crucial in reducing mental health stigma even though the impact varies based on cultural differences between individuals [48, 49]. Chatbots can also provide social and psychological support to patients where supportive real-world human interactions are not possible. For instance, monitoring the mental health condition of chatbot users living in Eastern countries would demonstrate that they have stronger emotions than depression compared to people living in Western countries. Chatbot data revealed that users from Eastern countries use words that are mostly associated with feelings of sadness. In the country, users from Western countries have a greater tendency to share vulnerable topics such as mental health. Chatbots do not broach topics that seek social support like social media platforms. Instead, they provide advice on daily life difficulties by patients with mental health problems. Instead, chatbots help overcome stigma by encouraging active listening and fostering a safe space [49]. Chatbots can effectively reduce medical health stigma among patients and acclaim effective and practical evidence-based treatments by providing a judgment-free, hospitable platform for patients through which they can communicate with like-minded people, share their medical concerns, and get proper assistance. This way, chatbot technology reduces stigma by presenting a comfortable sharing-sensitive ambience.

15.10 Summary of the Chapter

This chapter focused on medical health stigma to show how AI and machine learning are operating to eliminate such stigma. While reviewing literature relevant to this chapter, the various factors necessitating the need to overcome stigma were studied, along with the impact of stigma on the individual and society. From reasons of elimination of discrimination and ostracization, decrease in *disruptiveness* dimension, and increase in quality of life of patients, it was understood that the incidence of underreporting could be prevented. Moreover, the aggravation of mental health illnesses could also be prevented if this stigma can be controlled and properly managed. In line with this understanding, the role of AI and machine learning was explored to understand how these technologies can eliminate mental health stigma. Even though the direct contribution of these technology tools in reinforcing strategies for the management of stigma could not be found, their implication in effective diagnosis has been found. Hence, it was understood that these technologies help in overcoming stigma by means of accessing the mental health conditions of patients consistently at different stages, preventing the aggravation of the condition and generating a sense of empowerment among them. In this context, the significance of chatbots in reducing mental health stigma has also been studied.

References

1. Zoopi, L., What is mental health stigma?, in: *Medical News Today*, Nov. 2020. https://www.medicalnewstoday.com/articles/mental-health-stigma.
2. Brouwers, E.P.M., Social stigma is an underestimated contributing factor to unemployment in people with mental illness or mental health issues: position paper and future directions. *BMC Psychol.*, 8, 1, 36, Dec. 2020. doi: 10.1186/s40359-020-00399-0.
3. Ahmedani, B.K., Mental Health Stigma: Society, Individuals, and the Profession. *J. Soc. Work Values Ethics*, 8, 2, 4–1, 2011.
4. Thornicroft, G., *et al.*, The Lancet Commission on ending stigma and discrimination in mental health. *Lancet*, 400, 10361, 1438–1480, Oct. 2022. doi: 10.1016/S0140-6736(22)01470-2.
5. Kivimäki, M., *et al.*, Association between socioeconomic status and the development of mental and physical health conditions in adulthood: a

multi-cohort study. *Lancet Public Health*, 5, 3, e140–e149, Mar. 2020. doi: 10.1016/S2468-2667(19)30248-8.
6. Mayo Clinic, *Mental health: Overcoming the stigma of mental illness*, 2017. https://www.mayoclinic.org/diseases-conditions/mental-illness/in-depth/mental-health/art-20046477.
7. Reddy, S.N., Surabhi, D., Vali Buvvaji, H., Rama, V., Sabbella, R., The AI-Driven Supply Chain: Optimizing Engine Part Logistics For Maximum Efficiency. *Educ. Administration Theory Pract.*, 30, 5, 8601–8608, May 2024. doi: 10.53555/KUEY.V30I5.4428.
8. Stein, J.P., Messingschlager, T., Gnambs, T., Hutmacher, F., Appel, M., Attitudes towards AI: measurement and associations with personality. *Sci. Rep.*, 14, 1, 1–16, Feb. 2024. doi: 10.1038/s41598-024-53335-2.
9. Morley, J., *et al.*, The ethics of AI in health care: A mapping review. *Soc. Sci. Med.*, 260, 113–172, 2020.
10. Subu, M.A., *et al.*, Types of stigma experienced by patients with mental illness and mental health nurses in Indonesia: a qualitative content analysis. *Int. J. Ment. Health Syst.*, 15, 1, 1–12, Dec. 2021. doi: 10.1186/S13033-021-00502-X/METRICS.
11. American Psychiatric Association, *Stigma, Prejudice and Discrimination Against People with Mental Illness,* 2024. https://www.psychiatry.org/patients-families/stigma-and-discrimination.
12. Chan, K.K.S. and Fung, W.T.W., The impact of experienced discrimination and self-stigma on sleep and health-related quality of life among individuals with mental disorders in Hong Kong. *Qual. Life Res.*, 28, 8, 2171–2182, Aug. 2019. doi: 10.1007/S11136-019-02181-1/METRICS.
13. Gärtner, L., Asbrock, F., Euteneuer, F., Rief, W., Salzmann, S., Self-Stigma Among People With Mental Health Problems in Terms of Warmth and Competence. *Front. Psychol.*, 13, 877491, 2022.
14. Kowalski, R.M. and Peipert, A., Public- and self-stigma attached to physical versus psychological disabilities. *Stigma Health*, 4, 2, 136–142, 2019.
15. Miller, I., Golecki, H., Jensen, K., Understanding Incoming Bioengineering Student Perceptions About Mental Health and Wellness. *Biomed. Eng. Educ. 2023 4:1*, 4, 1, 57–72, Jul. 2023. doi: 10.1007/S43683-023-00120-8.
16. Livingston, J.D., *Mental Illness-Related Structural Stigma*, Mental Health Commission, 2013. https://www.mentalhealthcommission.ca/wp-content/uploads/drupal/MHCC_OpeningMinds_MentalIllness-Related SructuralStigmaReport_ENG_0_0.pdf.
17. Heath, J.K., Alvarado, M.E., Clancy, C.B., Barton, T.D., Kogan, J.R., Dine, C.J., The Context of 'Confidence': Analyzing the Term Confidence in Resident Evaluations. *J. Gen. Intern. Med.*, 37, 9, 2187–2193, Jul. 2022. doi: 10.1007/S11606-022-07535-Z/TABLES/3.
18. Kohrt, B.A., *et al.*, Reducing mental illness stigma in healthcare settings: Proof of concept for a social contact intervention to address what matters

most for primary care providers. *Soc. Sci. Med.*, 250, 112852, Apr. 2020. doi: 10.1016/J.SOCSCIMED.2020.112852.

19. Tsutsumi, A. and Izutsu, T., Quality of Life and Stigma, in: *Handbook of Disease Burdens and Quality of Life Measures*, Springer, New York, 2010.
20. Sharac, J., Mccrone, P., Clement, S., Thornicroft, G., The economic impact of mental health stigma and discrimination: A systematic review. *Epidemiol. Psichiatr. Soc.*, 19, 3, 223–232, Sep. 2010. doi: 10.1017/S1121189X00001159.
21. Jorm, A.F., Reavley, N.J., Ross, A.M., Belief in the dangerousness of people with mental disorders: A review. *StatPearls*, 46, 11, 1029–1045, Mar. 2012. doi: 10.1177/0004867412442406.
22. Ghiasi, N., Azhar, Y., Singh, J., *Psychiatric Illness and Criminality*, Treasure Island (FL), StatPearls Publishing, 2023.
23. Minaa, B., *Why Mental Health is a Social Justice Issue*, Flow Space, 2020. https://www.theflowspace.com/interpersonal-health/access-equity/minaa-b-owning-our-struggles-2937456/.
24. Trautmann, S., Rehm, J., Wittchen, H.U., The economic costs of mental disorders: Do our societies react appropriately to the burden of mental disorders?, in: *The economic costs of mental disorders: Do our societies react appropriately to the burden of mental disorders?*, vol. 17, no. 9, 2016.
25. Arias, D., Saxena, S., Verguet, S., Quantifying the global burden of mental disorders and their economic value. *EClinicalMedicine*, 54, 101675, 2022.
26. National Institute Of Justice, *Recidivism*, 2024. https://nij.ojp.gov/topics/corrections/recidivism.
27. NIH, *Ending Discrimination Against People with Mental and Substance Use Disorders: The Evidence for Stigma Change*, National Academies Press, Washington DC, 2016.
28. Kvaale, E.P., Gottdiener, W.H., Haslam, N., Biogenetic explanations and stigma: A meta-analytic review of associations among laypeople. *Soc. Sci. Med.*, 96, 95–103, 2013.
29. Cook, B.L., Hou, S.S.Y., Lee-Tauler, S.Y., Progovac, A.M., Samson, F., Sanchez, M.J., A Review of Mental Health and Mental Health Care Disparities Research: 2011-2014. *Sage J.*, 76, 6, 683–710, Jun. 2018. doi: 10.1177/1077558718780592.
30. Jorm, A.F., Effect of Contact-Based Interventions on Stigma and Discrimination: A Critical Examination of the Evidence. *Psychiatric Serv.*, 71, 7, 735–737, Jul. 2020. doi: 10.1176/appi.ps.201900587.
31. Sun, J., Yin, X., Li, C., Liu, W., Sun, H., Stigma and Peer-Led Interventions: A Systematic Review and Meta-Analysis. *Front. Psychiatry*, 5, 13, 915617, 2022.
32. Drishti, *Prev Next Mental Health Policies and Laws*, 2024. https://www.drishtiias.com/blog/mental-health-policies-and-laws#:~:text=The%20Mental%20Healthcare%20Act%202017,right%20to%20mental%20health%20treatment.

33. Walsh, C.G., *et al.*, Stigma, biomarkers, and algorithmic bias: recommendations for precision behavioral health with artificial intelligence *JAMIA Open*, 3, 1, 9–15, 2020.
34. Healthdirect, *Mental illness stigma*, 2024. https://www.healthdirect.gov.au/mental-illness-stigma.
35. Abdisa, E., *et al.*, Self-stigma and medication adherence among patients with mental illness treated at Jimma University Medical Center, Southwest Ethiopia. *Int. J. Ment. Health Syst.*, 14, 56, 2020.
36. Bharadwaj, P., Pai, M.M., Suziedelyte, A., Mental health stigma. *Econ. Lett.*, 159, 57–60, 2017.
37. Kumar, P., Nestsiarovich, A., Nelson, S.J., Kerner, B., Perkins, D.J., Lambert, C.G., Imputation and characterization of uncoded self-harm in major mental illness using machine learning. *J. Am. Med. Inf. Assoc.*, 27, 1, 136–146, Jan. 2020. doi: 10.1093/JAMIA/OCZ173.
38. Portela, D., *et al.*, Unsupervised algorithms to identify potential under-coding of secondary diagnoses in hospitalisations databases in Portugal. *Health Inf. Manage. J.*, 53, 3, 174–182, Sep. 2024. doi: 10.1177/18333583221144663/ASSET/IMAGES/LARGE/10.1177_18333583221144663-FIG1.JPEG.
39. Graham, S., *et al.*, Artificial Intelligence for Mental Health and Mental Illnesses: An Overview. *Curr. Psychiatry Rep.*, 21, 11, 116, 2013.
40. Oliver, D., *et al.*, Using Electronic Health Records to Facilitate Precision Psychiatry. *Biol. Psychiatry*, 96, 7, 532–542, Oct. 2024. doi: 10.1016/J.BIOPSYCH.2024.02.1006.
41. Kumar, B.P. and Anithaashri, T.P., Novel Patient Monitoring System using Artificial Neural Networks technique comparing with Time Series Analysis, in: *2022 International Conference on Business Analytics for Technology and Security (ICBATS)*, IEEE, pp. 1–6, Feb. 2022, doi: 10.1109/ICBATS54253.2022.9759071.
42. Tokmic, F., Hadzikadic, M., Cook, J.R., Tcheremissine, O.V., Development of a Behavioral Health Stigma Measure and Application of Machine Learning for Classification. *Innov. Clin. Neurosci*, 15, 34–42, 2018.
43. Yamashita, R., Nishio, M., Do, R.K.G., Togashi, K., Convolutional neural networks: an overview and application in radiology. *Insights Imaging*, 9, 4, 611–629, Aug. 2018. doi: 10.1007/S13244-018-0639-9/FIGURES/15.
44. Mohamed, E.S., Naqishbandi, T., Bukhari, S., Rauf, I., Sawrikar, V., Hussain, A., A hybrid mental health prediction model using Support Vector Machine, Multilayer Perceptron, and Random Forest algorithms. *Healthcare Anal.*, 3, 11, 100185, 2023.
45. Andrew, J., Rudra, M., Eunice, J., Belfin, R.V., Artificial intelligence in adolescents mental health disorder diagnosis, prognosis, and treatment. *Front. Public Health*, 11, 1110088, 2023, Mar 31.
46. He, H., Wen, C.K., Jin, S., Li, G.Y., A model-driven deep learning network for MIMO detection, in: *2018 IEEE Global Conference on Signal and Information Processing, GlobalSIP 2018 - Proceedings*, Institute of Electrical

and Electronics Engineers Inc., pp. 584–588, Jul. 2018, doi: 10.1109/GLOBALSIP.2018.8646357.

47. Warrier, U., Warrier, A., Khandelwal, K., Ethical considerations in the use of artificial intelligence in mental health. *Egypt. J. Neurology Psychiatry Neurosurg.*, 59, 1, 1–2, Dec. 2023. doi: 10.1186/S41983-023-00735-2/METRICS.
48. Williams, R.T., The ethical implications of using generative chatbots in higher education. *Front. Educ. (Lausanne)*, 8, 1331607, Jan. 2023. doi: 10.3389/FEDUC.2023.1331607/BIBTEX.
49. Chin, H., *et al.*, The Potential of Chatbots for Emotional Support and Promoting Mental Well-Being in Different Cultures: Mixed Methods Study. *J. Med. Internet Res.*, 25, e51712, 1, 2023, Oct 20.

16

Leveraging Sentiment Analysis to Encounter Mental Health Stigma: Insights, Strategies, and Impact

Uma Gulati[1]*, Astha Shukla[2] and Vivek Singh Sachan[2]

[1]Management, Institute of Technology and Science, Ghaziabad, India
[2]Business Management, CSJM University, Kanpur, India

Abstract

Sentiment analysis offers a powerful tool for addressing and overcoming mental health stigma by providing insights into public perception, tracking attitudinal changes over time, and guiding targeted interventions. This analytical approach allows for identifying prevalent misconceptions and negative beliefs that contribute to the stigma. Understanding these sentiments can guide efforts to correct misunderstandings and spread accurate information.

By categorizing sentiments as positive, negative, or neutral, this method provides insights into public opinion, consumer behavior, and social trends. Sentiment analysis is mainly used in multiple fields, including marketing, customer service, and social media monitoring, to compute reactions to products, services, events, or issues. Its ability to process large volumes of text data quickly and efficiently makes it an essential tool for understanding the mood and perspectives of a target audience, enabling more informed decision making and strategic planning.

Sentiment analysis allows organizations, researchers, and advocates to gauge public attitudes toward mental health issues. By computing large volumes of text data (such as social media posts, news articles, or forum discussions), it's possible to understand how people feel about mental health stigma—whether they view it positively, negatively, or neutrally.

By enhancing communication strategies, sentiment analysis helps craft messages that resonate with diverse audiences, promoting more open dialogue and community building around mental health issues. Furthermore, it supports policy and advocacy by informing policymakers of public attitudes and evaluating the

**Corresponding author*: umagulati.2001@gmail.com

Ridhima Sharma, Fazla Rabby, Rohit Bansal, Timcy Sachdeva and Jihene Mrabet (eds.) Confronting Mental Health Stigma with AI and Machine Learning, (405–424) © 2026 Scrivener Publishing LLC

impact of new initiatives. As a research and educational tool, sentiment analysis contributes valuable data that can shape training programs and advance understanding in the field, ultimately fostering a more supportive and informed society regarding mental health.

Mental health stigma remains a formidable barrier to seeking treatment, leading to social isolation and worsening health outcomes. This study investigates the potential of sentiment analysis—a natural language processing tool that interprets public opinion from text data—to combat this stigma. These insights enable the development of targeted intervention strategies, such as public health campaigns, educational initiatives, and policy reforms, all aimed at reshaping public discourse to foster a more supportive mental health environment.

The research also assesses the effectiveness of these strategies in reducing stigma and enhancing mental health literacy over time. Through the integration of sentiment analysis in mental health advocacy, stakeholders can gain a deeper understanding of stigma's variations and dynamics, enabling them to implement more effective, data-driven measures to counteract it. This approach not only helps in mitigating the harmful effects of stigma but also promotes a culture of acceptance and support for individuals facing mental health challenges. Ultimately, this study underscores the transformative potential of sentiment analysis in the ongoing effort to reduce mental health stigma and improve the overall well-being of affected individuals.

This chapter explores the insights, strategies, and impact of encountering mental health stigma through leveraging sentiment analysis. Additionally, it presents and briefly analyzes the challenges that sentiment analysis currently faces.

Keywords: Sentiment analysis, mental health, social trends, decision making, strategic planning, natural language processing (NLP)

16.1 Introduction

Mental health stigma remains one of the most pressing societal challenges of the modern age. It acts as a significant barrier to individuals seeking mental health treatment and receiving the support they need. Stigma surrounding mental illness manifests in various forms, including public stigma, self-stigma, and structural stigma, each contributing to negative outcomes for individuals affected by mental health disorders. Public stigma refers to society's collective attitudes toward individuals with mental illness, often characterized by discrimination, stereotyping, and marginalization. Self-stigma occurs when individuals internalize these negative perceptions, leading to feelings of shame, guilt, and diminished self-worth. Structural stigma, meanwhile, refers to institutional policies or practices that disadvantage individuals with mental illness, such as inadequate access to care or discriminatory workplace policies [1].

Despite increased awareness of mental health issues in recent years, stigma remains pervasive across cultures, affecting various facets of people's lives. Individuals often delay or avoid seeking treatment due to fear of judgment, social rejection, or discrimination. This contributes to a cycle where mental health issues worsen over time, making recovery more difficult. Therefore, it is crucial to develop innovative solutions to address and reduce stigma at multiple levels. This is where advancements in technology, particularly through sentiment analysis, have the potential to make a meaningful impact in the fight against mental health stigma.

With the advent of digital technology, the rise of social media platforms and other online communities has transformed the way people communicate and engage with each other. Platforms like Twitter, Facebook, Reddit, and blogs have provided spaces for individuals to discuss sensitive topics such as mental health in a relatively anonymous environment. This shift has brought mental health discussions into the public sphere, allowing individuals to share personal experiences, seek advice, and raise awareness about mental health conditions. Importantly, these platforms also offer a wealth of data on how society perceives and talks about mental health. This data, if analyzed properly, can reveal insights into public attitudes toward mental health, including identifying instances of stigmatizing language and tracking shifts in public perception over time.

Sentiment analysis is a crucial tool in natural language processing (NLP), a subset of artificial intelligence (AI) focused on enabling computers to understand and process human language. This technique, often referred to as opinion mining, is used to analyze the emotional tone of unstructured text, such as social media posts, news articles, reviews, and forums. By categorizing sentiments into positive, negative, or neutral, sentiment analysis allows researchers and policymakers to gauge public opinion on various topics. It provides insights into how people feel about specific issues, products, or events, enabling data-driven decision making. Sentiment analysis has become especially important in understanding public discourse on social platforms, where vast amounts of data are generated daily. As a result, it is widely used across industries to track trends, predict outcomes, and develop strategies to address public concerns, making it a valuable tool for both research and policy development. Additionally, advanced sentiment analysis techniques can also identify specific emotions such as anger, fear, sadness, and joy, providing a deeper understanding of how people feel about a given topic.

Sentiment analysis has become a valuable tool in several industries, including marketing, customer service, and politics, where understanding public opinion is critical for decision making and strategy development.

However, its application in the realm of mental health is relatively new but growing rapidly. The increasing use of social media as a platform for mental health discussions has made sentiment analysis an invaluable resource for researchers seeking to understand how society views mental health and how stigma operates in these online conversations.

By analyzing sentiment on a large scale, researchers can uncover insights into societal trends, identifying which mental health conditions are most stigmatized, the language used to describe them, and how public attitudes shift in response to societal events, policy changes, or public health campaigns. For example, when prominent figures discuss their struggles with mental health, sentiment analysis can track changes in public discourse, revealing whether these discussions lead to more compassionate and understanding conversations or, conversely, whether they reinforce negative stereotypes. Similarly, during mental health awareness campaigns or after high-profile suicides, sentiment analysis can provide real-time feedback on public opinion, allowing policymakers to adjust their strategies to be more effective.

Sentiment analysis is particularly useful in understanding mental health stigma because it can process vast amounts of unstructured data quickly and efficiently. Traditional research methods such as surveys and focus groups, while valuable, often have limitations in terms of scope and timeliness. They may not capture the full range of opinions or reach populations who are less likely to participate in formal research. In contrast, sentiment analysis can process millions of social media posts, blog entries, and forum discussions in real time, providing a comprehensive and up-to-date picture of public sentiment. It can also detect patterns that may not be immediately obvious through manual analysis, such as recurring themes in stigmatizing language or correlations between specific events and shifts in public perception.

Additionally, sentiment analysis allows researchers to go beyond simply identifying stigmatizing language and sentiments. It provides opportunities to measure the intensity of stigma and understand the context in which it arises. For instance, while a single negative comment about mental health might not be harmful on its own, a series of similarly negative comments clustered around certain mental health conditions could indicate a more entrenched stigma. Moreover, sentiment analysis can help identify which demographics or communities are most affected by stigma, allowing for more targeted interventions. For example, certain mental health conditions, such as schizophrenia or bipolar disorder, may be more heavily stigmatized than others, and sentiment analysis can help pinpoint where and how this stigma manifests, guiding public health efforts to address these issues specifically.

However, despite its potential, using sentiment analysis to combat mental health stigma also comes with challenges. One of the main challenges is the complexity of human language. Sentiment analysis algorithms, while powerful, sometimes struggle with the nuances of language, such as sarcasm, metaphors, and cultural differences in expression. These complexities can lead to misinterpretations or inaccuracies in sentiment detection. For example, a seemingly positive statement may, in fact, be sarcastic or subtly negative, making it difficult for algorithms to classify it correctly. Moreover, the context in which language is used can significantly impact its meaning. A word that is neutral in one context may be stigmatizing in another, and sentiment analysis algorithms must be able to account for these variations to produce accurate results [7].

Another challenge lies in the ethical considerations of using personal data for sentiment analysis. Mental health discussions often involve sensitive and private information, and researchers must be careful to ensure that individuals' privacy is protected. Collecting and analyzing data from public forums or social media without proper consent raises ethical concerns, particularly when dealing with vulnerable populations who may not fully understand how their data is being used. It is essential for researchers to adhere to strict ethical guidelines when conducting sentiment analysis on mental health data, ensuring that the benefits of their research outweigh the potential risks to individuals' privacy and autonomy.

16.2 Mental Health Stigma and Its Impact

Mental health stigma manifests in different forms: public stigma (negative societal attitudes), self-stigma (internalizing public attitudes), and structural stigma (policies that disadvantage individuals with mental illness). Research has long highlighted the damaging effects of stigma on people's mental health. According to Corrigan [14], stigma perpetuates discriminatory behaviors and limits individuals' access to necessary services, leading to social isolation, low self-esteem, and an overall reduction in quality of life. This persistent stigma has driven researchers to seek strategies for mitigating its impact.

According to the study "Mental Health Stigma and Service Use Among Black American Youth: A Systematic Review" [16], Black children face barriers in accessing mental health services due to persistent stigma and lower rates of service utilization compared to other groups. Stigma, both external and internal, prevents individuals from seeking necessary care, which worsens mental health outcomes. By using sentiment analysis to understand public discourse around mental health, researchers and policymakers can identify the roots of these stigmas, particularly within marginalized communities, and create targeted interventions that address cultural and societal barriers.

16.3 Sentiment Analysis: An Overview

Sentiment analysis, also known as opinion mining, refers to the process of using NLP to extract subjective information from textual content. By applying machine learning algorithms and linguistic analysis, sentiment analysis categorizes opinions into positive, negative, or neutral sentiments. It can also detect emotions such as joy, anger, sadness, or fear. This technique has become widely adopted in several fields, including business, marketing, and healthcare, to understand customer feedback, public sentiment, and societal trends [20]. Given the explosion of user-generated content on social media, blogs, and forums, sentiment analysis offers researchers and policymakers a powerful tool for understanding societal attitudes toward mental health.

Effectiveness of Anti-Stigma Interventions
Research on anti-stigma interventions, such as in the study "The Effectiveness of Anti-stigma Interventions for Reducing Mental Health Stigma in Young People" [23], highlights that adolescence is a critical period where stigma-related behaviors can exacerbate mental health issues. The study conducted a systematic review of existing anti-stigma strategies, finding that reducing stigma significantly improves mental health outcomes and help-seeking behaviors. By applying sentiment analysis tools to monitor the effectiveness of these interventions, researchers can track changes in societal attitudes, providing real-time feedback on the success of mental health campaigns.

Youth Mental Health and Community-Based Approaches
A key study, "Bridging the Gap: A Pilot Study of a Lay Health Worker Model to Decrease Child Mental Health Stigma" [13], explores a community-based intervention aimed at reducing stigma among African American children. The involvement of community health workers was shown to promote positive shifts in parental attitudes toward mental health. Sentiment analysis of social media discussions and public forums

where these interventions are discussed could provide insights into how these interventions are perceived and how they influence broader social trends.

Social Trends and Digital Discourse

Sentiment analysis allows researchers to delve into public discourse about mental health on platforms like Twitter, Reddit, and Facebook. By analyzing the tone, language, and context of online conversations, researchers can assess how mental health is framed in everyday dialogue. For example, the study "Program Considerations and Addressing At-Risk Populations in Active Minds Clubs: A Brief Report" [24] indicates that community-driven approaches to mental health, such as those found in youth-focused mental health clubs, can drive positive sentiment and reduce stigma. Analyzing online reactions to these programs can help refine strategies for reducing stigma and improving mental health outcomes for youth.

Leveraging NLP for Strategic Decision Making

Natural language processing (NLP), a subfield of artificial intelligence, has emerged as a transformative tool for organizations seeking to improve their strategic decision making. By analyzing and interpreting vast amounts of unstructured text data, NLP enables businesses to extract actionable insights, streamline operations, and predict future trends.

NLP has revolutionized strategic decision making by enabling organizations to harness the power of unstructured data. Through applications such as sentiment analysis, competitive intelligence, risk management, and predictive analytics, NLP provides decision makers with the tools to stay ahead in an increasingly complex and dynamic business environment. By addressing associated challenges and investing in robust NLP solutions, organizations can unlock the full potential of this technology and gain a competitive edge in their industries.

This chapter explores how NLP can be leveraged to enhance strategic decision making and the key benefits it offers [8].

1. Data-Driven Insights from Unstructured Data

One of the primary advantages of NLP is its ability to process and analyze unstructured data, which constitutes approximately 80% of all organizational data. This includes customer feedback, social media posts, emails, research papers, and industry reports. NLP tools can extract valuable information, such as customer sentiment, emerging market trends, or competitive positioning, from these sources. These insights help decision makers identify opportunities, address challenges, and prioritize investments.

For instance, sentiment analysis, a key NLP application, allows organizations to understand customer opinions about products and services. By analyzing reviews and social media mentions, companies can gauge customer satisfaction, identify pain points, and refine their offerings to align with consumer preferences.

2. Enhanced Competitive Intelligence
NLP enables businesses to monitor and analyze competitor activities more effectively. By processing publicly available information, such as press releases, industry news, and financial reports, NLP tools can uncover patterns and strategies employed by competitors. For example, topic modeling and keyword extraction techniques can identify recurring themes in competitors' communications, providing insights into their focus areas and market strategies.

Additionally, NLP-powered web scraping and news aggregation tools can track industry trends and regulatory updates, ensuring that decision makers stay informed and adapt to changes proactively.

3. Improved Risk Management
Strategic decision making often involves managing risks, such as financial, operational, or reputational risks. NLP can play a critical role in this area by identifying potential threats and anomalies in real time. For example, text mining algorithms can analyze legal documents, contracts, and compliance reports to detect potential liabilities or regulatory risks. Similarly, social media monitoring tools powered by NLP can identify emerging crises or public relations issues, enabling organizations to respond swiftly and mitigate damage.

4. Personalized Decision Support
NLP technologies, such as chatbots and virtual assistants, can provide decision makers with personalized and context-specific recommendations. These tools leverage natural language understanding (NLU) to process user queries and retrieve relevant information from organizational databases or external sources. For instance, an executive seeking insight on market conditions can interact with an NLP-based assistant to receive tailored reports and summaries, saving time and improving decision accuracy.

5. Forecasting and Predictive Analytics
NLP enhances predictive analytics by analyzing historical and real-time text data to forecast trends and outcomes. For instance, sentiment analysis on social media can predict consumer behavior, while analysis of industry

publications can indicate upcoming market shifts. These predictive capabilities empower organizations to make informed decisions about product launches, investments, and resource allocation.

6. Challenges and Considerations
While NLP offers significant benefits, it also poses challenges that organizations must address. Ensuring data quality, managing bias in algorithms, and protecting sensitive information are critical for the success of NLP applications. Additionally, integrating NLP into decision-making processes requires collaboration between data scientists and domain experts to align technical outputs with business objectives [9].

Ethical Considerations and Challenges
While sentiment analysis provides valuable insights into mental health stigma, it also raises concerns about privacy and the ethical use of personal data. Studies must ensure that they adhere to ethical guidelines, particularly when analyzing sensitive health-related conversations. Furthermore, ensuring that NLP algorithms account for cultural and linguistic nuances is crucial for producing accurate and meaningful results [10].

16.4 Sentiment Analysis in Mental Health Research

The application of sentiment analysis to mental health is relatively new but growing rapidly. Studies have leveraged sentiment analysis to understand how individuals perceive mental health issues, track changes in public sentiment over time, and identify the impact of stigmatizing language [17]. Social media platforms, such as Twitter and Reddit, have been instrumental in this research, providing vast amounts of unstructured data for analysis.

In a comprehensive review, Guntuku *et al.* [17] found that sentiment analysis of social media posts related to mental health conditions such as depression, anxiety, and schizophrenia revealed pervasive stigmatizing attitudes. By examining keywords associated with mental health, the researchers identified recurring patterns of derogatory language and negative sentiment. Furthermore, sentiment analysis has shown that stigma is not static; it fluctuates in response to societal events, media representations, and mental health campaigns [27].

The researchers conducted a co-citation analysis to uncover the intellectual structure of mental health stigma. Co-citation analysis is recognized as one of the most effective and efficient methods for knowledge mapping. It involves identifying pairs of papers frequently cited together in source articles. When multiple authors co-cite the same pairs of papers, clusters of related research naturally emerge. These clusters typically represent a shared theme or area of interest. Researchers can effectively map the structure of specialized research fields and even the broader science landscape by integrating co-citation analysis with techniques such as single-link clustering and multidimensional scaling. It helps in understanding the flow of ideas and the evolution of knowledge.

The researchers conducted a comprehensive search of the Dimensions database using the keywords "Youth" AND "Mental Health Stigma" to identify relevant literature. The search was limited to publication types such as articles, research papers, and book chapters to ensure the inclusion of high-quality academic resources. A total of 2,706 publications were retrieved, forming the dataset for further analysis [5].

To map the knowledge structure within the field, co-citation analysis was employed as the analytical approach. Co-citation analysis, which identifies patterns of relationships between authors or works based on their simultaneous citation by other documents, was carried out using VOS Viewer, a software tool designed for constructing and visualizing bibliometric networks. The unit of analysis for this study was "cited authors," and a minimum threshold of 50 citations per author was applied to focus on highly influential contributors to the field.

From the dataset, a staggering 213,632 authors were identified as being cited. However, only 685 authors met the citation threshold of 50 or more citations. For each of these 685 authors, co-citation links with other authors were meticulously calculated. These links represent the frequency and strength of co-citation relationships, highlighting intellectual connections and collaborations within the academic community.

The software selected authors with the highest total link strength, a measure that reflects the prominence and influence of authors within the co-citation network. The analysis revealed the formation of a co-citation network consisting of 685 items (authors), 5 distinct clusters, and 174,269 links. These clusters, representing groups of authors frequently co-cited together, signify different schools of thought or subfields within the broader research domain of youth and mental health stigma.

Each of the five clusters captures unique perspectives and thematic foci within the field. This clustering enables a deeper understanding of the diverse intellectual traditions, research methodologies, and theoretical approaches contributing to the discourse on youth and mental health stigma [11].

16.5 Social Trends and Mental Health Stigma

Sentiment analysis has played a key role in identifying social trends related to mental health. By analyzing public discourse, researchers have uncovered correlations between mental health stigma and broader social issues, such as politics, economic downturns, and cultural narratives [22]. For example, studies have shown that during periods of political unrest or economic uncertainty, negative sentiments about mental health tend to rise. Sentiment analysis has also shown that certain demographics, such as men and ethnic minorities, are more likely to express or experience mental health stigma [25]. A longitudinal analysis of mental health-related posts on Twitter by Weller [28] demonstrated how societal views on mental health shifted after major public events, such as the deaths of public figures due to mental illness or suicides. Such studies provide crucial insights into the dynamic nature of stigma, enabling organizations and policymakers to better understand when and why stigma increases and how to address it effectively.

The interplay between social trends and mental health stigma has been a subject of increasing focus in recent years. As society evolves, cultural, technological, and generational shifts influence perceptions of mental health, shaping both the persistence and reduction of stigma. This chapter also explores how social trends affect mental health stigma and the implications for individuals and communities [4].

Understanding Mental Health Stigma

Mental health stigma refers to the negative attitudes, stereotypes, and discrimination directed at individuals experiencing mental health challenges. It often leads to feelings of shame, social exclusion, and reluctance to seek help. Stigma manifests in two main forms: public stigma, which involves societal stereotypes and discrimination, and self-stigma, where individuals internalize these negative perceptions, affecting their self-esteem and recovery [6].

Impact of Social Media Trends

Social media has played a dual role in shaping mental health stigma. On the positive side, platforms like Instagram, Twitter, and TikTok have facilitated open conversations about mental health. Influencers and celebrities sharing their mental health journeys have normalized seeking help and encouraged empathy. Campaigns such as #EndTheStigma and

#MentalHealthAwareness have gained traction, reaching global audiences and promoting education [7].

However, social media also perpetuates stigma in some ways. The rise of toxic positivity—encouraging people to only focus on the positive aspects of life—can trivialize mental health struggles. Additionally, misinformation and oversimplification of mental health conditions on social platforms can reinforce harmful stereotypes, such as associating certain disorders with violence or incompetence.

Generational Shifts

Generational attitudes toward mental health have significantly influenced stigma. Younger generations, such as Millennials and Gen Z, are more likely to discuss mental health openly and seek professional help compared to older generations. This openness reflects broader cultural trends emphasizing authenticity, self-care, and mental well-being.

In contrast, older generations may still hold stigmatized views of mental health due to cultural norms that prioritize stoicism and view mental health struggles as personal weaknesses. Bridging this generational gap through intergenerational dialogue and education is critical for reducing stigma across age groups.

Cultural and Regional Influences

Cultural and regional factors play a significant role in mental health stigma. In many collectivist cultures, where community reputation is paramount, mental health challenges are often viewed as a source of shame. This stigma discourages individuals from seeking help, fearing judgment, or ostracization.

In contrast, individualistic cultures, particularly in Western countries, have shown a growing acceptance of mental health discussions, driven by advocacy and research. However, even in these societies, certain stigmas persist, especially surrounding severe mental illnesses such as schizophrenia or bipolar disorder.

Economic and Policy Trends

Economic trends and policy changes have also influenced mental health stigma. The inclusion of mental health in universal healthcare plans and workplace wellness programs has underscored its importance as a public health issue. Governments and organizations investing in mental health education and accessible care have contributed to destigmatizing mental health.

However, systemic inequalities, such as lack of access to mental health resources in low-income communities, perpetuate stigma by framing mental health care as a privilege rather than a right. Addressing these disparities is essential for fostering inclusivity.

Role of Education and Advocacy
Education and advocacy are crucial in combating mental health stigma. Schools, workplaces, and community organizations integrating mental health education into their programs can challenge stereotypes and normalize seeking help. Grassroots movements and international organizations like the World Health Organization (WHO) have been pivotal in raising awareness and promoting mental health literacy.

16.6 NLP and Natural Language Understanding in Sentiment Analysis

Natural language processing (NLP) is a field within artificial intelligence that focuses on the interaction between computers and human language. It allows machines to read, interpret, and generate human language [19]. NLP techniques, particularly sentiment analysis, have been instrumental in analyzing mental health-related data from social media, where human sentiments and emotional expressions are abundant. NLP techniques such as tokenization, lemmatization, and part-of-speech tagging enable machines to analyze the nuances of language and detect sentiment [2].

With the advancement of deep learning, neural networks such as Recurrent Neural Networks (RNNs) and transformers like BERT (Bidirectional Encoder Representations from Transformers) have further improved the accuracy of sentiment analysis. These algorithms excel in capturing context and understanding the subtleties of language [15]. In mental health sentiment analysis, these models have been used to detect the intensity of stigma, understand emotion-laden language, and identify hidden negative attitudes in seemingly neutral posts [12].

16.7 Strategies for Countering Mental Health Stigma Using Sentiment Analysis

Sentiment analysis offers a proactive approach to developing strategies for countering mental health stigma. By analyzing trends in public sentiment, mental health advocates and policymakers can identify the sources of stigma and develop targeted interventions. These strategies may include the following: One effective way to counter stigma is through awareness campaigns. Sentiment analysis can help organizations identify the most stigmatized mental health conditions and develop specific campaigns to address these issues. For example, data might reveal that depression is more stigmatized than anxiety, prompting campaigns focused on destigmatizing depression. Real-time sentiment tracking enables campaigns to adapt their messaging based on public reaction, increasing their impact and effectiveness [18]. The media plays a pivotal role in shaping public attitudes toward mental health. Research shows that negative portrayals of mental illness in films, television, and news media contribute significantly to stigma [26]. Sentiment analysis can be used to monitor media representations of mental health, identifying stigmatizing language and stereotypes. Organizations can then work with media outlets to promote more accurate and compassionate portrayals of mental health, contributing to a reduction in stigma. Sentiment analysis can serve as a tool for the early detection of mental health crises. By monitoring online discussions, researchers can identify individuals or communities showing signs of severe distress. Sentiment analysis of social media posts has already been used to detect individuals at risk of suicide or experiencing acute mental health issues, enabling timely intervention [3]. Mental health professionals can then provide support and resources to these individuals before their conditions worsen.

Sentiment analysis can also inform policy decisions related to mental health. By analyzing public opinion, policymakers can identify the most pressing mental health concerns and prioritize resources accordingly. Additionally, sentiment analysis can help evaluate the effectiveness of existing policies by tracking changes in public sentiment before and after policy implementation [21].

16.8 Challenges in Using Sentiment Analysis for Mental Health

While sentiment analysis offers valuable insights into public attitudes toward mental health, there are several challenges in its application. One of the key challenges is the inherent ambiguity of human language. Sentiments related to mental health are often expressed in subtle or indirect ways, making them difficult to detect using standard sentiment analysis techniques [25]. Additionally, cultural and linguistic differences can affect the accuracy of sentiment analysis models, leading to potential bias in the results.

Another challenge is the ethical considerations surrounding the use of personal data for sentiment analysis. Mental health discussions often involve sensitive information, raising concerns about privacy and consent. Researchers must ensure that their methods comply with ethical guidelines and protect individuals' privacy when collecting and analyzing mental health-related data [29].

Sentiment analysis, the computational process of identifying and categorizing sentiments in text, has shown great potential in supporting mental health assessments. However, employing sentiment analysis in this sensitive domain presents numerous challenges due to the complexity of human emotions, the variability in linguistic expressions, and the high stakes involved in mental health diagnoses. This review highlights key challenges based on existing literature. Human emotions are inherently complex, and they often cannot be easily categorized into predefined sentiment labels such as "positive," "negative," or "neutral." Expressions of mental health issues frequently include mixed emotions, sarcasm, or subtle nuances that traditional sentiment analysis tools struggle to interpret accurately. For instance, a phrase like "I'm fine" could signify genuine positivity or an attempt to mask negative feelings, depending on the context.

Furthermore, mental health-related texts often involve clinical terminology, idiomatic expressions, and metaphors, which are not typically covered in generic sentiment analysis training datasets. This complexity necessitates domain-specific models that are trained on mental health-specific corpora, which are often scarce or difficult to compile due to privacy concerns. Access to relevant and high-quality datasets is critical for building robust sentiment analysis models. However, in mental health, acquiring such datasets is challenging due to the sensitivity of the data and stringent privacy regulations, such as the Health Insurance Portability and Accountability Act (HIPAA) and the General Data Protection Regulation (GDPR). These regulations impose strict restrictions on data sharing, storage, and usage, limiting the availability of open-source datasets for research.

Additionally, datasets that do exist are often imbalanced, with a disproportionate representation of sentiments. For example, datasets might contain more expressions of mild anxiety than severe depression, leading to biases in model performance. Sentiments expressed in mental health-related texts are heavily context-dependent. The same word or phrase can have different meanings based on the user's history, cultural background, or situational context. For example, the word "tired" could indicate physical exhaustion, emotional burnout, or a symptom of depression, depending on the context. Most sentiment analysis models lack the capability to incorporate such context effectively, leading to potential misclassification of sentiments. Mental health expressions vary widely across different demographics, such as age, gender, and cultural backgrounds. A model trained on a dataset dominated by one demographic group may not generalize well to others, potentially leading to biased or inaccurate results. For instance, younger individuals might use informal language or slang on social media to describe their mental health, which traditional models might misinterpret. Using sentiment analysis for mental health assessments raises significant ethical concerns. Misclassifications can have severe consequences, such as overlooking individuals at risk of self-harm or incorrectly flagging someone as needing intervention. Additionally, concerns about user consent and potential misuse of personal data further complicate the ethical landscape. While sentiment analysis often focuses on text, mental health assessments typically require multimodal inputs, including audio, video, and physiological signals. Textual sentiment analysis alone may provide an incomplete picture, as certain emotional cues are better captured through tone of voice, facial expressions, or behavioral patterns.

16.9 Future Directions

The future of sentiment analysis in mental health research holds significant promise. As NLP techniques continue to evolve, sentiment analysis models will become more accurate in detecting the nuances of mental health-related sentiment. The integration of multimodal analysis, combining textual, visual, and audio data, will further enhance researchers' ability to understand public attitudes toward mental health [2].

Moreover, future research should explore the use of sentiment analysis in diverse cultural contexts. Mental health stigma varies widely across cultures, and sentiment analysis models must be adapted to account for these differences. Developing culturally sensitive sentiment analysis models will enable researchers to address mental health stigma in a more inclusive and effective manner.

16.10 Conclusion

Sentiment analysis offers a powerful and promising approach to understanding and addressing mental health stigma. By harnessing the capabilities of natural language processing (NLP), researchers can gain deep insights into public attitudes, social trends, and patterns of stigma related to mental health. These insights enable the development of more targeted and effective strategies for combating negative stereotypes and discrimination.

While challenges such as accuracy and ethical considerations remain, the potential for sentiment analysis to transform mental health advocacy and influence policy is significant. As technology continues to evolve, sentiment analysis will increasingly shape efforts to reduce mental health stigma, fostering a more inclusive and compassionate society. Ultimately, it will empower individuals and communities to confront and overcome the stigma associated with mental illness, improving mental health outcomes globally.

Despite its potential, sentiment analysis in mental health applications faces significant challenges that stem from the complexity of emotional expression, data limitations, context dependency, demographic variability, and ethical considerations. Addressing these challenges requires interdisciplinary collaboration among data scientists, mental health professionals, and ethicists to develop models that are accurate, fair, and respectful of individual privacy. Future research should focus on creating domain-specific datasets, incorporating context-aware algorithms, and ensuring the ethical use of sentiment analysis tools.

References

1. Shekhar, A.R. and Gupta, T., Sentimental Analysis of Social Media Data for Mental Health Monitoring, in: *2023 2nd International Conference on Futuristic Technologies (INCOFT)*, pp. 251–261, 2023, https://doi.org/10.1109/INCOFT60753.2023.10425161.
2. Baltrušaitis, T., Ahuja, C., Morency, L.-P., Multimodal Machine Learning: A Survey and Taxonomy. *IEEE Trans. Pattern Anal. Mach. Intell.*, 41, 2, 423–443, 2019. https://doi.org/10.1109/TPAMI.2018.2798607.
3. Coppersmith, G., Leary, R., Crutchley, P., Fine, A., Natural Language Processing of Social Media as Screening for Suicide Risk. *Biomed Inform. Insights*, 10, 1–10, 2018. https://doi.org/10.1177/1178222618792860.
4. Bharadwaj, P., Pai, M.M., Suziedelyte, A., Mental health stigma. *Econ. Lett.*, 161, 82–85, 2017. https://doi.org/10.1016/j.econlet.2017.06.028.
5. Gierk, B., Löwe, B., Murray, A.M., Kohlmann, S., Assessment of perceived mental health-related stigma: The Stigma-9 Questionnaire (STIG-9). *Psychiatry Res.*, 271, 494–499, 2018. https://doi.org/10.1016/j.psychres.2018.10.026.

6. Burton, C.L., Wang, K., Pachankis, J., Does getting stigma under the skin make it thinner? Emotion regulation as a stress-contingent mediator of stigma and mental health. *Clin. Psychol. Sci.*, 6, 3, 289–302, 2018. https://doi.org/10.1177/2167702618755321.
7. Ritsher, J.E.B., Otilingam, P.G., Grajales, M., Internalized stigma of mental illness: Psychometric properties of a new measure. *Psychiatry Res.*, 121, 1, 31–49, 2003. https://doi.org/10.1016/j.psychres.2003.08.008.
8. Marshall, C., Lanyi, K., Green, R., Wilkins, G., Pearson, F., Craig, D., Leveraging Twitter using artificial intelligence to explore mental health insights in the UK during the COVID-19 pandemic, in: *JMIR Infodemiology*, 2021, Advance online publication. https://doi.org/10.2196/preprints.32449.
9. Understanding the public stigma of mental illness: A mixed-methods, multi-level, exploratory triangulation study. *BMC Psychol.*, 22, 7, 123–135, 2024. https://doi.org/10.1186/s40359-024-0123-9.
10. The use and operationalization of "structural stigma" in health-related research: A scoping review. *BMC Public Health*, 24, 12, 567–578, 2024. https://doi.org/10.1186/s12889-024-0578-9.
11. How People Feel About Antipsychotics & Mood Stabilizers: Twitter/X Sentiment Analysis (2024 Study), in: *Mental Health Daily*, Retrieved from https://www.mentalhealthdaily.com/how-people-feel-about-antipsychotics-mood-stabilizers-twitter-x-sentiment-analysis-2024-study/.
12. Alshehri, F., Alshahrani, H., Alharthi, S., Sentiment analysis in mental health: Detecting emotion-laden language in social media. *J. Artif. Intell. Res.*, 11, 1, 72–78, 2020.
13. Chakawa, A., Bridging the gap: A pilot study of a lay health worker model to decrease child mental health stigma. *Community Ment. Health J.*, 58, 4, 542–555, 2022.
14. Corrigan, P.W., Druss, B.G., Perlick, D.A., The impact of mental illness stigma on seeking and participating in mental health care. *Psychol. Sci. Public Interest*, 15, 2, 37–70, 2016.
15. Devlin, J., Chang, M., Lee, K., Toutanova, K., BERT: Pre-training of deep bidirectional transformers for language understanding. Proceedings of the 2018 Conference of the North American Chapter of the Association for Computational Linguistics. *Hum. Lang. Technol.*, 1, 4171–4186, 2018.
16. Fields-Oriogun, B., Johnson, R.T., Nelson, K., Mental health stigma and service use among Black American youth: A systematic review. *BMC Public Health*, 24, 7, 556–573, 2024.
17. Guntuku, S.C., Yaden, D.B., Kern, M.L., Ungar, L.H., Eichstaedt, J.C., Detecting depression and mental health trends in social media using natural language processing. *J. Comput. Social Sci.*, 3, 2, 1–13, 2017.
18. Koh, P.W., Thaker, S., Lim, Y., Real-time sentiment tracking of mental health campaigns: Applications and ethical considerations. *Social Media Soc.*, 6, 1, 20–36, 2020.

19. Manning, C.D., Surdeanu, M., Bauer, J., Finkel, J., Bethard, S.J., McClosky, D., The Stanford CoreNLP natural language processing toolkit. Proceedings of the 52nd Annual Meeting of the Association for Computational Linguistics. *Syst. Demonstrations*, 52, 55–60, 2014.
20. Pang, B. and Lee, L., Opinion mining and sentiment analysis. *Found. Trends Inf. Retr.*, 2, 1–2, 1–135, 2008.
21. Pestian, J.P., Matykiewicz, P., Linn-Gust, M., South, B., Uzuner, O., Wiebe, J., Cohen, K.B., Brew, C., Suicide risk assessment with natural language processing. *J. Am. Med. Inf. Assoc.*, 23, 6, 1085–1092, 2016.
22. Ritterband, L.M. and Thorndike, F.P., eHealth in clinical practice: A vision of the future. *Clin. Psychol. Rev.*, 45, 17–27, 2016.
23. Song, H., Rojas, K., Ma, Y., The effectiveness of anti-stigma interventions for reducing mental health stigma in young people. *Psychiatry Res.*, 319, 114982, 2023.
24. Stern, A. and LaChapelle, S., Program considerations and addressing at-risk populations in Active Minds Clubs: A brief report. *J. Coll. Stud. Dev.*, 63, 3, 286–294, 2022.
25. Tausczik, Y.R. and Pennebaker, J.W., The psychological meaning of words: LIWC and computerized text analysis methods. *J. Lang. Social Psychol.*, 29, 1, 24–54, 2010.
26. Wahl, O.F., *Media madness: Public images of mental illness*, Rutgers University Press, New Brunswick, New Jersey, 1995.
27. Wang, Y., Ng, R.T., Lin, J., Tracking fluctuations in public sentiment about mental health: A computational approach. *Soc. Psychiatry Psychiatr. Epidemiol.*, 55, 3, 381–392, 2020.
28. Weller, M., Smith, L., Johnson, P., Longitudinal analysis of mental health-related posts on Twitter: A case study of changing perceptions. *Internet Interv.*, 2, 3, 235–243, 2014.
29. Williams, K., Lee, C., Kim, S., Ethical concerns in social media-based mental health research: Considerations for future work. *Digit. Ment. Health J.*, 5, 2, 112–126, 2020.

Index